media education
an introduction

Edited by
Manuel Alvarado and Oliver Boyd-Barrett

bfi

BFI Publishing
in partnership with

The Open University
On behalf of the Media Education Course Team

First published in 1992 by the
British Film Institute
21 Stephen Street
London W1P 1PL

British Library Cataloguing in Publication Data

Media education.
  I. Alvarado, Manuel, *1948–* II. Boyd-Barrett, Oliver
  302.234071041

  ISBN 0-85170-295-3

Set in Plantin by
Rowland Phototypesetting Ltd
and printed in Great Britain by
St Edmundsbury Press Ltd, Bury St Edmunds, Suffolk

Cover design: Jonathan Davies and Geoff Wiggins
Cover photograph courtesy of Young and Rubicam Italia SPA

The *Media Education: An Introduction* Pack comprises the
following linked components:

– this Reader
– a 75,000-word Work book
– a 60-minute video cassette
– a 60-minute audio cassette
– 40 slides

Obtainable singly, or as pack E555, from:

LMSO
Open University
P.O. Box 188
Milton Keynes
MK7 6DM

Contents

•

vii

Acknowledgments

This Reader has been edited by Manuel Alvarado (BFI) and Oliver Boyd-Barrett (OU, joint chair) in collaboration with, and on behalf of, the Course Team:

Cary Bazalgette (BFI, joint chair) Christine James (BFI)
Julian Bowker (BFI)   Paul Manners (OU)
Jim Cook (BFI)   Barbara Mayor (OU)

Part IA researched and introduced by Jim Cook and Oliver Boyd-Barrett; Part III commissioned by Julian Bowker and Oliver Boyd-Barrett and introduced by Christine James; Part IV commissioned and introduced by Julian Bowker and Christine James.

The Team would like to thank the following for their contributions to the Reader:

Wendy Bradshaw and Tana Wollen (BFI);
Neil Mercer and Peter Scrimshaw (OU);
Hossein Zand (developmental testing, OU);
Philip Simpson (external assessor);
Jonathan Davies and Geoff Wiggins (design);
Jon Davison (photographs);
Roma Gibson and John Smoker (production);
Ron Hawkins (editorial);
Kathleen Luckey, Michele Marsh, Alpa Patel, Yvonne Salmon, Joan Woodhead;
The staff and children of:
Wykebeck Primary School, Leeds, Yorkshire;
Northumberland Park Community School, Haringey, London;
Beacon Community College, Crowborough, Sussex;
Ifield Community College, Crawley, Sussex.

Notes on Contributors

Dave Allen   Lecturer in Education, Portsmouth Polytechnic, Hampshire.

Manuel Alvarado   Head of Education, BFI.

Cary Bazalgette   Deputy Head of Education, BFI.

Judy Bennett   TVEI Advisory Teacher for Media Education, Redbridge, Essex.

Robin Bower   Headteacher, Peak Forest Church of England Primary School, Buxton, Derbyshire.

Julian Bowker   Education Officer, BFI.

Oliver Boyd-Barrett   Sub-Dean, School of Education, Open University.

Wendy Bradshaw   Education Officer (Training), BFI.

Gill Branston   Lecturer in Education, West Glamorgan College of Higher Education, Swansea, Wales.

Steve Brennan   Advisory Teacher for Media Education, Wigan, Lancashire.

Jude Brigley   Teacher of English and Media Studies, St Ilan Comprehensive, Caerphilly, Wales.

David Brockie   Lecturer in Teaching and Learning, Department of Education, University of York.

David Buckingham   Lecturer in Department of English and Media Studies, University of London Institute of Education, London.

Edward Buscombe   Head of Trade Publishing, BFI.

Tony Carroll   Teacher of Art and Media Studies, Ifield Community College, Crawley, Sussex.

Richard Collins   Senior Research Associate, University of London Goldsmith's College, London.

Jim Cook Education Officer, BFI.

Angela Devas Lecturer in Media Studies, Acton College, London.

Kate Dewar Teacher, Wykebeck Primary School, Leeds, Yorkshire.

Eddie Dick Education Officer, Scottish Film Council, Glasgow, Scotland.

James Donald Senior Lecturer in the School of Cultural and Community Studies, University of Sussex.

Peter Frazer Teacher of English and Media Studies, Latymer School, Edmonton, London.

Dot Frogatt Advisory Primary Headteacher, Sussex.

Nicholas Garnham Head of Centre for Communication and Information Studies, Polytechnic of Central London.

Andrew Goodwin Freelance Lecturer and Writer based in San Francisco, USA.

Jenny Grahame Advisory Teacher for Media Education, English and Media Centre, London.

Stuart Hall Professor of Sociology, Open University.

James D. Halloran Emeritus Professor, Centre for Mass Communication Research, University of Leicester, Leicester.

Jim Hillier Lecturer in Film Studies, University of Reading, Berkshire.

Marsha Jones Teacher of Sociology in a Leicester Community School.

David Lusted Freelance Lecturer and Media Education Consultant.

Paul Manners Producer, BBC (Open University).

Angela McEwan TVEI Advisory Teacher for Media Education, Renfrewshire, Scotland.

Len Masterman Lecturer in Adult Education, University of Nottingham.

Neil Mercer Head of Centre of Language and Communications, Open University.

Ben Moore Advisory Teacher for Media Education, Newcastle, Northumberland.

Jan Mulreany Freelance Educational Consultant, Brighton, Sussex.

Graham Murdock   Reader, Department of Sociology, University of Loughborough.

Sue Van Noort   Teacher, Kettlebridge Nursery First School, Sheffield, Yorkshire.

Guy Phelps   Principal Examiner, British Board of Film Classification, London.

Cathy Pompe   Freelance Advisory Teacher, Cambridgeshire.

Norrie Porter   TVEI Advisory Teacher for Technology, Redbridge, Essex.

Peter Scrimshaw   Lecturer, School of Education, Open University.

Julian Sefton-Green   Teacher of Media Studies and English, Northumberland Park Community School, Haringey, London.

Roy Stafford   Freelance Media Education Consultant, Keighley, Yorkshire.

David Sudbery   Head of English and Teacher of Media Studies, Beacon Community College, Crowborough, Sussex.

David H. Tripp   Lecturer, School of Education, Murdoch University, Western Australia.

Garry Whannel   Senior Lecturer at Roehampton Institute, London.

Paddy Whannel   died 1980. Was Head of Education, BFI, 1957–1971.

Judith Williamson   Freelance Writer and Lecturer.

General Introduction

This collection draws together a wide and unique range of accounts of education about the media for young people between the ages of 4 and 18. Those who are new to the area of media education will find here some of the very best insights into its nature and purposes, its theory, content, and practice. Those who are already familiar with media education will find a rich seam of source material, available to them to mine with whatever conceptual approaches or methodologies they bring with them. All are likely to encounter challenging new approaches to conceptual structures, teaching pedagogy and practice, and to the evaluation of practice which may just revolutionise their own work or, at the very least, will aid them in the process of professional self-evaluation and development.

The genesis and development of any new subject is in part a history of contest for curriculum space and of struggle between competing traditions and ambitions. Media education has been no exception. In the first section we reprint extracts from texts published over the last quarter of a century which have been far-sighted and influential in their struggle for media education. They trace the changing intellectual and cultural attitudes between the media and the teaching about media. As such they provide invaluable resources essential for the construction of any history of media education and for the construction of a professional identity for any practitioner.

Most of these articles are now difficult to locate and obtain. They range from an early book, published in 1964, actively promoting teaching about the mass media in the context of a broader affirmation of popular culture – Stuart Hall and Paddy Whannel's seminal work, *The Popular Arts* – through articles published in a key journal of the 1970s *Screen Education*, to the official documents and responses of the late 1980s that emerged from the Department of Education and Science and the British Film Institute's Education Department.

The differences in tone, style, and stance adopted in such a diverse range of intellectual and political statements are reflected by a heady mixture of argument, assertion, and polemic mixed with semi-manifestos and programmatic listings. Our view is that it is important for students and teachers of the media to understand the history of these debates, not only for their intrinsic interest but also for the invaluable contextual insights they offer to current thinking and future strategies.

There are many possible routes through these materials (both for this

1

and for later sections). Teachers, in particular, may be interested in navigating their way by the compass of any of a variety of key issues and concepts, including ideology, pedagogy, the role of practice, or, indeed, the allegedly subversive potential of media education for education structures. Another technique is to set up key questions, and then to interrogate, comparatively, a range of articles for the answers they appear to offer, and to trace developments in these answers over time – for example, how best to mount the case for the importance of teaching about television, or, is media education primarily content-based or skills-based, and what are the criteria that can best help select which content and which skills? Readers will find that history is often a resource that can be drawn upon for ideas about how to formulate responses to current preoccupations.

The development of new curriculum structures in many national education systems has both extended and narrowed opportunities for media education. Media education may be enshrined within such subjects as mother tongue teaching, art, or technology. However, it is often a limited, and limiting, view of media education that prevails, one that tends to perceive the subject as concerned primarily with the non-fictional. That most of the population receive most of their narrative and fictionalised dramatic experience through the mass media is a consideration that is unfortunately overlooked in this perspective. In the UK the responses to the National Curriculum Council of bodies such as the British Film Institute and others, together with the range of positions reflected in this volume, are testimony to the work that is still required before media education is adequately represented to the curricula of the schools of this country.

Whereas the first section of Part I looks at the development of a variety of approaches to media education, the second section looks at the major traditions of study of the mass media within higher education which in turn feed, by a variety of direct and indirect means, the teaching of media education within schools. Jim Cook introduces the 'interpretive' tradition, rooted within English, then extending forward through film studies to television studies. This tradition focuses its attention above all, though not exclusively, upon the text and textual analysis. By contrast, the social science tradition outlined by Oliver Boyd-Barrett is as much or more concerned with context, in other words, the social, political, economic, or organisational, professional, and cultural determinants and influences that help account for the generation and production of any given media communication, as well as the factors that enter into audience response, comprehension, and negotiation with the meanings generated by texts and their media environments.

While the trajectories (now converging) of the 'interpretive' and 'social science' traditions have been essentially intellectual or conceptual, media education within the art school tradition is marked by a more institutional inflection. This is outlined in Manuel Alvarado and Wendy Bradshaw's piece which traces the shift from a 'film-making as a creative art' position to the wider-ranging and more vocationally inspired activities of practical media activities developed in many educational establishments in the 1980s.

Part II consists of a single essay in which Cary Bazalgette describes in detail a sophisticated model for organising educational work on the media.

The key aspects which form the core of this model have been refined over a number of years as the subject itself has been defined and developed: they were codified and first published in their present form in the BFI Education Department's *Primary Curriculum Statement* in 1989, and further presented in the Department's *Secondary Curriculum Statement* published two years later.

The six interrelated key aspects of category, language, technology, agency, representation, and audience provide a structure and a conceptual framework for teachers, not only for preparing syllabuses but also for developing an analytically flexible template for understanding pupils' talk and writing. Against these key aspects a teacher can constantly reference the progression of pupil activities and work. The key aspects themselves are open to challenge and revision as social and technological agendas change, but they offer a model which can also be adapted and deployed for the consideration of and work with media in other areas of the curriculum.

We decided that, before embarking on the presentation of a wide range of accounts of contemporary classroom practice, in Part III, it would be useful to try to answer the essential questions: How can a teacher know and analyse what is going on in the classroom? How can he or she evaluate their own initiatives? How can a teacher as action researcher engage productively in such a process? One purpose of this Reader is to reveal the limitations as well as some of the strengths of the anecdotal or subjective account, and to introduce methodologies for the exploration of classroom practices.

The view of media education that has influenced our approach to selections for this volume is one that stresses the importance of listening to and understanding the media knowledge and experience which children and young people bring with them to the study of media. Equally, it is important to maintain this understanding throughout classroom practice. The context of the classroom itself, and in particular of the linguistic context of dialogue between teachers and students, are factors that have considerable influence both on what children say and on what teachers perceive. Neil Mercer's introduction to the work of Vygotsky presents one influential approach to accessing and influencing this linguistic context. Analysis of what is happening linguistically in classroom dialogue is one part of the wider necessity for continual evaluation and professional development to which the tradition of action research, addressed in Peter Scrimshaw's contribution, is committed. Video representations of classroom practice have become increasingly important tools of action research and analysis, and Paul Manners' carefully structured account 'Filming in the Classroom' provides an invaluable and unique account of the complexities of video representation and of how these can best be tackled.

The formal study of media education has been rich in theory and advocacy, but not always so strong in the provision of reflection about and accounts of classroom, curriculum, or institutional practice. That deficiency is one which has begun to be addressed in the late 1980s and early 1990s, partly in response to the challenges and opportunities of new curricula in Scotland, England and Wales, and Northern Ireland, and partly to the need for practitioners to think through the implications of the role of media education for other aspects of the curriculum, including art and technology, as well as subject areas such as history and geography. The generation by the BFI of curriculum development materials has been prominent in this more classroom-focused thinking. Part IV of our volume builds on such initiatives in bringing together a wide-ranging set of accounts of educational and institutional practice, as well as accounts which relate to general curriculum development either of media education as such, or the role of media education in cognate areas. These were selected not because they represented the last word in what we though practitioners' accounts necessarily 'ought' to look like, but because they strongly represented the current diversity of experiences, context, teaching objectives, issues, and themes. In some cases they were specifically commissioned for inclusion in this Reader, in other cases they have been culled from other publications or projects. They had one characteristic in common: they commended themselves to the editors as likely to inspire in a whole variety of ways further strategies of professional change and development.

This Reader is one outcome of an initiative of the British Film Institute, in collaboration with the Open University's Centre for Language and Communications, in the development of a highly original media education pack which comprises, in addition to this volume, video and audio cassettes, a workbook, and slides. The pack was designed to meet the growing demand, and the growing complexity of demand, for INSET provision in media education, and to take account both of the changing nature of the field and of the decline in in-service training and advisory provision. This pack is recommended to those readers who would like to increase their knowledge and experience in media education. The Reader itself is designed as an integral whole which need not be read or studied in connection with the other components of the pack, but which will contribute significantly to its objectives.

We recognise that this volume, like the pack of which it is a part, is specifically addressed to what we perceive as the needs and demands of the UK market. As such, it cannot be as responsive, in equal measure, to the needs and demands of media education in other parts of the world. Nevertheless, we have been encouraged by signs of considerable commonality of concerns among different countries, notably Canada and Australia. This is not to say there are not some important differences: the experience of Latin America, for example, suggests that the churches play a more prominent role, and state education systems less of a role, in promoting media education, and that media education tends to be seen more in the context of trends towards cultural globalisation and the tension which these pose for principles of national sovereignty and autonomous development. On the other hand, it is clearly the case that any provision of media education is likely to need to give an important place to the interpretation of texts and the methodologies available for accomplishing this in the classroom, as well as to issues of practice and the relationship of practice to pedagogy and theory. Many such differences and similarities became clear to us in the context of the international conference on media education organised by the BFI, UNESCO, and the Centre de Liaison de l'Engseignement et de Moyens d'Information, held in Toulouse, France, in 1990, entitled 'New Directions in Media Education'. Educators from forty-five countries attended that conference to discuss the full range of issues presented in this volume. Not only has that experience fed into this Reader and the BFI/OU pack, but it is also one which we think very appropriately signals the beginning of a new era for media education globally, one which we believe this volume represents and to which it is intellectually dedicated.

Manuel Alvarado   *British Film Institute*
Oliver Boyd-Barrett   *Open University*

PART Iᴀ
The Development of the Subject

THE POPULAR ARTS

STUART HALL &
PADDY WHANNEL

Teachers: Mike Smart. Mark Parnham. Jean Richardson

Photo: John Bettinson

BADNEWS

Glasgow University Media Group

Photo play at Horniman School. Forest Hill

Photo: Jon Davison

Between theory and practice

Dominant Attitudes to Mass Media
Introduction

As characterised by James Halloran and Marsha Jones, as well as by Graham Murdock and Guy Phelps, the dominant attitudes to the mass media within education took the form of either negative evaluations or else a concentration on possibly respectable elements of popular culture. Jim Cook, Jim Hillier, Stuart Hall, and Paddy Whannel all cautioned against these essentially evaluative positions and argued for a more systematic study of film and television.

The pieces in this section are included as a necessary and salutary reminder that current attitudes and positions are frequently continuing parts of different and often quite antithetical histories. Thus the inoculation approach, seeking to protect the young, can still fuel anxieties about media phenomena such as, at the time of writing, Ninja Turtle 'commoditoys'. More positively, Stuart Hall and Paddy Whannel's concern with, and belief in, the diversity of audience readings and uses of similarly varied media artefacts is essentially a premise on which this book is based.

It is particularly worth dwelling on the *Screen* extract from Paddy Whannel, both for the lucidity of its analysis of the problems facing a new knowledge and curriculum subject and also to wonder at its prescience. Twenty-two years later, as many subsequent extracts will indicate, we are still quite properly working through the agenda and sets of questions posed here.

The Inoculation Approach

James D. Halloran and Marsha Jones

From *Learning About the Media: Communication and Society* (UNESCO Papers), Paris, UNESCO, 1986, pp. 55–60.

This approach to the study of media education is chronologically the earliest, and has influenced the successive ways of considering teaching about mass communication. It is an approach which in some countries dates back to the inception of the mass communication process. In Germany, for instance, it began in the seventeenth century, with the appearance of the first newspapers. In Great Britain it is newer, and is usually traced to some of the ideas in the philosophy of education at the beginning of this century. 1

The approach, which has been termed the 'inoculative' or 'moral' one, essentially arose from a deep concern among educators and literary critics that young people needed to be protected against what was considered to be the very harmful and powerful influences of the mass media. Young people were seen as sensitive and malleable, and hence capable of being exploited by the new media products. Some experiences in Great Britain . . . have been selected as illustrations of this approach. 2

Great Britain

In Britain, this kind of media education emerged from a classical tradition of literary criticism. It was based on the premise that modern society and its manifestations were alien to the essentials of 'human nature'. Because of technological development and concomitant mechanistic relationships, it was felt that modern technological society was alienating; its products were therefore likewise alienating, especially those which were mass-produced and communicated *en masse*. 3

This view was most forcefully expressed by F. R. Leavis and Denys Thompson. The tone of their criticism is conveyed by the following extracts: 4

> The great agent of change, and from our point of view destruction, has of course been the machine-applied power. The machine has brought us many advantages, but it has destroyed the old ways of life, the old forms, and by reason of the continual rapid change it involves, prevented the growth of the new. Moreover, the advantage it brings us in mass production has turned out to involve standardisation, levelling down outside the realm of mere material good.[1]

This 'levelling down', in their view, had potentially disastrous consequences for young people: 5

10

Those who in school are offered (perhaps) the beginnings of education in taste are exposed, out of school, to the competing exploitation of the cheapest emotional responses: films, newspapers, publicity in all its forms, commercially catered fiction – all offer satisfaction at the lowest level, and inculcate the choosing of the most immediate pleasures, got with the least effort.[2]

It is interesting to note that the authors assume that 'high culture' is   6
preferable, partly because it can only be acquired with greater mental effort than 'popular culture'. From this rather pessimistic perspective, 'mass' or 'popular' culture was considered to be merely a distraction; young people were to be provided with the right kind of apparatus to defend themselves against its effects. Their opinion of the popular press is made clear in the following passage:

As for 'distraction', that is best exemplified by the popular newspaper – if 'dissipation' is not the better word. . . . in the popular newspaper the tendency of the modern environment to discourage all but the most shallow and immediate interests, the most superficial, automatic, and cheap mental and emotional responses is exhibited at perhaps its most disastrous.[3]

This critical position was taken on board primarily by teachers of English   7
literature, who interpreted the message as a directive to protect young people against the corrupting influence of the mass media, especially the cinema, which was very popular with young audiences at the time.

Paradoxically, it was agreed by some critics that not all cinema was   8
harmful; in fact, some of its products could be viewed as genuine expressions of art, and could be used as criteria against which to measure the less worthy products. Therefore, young people were to be armed with the conceptual apparatus to discriminate between products of the media organisations. This had particular implications for the role of the educators:

The moral for the educator is to be more ambitious: the training of literary taste must be supplemented by something more. . . . An education that conceives seriously its function in the modern world will, then, train awareness (a) of the general process of civilisation, and (b) of the immediate environment, physical and intellectual – the ways in which it tends to affect taste, habit, preconception, attitude to life and quality of living. . . . We cannot, as we might in a healthy state of culture, leave the citizen to be formed unconsciously by his environment; if anything like a worthy idea of satisfactory living is to be saved, he must be trained to discriminate and resist.[4]

This profound distrust of the media was evident in the official ideology   9
of education, as the reports on Secondary Education of Spens (1938), Crowther (1959), and Newsom (1963) demonstrated.

Spens spoke of 'the hoarding, the cinema and . . . the public press . . .   10
[as] . . . subtly corrupting the taste and habit of the rising generation'.[5]

11

The Crowther Report, taking a similar position in relation to the education of secondary pupils, suggested:

> Because they [mass media] are so powerful they need to be treated with the discrimination that only education can give. . . . There is also . . . a duty on those who are charged with the responsibility for education to see that teenagers, who are at the most insecure and suggestible stage of their lives, are not suddenly exposed to the full force of the mass media, without some counterbalancing assistance.[6]

The Crowther Report referred to the bewildering and bludgeoning nature of the impact made by the mass media of communication as the reason why 'so many intelligent young people should [not] be left without a guide through the maze'.[7]   11

The Newsom Report responded more positively to the mass media as providing potentially useful educational resource material. The report emphasised that popular journalism should be more widely and systematically studied in secondary schools, and that studies of film and television would supplement work on literary texts. For almost the first time, recognition was being given to the place of media in pupils' lives. Although the emphasis remained largely one of inculcating discrimination, it was acknowledged that television had a particularly important role to play in increasing knowledge and in allowing children to glimpse the world beyond their own personal experiences: 12

> Here we should wish to add a strong claim for the study of film and television in their own right, as powerful forces in our culture and significant sources of language and ideas. . . . the most important and general use of these media, however, as major means for the mass communication of cultural experiences, is not generally dealt with in schools. . . . little attention is paid to the degree to which film and television enter into and influence the lives of our pupils and to these media as legitimate means for the communication of personal experience alongside literature, music and painting.[8]

However, Newsom was still advocating that education should provide an inoculatory 'counterbalance' to the new products of the expanding 'leisure industry':   13

> We need to train children to look critically and discriminate between what is good and bad in what they see. They must learn to realise that many makers of films and of television programmes present false or distorted views of people, relationships, and experience in general, besides producing much trivial and worthless stuff made according to stock patterns.[9]

Newsom emphasised the distinction between 'good' and 'bad' products of the media, and the advantage of utilising worthy products for enriching children's education: 14

12

By presenting examples of films selected for the integrity of their treatment of human values, and the craftsmanship with which they were made, alongside others of mixed or poor quality, we can not only build up a way of evaluating but also lead pupils to an understanding of film as a unique and potentially valuable art form in its own right, as capable of communicating depth of experience as any other art form.[10]

The inoculatory, or moral, approach to the teaching of mass media held sway in Britain until well into the 1970s, and is still in existence today. The study undertaken by Murdock and Phelps[11] demonstrated clearly that there was an 'experiential gap' between the lived experiences of teaching staff in secondary schools and their pupils, which was exemplified by differences in their media preferences and behaviour. Staff demonstrated differing levels of media orientation and attitudes, which they transferred to their classroom teaching.

Notes

1. F. R. Leavis and Denys Thompson, *Culture and Environment*, London, Chatto and Windus, 1933.
2. Ibid. p. 3.
3. Ibid. p. 102.
4. Ibid. pp. 4–5.
5. *Report on Secondary Education* (Spens Report), London, HMSO, 1938, pp. 222–3.
6. *15–18* (Crowther Report), London, HMSO, 1959, vol. 1, para. 66.
7. Ibid. para. 510.
8. *Half Our Future* (Newsom Report), Central Advisory Council for Education, London, HMSO, 1963, para. 474.
9. Ibid. para. 475.
10. Ibid. para. 476.
11. Graham Murdock and Guy Phelps, *Mass Media and the Secondary School*, London, Macmillan/Schools Council, 1973.

Teachers in the Classroom:
Using Mass Media Material

Graham Murdock and Guy Phelps

From *Mass Media and the Secondary School*, London, Macmillan/Schools Council, 1973, pp. 38–42.

A number of teachers also make frequent use of mass media material in their classroom teaching, but unlike the proponents of the 'inoculation' approach, they treat it in a positive rather than a negative way. Thus, Frank Whitehead's stress on media-based teaching as a necessary preventative inoculation against a creeping disease is replaced by Michael Marland's argument that 'the basis of all our teaching must be adding, enriching, and encouraging – not deleting, criticising and inhibiting'.[1] Underlying this sort of approach is a definition of culture and a view of the process of media influence which is almost the complete opposite of that behind the 'inoculation' approach. This alternative view owes a great deal to the work of Richard Hoggart.

Whereas most commentators are middle-class observers taking a bird's eye view of working-class culture, Richard Hoggart writes as an insider, and bases his widely known book, *The Uses of Literacy*, firmly on his own experience of growing up in Hunslet in the 1930s. Drawing on this experience, he maintains that it was not the case that the traditional rural folk cultures were destroyed overnight by the twin processes of industrialisation and urbanisation, and replaced by a uniform, media-based mass culture. Rather, he argues, the migrant workers brought many of their folk traditions with them to the cities and, out of the meeting of these remnants and their new experience of the work situation and city life, they forged a strong and vigorous popular culture which expressed their distinctive sense of themselves as workers in particular industries and as people living in specific localities. According to this argument, therefore, the activity of producing a culture ceases to be exclusive to one particular privileged group, and becomes instead an integral part of the social life of all groups. Cultures in this sense are made up of the patterns of beliefs, values, ideas, and emotions, together with their characteristic forms of expression, through which groups define, interpret, and respond to their experience of social life and social change. Cultures represent a repository and distillation of the group's common social experience, a series of 'master patterns' of meaning and expression which permeate the whole texture of family and neighbourhood life and provide most individual members with their definition of the situation. Despite the considerable amount of economic and social change since 1945, these situational neighbourhood cultures continue

14

to provide the basic framework through which many working-class people look at and respond to their social experience.

Far from providing an entirely passive, zombie-like audience, therefore, these people – like others – constantly measure what is offered to them against the standard of their personal experience, and consequently they tend to be quite selective. As Hoggart puts it:

> The 'common man' . . . is not much deceived; he has some awareness of his own difficulties in judging and coping; he has a much more sensitive awareness of the fact that he is being 'got at', being 'worked on'. He has suspected 'fancy talk' for generations. He can 'see through' most appeals, and is on constant watch against being 'taken in'.[2]

This viewpoint leads logically to two further propositions. First, the impact of media material comes to be seen in terms of a complex interaction rather than a simple reaction, and the important question to ask becomes: what do people *do with* the material they select? rather than, what does the material *do to* the people who receive it? Secondly, the stress on the essential homogeneity of mass media products is replaced by recognition of the differences between superficially similar sorts of products and between elements within the same product. As Stuart Hall and Paddy Whannel put it in their book, *The Popular Arts*:

> In terms of actual quality . . . the struggle between what is good and worthwhile and what is shoddy and debased is not a struggle against the modern forms of communication, but a conflict within these media.[3]

Instead of falling back on the rigid hierarchical division between the élite culture of the literary tradition and newer media-based cultural forms, which reinforces the gap between middle-class and working-class life and thought, Hoggart proposes that all cultural artefacts should be ranged along a continuum marked 'authentic' at one end and 'phoney' at the other. 'Our job', he argues, 'is to separate the Processed from the Living'.

> The crucial distinctions today are not those between the *News of the World* and *The Observer* . . . between the 'Top Ten' and a celebrity concert, or between 'skiffle' and chamber music. The distinctions we should be making are those between the *News of the World* and the *Sunday Pictorial*, between 'skiffle' and the 'Top Ten'.
> This is to make distinctions between the quality of life in each thing of its own kind – distinctions which require an active discrimination, not the application of a fixed 'brow' or educational scale.[4]

Hoggart's central concern is with the way in which we can use all kinds of communications, the new media as well as traditional literary or oral forms, as a way of 'speaking to each other'. A successful or good cultural artefact is therefore one which embodies a deeply felt and authentic experience and which strikes genuine chords in the audience. Thus, he argues, the *Daily Mirror* of 1945 was a better paper than the *Daily Express* because it 'was much more in touch with the prevailing mood' of 'ordinary people', and spoke directly to them about their hopes for the future.[5] This kind of open-ended, relativistic approach leads very rapidly to a complete redefinition of what is meant by culture and, from this, to a reassessment of what counts as valid knowledge in the school curriculum in general and the English lesson in particular. Once the idea of a cultural continuum is accepted, the teacher is necessarily obliged to regard mass media artefacts as potentially valid forms of cultural expression in their own right, and to incorporate them as a necessary and integral part of his teaching. Perhaps the clearest expression of this position, by a practising teacher, has come from Michael Marland:

> It can be said with confidence . . . that no middle-school English course would be complete today without the integration of the newer media into the classroom consideration. Last night's television play and today's newspaper must take their place in a continuum that ranges from the most trivial of reading matter to the most major literature.[6]

Another statement of the same basic position can be found in a recent article by Robert Shaw, former head of English at a leading Leeds grammar school. He describes the basic aim of his teaching as developing 'a critical awareness of the way language and the other media of communication work', and goes on to argue that:

> The English teacher, traditionally the high priest of culture and entrusted with a special responsibility for communications, has some duty to attempt to introduce the new media of 'popular culture' into the classroom, not simply as audio-visual aids or in . . . artistically acceptable forms, but in . . . representative examples.[7]

A version of this same viewpoint was put to us by a young music mistress in a large mixed comprehensive school in London:

> I think it is essential that any music teacher today should take account of the vast amount of music the pupils hear through the mass media. I do not mean that entire lessons should be given over to 'pop' but that it should be treated as a branch of music, with an equal right to be enjoyed as much as any other. The teacher must then go on to help the children decide for themselves what they like or dislike *within each type*. [her italics]

The emphasis here is on the teacher being aware of and open to the nature of pupils' everyday cultural experiences and attempting to build bridges between the classroom and the world of leisure. This strategy has recently been endorsed in the report of a Schools Council working party on music and the young school-leaver. The report concluded that:

The school should make every effort, without lowering its own standards or losing its ideals, to bridge the gap between the music offered in an educational context and the music that young people claim as their own and that they spontaneously and actively enjoy.[8]

This was not the first time that this viewpoint had received 'official' sponsorship. Over eight years before, the Newsom Report had argued that cinema and television are a 'unique and potentially valuable art form . . . as capable of communicating depth of experience as any other art form' and that consequently they should be studied 'in their own right' and not simply 'used as visual aids for the presentation of material connected with other subjects'.[9] This in turn served to reiterate and reinforce the policy that the British Film Institute's Education Department, under the leadership of Paddy Whannel, had been pursuing since the mid-nineteen-fifties.

Notes

1. Michael Marland, 'Mainstream', in Denys Thompson (ed.), *Directions in the Teaching of English*, London, Chatto and Windus, 1969 edn, p. 86.
2. Richard Hoggart, *The Uses of Literacy*, London, Chatto and Windus, 1959, p. 227.
3. Stuart Hall and Paddy Whannel, *The Popular Arts*, London, Hutchinson, 1964, p. 15.
4. Richard Hoggart, 'Culture: Dead and Alive', in Richard Hoggart (ed.), *Speaking to Each Other*, vol. 1 *About Society*, London, Chatto and Windus, 1970, pp. 131–2.
5. Richard Hoggart, 'Mirror for What People?' *New Society*, 27 October 1966, p. 657.
6. Michael Marland, op. cit. p. 74.
7. Robert Shaw, 'Meaning in English at the Leeds Modern School', in G. Summerfield and S. Tunnicliffe (eds), *English in Practice: Secondary English Departments at Work*, Cambridge, Cambridge University Press, 1971, p. 142.
8. Schools Council, *Music and the Young School Leaver: Problems and Opportunities* (Schools Council Working Paper 35), London, Evans/Methuen Educational, 1971, p. 31.
9. *Half Our Future* (Newsom Report), Central Advisory Council for Education, London, HMSO, 1963.

The Institutionalisation of Film and Television Study

Jim Cook and Jim Hillier

From *The Growth of Film and Television Studies 1960–1975*, London, BFI Occasional Paper, 1976.

Film Study Before 1960

. . . What work was taking place seems to have stood very firmly, not [1] surprisingly, within the cultural tradition of Arnold and Leavis. . . . Fundamentally, this tradition was also the context for most of the critical and theoretical writings on the cinema which existed at that time. The film teaching of this period emphasised many of the concerns of established film books such as Ernest Lindgren's *The Art of the Film* and film histories such as those by Paul Rotha and Arthur Knight:[1] a clear view of the historical development of the cinema, a stress on changing technology and techniques, on craftsmanship and on quality. The term 'film appreciation' belongs essentially to this period and this approach, emphasising both learnable facts and techniques and the appreciation of a good cinema. The protective or inoculative approach to cinema remained strong, one result being that the mainstream of popular American cinema (as opposed to the supposed technical innovators such as Griffith or Welles and the 'poets' such as Flaherty) was virtually ignored.

An important aspect of this approach to film study was the interest in [2] film-making. One of the reasons why study centred on techniques was that it was seen as a prelude to students making their own films based on their study. This resulted in carefully scripted story films, shot and edited with as much technical skill as could be mustered. . . .

The Thematic Approach to Film Study

. . . Just as in English teaching there was a move away from the teaching [3] of formal grammar to an approach to language and literature through human and social themes, so in film study there was a shift away from film grammar and history towards an exploration of film through themes. This approach retained an emphasis on personal experience and relevance but aimed also at beginning a more systematic thinking about film.

The best account of this development of the thematic approach remains [4] *Talking About the Cinema* by Jim Kitses and Ann Mercer.[2] Observing that most of their further education day-release students judged films solely in terms of their entertainment value, they wrote:

> It is primarily because of this entertainment bias that we have found
> the theme to be an important organising principle in our teaching.

In taking 'Young People', or 'Personal Relationships', or 'War' and bringing in film materials that treat the subject differently, we have wanted to establish that films *do* have a connection with reality. We have seen this as a first priority in our courses: at the beginning we have planned our lessons so that students are encouraged to find links between the films they see and the life they experience outside. In this way, we have wanted our students to recognise that films can be personally meaningful and judged on other grounds than those of 'entertainment'.

This orientation to film study, or the use of films in study, became, in the 1960s, the dominant approach to film teaching at the secondary level. . . .   5

. . . In practice, the discussion of extractable themes or issues tended to predominate at the expense of consideration of their embodiment in the work – what Kitses and Mercer describe in their work as the balance 'between the objective demands of the study of an art and the personal needs of the students' is upset, to the detriment of any learning about *film* since when this happens one is no longer 'talking about the cinema'. A related problem, as in most thematic approaches, is that if 'style' is felt to be getting in the way of discussion of themes, then certain kinds of film experience are favoured over others. Kitses and Mercer themselves noted the limitation of the thematic approach's possible 'drive towards naturalistic and social films: highly stylised fantasies or more personal and introspective experiences will not "fit" '. . . .   6

Film-Making

In essence, the new approach to film-making meant a move away from our film grammar 'rules' and the carefully scripted, 'well-made film' towards the use of the cine camera as a means of personal expression and of exploration, both of what the camera can do, and also of the properties endemic to it which allow for particular results to be obtained.   7

Although never explicitly theorised at the time, and depending upon the emphasis placed on it, this type of work could in fact either endorse dominant notions of realism – the camera catching 'truth' – or else act as critique of them.   8

One of the main sources of the impact of this new approach was that it opened up film-making as a valid educational exercise for those teachers who doubted the value of the kind of school-made film which had been fundamentally an imitation of the professional product and whose relevance to students' experience seemed slight. Mainly because of this, this approach to film-making is still widely practised, although some of the more interesting developments of this position – exercises, enquiry, rather than finished films – have been in work on media other than film, particularly in practical work with video cameras. . . .   9

Television and Media Studies

The term 'screen education' implies study of media other than film, especially television. Until recently, progress in television and other media studies   10 has been relatively slow and unsystematic. This stems from two causes: firstly, even more than film, it has lacked and still does lack any distinct theory and/or critical tradition, and secondly, linked to this, there has hardly existed in Britain any tradition of studying the ideological nature of institutions.

Some of the problems relating to defining and studying media studies were summarised by Manuel Alvarado in the following terms:

> 'Media' is a very general term and can be used to include a large range of aspects of twentieth-century life. Certainly, one would expect the worlds of advertising, fashion, 'pop' music, photography, film, news-papers, radio, television to be encompassed under that general heading as aspects of what we would term 'mass culture', but in many schools the whole area is likely to be treated in a very negative fashion ranging from excluding discussion to discussing the media in order to 'inoculate' the children against its inherent evils. One of the chief justifications for teaching 'Media' positively is that the media are responsible for being, in Ed Buscombe's words, 'the major source of most people's information about the world or at least about social and political events as well as the minutiae of personal behaviour and life styles'. . . .
>
> If so little positive practical work and so little useful research has been established the questions remain of 'what' and 'how' does one study and teach 'Media'? If criteria can't be borrowed from established disciplines like literature and music (as has been the case with Film Studies) and if there isn't an established body of 'ideas' and 'facts' to be transmitted, the teacher has to start thinking in terms of reorganising the curriculum and reconceptualising his/her whole definition of the term 'knowledge'. For the moment all that can be done is to point at what seem to be the most interesting ideas and areas to develop. One area that needs developing is the notion of the 'process' of the media – of the way in which the media take an event, edit it, 'produce' it and timetable it for relaying. The fundamental transformation that must occur in the process of 'mediation' – the way that messages are 'encoded' and meanings generated – would appear to be one of the most important and urgent tasks for both researchers and teachers to investigate. What is very clear is that, despite what the media organisations might claim about being ideologically free, unbiased and objective, by its very nature the process that they are engaged in is one which requires a high degree of selection and organisation of the many elements involved in that process of production.

Notes

1. Ernest Lindgren, *The Art of the Film*, London, Allen and Unwin, 1948; Paul Rotha, *The Film Till Now*, London, Jonathan Cape, 1930; Arthur Knight, *The Liveliest Art*, New York, Macmillan, 1957.
2. Jim Kitses and Ann Mercer, *Talking About the Cinema*, London, BFI 1966 (revised and expanded 2nd edition 1974).

Film Education and Film Culture

Paddy Whannel

From 'Film Education and Film Culture', *Screen*, vol. 10, no. 3, May/June 1969, pp. 50–7.

We need to make two claims. We have to argue first of all for the *idea* of   1
the study of film as art and entertainment as a distinct discipline having its
own particular problems. Secondly, we need to establish centres at all levels
in education, but especially within higher education, where such a study
can take place. The general case for film study is best put in these terms:
the cinema is a significant feature of contemporary culture representing the
most developed and distinctive form of art produced by technology with
the unique feature that its growth, from its most primitive beginnings, is
preserved for study on celluloid. Other secondary arguments, such as those
in the Newsom Report which make special reference to young people, can
be brought to bear, but it is important to recognise that they are secondary.
One such is the argument that the quality of the varied uses of film now
in existence is dependent on the development of the study of film in its
own right. The teacher of, say, social studies using pieces of poetry, sections
of novels and plays, and so on is drawing upon a rich and established
literature culture. Unless an equivalent film culture is developed the uses
of film will remain partial and thin. . . .

In trying to define what might be involved in the academic study of film,   2
the most useful parallel has always seemed to be with literature. Film, like
literature, has its different forms and genres, its authors and its texts. The
parallel has the merit of simplicity, of making clear, especially to those
outside the film-teaching movement, the distinction between film as aid
and the study of film as art. The central importance of studying the work
of the cinema's great directors can be readily understood as the equivalent
of the study of important novelists and dramatists. The parallel also makes
clear the distinction between film, which has a history, a certain formal
coherence and an emerging scholarship, and television which has none of
these things, or at the best has them in a very rudimentary form.

But while the parallel with literature has its uses, it also evokes the charge   3
of being 'purist' or 'élitist' or being 'too narrow'. One can see why this
should be so. The advocate of film study is faced with the dilemma of
advancing its claims as one of the humanities at a time when the humanities
are in crisis. The literary culture, so long at the centre of our educational
and political systems, is being challenged on all sides. There is the major
challenge from outside of the scientific culture. Also, within the arts there
are developments, especially in the fields of music and the visual arts,
which, in enlisting the aid of technology and being open to a high degree

of cross fertilisation between popular and avant-garde forms, undermine the old literary-based distinctions between highbrow, middlebrow, and lowbrow. Even within education, the assumptions made about the humanising role of literature are under pressure. By and large, the literary culture, with its emphasis on good taste and a refined personal sensibility, *is* narrow. Nothing could be less desirable than to impose such a strait-jacket on the cinema which is, after all, not only an art, but also an industry and a form of mass entertainment. The problem is, therefore, to define the content of film study sufficiently rigorously to give it coherence without suffocating it by too narrow a framework.

We should also be able to define it as a subject independent of how it 4
might be taught and what teaching strategies might be used for different age-groups. The following rough sketch of a possible framework I put forward very tentatively in the hope that it might provoke discussion.

Criticism
It would still seem sensible to regard the illumination of particular texts as 5
the controlling element, so that criticism would be at the centre of the study, although this does not mean that the bulk of the time should be devoted to it. The emphasis should be on description and elucidation rather than on evaluation, and the level of *information* should be high. There is a need to develop systematic approaches and to find more objective bases for critical analysis than personal taste and sensibility. At present the various ideas clustered round the notions of author and genre would seem to present the most useful starting points.

Theory
This is a sparsely documented field. There is a need to re-examine and 6
carry further where possible such existing theories as the traditional film grammar approach. Much must be derived from other fields, such as the work in aesthetics and more specialised studies like semiology and com-munications theory.

Contextual Studies
Assuming the core of the work is the study of particular directors, this 7
must then be related to the context within which a director works and which conditions his work. Areas to be covered here include the structure of the industry, the production system, the entertainment forms available, and the critical climate. Here again the aid of other subject disciplines, such as sociology and economic history, must be sought. . . .

Research and experiment in teaching method must go hand in hand with 8
the attempt to define the content of film study and the nature of film art. There is as much solid work to be done in the former as in the latter. If the film-teaching movement has suffered in the past from being too isolated from criticism, it has also been too isolated from developments within education. There is much to be gained from the experience of other subject specialists, and useful lessons could be drawn from a study of how other disciplines found a place (or in some cases did not find a place) within the

22

educational system. One fundamental question which can only be mentioned in passing here illustrates this. What is the role of practical and creative work in film study? This raises questions not only about the function of such work within a subject conceived as a liberal study, about its relationship to the critical and historical treatment of the subject, but also about the kind of institutions appropriate for film study within higher education. Part of the answer will be found in developing and evaluating the work in the experimental use of audio-visual equipment pioneered by teachers like Douglas Lowndes at Hornsey and Albert Hunt at Bradford. It is notable, for example, that this work has developed alongside the growth of thematic teaching and parallels the shift from the production of the set play to forms of improvised drama with English. It would be interesting, therefore, to consider what forms of practical work would be appropriate to courses that were based neither on themes nor on film grammar. But there is then the question of the relationship of film study as it emerges as a university discipline to the schools, such as the Royal College of Art, offering professional film training. If and when a National Film School is established this issue will be sharpened. Would such a school be the appropriate centre for producing critics, scholars, and potential film teachers? This was not envisaged by the Lloyd Committee, and none of the existing schools regard this as their function, although some provision is usually made for the study of film criticism and history. Is the drift, therefore, towards a School or Schools offering professional training, with the scholarly work taking place inside the university? What then would be the place of practical film-making within a university department? To answer such questions involves us not only in examining the work as it emerges in this country, but also in looking at institutions abroad, such as the large schools in Eastern Europe, the Film Department at UCLA in America, and smaller schools such as the Swedish Film Institute. But more than that, for the division between scholar and practitioner goes deep within the educational system, so that it becomes relevant to look at, for example, the growth of art education with its classic distinction between the departments of fine arts, which aim to produce art historians and critics, and the schools of art which exist to produce artists.

The Media and Society

Stuart Hall and Paddy Whannel

From *The Popular Arts*, London, Hutchinson, 1964, pp. 23–8.

So much of the criticism against the mass media seems uninformed, the 1
attacks misdirected, at times little more than an outburst of irritation and
anger at a *whole* situation, where the products of the media serve as a
scapegoat.

If we are going to deal adequately with the problem as it affects the 2
classroom we must define it carefully; even the more considered statements
contain assumptions that should be carefully examined. These assumptions
appear to group themselves around three broad and seemingly contradictory approaches. As an example of the first approach we might take the
resolution passed at the NUT Annual Conference in 1960:

> Conference, whilst recognising the vital part played by teachers in
> developing the moral and cultural standards of the nation and its
> children, considers that this is a task in which others must co-operate.
>
> Although today more young people than ever are actively engaged
> in intellectual pursuits and appreciate or participate in the creation of
> art, literature, music or drama, Conference believes that a determined
> effort must be made to counteract the debasement of standards which
> result from the misuse of press, radio, cinema and television; the
> deliberate exploitation of violence and sex; and the calculated appeal
> to self-interest.
>
> It calls especially upon those who use and control the media of mass
> communication, and upon parents, to support the efforts of teachers
> in an attempt to prevent the conflict which too often arises between
> the values inculcated in the classroom and those encountered by young
> people in the world outside.

This was an important resolution. It was the first time the issue had 3
arisen in such a form at a major conference and it led directly to the NUT
Special Conference, *Popular Culture and Personal Responsibility*, which
attempted intelligently to bring together teachers, critics, controllers of the
media, and creative artists working within them. But it is unfortunate
that the resolution puts the entire blame on the providers. The prime
responsibility of the providers should, of course, be clear. Nevertheless, it
would have been encouraging if the resolution had recognised that teaching
has a more positive role, and that there are educational inadequacies to
account for as well. No doubt if the Conference had listed the 'values
inculcated in the classroom' they would have been unexceptional. However,

we could benefit from a more precise statement of what those values are, and of how they have stood the passage of time. And there is surely something to say about the *way* those values are handled, and of what often prevents them from making a serious impact upon young people. It is not only that these values are under pressure from newer, perhaps more meretricious, ones. It is that they are often handled in such a way that they fail to connect. They are offered as valid because they fell within a tradition, not because they are still active and alive and relate to contemporary experience. One of the reasons why the Special Conference itself was only a partial success was that many teachers present were too eager to think in terms of censorship and control, to defend the *restrictionist* approach, and to attribute to education a purely passive role.

In this respect the terms used in the Crowther Report (1959) are preferable: 4

> There is undoubtedly a duty on those who wield such great power to use it responsibly. That is a matter for the whole community, and not especially for educationalists. There is also in our view a duty on those who are charged with the responsibility for education to see that teenagers, who are at the most insecure and suggestible stage of their lives, are not suddenly exposed to the full force of the mass media without some counterbalancing assistance.

The Crowther Report does establish a better balance of blame than the   5
NUT resolution, but a more fundamental objection can be made to both statements in the way they define the problem itself. Both passages imply a clear distinction between the two cultures – the culture of the mass media, and the traditional culture of the sophisticated arts – and both see these as standing in opposition to each other.

The language of the Crowther Report is that of threat and menace –   6
young people 'exposed to the full force of the mass media'. In the NUT resolution, the 'counter-balancing assistance' is defined exclusively in terms of the traditional culture – 'art, literature, music or drama'. . . .

The opportunist teacher who embraces the leisure interests of his pupils   7
in the hope of leading them to higher things is as frequently unsympathetic to the really valuable qualities of popular culture as his colleague who remains resolutely hostile. In neither case is there a genuine response, nor any basis for real judgements. Young people are especially sensitive to the insincerity that is often at the root of such opportunism. Even when this doctrine is presented in its more progressive dress as 'beginning with the child's interests' it remains unsatisfactory. The assumption is that we can begin with jazz but with the intention of moving towards concert music; we can begin with the cinema but only as a stage in developing an interest in the theatre. Now jazz music and the movies have their own special virtues but it is doubtful if these can be revealed when they are regarded as only stepping-stones in a hierarchy of taste. If these virtues are not revealed, if in handling jazz and films we do not confront their essential qualities, then their study will not result in a real growth of awareness.

It is, therefore, on a training in discrimination that we should place our   8

25

emphasis. We should think of this as a training for a greater awareness, for a sharper attention to subtle meanings. In this sense it should be distinguished from 'raising the level of taste'. Taste-changing goes on all the time. Calendars with kittens in baskets are replaced by prints of Van Gogh's *Sunflowers* and these in turn by Buffet reproductions. But these shifts in fashion can take place without any great increase in pleasure or understanding.

We must also stop talking about the various kinds of art and entertainment as if they were necessarily competitive. Popular music, for example, has its own standards. Ella Fitzgerald is a highly polished professional entertainer who within her own sphere could hardly be better. Clearly, it would be inappropriate to compare her to Maria Callas; they are not aiming at the same thing. The popular singer, especially one with a jazz background, uses her voice in ways that would be illegitimate for a concert singer. Equally, it is not useful to say that the music of Cole Porter is inferior to that of Beethoven. The music of Porter and Beethoven is not of equal value, but Porter was not making an unsuccessful attempt to create music comparable to Beethoven's. Different kinds of music offer different sorts of satisfaction. If we can begin to recognise different aims and to assess varying achievements with defined limits we shall get rid of much of the mishmash in between.

A true training in discrimination is concerned with pleasure. It places its emphasis on what can be gained from the best that is available. It is careful not to define the best in narrow terms: by 'best' it will mean Tony Hancock rather than the *Brains Trust*, *The Gunfighter* rather than the filmed classic, *Born Yesterday* rather than *Lust for Life*. Already, useful work is being done in this field in a number of schools and colleges, particularly in relation to the cinema. (We will draw upon this in later chapters.) There is, however, an earlier tradition derived primarily from the textbook *Culture and Environment*, written by F. R. Leavis and Denys Thompson and published in 1933. Within this tradition a great deal of valuable work has been done, especially in the teaching of English, and anyone concerned with the problems of education and the cultural environment owes an immense debt to these pioneers. But this work is based on a conservative, indeed pessimistic, view of society. It contrasts the organic culture of pre-industrial England with the mass-produced culture of today. This is a perspective that has produced a penetrating critique of industrial society, but as a guide to action it is restrictive. The old culture has gone because the way of life that produced it has gone. The rhythms of work have been permanently altered and the enclosed, small-scale communities are vanishing. It may be important to resist unnecessary increases in scale and to re-establish local initiatives where we can; but if we wish to re-create a genuine popular culture we must seek out the points of growth within the society that now exists. With the growth of larger political and economic units, the increase in social mobility, and the declining role of the family, the media might be made to provide a range of imaginative experiences which could help young people to grapple with some of the problems they face as a result of maturing quickly and moving at an early age into a more open society. At any rate, we cannot begin to conceive of creative uses of the media if we are

26

thinking wistfully of a past age which it is all too easy to picture in dangerously romantic terms. 'All that can be done, it must be realised,' wrote Q. D. Leavis, 'must take the form of resistance by an armed and conscious minority.' This is too limiting a view – especially for those who teach the majority school population. To be fair, of course, *Culture and Environment* dealt exclusively with the written word, and its destructive criticism of advertising and popular reading-matter has to be seen in the context of the positive teaching of literature. But once we take in the cinema, for example, we can no longer think in defensive terms. No one has to be defended against de Sica, Bergman, or Antonioni.

What continues to be important in the *Culture and Environment* tradition is the emphasis on analysis and the concern for humane values. Analysis as a discipline and method is still rather suspect in the teaching profession. It is true that some of the work done under the heading of literary analysis is niggling and mean-spirited. But we should not spurn a method merely because it has been misapplied. It is sometimes assumed that analysis, with its insistence on close attention to the text and its preoccupation with style, turns the study of literature into an exercise for pedants, excluding all the values that make it a humanising influence. But the text is studied to see what the writer has to say, the style is examined to reveal those very values. The point is made by Dr Leavis in his essay 'Sociology and Literature':

> For to insist that literary criticism is, or should be, a specific discipline of intelligence is not to suggest that a serious interest in literature can confine itself to the kind of intensive local analysis associated with 'practical criticism' – to the scrutiny of the 'words on the page' in their minute relations, their effects of imagery, and so on: a real literary interest is an interest in man, society and civilisation, and its boundaries cannot be drawn; the adjective is not a circumscribing one.
>
> *The Common Pursuit*

Alongside this kind of analysis the teacher will, of course, make provision for all sorts of practical and creative work – painting, imaginative writing, drama, film-making, and so on. But in the hands of a teacher generous and open in his own responses, analysis can also be creative. The work of David Holbrook in English teaching is relevant here; also articles in the journal, *The Use of English*. Raymond Williams's *Reading and Criticism*, published in 1950, provides a useful introduction to its application at adult education level. Some work along these lines is also being carried out in the study of the cinema, and the BFI pamphlet *Film Teaching* describes four courses. We need not accept either the particular judgements of these writers and teachers or the social philosophy that underlies them to see the value and relevance of their work and how it can guide our handling of the art and entertainment provided by the more recently developed communications media. It would, of course, be foolish to make large claims for this popular culture. The cinema, by far the most mature and expressive of these forms, has produced remarkable work in its short history; but it cannot be compared to literature either in volume or quality of achievement. Nevertheless, the best films do offer experiences comparable in kind to those offered by literature, and they can be discussed with similar profit.

Notes

1. F. R. Leavis, *The Common Pursuit*, London, Chatto and Windus, 1952.

Film
Introduction

Elaborating on the problems and limitations, described by Cook and Hillier above, of using audio-visual material in order to extract themes from it, Cary Bazalgette demonstrates both the intellectual problems with a position which argues that meanings are self-evident, and the pedagogic difficulties to which such an assumption can lead. She argues that meanings are constructed, and that it is a task of media education to enable students to recognise this by teaching them to deconstruct and reconstruct media texts.

Although these arguments are still pertinent, the situation out of which they arose was quite specific: an analysis of the ways in which film had been incorporated into the Certificate in Secondary Education (CSE) examinations in English. By contrast, the other piece, which we have taken from *Screen Education*'s 1974 special issue on film, is globally general in its attempts to describe the 'field' of film study.

As such it is both a fascinating example of the intellectual confidence that a nascent 'subject' can engender, and more pragmatically a useful and still valid checklist of areas of connection and crossover for anyone teaching any elements of media study and education at whatever level. As identified in *Primary Media Education – A Curriculum Statement*, BFI 1989, and elaborated in the Part II of this Reader, the core areas of agencies, categories, technologies, languages, audiences, and representations derive from models such as this.

The Myth of Transparency in Film Study:
An Analysis of the ways Film has been
Incorporated into CSE Examinations in English

Cary Bazalgette

From 'The Myth of Transparency in Film Study: An Analysis of the ways Film has
been Incorporated into CSE Examinations in English,' Screen Education,
no. 10/11, Spring/Summer 1974, pp. 8–14.

This use of film [to illustrate set books] is widespread in English teaching, 1
and is still seen by many teachers as the only justification for all the financial
and logistical complications of hiring and showing a feature film. When
local cinemas, libraries, or film societies are showing a particular film of a
set book, the local schools are often invited to send groups of children
along. This may be seen as a far cry from film study proper, but it is
important, nevertheless, because it serves to reinforce the idea, which has
wide currency, that the meaning of visual images is always immediately
explicit. . . .

The assumption here seems to be that works of art are transparent; that 2
in them one 'meets' characters just as one meets them in real life and
without any need for techniques of criticism to understand them. There
seem to be two main reasons for the extension of this assumption to film
study. One is that when using film, most teachers are uncertain about how
to approach it, since they have little experience of studying film themselves.
Furthermore, they usually have to use it in conditions which are hardly
conducive to such elementary procedures as previewing, watching the film
more than once, or using the still-frame device to initiate discussion of
particular images. They will normally see a film once, in a room with sixty
or ninety or even more students, with imperfect sound and blackout. In
such a situation, a simple level of narrative is likely to be the only possible
frame of reference. . . .

What I should like to question fundamentally is the notion that it is 3
somehow easier, 'less academic', for the CSE-level student to study literary
or cinematic texts in this way, starting as it were beyond the artefact, with
a given meaning whose sources are never illuminated. Many of the questions from CSE papers that I have cited seem to me to be in fact immensely
difficult. To explain 'why a character made a vivid impression on you'
seems to be first of all an extremely vague assignment, and secondly one
that to answer in any useful sense at all (other than by using a good deal
of paraphrase) needs a fairly sophisticated critical vocabulary. Similarly,
the demand 'Write an essay describing in detail how Polanski treated any
two of the scenes printed in your extracts. How successful was he?' might
be an easy task for a *Sunday Times* reviewer; less so, I imagine, for the

student who has to manipulate the invisible criteria that lurk behind the word 'successful'. . . .

The fear is that 'by concentrating on technique' one will somehow steril-   4
ise the students' instinctive response; they will no longer be able to 'react naturally' to a film because they will be too busy analysing the techniques used in it. The argument seems to me to have a basic flaw. I am suspicious of a teaching approach that reverences the natural, instinctive, emotional response to such an extent that it separates it from, and evaluates it above, any understanding of the means by which this response has been gained. Any response, however instinctive, is based on a subconscious understanding of stylistic conventions: why is it better for this understanding to remain subconscious? Such an approach, in fact, must ultimately *limit* instinctive response. I would also suggest that in many classrooms the response that is sought is not necessarily the students' immediate emotional response, but one that is acceptable to the teacher, and that is based on sets of definitions already offered by the teacher, for example, 'What does this film tell us about the war?' . . .

But if students are not trained to ask basic questions about the images   5
which confront them, if they are not asked to examine the knowledge and assumptions which they already possess, they are being denied the opportunity to develop the most simple and essential critical tools. They are being trained instead to accept given definitions and, very often, given moral postures as well. They are, in fact, being specifically trained *not* to articulate their own responses.

31

The 'Field' of Film Study

Editorial Board, *Screen Education*

From *Screen Education*, no. 10/11, Spring/Summer 1974, pp. 52–7.

Introduction

The general introduction to this section of *Screen Education* explains in   1
some detail why individual members of the Editorial Board set themselves
the exercise of elaborating what constituted for them the 'field' of film
study. The following collation was made collectively through a further
series of discussions by the Editorial Board.

Broadly, two considerations predominated in attempting to outline col-   2
lectively the 'field' of film study:

- Empirical observation of what has been taught: the syllabuses printed
  earlier; board members' own experience, etc.
- Speculation as to *why* certain areas had been taught, and, in terms of
  the subject 'film', what the extensions might be by implication from
  what *has been* taught to what *could be* taught.

In an effort to prevent this speculation becoming arbitrary and volun-   3
taristic, an attempt was made to ground it in considerations derived from
critical writings and study of the cinema over the last fifteen years. Thus
the 'field' is an attempt to be comprehensive about what might constitute
the subject 'film'.

Main headings, sub-heads, and links are printed alphabetically for two   4
reasons:

- Any other order would suggest a hierarchy of priorities, and to establish
  what such a hierarchy might be in terms of anything other than subjective value judgements seemed too complex a task for the Board to
  embark on at this stage.

  It might be possible to elaborate a hierarchy in terms of the suitability/
  non-suitability of various areas of the subject vis-à-vis student levels of
  intelligence and attainment, educational priorities and methodologies,
  etc., and these are hinted at below and exemplified implicitly in the
  syllabuses printed elsewhere in this issue. Broadly, however, in elaborating the 'field' of the subject, these considerations were *consciously*
  omitted.

- It is recognised that probably neither are the outlined areas of the 'field'
  exhaustive nor the implications of the links fully worked out. The
  list is basically a first draft for a collation of the elements potentially

comprising the field of film study, and before any attempt at creating a hierarchy from it could be attempted one would have to be certain whether, as it stands, the list itself is complete or not.

Bearing this in mind, the glossed notes on the various elements comprising the 'field' should be read as explanatory for this draft and not as having any assured, absolute validity. The gloss against each main heading attempts to explain why the area is included as a main heading; and the gloss against each of the links attempts to sketch out the cross-references that could be made. 5

Connected with the refusal to suggest a hierarchy of main headings, it should be noted: (i) that in most cases each link is a main heading itself elsewhere; (ii) that for any one set of links a particular methodological emphasis could just conceivably treat each one separately as they are outlined below, or else, more realistically, either collapse the whole set or single out one element for particular consideration. 6

Authorship	Although recently subjected to potentially radical assessment and modification, notions of personal authorship still constitute one of the key critical concepts of the 1960s, since it was through an application of them that the first systematic attempts were made to produce knowledge about the popular commercial industrial cinema. 7
Sub-heads	Genre – convention/code – context. Industrial context. Notion of creative artist – personal vision and style, etc.
Links	
Genre	Qualifies the notion of an individual creator; links the artist to a context of conventions – narrative, visual, etc.
Images	Qualifies an exclusively literary thematic consideration of a director's work, i.e., his ideas.
Industry	Studying the context in which movies are made again qualifies any over-simplistic notion of the creative artist and acts as a potential counter-emphasis.
National Cinema/ Movement	Analogous to the link with genre, the link here forces considerations beyond personal vision into those of cinematic and cultural conventions. The interplay of the two can be studied also.
Technology	The determining effect of technology on personal style can be considered. Particular 'techniques' favoured by individuals: deep focus, montage, colour, scope, light-weight camera, etc.

Genre/*Movie Cycles*

Along with authorship, genre is the other key concept developed in order to understand the workings of popular 8 cinema. Potentially quite difficult to handle, it (*a*) confronts directly the cultural context in which movies are made and which they in turn reflect; and (*b*) forces considerations of form and style beyond those elaborated by any one individual.

Sub-heads	Conventions.
	Film history.
	Iconography.
	Society/history/culture (can overlap into other areas of popular culture).
	Stars and star system.

Links

Images   The development of visual conventions, not created by any one individual but common to a body of films (cf. the emphasis given to Images when linked to work on Authorship).

Industry   The extent to which genres develop through a repetition of types of film known to be popular and successful.

Technology   The extent to which changes and developments in technology – sound, colour, scope, etc. – bring about changes and modifications in the form of the genre.

History   As traditionally taught, film history was conceived as a   9
linear progress from Lumière to Wells, and many potentially interesting areas to study were buried beneath the factual details of chronological 'development'. Rather than *a* history of the cinema, particular histories seem more important:

> e.g. technology: sound, colour, scope, video, etc.
> author⎱   early films compared with later
> genre ⎰   ones.
> industry: the period of absolute studio control compared with that of later more independent production.

At a more advanced level it is possible to study the notions of *a* film history, e.g., through a consideration of the writings of someone like André Bazin, but at CSE level history is probably most manageable when it is invoked as a dimension or aspect of other areas under consideration.

Ideology   This is one of the areas referred to earlier as being almost   10
certainly not adaptable to *formal* incorporation into CSE courses. It is probably best realisable as an *emphasis* in other areas, and it is for this reason that the notes on some of the links here are effectively the same as the notes on them under later main headings. In particular

Industry and Images overlap and interlock.

Its importance is that it clearly sets any consideration of film into a broader social context.

While deriving ultimately from quite complex writings on Marxist aesthetics, it is sufficient to note here the usefulness of the notion in demystifying certain prevalent and over-simplified ideas about art in general and film in particular:

(i) the idea of the art object as something to be contemplated and 'appreciated' but not related in any systematic way to a wider social context;

(ii) the idea that when relations between film and 'real life' *are* made, they are made in terms of film's realism, its ability to reflect life directly and open a window on the world.

Sub-heads	Codes and conventions.
	Film production and economic/political systems.
	Film and socio-cultural norms.

Links

Genre	As 'coded' readings of society, e.g., the Western studied as myth-history.
	NB. There is a danger here in that an over-simplified approach simply ends up by downgrading the movies: they got the 'facts' wrong, history got them right.
History	How a particular set of films, e.g., 'psychological' Westerns of the fifties or 'Swinging London' movies of the mid-sixties, may reflect aspects of the society at the time in which they were made. Such studies would be examples of the particular histories referred to in the notes under History.
Images	This constitutes a central link and is probably the most practically realisable way of studying the interrelationship between films and the social context in which they were made and in a complex way reflect. For example: (i) a study of the star system, the projection of star images, the rhetoric of film advertising, cultural 'appeals' in movies; (ii) a study of how technological processes can help determine the form of the image: deep focus, monochrome, glossy colour, etc.
Industry	Again a useful practical way in which to 'study' Ideology: the formula for success of genres; commercial considerations; interference and imposition by a studio on a director's plans, e.g., size of production, choice of star; a studio's identification of themselves with a particular type of film; their image.
National Cinema/ Movement	An identification of cultural mores in the movies; attempts can be made through a consideration of recurrent images (cf. Genre and Images links) to study how

	aspects of the culture are encoded and reflected in the movies.
Technology	An extension of the points made in the notes on the Images link: How the range of technology is promoted as continually increasing cinema's 'realism'; why particular technological innovations are introduced at a particular time, e.g., wide-screen scope to combat small-screen TV.
Images	Central as a prime constituent of the language of cinema. 11
Sub-heads	Conventions – iconography.
	Codes of cinema/film: the idea of a film language.
	General question of reading images – codes of narrative, culture, etc.
	Mise-en-scène: style and meaning.
	Narrative.
	Realism – Expressionism – other isms?
Links	
Authorship	The typical images/mise-en-scène of a director.
Genre	The iconography of a genre.
Industry	The star system; creation of 'Images' and types; the rhetoric of advertising and publicity.
Technology	A study of the various factors which materially determine the form of the image: processing, film stocks, etc.
Industry	Of central importance in locating film in its commercial, 12 industrial, and social context, a study of the industry is a particularly useful way to make points about film's relation to and reflection of dominant social and cultural mores (cf. the introductory notes above on Ideology).
Sub-heads	Genre.
	Processes/stages of production: film as collaborative enterprise, division of labour, etc.
	Publicity/advertising.
	Star system: fans/audiences.
	Structure: ownership of production, distribution, exhibition, and finance.
	Technology.
	Television.
Links	
Authorship	Extent of studio control/interference; factors affecting size of production, choice of stars, etc. Probably best studied as particular case histories, e.g., *Gone with the Wind*.
Genre	Recurrent variations on a pattern/formula known to be commercially successful. A consideration of the extent to which this ensures the continuation of genre movies.
History	A study of the state of the Industry at any particular time and an attempted assessment of the potential influence this may have had on movies then being made. Studies

	could be of the industry in general, particular studios, or particular individuals (studio bosses, producers, stars, etc.).
Ideology	(See also the notes under the Industry link in the Ideology section.) Further areas to study could be the various markets/types of audiences films are aimed at; the industry's response to cultural changes, e.g., sexual permissiveness, politicisation of the young, 'revolution', etc.
Images	As above: projection of star images, advertising, etc.
National Cinema/ Movement	A study of the conditions partially determining the type of cinema and films made: sophistication of plant, state or private ownership of studios, backgrounds (professional and social of 'creative' personnel, etc.).
Technology	The range of it and various determining effects on films made.

National Cinema/Movement

Analogous to genre, studies in this area are a useful way of grouping movies and making connections with the culture. Far more so than with genre, however, there is a potential danger of the sociological element becoming dominant and swamping other concerns. 13

Sub-heads	Origins/influences.
	Politiques/manifestos, i.e., conscious statements of aims.
	Relation to other arts.
	Sociology: relation to history/culture.
	Styles.
	Subjects.

Examples of movements within National Cinemas
  British documentary in the thirties
  Cinéma vérité
  French new wave
  German expressionism
  Italian neo-realism
  Soviet films of the twenties

Links	
Authorship	Studies of particular individuals within a National Cinema/Movement.
History	Growth of the form, and the extent to which it parallels and reflects changes in the culture.
Ideology	*How* the films seem to carry, encode, reflect aspects of and attitudes to the society in which they were produced.
Industry ⎫ Technology ⎭	An inflection of all the aspects already mentioned (organisation, resources, etc.) directed towards a study of one particular National Cinema of Movement.

Technology

Technology is a further area which, although it is central to the 'field' of film study, is probably not easily taught as such except perhaps in film schools. Like History and Ideology, at CSE level it is probably best 'taught' as a 14 dimension of other areas. Its value is that, in a variety of ways, it draws attention to the material level of film and film production.

The problems which work in this area raises are those of the relationship between film-making and film study.

Sub-heads	Film: Colour, monochrome.
	Film gauges.
	Film stocks.
	Lenses.
	Mobility/immobility of equipment (perhaps especially in a study of Documentary).
	Processing.
	Screen ratios.
	Sound.
	Television.
Links	
Genre	Changes affecting conventions and iconography: sound, colour, scope, etc.
History	(i) What was available/possible at any particular juncture and how this affected what was made; (ii) Developments over a period of time in particular pieces of equipment, e.g., increasing mobility of cameras.
Ideology	A study of how and why broadly successive developments in technology are introduced as bringing added realism to film. Why particular innovations were introduced at particular times.
Images	How the 'look' of an image is in part technologically determined: deep focus, scope, etc.
Industry	The range of technology drawn on in making a film. The commercial reasons for changes and developments, e.g., the introduction of scope to combat competition from the small screen of television.
National Cinema/	The determining effects of the particular technology available on films made.
Movement	The use made of particular aspects of technology to achieve a desired effect, e.g., lightweight cameras and the cinéma vérité movement.

Television
Introduction

As Jim Cook and Jim Hillier point out, it was always recognised that television presented particular problems and challenges both for the understanding of its operations and for making it teachable. In general, given the well-established suspicion of mass media products, and in particular because television is deemed to invade the domestic sphere, serious study of TV had to battle for a long time against negative dismissal or a particularly tenacious version of the inoculation approach, or both. For an indication of the extent to which television is still construed as at best ephemeral and at worst a trivialiser of the issues it deals with, consider virtually any review of any programme in the quality press.

Even when television is treated with liberal sympathy, as in the extract from the Bullock Report, such an endorsement is something of a mixed blessing, since its emphasis on appreciation sidesteps issues of study and analysis in favour of assumed consensual values. Like the 'transparency trap' described by Cary Bazalgette, the entailments for teaching from such a position are hazardous.

In 1974, the same year as the Bullock Report (and, indeed, as its Film Study issue), *Screen Education* published Ed Buscombe's report of his secondment as an IBA Schoolteacher Fellow researching the development of TV studies in schools and colleges. Here for the first time issues of ownership and control were thought through along with the more 'traditional' concern with television's texts, and all of this framed within a concern for pedagogy and the teachability of television studies.

Writing six years later, Len Masterman is also centrally concerned with what is taught and what it is possible to teach. Echoing Buscombe he argues that the entire range of television output should be subject to a 'mode of enquiry' based on a tripartite model of observation and description, interpretation, and analysis, with the overall educative aim of exposing the mediations and ideological constructs behind the seemingly transparent flow of images and sounds.

The bewildering diversity of intellectual approaches that could be taken in furthering such an enquiry are summarised by Andrew Goodwin and Garry Whannel with the implication that, while in the 70s and 80s they all followed each other too quickly and too often in a rather ill-digested fashion, now they are worthy of strategic reconsideration, depending upon what aspects of television it is that one wants to study and teach.

39

Resources

The Bullock Report

From *A Language for Life* (Bullock Report), London, HMSO, 1974, Part 7, para. 22.14.

22.14 One of the most powerful sources of vivid experience is the general output programmes of television, particularly documentaries and drama. Many teachers are already basing a good deal of classroom work on such programmes. In some primary schools they use after-school programmes as a stimulus for talking and writing, and assemble collections of books to exploit the interest the programmes arouse. In secondary schools the practice is more widespread, and we met teachers who brought the experience of the television screen into the classroom, preparing for evening programmes and following them up the next day. Some classes were reading the texts of television plays with enjoyment and others were writing scenes for themselves. In a few schools we came across serious study of the medium of television itself. We were impressed by such work as we did see but are concerned that a decade after the publication of the Newsom Report there is still little evidence of the kind of study it recommended: 'We should wish to add a strong claim for the study of film and television in their own right'. We believe that in relation to English there is a case for the view that a school should use it not as an aid but a disseminator of experience. In this spirit we recommend an extension of this work. Although there is unquestioned value in developing a critical approach to television, as to listening and reading, we would place the emphasis on extending and deepening the pupils' appreciation.

Television Studies in Schools and Colleges

Edward Buscombe

From 'Television Studies in Schools and Colleges', *Screen Education*, no. 12, Autumn 1974, pp. 6–13.

It is imperative that those who wish to study television should put forward the strongest possible arguments for doing so, arguments that will justify their demand for access to the facilities. We have seen how the case for film studies has altered over the years, how there has been a shift away from using film to train the responses of students to artistic experience and towards increasing their understanding of how film relates to society. How much of this is relevant to television? The first thing to be said is that, although, as Murdock and Phelps have demonstrated, the 'inoculation' approach is still with us, there is little profit in recommending the study of television as a way of turning people against it. Starting from the premise that television is meretricious is not a good way of understanding it. The establishment of a new area in the curriculum will require from those who are to undertake it a high degree of energy, commitment, and hard work. One of the major problems confronting the development of the subject is that it is on the teachers themselves that a large part of the burden will fall, not only of exploring ways of teaching it but also of actually constituting the subject. It is not the case that there already exists a large body of knowledge about television which the teachers will simply have to impart to their students. On the contrary, our present knowledge is sketchy, and since television is only just beginning to be studied seriously in universities and polytechnics teachers cannot anticipate that a very large quantity of research will be forthcoming in the immediate future. For the time being much will rest on the enthusiasm of teachers working in the classroom; if they don't even like television they are not likely to be of much use.

Nor is it realistic to suppose that we can get very far by searching among the total output of television for the 'best that has been thought and said'. Some work has been done on television on just this basis, concentrating on 'serious' plays, or programmes such as *Panorama*. The problem here is that not only will the teacher's students probably not watch these programmes from choice; even more importantly, one cannot hope to understand television as a whole without understanding all its parts. This does not imply the acceptance of television as it is, but if we wish to have any hope of improving it we need first of all to know what kind of a thing we are dealing with. Television commercials, quiz shows, light entertainment programmes, soap operas, and other despised genres all repay close attention, and not just because some of them may be 'good of their kind'.

41

The implications of this will be examined more closely in the following section, which deals with the 'what' rather than the 'why'. But there are one or two more things to be said at this point on the subject of why study television. One answer might be, just because it's there. Research shows that American children already spend more time watching television than they do in school, and there is reason to suppose that British children will soon reach this stage if they have not already done so. Television is a major, perhaps *the* major, source of most people's information about the world, or at least about social and political events as well as the minutiae of personal behaviour and life styles. The mere fact that television is there may not really be a reason for studying it. Children spend more time asleep than they do watching television, but that is not an argument for studying sleep in schools (though the unconvinced might retort that sleeping and watching television are pretty much the same thing). But despite the disagreements among social scientists about the actual effects of television, there can be no doubt that it is a major factor in our cultural experience. For this reason alone it seems absurd that it should be almost totally excluded from the classroom.

But the argument cannot be left there. 'The philosophers', as Marx said, 'have only interpreted the world in various ways. The point, however, is to change it.'[1] If television is such an important part of our lives then it is too important to be left to the programme-makers and executives. It is said above that the development of television studies requires us to be interested in all aspects of television. But this does not imply that the present state of television be simply accepted as either desirable or unalterable. If we do not wish to dismiss television as rubbish neither do we wish to embrace everything that the programme-planners give us. In fact, we should not want to be 'given' anything at all. Television at the moment is a closed shop, in more than the ACTT[2] sense. It is controlled and operated by a comparatively small number of people. The very much greater numbers for whom the programmes are produced have virtually no say in the decisions taken. There is no public representation on any of the controlling bodies (of course, there are members of the public on some of them, but they do not represent anyone but themselves). This is not the place for an essay on the need for publicly responsible and responsive broadcasting, but if one accepts the arguments put forward by Nicholas Garnham in *Structures of Television* (BFI Television Monograph 1973), as I largely do, then one justification for television studies becomes clear. A knowledge and understanding of television in the public at large is a prerequisite for public control over the medium. Such knowledge will not in itself bring this control, for this will need political action. But it is a necessary first stage. . . .

It is no part of my argument, therefore, that television should be studied because it is more important than anything else, nor because it is easier than other things. Rather, it should be studied because it is *one* important medium of communication, which people need to better understand and control. But the introduction of television study into schools might also have some effect on the educational system. This is not the place for a lengthy examination of what is wrong with our present system, but it can

3

4

5

scarcely be denied that all is not well. In some London schools the situation is close to breakdown, with absenteeism rife among staff and students, acute problems of discipline, and a generally low morale. The study of television will not in itself put these things right, but the nature of the subject is such that it might well have some effect. One of the reasons why film studies have been regarded with suspicion by some teachers is that it is felt to be a 'soft option', by which is meant that the students like it. Of course, its detractors would maintain that students like it because they aren't required to do any 'work', but it might be useful to enquire why the 'work' they have to do in other classes is disliked. Presumably it is because they do not see that the effort expended is commensurate with the potential rewards to be obtained. I am not contending that television should be taught simply because it might prove popular, although for many teachers, particularly the hard-pressed ones trying to cope with reluctant ROSLA (Raising of the School Leaving Age) classes, this might be reason enough. Still, the potential popularity of the subject ought not to count against it, certainly not when in many areas of the educational system it is becoming increasingly difficult to interest students in anything at all. And certainly not when this popularity may be a reflection of the fact that students find they are getting something useful out of it. That in fact they *are* working, in the sense of actually learning, and enjoying it, whereas in other subjects, they are often working but not really learning, and so not enjoying it.

But I think it can be claimed that another consequence besides popularity 6 might follow from the introduction of television studies. Despite an increase in liberalisation since the war, our educational system is still extremely authoritarian. The basic classroom situation is still that of a teacher out in front telling things to his class, which they are expected to receive passively. In many subjects and many schools there is very little two-way communication. Education thus reflects, indeed prepares people for, the largely authoritarian structure of society as a whole, in which work is organised hierarchically. Schools, just like industry, are run by a very few people telling the rest what to do.[3] I am not arguing that teachers should not know more than their students, only that there are better ways of imparting knowledge than the one commonly practised. In teaching about television it ought to be less easy simply to reproduce such a situation. This is not because the teachers would be little better informed than their classes (this is unfortunately likely to be the case in some instances, but isn't therefore desirable); rather, it is because of the nature of the teaching methods which seem most suitable for the subject. This will be more fully discussed in the next section, but it can be said here that the system of teachers delivering lists of facts to their classes is not very appropriate for television studies. One would not be teaching simply information. Television is not just a picture on a screen but a process of production. The best way to learn about such a process is to carry it out for yourself. Television teaching, I would argue, needs always to contain some practical work in which the members of the class co-operate in the production of some material, and thereby learn, if only by analogy, how television programmes are put together, how they come to be what they are. In this way the old, rigid pattern of instruction will be broken down and replaced by a new type of learning situation, of simulation. Such a situation would not be any great novelty; it is already being practised in certain schools and in certain subjects. Nor should one assume that a new subject would necessarily dictate new teaching methods. One knows only too well how hard teachers cling to the old methods, and it would be quite possible to teach about television in a way that was as rigid and inflexible as ever. But at least with television it should be easier to show that such methods would be very bad ones for the subject, and that the kind of resources available make the old methods unnecessary. . . .

The question remains, exactly what kind of analysis can the teacher carry 7 out? We do not as yet have anything approaching a theory of television which is capable of supporting any analysis we might make; and there is not even, as there is in film studies, a tradition of close textual reading. It is precisely the latter, I think, which needs to be established. A theory of television, just as a theory of cinema (assuming that such a thing is indeed possible), will need to be so complex and intricate that it will be a long time coming. But this does not mean that in the interval there are not useful things to be said about television programmes. Those things are more likely to be helpful the more they get away from purely personal impressions and the more they are grounded in a rigorous methodology which is at least conscious of the assumptions it makes even if it cannot always demonstrate their validity. The analysis of television can profit from the experience of film studies.

Notes

1. Karl Marx, 'Theses on Feuerbach', in *Basic Writings on Politics and Philosophy*, London, Collins Fontana, 1969.
2. Association of Cinematography, Television and Allied Technicians which has now become the Broadcasting Entertainment and Cinematograph Technicians Union (BECTU).
3. For a very good description of this situation, and a critique, see Douglas Holly, *Beyond Curriculum*, especially the chapter 'Conventional Secondary School Practice', London, Paladin, 1974.

The Case for Television Studies

Len Masterman

From *Teaching about Television*, London, Macmillan, 1980, pp. 7–13.

So far I have tried to draw attention to two observable trends in media education. First of all an increasing awareness by teachers of the problems associated with the use of film material in the classroom, an awareness which has led to a growing feeling that television might be a more appropriate and important medium for study. The second trend concerned an observable movement towards the umbrella subject of media studies in which the study of television would play an important part. I have attempted to draw attention to the epistemological fuzziness surrounding media studies, to point to some of its deficiencies in existing classroom practice, and to look at some of the problems raised by one version of the subject in which the study of the media as consciousness industries would provide the containing framework. It now remains to ask whether the medium of television itself can offer to the teacher a framework for disciplined study. 1

The need for a sound theoretical base capable of standing close scrutiny is paramount. At the moment the study of television in schools lacks not only intellectual coherence but even very much in the way of simple mechanical co-ordination. There are exceptions,[1] but, whether television is taught independently or within the context of the mass media, the tendency appears overwhelmingly to be for teachers to go very much their own way, guided principally by their own tastes and judgements and by a generalised desire to encourage discrimination and visual literacy. The proliferation of Mode III examinations (courses devised and assessed by teachers), while bringing tremendous advantages in its encouragement of teacher independence and initiative, has tended to contribute to the current chaotic heterogeneity. As a result, television courses at the moment are largely uninfluenced by one another, and good practice remains isolated within individual schools. The lack of course co-ordination, together with the familiar difficulty for overworked teachers of making space for themselves in which they can seriously reflect upon their own practice, has been responsible for television being taught in something of an intellectual vacuum. Yet there is evidence that some teachers are moving away from 'discriminatory' television teaching towards new approaches, and that if only the right questions could be posed it might be possible to find a surprising amount of agreement about what might constitute the way ahead. The purpose of the rest of this chapter is to pose these questions and to suggest answers which might illuminate the way in 2

45

which television teaching might develop in schools within the next decade.

To what extent can the study of television be constituted as a viable intellectual discipline? Before we can answer this question we must ask another: what is it that constitutes any discipline? Most fundamentally a discipline is characterised by *an agreed field of study or enquiry*, and is further defined by an *intellectual framework which delimits the questions to be asked*. Information is elicited from the field through a *distinctive mode of enquiry* and the purposes of this enquiry must be '*important*' or '*serious*' in ways which need no elaborate justification. Jerome Bruner has also argued that at the core of any discipline lie *concepts* and *principles* 'as *simple* as they are *powerful*' which 'may be taught to anybody at any age in some form'.[2] Can these considerations lead us to a more disciplined study of television? It is to this question which we must now turn.

The Field of Study
The primary object of study in television studies is observable and circumscribed; it is the continual flow of information which is communicated to us by television. What are the characteristics of this body of information? Most importantly the study of television is based upon the premise that televisual information is *non-transparent*. As Nell Keddie has pointed out,[3] this is also true of film studies, but the need to emphasise and demonstrate non-transparency is even more urgent in television since it is an apparently less synthetic medium than film, with an apparently closer relationship to 'real' events. A 'window on the world' view of the medium would make the study of television impossible; one would not be studying it but other things – news, sport, or light entertainment. The case for the study of television rests upon the significance and potency of a mediating process which exists independently of the existence of the event being televised.

Televisual communication is also characterised by its greater diversity – it serves the functions of the newspaper, theatre, cinema, sports arena, and music hall all rolled into one. This apparent hindrance to its disciplined study (it is difficult to imagine any but the woolliest of conceptual structures being able to comprehend such diverse functions) again forces attention upon a major generic function of television which is to provide a field for the embodiment and revelation of beliefs, values, and attitudes. This it must inevitably do. In practice one can say much more – that in every country in which it operates *television has an ideological function*, as James Halloran has succinctly pointed out:

> Generally throughout Europe television serves the nation-state, whatever the politics of the state. . . . On the one side there are the broadcasters with their professional ideologies, occupational routines, and self-protecting mythologies, who have been socialised into a profession within given socio-economic systems. These professionals select, process, and present the message. On the other side, there are individuals who make up the non-participating audiences and who receive the messages in relative isolation. It is seen by many as an elitist, literary set-up where a small group of educated, articulate people who more or less share the same codes of the dominant culture

3

4

5

– encode messages for consumption by others who have different codes . . . generally the receiver will not be in a position to recognise all the professional rules and practices.[4]

Stuart Hood has drawn the connection between television's ideological function and the carefully fostered illusion of transparency:

> Since one of the principal functions of television is to convey the dominant ideology of society, the impression of immediacy or lack of intervention is important. What appears to be immediate is less likely to be questioned.[5]

Roland Barthes's notion of myth – 'depoliticised speech' – takes the logic of the argument a stage further. When constructed meanings operate under the guise of 'givens', when ideological dimensions are suppressed, and speech depoliticised, then 'Nature seems to spontaneously produce the represented scene'.[6] Myth transforms ideological representations into natural ones. The study of television necessarily becomes the study of myths through the suppression of ideological functions and mediating processes. *Television education is therefore a demythologising process which will reveal the selective practices by which images reach the television screen, emphasise the constructed nature of the representations projected, and make explicit their suppressed ideological function.* Such an education will also necessarily be concerned with alternative realities – those constructions implicitly rejected, suppressed, or filtered out by the images which appear on the screen.[7]

If this theoretical formulation seems remote from the kinds of activities which are normally considered to be within the capabilities of a mixed-ability comprehensive school class, it is because the sphere of ideology is one which pupils will approach as the final stage of a three-level process of analysis. The teacher's first task is to encourage his pupils to generate from images *descriptions* of what they see at a *denotative* level. This, it is suggested, may be achieved by increasing awareness of the multiplicity of ways in which television images communicate their meanings. Secondly, he may encourage pupil *interpretation* by drawing attention to the *connotative* levels of meaning in cultural images and objects. What does each denotative quality *suggest*? What associations do that colour, that shape, that size, that material have? Discussion, at first free-flowing and open-ended, will gradually become less so as definite patterns and clusters of associations become evident and the group move into interpretation at the *third* level, that of *ideology*, 'the final connotation of the totality of connotations of the sign' as Umberto Eco has described it. What does this programme *say* through its complex of signs and symbols? What values are embodied here, and what does it tell us of the society in which it finds a place? Who is producing this programme, for what audience, and with what purpose?

To recapitulate: in television studies the field of investigation is constituted by the flow of information communicated to us by the medium. In spite of the apparent transparency, neutrality, and diversity of function of this information it is both mediated and ideological. Mediation and ideology are themselves inextricably intertwined. Mediation is an ideological pro-

47

cess, whilst ideology becomes 'visible' the moment that mediation processes are pinned down. The nature of that mediation and ideology can be partly revealed by a three-step process of analysis in which television information is examined at the levels of its denotative and connotative meanings before revealing itself as an ideological construct. For a fuller understanding of the constructed nature of the television image, however, further interrogation is necessary both of the images themselves and of the contexts within which they are embedded. Attention will need to be drawn to such diverse containing frameworks as the contextualising remarks of announcers, linkmen, comperes and presenters; articles relating to television programmes in the press or in *Radio Times* and *TV Times*; the visual codings and conventions of the medium; and the routine professional practices of those who work within it.

Of all the questions that can be asked of the television image it is those which reveal it as a mediated and ideological construct which provide the most significant structures within television studies' conceptual framework. Many other questions can, and often will, be asked by the student of the television image; for example,

> What other programmes are like this one? What connections can be made between this programme and others featuring the same star/ production team/writer? What insights does this programme give us into the problems and people it depicts? How does this programme compare with the novel or play it derives from? Do I like this programme? Does the programme/film/play/documentary have any kind of organic unity? Is it of greater or less value than comparable programmes?

These questions simultaneously open out further perspectives and delimit additional areas of enquiry. They are questions of *secondary significance*, however, since they are most properly applied only to part of the total output of television and not to all of it.

This is perhaps an appropriate point to stress that the discussion of questions ought in itself to play a significant role in television education. How many questions is it possible to ask of a television picture? What are the differences between these questions? Can they be categorised? Or arranged into a hierarchy? These and other methodological problems ought not simply to be the concern of the teacher, but should be thought through and understood by pupils as well, for it is they who will ultimately be confronting the primary source material and who will need to be aware of the wide variety of tools at their disposal for making sense of it.[8]

The Mode of Enquiry

Some indication has already been given of the kind of enquiry in which television studies will engage. What will be the process of this enquiry? The task of the student of television is to *observe* and *describe* the images he sees, and *interpret* them at their connotative and ideological levels. This will involve the *analysis* of the codings, conventions, and mediating processes which shape television images. As I have stressed, however, this

48

mode of enquiry cannot reveal mediating frameworks which exist outside of the medium itself; it cannot directly disclose those images which have been excluded from the screen, and it cannot inform us directly of the many constraints and influences operating upon the form of a particular communication, though in both areas legitimate inferences can often be made on the basis of the images themselves. Our mode of enquiry will need to incorporate a sensitivity to its own limitations, and an awareness that these less accessible strands will need to be woven into any coherent understanding of television images. Hence the importance attached in this book to simulations in which pupils themselves become mediators and the acts of selection which make the television image a 'preferred' one can be replicated in the classroom.

Core Concepts and Principles

Teachers of the mass media will find it a useful exercise to try to formulate the 'simple' and 'powerful' concepts which lie at the heart of their work. The difficulties of achieving this *across* the media have already been touched upon. Central to the study of television there seem to me to be a number of core concepts: total communication, connotation, mediation, and ideology; and a number of subsidiary ones such as genre, iconography, and coding. Most of these – the concepts if not necessarily the words – seem to me to be capable of being passed on to the youngest of pupils in intellectually respectable versions via a spiral curriculum of the kind suggested by Bruner. The brief for television education in primary and secondary education must be to find ways of introducing and deepening these concepts through the use of material appropriate to different age ranges.

The Importance of Television Studies

One of the most persistent arguments which the television teacher will meet from colleagues and parents is this: 'I find your work very interesting, most stimulating, etc., but do you *really* think it's important? I mean, a lot of the material you're handling is pretty trivial stuff; and kids watch too much of it anyway, without our needing to bring it into the classroom. Surely there are more important things for them to be doing in school.' According to Murdock and Phelps's survey[9] this view is still widely prevalent in schools, let alone amongst parents: 80 per cent of grammar schools and 42 per cent of the comprehensive schools surveyed felt that the study of the mass media had little or no legitimate claim to classroom attention. This whole question, then, is neither remote nor academic, but one that the television teacher will meet every day in the course of his work. In the last resort, any answer to the question 'Why is the study of television important?' must be a personal rather than a definitive one; in offering my own answer I do so in the recognition that the individual teacher will wish to add arguments of his own, and delete those with which he cannot agree.

The study of television is important because the medium itself is important. The Bullock Report is simply the latest of a number of sources to draw attention to the fact that most pupils spend far more time watching television than they do in the classroom.[10] To teach about television is to value this important and concrete part of pupils' experience and to assume its prime importance in real pupil learning. It is to attack a countervailing tendency in education to distrust the experience and judgement of the pupil, a process which whittles away the significance of his opinions, his dignity, and ultimately his identity. One of the most damning indictments of schooling is that it can instil a conviction in pupils that neither they nor their experience are of any importance. A belief that one is not worthy of anything better is, of course, a precondition for the passive acceptance of slum houses, boring repetitive jobs, and social and political subservience. Television studies assumes the prime importance of the experience of the learner, attempts to raise his consciousness by demythologising this experience; encourages him to posit alternatives; demonstrates the importance and strength of group experience; and continually fringes out from what is concrete and 'known' to a consideration of the wide range of social, aesthetic, industrial, political, and philosophic issues raised by particular programmes.

Television is a major source of most people's information about the world. Because we live in a socially segregated society with total institutions for deviants, and socially segregated housing and schooling areas, the medium is often our *only* source of information about a wide range of social problems and deviancies. Hartmann and Husband[11] have drawn attention to the importance of the frames of reference within which such issues are presented by television, and which need very careful scrutiny before any understanding of the issues involved can be reached. The study of television is vital not simply because it is such a pervasive and influential medium, but, as we have seen, because of its apparent transparency and naturalness. Knowledge of the mediated and constructed nature of the television message, and of the ways in which pictures are used selectively, ought to be part of the common stock of every person's knowledge in a world where communication at all levels is both increasingly visual and industrialised. Television education is therefore part of an education for responsible citizenship. The case for its serious study seems to me to be very strong – even unanswerable; the fact that the medium continues to be ignored by vast numbers of schools in spite of a whole string of recommendations from official reports over the last twenty years is indeed an indictment of the conservatism and inflexibility of many educational establishments and of their inability to respond to developments and trends of major significance within society.

Notes

1. The ILEA, for example, is making an outstanding attempt not only to co-ordinate but to develop television work in schools, whilst in Lincolnshire co-operation between the local authority and two local colleges of education has resulted in the setting up of television facilities which are widely used by local schools.
2. Jerome Bruner, *The Process of Education*, Cambridge, Mass., Harvard, 1960, pp. 12–13.
3. Nell Keddie, 'What are the criteria for relevance?' *Screen Education*, no. 15, Summer 1975, p. 4.
4. James Halloran, 'Understanding television', *Screen Education*, no. 14, Spring 1975.

5.   Stuart Hood, 'Visual literacy examined' in Bryan Luckham (ed.), *Audio-Visual Literacy* (Proceedings of Sixth Symposium on Broadcasting Policy), University of Manchester, 1975.

6.   Roland Barthes, *The Rhetoric of the Image*, Working Papers in Contemporary Cultural Studies, Spring 1971, Birmingham University.

7.   The precise nature of the media's ideological function has been the subject of much debate. Some writers – following Marx's, 'the ideas of the ruling class are in every epoch the ruling ideas' – identify the dominant ideology as the pattern of ideas and beliefs of the dominant class, a position which leads to a view of media products as monolithic expressions of ruling-class values. But as Sylvia Harvey has observed, 'The notion of a single ruling-class ideology organising and uniting the organs of mass communication ignores both the presence of divisions within the ruling class and the extent to which the ideology of free speech does open up a space for progressive journalists and media practitioners' (*May 1968 and Film Culture*, London, BFI, 1978). More recent Marxist thinking has therefore suggested a more complex view of ideology as a process through which ruling-class ideas become transmuted into 'natural' representations and common-sense notions. This development has been clarified by Barthes' concept of Myth, but owes most to a resurgence of interest in the work of Gramsci whose concept of *hegemony* moved beyond notions of imposition of ruling-class ideas to an understanding of how a dominant class's definitions of reality come *by consent* to constitute the lived reality of a subordinate class and to define the limits of common-sense for that class and for society as a whole. Common sense is, as Geoffrey Nowell-Smith has suggested, 'the way a subordinate class in society lives its subordination'. This view of ideology involves an obvious paradox. For common-sense is, in its own terms, by definition, un-ideological, a-political. The process of ideology, therefore, works most crucially in the very area where its existence is most strenuously denied. It is to be understood, in Stuart Hall's words, 'not as what is hidden and concealed but precisely as what is most open, apparent, manifest . . . the most obvious and "transparent" forms of consciousness which operate in our everyday experience and ordinary language: common-sense'.

8.   See Neil Postman and Carl Weingartner, *Teaching as a Subversive Activity* (Harmondsworth, Penguin, 1971) for a detailed discussion on the importance of questions in the school curriculum.

9.   Graham Murdock and Guy Phelps, *Mass Media and the Secondary School*, London, Macmillan/Schools Council, 1973, ch. 5.

10. *A Language for Life* (The Bullock Report), London, HMSO, 1974, ch. 2, para. 5. The *difference* between viewing and classroom hours may surprise even television teachers. Bullock gives the average figure of 25 hours viewing per week for pupils between the ages of 5 and 14. This gives an annual total of 1300 viewing hours. Assuming that pupils between 5 and 14 are in the classroom for 4½ hours each day (rounding down to discount time spent in assemblies, sports, etc.) and for 40 weeks each year, this gives an annual total of 900 hours spent in the classroom. *Children between 5 and 14 therefore on average spend 44 per cent more time watching television than they do in the classroom.*

11. Paul Hartmann and Charles Husband, 'The mass media and racial conflict' in Stan Cohen and Jock Young (eds), *The Manufacture of News*, London, Constable, 1973.

51

Understanding Television

Andrew Goodwin and Garry Whannel

From *Understanding Television*, London, Routledge, 1990, Introduction pp. 4–6.

One problem that might explain the delay in 'cashing in' the advances of the 1970s is that those developments remain extremely uneven. They range from relatively prosaic efforts to undertake sociological studies of television through to wordy engagements with the outer conceptual reaches of psychoanalytic theory. And many of these theoretical advances remain as yet unconsolidated. One perhaps necessary side-effect of the explosion of cultural theory in the 1970s was a tendency for media analysis to latch on to new ideas in an almost ephemeral fashion that resembled television more closely than scholarship. Students of television grappled with the implications of, say, the structuralist analysis of Louis Althusser[1] . . . only to discover that the academy went '*post*structuralist' that very same week. New theories of ideology and culture often seemed to be uncovered, developed, critiqued, and abandoned within a matter of months. (One explanation for this lies in the poverty of British theory, which often latched on to developments abroad very late, only to discover that they were already out of date.)

We exaggerate this 1970s trend in order to make a serious point: that one effect of this emphasis on new theory was the premature abandonment of many potentially fruitful concepts and paradigms. One only has to think of the way in which the ideas of the German Marxists of the Frankfurt School were first rediscovered, then parodied and critiqued (as parody), and finally discarded. In the process, a number of important insights were lost, and any attempt to re-engage with them could quickly be dismissed as thoroughly *passé* in the fast-moving world of 1970s media theory.

A great deal of 1970s analysis of television and the media has yet to be fully worked through. There is the question not only of those paradigms that might usefully be re-evaluated, but also the problem of inadequate theoretical projects which remain abandoned by the analytical roadside, like clapped-out old cars. Their breakdown has yet to be fully understood. The debate about 'realism' is one such abandoned rust-bucket. In the 1970s the theoretical air crackled with concepts that derived from Marxism, feminism, psychoanalysis, and cinematic and literary theory, and academic journals like *Screen* and *Framework* published numerous articles analysing television in these terms. Eventually this work collapsed under the weight of its own theoreticism and the debate about realism and modernism was simply abandoned in favour of a new (and apparently *unrelated*) discussion about '*post*modernism', which takes place as though the early 1970s positions never existed.

One problem for 1970s work was an understandable infatuation with theory at the expense of empirical analysis, and a related tendency (clearly determined by the politics of academia) to fetishise 'originality'. An original theory was often more exciting and prestigious than an explanatory one. It is generally agreed that one problem in evaluating competing theories developed in the 1970s was the lack of concrete analysis involved in merely applying theories to texts and thus producing dozens of (sometimes contradictory) 'readings'.

In the 1980s there was a tendency to move back towards the empirical: towards testing out critical debates through an engagement with the site of production;[2] towards a testing out of critical theories via closer readings of the text;[3] and towards a testing out of textual readings through a study of actual audiences.[4] There has also been a related interest and commitment to the *popular*. That is to say, where theory in the 1970s often looked at popular television to discover whether or not it measured up to certain pre-given theoretical and political criteria, the 1980s have seen a shift towards taking the popular on its own terms, and beginning with actual public taste cultures (in order to understand them better), rather than abstract theories.[5] This period has thus seen a shift from a focus on 'serious' television (drama, documentary, news, current affairs) to popular entertainment forms (soap opera, situation comedy, pop music video, sport, game show, and so on). This approach has its advantages (and does, after all, derive from a theory – a paradigm built on the writings of Antonio Gramsci), but it also has its detractors.[6]

A further and more difficult shift in 1980s approaches emerged out of a perceived change in television itself. This was the debate about postmodernism. This term is notoriously difficult to pin down, but can be summarised in this context as a concern with a number of ways in which contemporary television is seen to defy the old modes of analysis deriving from literary and cinematic theory. Critics point to programmes like *Miami Vice*, *Late Night With David Letterman*, *The Singing Detective*, and *Max Headroom*, and to new forms and services like music video and MTV, as examples of television that is qualitatively different from the texts of the 1970s.[7] While these critics certainly can't be said to agree among themselves, the common themes in such analyses are a concern for television's recent incorporation of avant-garde modernist devices, its 'flatness' and emphasis on surface style, its abandonment of traditional narrative; and its tendency to be self-reflexive and about itself (rather than a mediation between itself and an extrinsic 'reality'). Many critics now argue that this postmodern aesthetic requires new ways of 'reading' and understanding television.

Clearly a further important trend (and perhaps a related one) in the 1980s concerns not the text–reader relation addressed by postmodern critics, but the text–institution relation that is radically altered by the growing deregulation of television, on both sides of the Atlantic. The 1986 Peacock Report on broadcasting offered a challenge to British assumptions about the organisation of television as a public service. In the context of British television this has meant a radical questioning of the assumptions that analysts once took for granted. It has also meant an engagement with the proliferation of sites of distribution, as television becomes available not as a text transmitted by a national duopoly, but as a product available through a multiplicity of marketplace sources – home video and cable and satellite TV now supplement the public service institutions of television.

Notes

1. Louis Althusser, 'Ideology and ideological state apparatuses', in *Lenin and Philosophy and Other Essays*, London, NLB, 1971.
2. Cf. Jane Feuer, Paul Kerr, and Tise Vahimagi, *MTM: 'Quality Television'*, London, BFI, 1984; John Ellis, *Visible Fictions*, London, Routledge, 1982.
3. Cf. Harold Newcomb (ed.), *Television: The Critical View*, New York, OUP, 1987; Len Masterman (ed.), *Television Mythologies: Stars, Shows and Signs*, London, Comedia, 1985.
4. Cf. Dorothy Hobson, *'Crossroads': Drama of a Soap Opera*, London, Methuen, 1982; Ien Ang, *Watching Dallas*, London, Methuen, 1985; Justin Lewis, 'Decoding TV News', in Phillip Drummond and Richard Paterson (eds), *Television in Transition*, London, BFI, 1985; David Morley, *Family Television: Cultural Power and Domestic Leisure*, London, Comedia, 1986.
5. Cf. Tony Bennett *et al.* (eds), *Popular Television and Film*, London, BFI, 1981; Richard Dyer (ed.), *Coronation Street*, London, BFI, 1981.
6. Cf. Carl Gardner and Jenny Shepherd, 'Transforming television – Part One, The limits of left policy', *Screen*, vol. 25, no. 2, March/April 1984; Judith Williamson, 'The problems with being popular', *New Socialist*, no. 41, September 1986.
7. Cf. Todd Gitlin, 'Car commercials and *Miami Vice*: we build excitement', in Todd Gitlin (ed.), *Watching Television*, New York, Pantheon, 1987; Larry Grossberg, 'The in-difference of television', *Screen*, vol. 28, no. 2, March/April 1987.

Practice
Introduction

Implicit in a number of the extracts thus far selected is a notion that, at the very least, teaching about the media proposes a different relation between the teacher/the taught/the subject from that of knowing teacher/ empty vessel student/neutral knowledge. The title of the Richard Collins article and of the anthology from which it is taken attest to the rather stronger claims which were argued for media studies in the late 70s and early 80s. At this time the argument was being made that media studies, especially in its emphasis on practice, challenged both 'constructions of school knowledge and authoritarian classroom relations'. These challenges were seen to relate both to what was taught and to how it was taught.

Collins is concerned to challenge these assumptions, arguing that neither an emphasis on creativity nor on production *per se* are particularly educational, since products of the former are not amenable to analysis and products of the latter can only be judged by how like or unlike the real (professional) thing they are. He concludes that simulation exercises, defamiliarising the dominant conventions, are the only genuinely educational activities of 'practice'.

In his overview piece, David Buckingham summarises some of the developments and entailments of the Collins deconstruction approach. On the one hand it can link to cross-curricular media education initiatives of 'open-ended inquiry, in which genuine practical experimentation is seen as a means of generating and testing new hypotheses'; on the other it can degenerate into experimentation for its own sake. To guard against this tendency Buckingham reminds us that practical work should always produce artefacts as well as clarify processes, that is, such work should not simply involve deconstruction exercises but create texts made with finite audiences of real people in mind as well.

Roy Stafford summarises more recent versions of the arguments for practical work and identifies four different types of worry which are expressed: it can become self-indulgent (the creativity worry); it becomes obsessed with equipment (the technicist worry); it is all exercises (the deconstructionist worry); it mimics professionals (the simulation worry). He subsequently goes on to describe interesting work carried out in the new circumstances generated by CPVE (Certificate in Pre-Vocational Education) and GCSE (General Certificate of Secondary Education) courses, without necessarily fully countering these worries. He does, however, usefully recast and extend the notion of creativity to include considerations of how to assess the *collective* enterprise and collaboration required by practical work. The issues opened up here under the rubric of creativity become equally salient at 18+ when they are incorporated into notions of training.

Media Studies:
Alternative or Oppositional Practice?

Richard Collins

From Geoff Whitty and Michael Young (eds), *Explorations in the Politics of School Knowledge*, Driffield, Nafferton, 1976, pp. 169–74.

Two of the most important ideas, which have been regarded as broadly   1
progressive and making for change in post-war education, are those of
'relevance' and 'child-centredness'. Essentially, these ideas have supported
attacks on the constitution of school knowledge as an initiation of the
child into what R. S. Peters calls 'public tradition', mediated through an
extremely reified categorisation of knowledge. The entailments of constituting school knowledge as a set of discrete subjects, preoccupation with
'standards', hard knowledge, and civilisation will need no rehearsal here:
Michael Young's definition (with perhaps the rider that there is a bias
towards a particular kind of 'unrelatedness' in the academic curriculum,
towards a positivistic construction of knowledge)[1] aptly characterises the
tradition against which educational change in Britain has been defined:

> Literacy, or an emphasis on written as opposed to oral presentation,
> individualism, or avoidance of group work or co-operation, which
> focuses on how academic work is assessed, and is a characteristic both
> of the process of knowing, and of the way in which the 'product' is
> presented, abstractedness of the knowledge, and its structuring and
> compartmentalising independently of the knowledge of the learner,
> finally (and linked to the former), is what I have called the unre-
> latedness of academic curricula, which refers to the extent to which
> they are 'at odds' with daily life and common experience.[2]

Media study, in so far as it has been espoused by progressives in British   2
education, has been taken up, because it offers contradictory possibilities to
those of the academic curriculum and its schooling in the 'public tradition'.

Jim Grealy, for instance, argues, in an article largely concerned with   3
establishing school as part of the ideological apparatus of the state, that
media studies is well suited to challenging conservative constructions of
school knowledge and authoritarian classroom relations:

> The subject as a closed system of knowledge can be undermined by
> the stress laid by media studies on the continuity between what the
> pupils study in the classroom, and what they watch and use out of
> school. Also, the normal hierarchical way of teaching, information
> conveyed from teacher to passively receptive pupils, is very difficult

to sustain in a media studies course, with its emphasis on practice, as well as 'theoretical' teaching.[3]

It is to the question of practice, as opposed to 'theoretical' knowledge, that I want to turn. In media studies practice is seen as offering an aspect of 'child-centredness' to a subject which, although evidently part of the child's world through his or her consumption of television, radio, press, or cinema, has its abstract features, and involves the acquisition and understanding of knowledge outside 'daily life and common experience'. Further, child-centred educational practice is seen as breaking radically with the customary hierarchical and authoritarian relations of school. Child-centredness, and its necessary relevance, rewrite the 'hidden curriculum', or so the arguments go. Practice, the use of film, tape recorders, and particularly television equipment, in programme-making and exercises, has come to constitute part of the accepted definition of media studies, and has been 'naturalised' as part of the subject area.

It is difficult, though, to generalise about practice: facilities differ, and those available in British educational institutions range from a colour television studio, through a single television camera with monitor and VTR (videotape recorder), to still camera and tape recorder, and facilities go far towards defining the kind of work that can be done. One major argument for practical work is that, in programme-making, students experience situations analogous to those of professional media workers, and that this experience of programme-making informs understanding of broadcast television. Clearly, the analogy has pertinence, in so far as the facilities used by the student are like those of the professional. The argument loses force when one video rover stands in for White City Television Centre, although simulations and games like *Radio Covingham*,[4] in which participants play the role of journalists on a local radio station, and receive inputs of news agency handouts, listeners' letters, interviews, press releases, etc., which they order into a news programme of predetermined length, offer interesting possibilities with the minimum of equipment.

There are a variety of ways of 'doing practice', between which I think it is important to discriminate. For there is, it seems to me, no guarantee that working in this way will necessarily have the progressive implications that Grealy and others find in it. For practice is often constructed as an *imitation* of broadcast television, and child-centredness does not necessarily oppose reproduction of these dominant forms of seeing and ordering the world, and the view of the world inscribed in the way professional broadcasters do things. To construct television study and television practice on a premise of child-centredness is to invite the reproduction of the relation of dominance between interviewer and interviewee, aspiration towards perfection of programme production, and disappointment when work does not equal that of professionals, with consequential reinforcement of the mystique of professionalism and the authority of the BBC and commercial companies. These professional practices, of course, are learned by children in consumption of broadcast television, whose specific conventions naturalise themselves as a definition of television, and will be reproduced in child-centred classroom practice.

7

'Doing practice' has, perhaps, three major rationales:

- Practice as an artistic form and end in itself.
- Practice which takes television (or whatever) as a mimetic system, which presents information without fundamental transformation of the information in the process of reproduction. The end of this mode of practice is the acquisition of the technical skills necessary to use television (or whatever other medium is in question) as an audiovisual aid, the contents of which have a one-to-one relation to the real world which it represents.
- Practice as an instrument of study. Programme-making as analogy or simulation; exercises in the systematic variation of conventions to determine the specific effect of particular conventions.

8

The first rationale sees the producer(s) of programmes as an artist, a privileged creative individual (although, when production is performed collectively, the individualistic ideology is usually salvaged by constructing the collective hierarchically, with a director, who 'makes' the programme), who expresses himself (and it usually is 'himself') through the artefact and its production. Much broadcast television is like this. Its fullest definition, and, one hopes, its nadir, comes in Ken Russell's programmes named after other artists, *Elgar*, *Mahler*, etc. In broadcast television the élitism of this procedure is naked: in education the intrinsically individualistic and élitist notion of the artist is dressed up in populist clothes. Lightweight portable television equipment, e.g., the video rover (or, in another medium, simple and cheap reprography of written material), makes possible, it is argued, a new form of self-expression, uninhibited formally by heavy studio equipment or the baggage of *The Grammar of Television Production*,[5] and liberated from the expense of studio production. For the video freak, there are limitless possibilities of personal statements, creativity, demanding no legitimation beyond 'I did it', 'I like it'. This form of practice constitutes everyone behind a video rover as an artist, or behind a Xerox machine as a Pulitzer, and maintains the privileged status of the role, while purporting to democratise it. Central to this form of practice is a necessary anti-reflective and unanalytical stance towards the rhetoric of the medium in question (i.e., its signifying codes and their articulation). Indeed, this is part of the point: art objects, whatever they be, videotape or marble, are by definition removed from analysis and the province of reason to a realm of instinct, feeling, the subjective, personal, and artistic. This seems to me to be the antithesis of study, and hostile to the production and dissemination of knowledge.

9

The second rationale constitutes the medium used as transparent, that the process of representation is one of unmediated reflection of an anterior world. And, again, this is a view which is current among media workers; the dominant ideology of broadcast television is governed by the naturalist fallacy of television offering a window on the world. It seems to me that study of the mass media must have, as a principal concern, definition of the specific structuring and organising properties of the media, of the ways in which information represented on television, or in a newspaper, have been transformed in the process of representation. For instance, the nature of reportage operating as a system of exclusions: television excludes phenomena temporally, by shooting a world of infinite duration for finite periods and by editing, and spatially, by using particular camera and microphone positions, angle of view of the camera lens, or angle of acceptance of the microphone. This kind of emphasis would confront directly one of the most pervasive mystifications and legitimations of contemporary broadcasting and journalism. Unless the conventions and mediations of the television system are articulated and brought into consciousness, or, to refer to another medium, the news values of journalists foregrounded, then study of television or newspapers cannot be said to be performed. Practice without attention to the mediated nature of communication subverts this articulation and bringing to consciousness, and opposes proper media study.

The third mode of practice seems to me to be educationally the most appropriate kind, and involves simulation exercises, or the systematic variation of elements in a message. For example, one might hypothesise that the convention of 'voice over' may be an important determinant of the meaning of a television message; this hypothesis can be tested by varying the elements in the message, using silence, voice over, music, narrator in or out of shot, etc., in a particular exercise. I say 'exercise', because other definitions, like programme-making, assimilate the activity to the category systems of modes 1 or 2. Even if a programme is presented and conceived as a simulation, it may be difficult for participants to think themselves outside the terms of the simulation situation, and constraints which are present solely to strengthen the desired analogy between imitation and the real thing, rather than as natural or necessary elements. For example, programme-making which follows the organisational patterns of broadcasting may offer insight into the relations between members of the broadcasting hierarchy, or it may also 'teach' fallaciously that a director is necessary to programme production, and that he is 'responsible' for the programme.

The third mode of practice, then, specifically constitutes itself as an instrument of study, interrogating the structures and conventions of programmes, the codes and their articulation in variations of elements of the message, and questioning professional practice, and the production situation, through simulation. Problems of practice, though, are not solely or simply theoretical, for the dominant tendency in the provision of video equipment to education is to place the instruments of *reproduction*, not production, in the hands of teachers and learners. Thus, the provision of AVA and video equipment in schools and colleges tends to enforce patterns of reception and consumption, not of production and origination. We have more television receivers, videotape recorders, and slide projectors than we have microphones or television and still cameras. The emphasis and implicit rationale is akin to that of early education: teaching reading, not writing, learning to be an object, not a subject. Raymond Williams, in *Television: Technology and Cultural Form*,[6] makes this connection very neatly, saying that literacy was one of the defining characteristics of élites, often of a priestly caste, just as 'media literacy' remains the prerogative

10

11

of a contemporary élite, what Nicholas Garnham called 'The New Priesthood'.[7]

Given the way contemporary mass communications enforce a skewed pattern of production and consumption, a subject/object relationship between the new priesthood and the laity in the living room, it is tempting to applaud all efforts to redress the balance, and to put the means of production into people's hands, to enable children, community groups, or just anyone, to get their hands on a video rover, and do their own thing, even if it is a 'practice one'. But such strategies are open to the danger of constituting themselves as alternative, not oppositional (to employ a distinction of Raymond Williams),[8] i.e., they become activities which 'can be tolerated within a particular effective and dominant culture'. Indeed, one could claim that pressure to consume (more video rovers, more film stock, more hardware) actually strengthens the dominant culture, and consolidates the position of Kodak, Philips, and Sony (buying a state capitalist Praktika, or a Co-op Tandberg makes little difference). 12

Doing your own thing with a videopack is a questionable advance in media literacy, although it is an activity that has its champions. Staying at home, the argument runs, and gaping at the tube in the corner, equals reading 'the media'; cheap portable television equipment enables people to 'write' electronically, and to become literate in the medium. In some sense, of course, that is true, and an advance. Being able to write electronically is better than merely reading. But, one asks, who writes, who reads, and what is written and read in the new formation? In what sense are the existing powerful relations of knowledge and control changed? I don't think wider dissemination of television equipment will very much change the relations of production and consumption of information, which are overwhelmingly dominant, or those between broadcast television and its audiences. After all, the means of production of radio have been public for a long time, and tape recorders have never been so cheap. Neither a great social and political change has ensued, nor greater understanding of the conventions and techniques of communications through recorded or broadcast sound. 13

Notes

1. For positivism of coelacanthean vintage, see Terence Miller's (Director of North London Polytechnic) statements, reported in the *Guardian* (9 June 1975), that, *inter alia*, sociology has the epistemological status of alchemy, and grants should be weighted in favour of students studying 'hard' subjects like physical science, technology, etc.
2. Michael F. D. Young, 'An Approach to the Study of Curricula as Socially Organized Knowledge' in *Knowledge and Control*, London, Collier-Macmillan, 1971, p. 38.
3. Jim Grealy, 'Film Teaching and the Ideology of the Educational System', *Screen Education*, no. 15, Summer 1975, p. 18.
4. 'Radio Covingham', published by ILEA Media Resources Centre, described in Manuel Alvarado, 'Simulation as Method', *Screen Education*, no. 14, Spring 1975.
5. D. Davis, *The Grammar of Television Production*, London, Barrie and Rockliff, 1960.

6. Raymond Williams, *Television: Technology and Cultural Form*, London, Fontana, 1974.
7. Joan Bakewell and Nicholas Garnham, *The New Priesthood*, London, Allen Lane, 1970.
8. Raymond Williams, 'Base and Superstructure', *New Left Review*, no. 82, 1974.

Practical Work

David Buckingham

From 'Theory and Practice in Media Education', in *Communication and Education* Unit 27, Milton Keynes, Open University, 1987, pp. 31–36.

Practical Work as Self-expression

The use of media as a means of self-expression has two main sources – on the one hand the tradition that developed in art colleges, and on the other, youth and community work. While the former has been particularly influential in higher education,[1] the latter is perhaps more pertinent to schools. Nevertheless, there are shared emphases here on the potential offered by media technologies for individual and group creativity. What distinguishes the youth and community work tradition is that this emphasis acquires a political inflection. Media work in this context is seen as a means of community development and as assisting the democratisation both of local politics and of the media themselves.

Tony Dowmunt, for example, answers the question 'Why use video with young people?' as follows. Firstly, he argues that video is easy to use, and because it has 'a lot of magic and glamour about it' it can easily motivate children 'whose other experiences of learning may have led them to being labelled, or feeling themselves to be, failures'. At the same time, this process can also lead to 'a closer understanding of how TV is made', and this 'more active involvement with the medium' can help young people develop a more questioning attitude towards broadcast television. Thirdly, Dowmunt suggests, video can be a powerful means of assisting 'personal and group development'. For instance, a group might use video to role-play or rehearse incidents from their everyday lives. He argues that video work can help young people to learn to function as part of an interdependent group, making use of each individual's skills. Finally,

> by using video in particular ways, young people can put themselves in a different relationship with the adult world, one in which they have more power. . . . A lot of young people have found that making a videotape and showing it is one of the few ways open to them of bringing their point of view to an institution or group of adults who have power over them.[2]

The use of video in community work appears to have originated in the left political movements of 1968 and after. Willener *et al.*, in a book symptomatically entitled *Videology and Utopia*,[3] provide a valuable insight into this use of video as a means of 'cultural animation' in France. Describing the use of video by a range of groups – including young people, women, industrial and migrant workers, and community groups – they develop an elaborate and almost mystical theory of its potential as a means of liberation and social change. For these authors, the promise of the 'videotopia' is one in which the specific potentialities of video as a means of feedback will enable 'the people' to appropriate communications media for progressive social goals.

Subsequent accounts have pointed to the lack of evidence to support such claims, however. Caroline Heller, in a controversial report for the Arts Council of Great Britain,[4] points out that the barriers to democratising broadcasting are political rather than technical, and that the experience of amateur production may well have the opposite effect – of developing a deeper respect for the achievement of the professionals. She draws attention to the fact that low-gauge video is a relatively expensive medium, and that the equipment is not designed for heavy use. Furthermore, while shooting may be easy, editing is both expensive and difficult (although this is certainly less true today). Heller suggests that, as a result, the main beneficiaries of community video may well have been the multinational corporations who produce the equipment. Community activists might be better advised to look to cheaper and smaller-scale media to further their aims.

The broad rationale that Dowmunt's book exemplifies has also come under particular criticism from media studies teachers. Len Masterman,[5] for example, challenges the view that practical work can provide critical insights into television *viewing*, or improve students' 'self-image'. He paints a depressing picture of 'an endless wilderness of dreary third-rate imitative "pop" shows, embarrassing video dramas, and derivative documentaries courageously condemning war or poverty, much of it condoned by teachers to whom technique is all and the medium the only message'.

Bob Ferguson,[6] in a similarly scathing attack, argues that this emphasis on creativity has been linked to a 'romanticisation of the working class'. The early development of media studies as a subject for the 'less able' led to its becoming 'a potential means of keeping recalcitrant, apathetic, or bored students occupied'. As a result, it tended to avoid work that was seen as too intellectually demanding, and this led to a 'poorly structured approach' that institutionalised low expectations of students.

In my view, both writers somewhat unfairly denigrate practical work on the basis of what amounts to bad teaching. There is obviously no reason why practical work should be inherently undemanding, or inevitably of poor quality. Nevertheless, Ferguson's argument does raise the central problem of *evaluation*. He argues that teachers have often lacked clear aims, and therefore also criteria for evaluating and thus improving their own and their students' work: 'Genuine constructive criticism based upon criteria which are drawn up by the teacher and student is essential for the development of practical work. The act of agreeing criteria for judgement immediately brings theory closer to practice.'

Practical Work as a Method of Learning
Similar problems apply in the second approach to practical work, its use as a *method of learning* that applies across the curriculum. This approach was developed by the Schools Council *Communications and Social Skills*

project.[7] There are clearly considerable areas of overlap here with the kind of work I have already described. For example, the project directors claim that their approach is particularly effective with 'underachievers' who find it difficult to learn using conventional verbal and mathematical modes, and who therefore suffer from a poor self-image as learners. In emphasising the value of engaging in group activities involving collective decision-making, this approach shares the view of practical work as a means towards 'personal and group development'. At the same time, it raises even more clearly the central question about the reasons for using audio-visual media for such purposes.

If media are capable of motivating certain children in ways that conven-   9
tional methods cannot, why does this happen? What are the significant differences between approaches that fail and those that appear to succeed? Lorac and Weiss emphasise the fact that media production is a group activity, and that finished products can be shown to a range of audiences. Yet, in that case, isn't drama an equally suitable method to achieve the aims they describe? Indeed, drama is preferable in many respects: it is significantly cheaper, less complex in terms of the technology, and no less accessible for students who find reading and writing difficult.

What the media do possess, and what drama to some extent lacks, is   10
social status – what Dowmunt calls 'magic and glamour'. Lorac and Weiss ignore this factor, but it is crucial in the success of many of the cases they report. For example, here they describe a videotape produced by a group of non-exam fifth-form students:

> . . . here they have worked hard to produce sentences that are very close indeed to the written mode. This is presumably because they know how television announcers are expected to talk. . . . The choice of a statement like 'In this programme we intend to . . .' suggests a willingness to usea form of grammar and vocabulary that is hostile to the roles in which many working-class youngsters see themselves. . . . It is interesting that in the finished programme and [in discussion] the children's accounts seemed to change too.

This could be seen, as it is by Lorac and Weiss, as a very positive   11
example of children adopting another linguistic code and thereby extending their linguistic repertoire. Yet their account has the disturbing implication that, if using media forces children to adopt forms of language thatare (to use the authors' terms) 'hostile' to the way in which they see themselves, this is something to be celebrated. Should children not be asked to question why it is that television announcers are 'expected' to talk in particular ways and not others? Should they not be encouraged to produce work using language that is not 'hostile' to the way in which they see themselves? In this sense, the success of the project appears to result from encouraging an uncritical emulation of professional practice. The models that children are encouraged to follow are precisely those of dominant media institutions – models that, as I have indicated, cannot be seen as either neutral or inevi- table. While I agree that it is crucial for students to be able to use dominant forms of language, this extension of their linguistic repertoire should

involve a recognition of the value of the students' own language, and a more analytical *questioning* of the relationship between forms of language and forms of power.

Practical Work as Deconstruction

It is this kind of questioning that informs our third approach here, the use of practical work as 'deconstruction'. Len Masterman, for example, having rejected the prevailing use of video as 'doing your own thing with a porta-pak', argues that it should be used primarily to assist in the study of television itself – for example, in simulating TV news production or inter-viewing techniques. He suggests that it may also be particularly valuable as a means of investigating the established 'codes' of television, since 'it allows individual conventions (of framing, camera-positioning, editing, etc.) to be isolated, experimented with and broken while variations in their meaning are explored'. Bob Ferguson likewise emphasises the value of 'rule breaking' as a means of pointing out and questioning such conventions. In 'deconstruction', he suggests, 12

> one concentrates on making brief, often modest media artefacts which are designed to highlight a form of construction usually accepted unquestioningly as the norm. One is here encouraging students to manipulate televisual or filmic language for a *specific purpose*. Not to express oneself, but to manufacture a meaning through the conscious manipulation of production techniques and norms.

This approach, which Masterman suggests may well be more appropriate in higher education, runs the risk of 'theoreticism' – of emphasising theor-etical concerns at the expense of the students' motivation to produce their own messages. There are clearly dangers in an exclusive emphasis on critical analysis, which constantly seeks to deconstruct dominant forms yet fails to encourage students to develop and to interrogate their *own* position. 13

It is interesting in this respect to compare media studies with more established areas of the curriculum. For instance, the value of practical work in science and technology subjects is rarely questioned. While, in some instances, 'experiments' may serve merely to illustrate theoretical principles, recent developments in these areas have emphasised more open-ended inquiry, in which genuine practical experimentation is seen as a means of generating and testing new hypotheses. In English teaching, priority has traditionally been given to students as producers of language – analytical work, in the form of language study, has been a relatively recent development in schools, and has consistently been seen as part of the broader context of language *use*. Christopher Williams, discussing practical work in higher education, argues that certain versions of theory can enhance tendencies towards pretentiousness, and may even make it impossible for students to produce work at all. Certain critiques of docu-mentary realism, for example, can lead to highly 'theoretical' films that refuse to represent the real world in any form. This is perhaps less of a risk in schools, but it would certainly be counter-productive to reject what for many students is an important reason for choosing media studies – the 14 desire to construct their own meanings in film and video. Both Masterman and Ferguson do acknowledge this, although somewhat marginally. Ferguson, for example, argues that deconstruction can serve a double purpose, not only encouraging students to interrogate the dominant codes of television but also enabling them to realise alternative possibilities for code construction. He suggests that

> it is important to show how practical work can extend comprehension of the structures, practices, and production values of the broadcasters whilst at the same time opening up a potential means of communication which allows for the development of oppositional, informational, and expressive message making.

While I agree with Ferguson and Masterman that it is important with practical work to be very clear about one's aims, I would also emphasise the importance of allowing students the opportunity to determine their own concerns and devise their own messages. While deconstruction exercises are clearly valuable, they tend to be heavily teacher-directed, and can reduce practice to a mere illustration of theory. If practice is to inform and help to develop theory, it needs to be able to move beyond merely testing hypotheses: there needs to be a more dialectical relationship. The recent growth of the independent film and video sector may prove significant here. The many independent workshops, funded by Channel 4 and other sources, are contributing to the growth of an alternative, or oppositional, film and video culture in which hitherto excluded voices such as women and black people have a powerful voice. Making their products available to schools may well indicate to students that there are alternatives to the dominant forms of television, through which their own concerns can be represented and can reach an audience.

This sense of audience is particularly important in practical work, yet it has often been neglected. For different reasons, each of the approaches I have outlined tends to regard the *process* of production as more important than the product itself. In so far as products do emerge, they are primarily orientated towards teachers, or towards the group itself. What is often seen as more important is the understanding generated by the process – whether it is an understanding of the media themselves, or a broader form of 'personal and social development'. Nevertheless, Tony Dowmunt and Lorac and Weiss suggest that one of the advantages of media products is that they can be directed towards a wider audience; and this attempt to address one's ideas to a specific audience can encourage students to be clear about what they want to communicate.

Thus, while I have argued against encouraging students merely to emulate professional practice, I am not suggesting that such practices should (or indeed can) be rejected completely. There is a danger in the deconstruction position of establishing an *absolutist* distinction between 'dominant' and 'oppositional' forms. Yet the facts that students may appear to reproduce dominant conventions, in the manner described by Masterman, does not necessarily mean that they are doing so unquestioningly, or that they passively accept those conventions. In this sense, it is crucial that any evaluation of practical work should be undertaken by the students *in terms of their own intentions*. And if the intention is to communicate with a specific audience, a certain standard of technical quality is obviously important. In this sense, practical work can demand a high degree of facility in exploiting the specific qualities of a given medium. Developing such a facility can be a disciplined process that is the very opposite of the 'poorly structured approach' Ferguson rightly attacks.

Finally, it has not been my intention in this section to proclaim a theoretical purity for media studies, or to suggest that practical work should only be undertaken within it. The work of the Schools Council project makes a strong claim for the value of practical work in many other curriculum areas. While not wishing to refute that claim, I would argue that the use of media production, like the use of educational television, needs to be critically informed by the perspectives developed within media studies. In particular, it is not sufficient to regard practical media production as a purely neutral or instrumental process: just as we would not wish students to accept educational television at face value, so practical production should be a process in which students are encouraged to question accepted professional practices and to develop practices informed by their own perspectives and concerns. The challenge for media studies teachers posed by the currently increasing polarisation between education and training – for example, through the intervention of the Manpower Services Commission in education – is to ensure that practical work, wherever it occurs in the curriculum, is informed by a critical analysis of the media, rather than by an unquestioning acceptance of dominant forms. To return to the questions raised at the start of this section, the ability of media studies to combine the theoretical and the practical, 'consumption' and 'production', and to question the distinctions between them, may prove to be a significant part of its contribution to the future of education.

Notes

1. Christopher Williams, 'Film making and film theory in higher education', in Christine Gledhill (ed.), *Film and Media Studies in Higher Education*, London, BFI, 1981.
2. Tony Dowmunt, *Video with Young People*, London, Interaction, 1980.
3. A. Willener, G. Milliard and A. Ganty, *Videology and Utopia*, London, Routledge, 1976.
4. Caroline Heller, 'The resistible rise of video', *Education Broadcasting International*, vol. 11, no. 3, 1978.
5. Len Masterman, *Teaching About Television*, London, Macmillan, 1980.
6. Bob Ferguson, 'Practical work and pedagogy', *Screen Education*, no. 38, Spring 1981.
7. C. Lorac and M. Weiss, *Communications and Social Skills*, Exeter, Wheaton, 1981.

Redefining Creativity:
Extended Project Work in GCSE Media Studies

Roy Stafford

From David Buckingham (ed.), *Watching Media Learning*, Brighton, Falmer, 1990, pp. 81–5, 89, 95–7.

Introduction

Practical work has had a long and difficult history as part of media education. Media theorists have always treated 'hands-on' experience with suspicion, fearing a fall into what Len Masterman once called 'the technicist trap',[1] the promotion of product and technology over process and ideology. The great risk with practical work, it is argued, is that students will simply learn to ape the professionals, and that a critical, analytical perspective will be lost. Conversely, some progressive educationists have adhered to notions of creativity, in which the purity of the experience of practical work has appeared to be unsullied by the dirty work of critical reflection.

A compromise appeared to have been reached in the early 1980s whereby media educationists agreed that practice and theory must be synthesised, that one should not be discussed without the other. In effect, however, this often meant that practical work was reduced to a practical *exercise* – a means of 'proving' media theory, often through 'code-breaking'. What was lacking from this analysis and its attendant pedagogy was any theoretical understanding of practice itself. Care was taken to delineate the different concepts which made up the core of media theory but similar care was not lavished on practice.

This consensus has been broken because of three separate but interlinked developments which have taken place in the last few years:

- Curriculum development has gradually moved in favour of student-centred, resource-based, activity learning. There has been a shift away from traditional academic exercises requiring close teacher control towards more open-ended projects and case studies. Students may be expected to work in groups without supervision and may be involved in simulated and actual work experience.
- The 14–19 Curriculum has been pressurised to become more 'vocational', and this has meant an increasing interest in the vocational and practical aspects of media education. New 'A' level and GCSE courses in Communications and Media Studies have brought practical work components into traditional Humanities syllabuses, while new courses under the aegis of CPVE, CGLI and BTEC[2] have seen the development of media education within pre-vocational and vocational courses aimed at employment in media industries.

– Developments in electronics technology have made available high-spec but low-cost equipment in audio, video, photographic, and computing applications. The constraints on student work are lessening and the argument about not aping professional practice is becoming more difficult to pursue. Previously, the institutional constraints of the classroom, added to the limitations of equipment, meant that only part of the production process could be undertaken realistically. It is now possible to organise student 'commissions' for real clients which can be undertaken within open-ended project time. In video production there are now a number of schools and colleges which can engage in sophisticated production and post-production work and the 'non-professional' quality of the finished product is a function only of the tape format and not the production methods.

Practical work has also been formally recognised in the most significant curriculum development in media education during the last few years, namely GCSE Media Studies. Here, practical work occupies between one-third and half of the overall assessment. In 1988, 10,000 candidates were assessed on practical work, and numbers are likely to increase at least in the short term. Clearly, any confusion over the role of practical work makes even more difficult the knotty problem of devising assignments and appropriate assessment methods. The earlier notions of practical work are no longer tenable. What must replace them?

This paper puts forward a tentative proposal for a new view of practical work and in particular video production. It argues that practical media work requires a range of skills and understandings which may be unique to the field. In particular, the necessity for group work in most forms of media production and the development of creative skills in a particular institutional/industrial context requires media teachers to recognise a set of skills and understandings which have previously been ignored. This paper is therefore concerned to excavate in order to produce the buried outlines of a pedagogy for practical work.

Critical Perspectives on Practical Video Work
The first portable video equipment became available to schools and colleges around 1974–75. Relatively difficult to operate and offering a monochrome image, the new medium did not find immediate favour with teachers who had previously sought to develop a good standard of work on Super 8 cine film. However, it did attract those who appreciated the facility to obtain images without the time-lag of film-processing and also the relative cheapness of longer shooting with reusable tapes. Much of the classroom work which utilised the new video technology was undertaken with the pupils who represented a major problem for schools in the mid-1970s, namely the 'low-achieving' 15-year-olds 'caught' by the raising of the school leaving age to 16. In further education a similar group of students on basic skills courses was often offered practical video work as a 'non-academic' activity. Much of the work was poorly organised, under-resourced and lacking any form of assessment. Some work had real educational value but too often it was seen in a rather patronising way as a means of keeping 'difficult'

students occupied. In the 'failure' of the productions themselves it also reinforced the lack of achievement for these students.

Writers promoting a critical form of media education were understandably dismissive of work which they saw as ignoring analytical skills. Bob Ferguson details this early history in an influential article, published in 1981.[3] The flavour of his polemic can be tasted in the following extract describing typical practice:

> . . . the camera was often 'squirted' at its subject and the dizzy, boring and incoherent results thus obtained could be justified as experimentation. When plots were attempted they were puerile. . . . The results, if seen by the unconverted, seldom convinced them of the desirability and effectivity of practical work in film and video.

Ferguson identifies two possible justifications for this kind of work. Firstly, some teachers imported the notion of 'creativity' from English teaching (cf. 'creative writing') in order to fill the intellectual gap in practical work. Secondly, and very differently, some teachers saw practical work as a means of emulating professional practice and 'learning through doing' that film and television production is a complex business. Ferguson compares these approaches unfavourably with a third approach, namely 'deconstruction' or 'rule-breaking exercises'. This is an analytical activity, which involves students manipulating meaning rather than creating it. Ferguson sees it as open-ended in the sense that it 'does not have to embrace a single mode of televisual, filmic or dramatic construction as *correct*'. It is a means of interrogating media conventions which allows students to refuse dominant, transparent production styles and messages. This view of practical work as rule-breaking – for example, in the form of interview exercises or audio-dubbing of re-edited footage – became the orthodoxy for many media educationists in the early 1980s.

Ferguson himself had been a successful proponent of practical film work at Hornsey College of Art in the late 1960s.[4] Yet in 1981 he argued that 'For the students involved [this work was] more of a social than an educational undertaking.' He appears to be rejecting his previous work as based on experiential rather than cognitive learning, and as symptomatic of the weaknesses of a 'liberal studies' approach. Many media teachers in the early 1980s turned against both the 'progressive' pedagogy of liberal studies and the skills-based, 'active' learning approach characterised by the various schemes promoted by the Manpower Services Commission.

Len Masterman's influential book *Teaching About Television*,[5] published in 1980, shares Ferguson's misgivings about many of the justifications previously offered for practical video work. He also recognises the poor quality of most attempts to emulate professional production. However, he sees the importance of establishing a pedagogy for practical work which recognises the potential of video as an expressive medium, but one which must be used in relation to students' own language and culture and which 'harnesses group resources'. He suggests a whole range of potential activities, which includes both code-breaking exercises *and* more extended projects and simulations.

In *Teaching About Television*, Masterman devotes seven pages to practical 11
television work and, despite his misgivings, looks forward to video as 'an
integral part of a more total liberating education'. Yet in 1985, in his
equally influential book, *Teaching the Media*,[6] practical work is allowed just
over a page. Practica! work is now 'not an end in itself, but a necessary
means to developing an autonomous critical understanding of the media'.
Extensive and time-consuming projects are far less significant than code-
breaking and (closed) simulations. It is perhaps unfair to characterise a
significant change in Masterman's position with just a few quotes, but
the tone of his writing suggests a conversion to the orthodoxy, in which
deconstruction exercises became the *only* acceptable form of practical work.

Ferguson and Masterman have spread this approach to practical work 12
through their writings and teacher education programmes, and to a certain
extent they have been supported by the British Film Institute Education
Department in its reluctance to engage with practical work beyond the
closed exercise. However, it would be wrong to give the impression that
the orthodoxy has remained unchallenged.[7] Jim Hornsby, writing a BFI
Advisory Document in 1984,[8] recasts some of the earlier arguments. He
identifies the 'creativity' approach and renames it 'aestheticist'. The fears
of technical instruction which developed in media educationists as they
gazed in horror at those institutions which invested heavily in sophisticated
video technology under the aegis of the MSC (especially from 1984 with
its Technical and Vocational Education Initiative) are neatly summed up
in the disparaging term 'technicist'. Against these despised forms, Hornsby
identifies two 'oppositional' or 'alternative' media education approaches,
deconstruction, and 'progressive content'.

Hornsby sees two weaknesses in deconstruction. Firstly, such exercises 13
can be reduced to simply proving a theoretical point, and in doing so
students may be involved in producing a meaningless statement. He argues
that learning to use conventional codes and understanding why they produce meaning can be more productive. Secondly, he turns the professional
emulation argument around by pointing out that:

> deconstruction exercises also risk ignoring the fact that practical media
> work in an educational context is always, obviously, distinct from
> professional practice. In my view, exercises should therefore be struc-
> tured in terms of the real reasons for this difference rather than from
> a perceived need to deconstruct professional conventions.

This seems to me an argument for addressing the institutional constraints
of the school/college and the perceived position of the students.

This argument also carries through to the other form of 'oppositional 14
practice', the attempt to develop student projects concerned with issues
which are seen to be handled unsatisfactorily by broadcast television. There
is almost an inverse form of theoreticism here. Formal considerations are
virtually ignored, to be replaced by concerns over representation. Students
are encouraged to tackle 'images of women' or 'youth culture' without any
consideration of the forms used by broadcast media or the institutional

practices which inform them: it is assumed that students will somehow naturally contest the meanings of the professionals.

Hornsby's argument is aimed at rescuing practical work from the reductivism that sees it only as a single practice, and as an adjunct to theory. While the value of deconstruction exercises is not in doubt, some of the assumptions about creativity and simulated professional production which have recurred in this debate are in need of reappraisal. This view is supported by some recent writing which explicitly refers to GCSE projects. Jane Arthurs, writing in 1987,[9] offers a very clear reading of Hornsby and an illuminating personal experience:

> I never really understood what was meant by continuity editing and why it is a deeply ideological process until I tried to replicate it myself. . . . Theory does not in itself generate practice . . . practice derives from relations with the real world and from this actively constructs meaning. The implications for devising student projects are that productions should arise out of the immediate context of students' lives.

This less reductive view of the relationship between theory and practical work is one I hope to develop in this chapter.

The Practical Project

The Practical Project was introduced early in the spring term. The pattern of teaching changed so that work on 'core concepts' continued in one period, while the other period (on a Friday afternoon – such is the timetabling fate of new subjects) became an open workshop reserved for the practical project. The project was quickly identified as an 'open' commission and easily distinguished from the 'closed' exercises associated with the coursework assignments.

The GCSE syllabus requires that students work individually or collectively on a theme and that the assessment schedule must clearly show where they have received assistance. I provided thematic titles which I thought might allow students to choose something that they felt able to make a statement about: 'London 1990', 'Springtime', 'Holidays', 'In Vogue' and 'On the Street'. Most opted for one of the last two. I left them to form their own groups and to formulate their ideas. They did not have to attend each class but I did require them to come and discuss their project as soon as they had a working title. From then on I expected them to come to me for advice on how to use technology or to book equipment or facilities.

In practice, some students were always there, while others I hardly saw. I did monitor the progress of each project as carefully as I could (partly by fishing for information on the college grapevine, partly by quizzing the regular attenders). As the deadline approached I tried to restrain my teacherly instincts to rush in and make things happen. I attempted as surreptitiously as possible to make helpful suggestions, to demonstrate techniques, to discuss with groups what they had planned. I was determined that the groups would work on their own ideas, but I was also determined that no group should fail for lack of support. In the event, I didn't have to 'rescue' any group. I spent most time with a group who were quite competent at organising themselves, but rather lacking in ideas, and who produced the most conventional videotape. Despite the help I gave, the finished products were seen very much as the 'property' of the groups and not an exercise they had performed for me: this is certainly clear from the account of two groups' work which follows.

[Two projects are described in the next section. Three students made a rap video on the theme of 'Springtime'. One wrote the lyric, another sang and organised the dancing. In the second project, five students produced a survey of commercial rap videos, including a look at associated fashions and a discussion of the importance of rap as a youth culture. Both projects suffered production delays caused by absences, indecisions, and so on. They were completed under pressure at the last minute.]

Conclusion: Rethinking 'Creativity'

The pedagogy adopted in these two projects was chosen to complement the closed exercises in rule-breaking or analysis of codes undertaken elsewhere in the course. So what are the benefits of such an approach and how might they be judged against the 'orthodoxy' represented by Ferguson and Masterman? Do they fulfil Hornsby's criteria?

The key term here appears to be 'creativity'. This term has often been used pejoratively to describe activities concerned with a mere expression of 'feeling'. It does have another meaning, however, which seeks to embrace all the skills and understandings that might be involved in any form of practical activity.

It was only when I began to reflect upon the experience of teaching on the GCSE course that I realised the importance of the curriculum debates around Vocational Preparation[10] and specifically CPVE in developing my own ideas on practical work. I have intimated above that the orthodox approach to practical work in media education was partly influenced by a recoil from the development of skills-based curricula during the early 1980s. Indeed, I shared in that concern[11] but I felt then as I do now that vocational education is important and that retreating towards a purely analytical 'subject discipline' would not help to promote media education more broadly.

That retreat or, more correctly, refusal to occupy the battlefield was misguided and misconceived for a number of reasons. Firstly, the force of curriculum change was too great and GCSE itself is heavily imbued with ideas of resource-based, active learning. Secondly, the new curriculum model was not monolithic. It is possible to discern a considerable difference between those documents emanating from the educationists within the Further Education Unit (FEU) of the Department of Education and Science and those with an FEU label but a parenthood in the Manpower Services Commission (now the Training Agency).[12] Here, for instance, is an extract from an FEU Discussion Paper of 1985[13] promoting a 'creative curriculum':

> The creative curriculum is one in which:
> There are opportunities for students to develop their creative abilities

74

by pursuing their individual skills and interests in an environment which values experimentation;

A premium is placed on self-directed learning, in which the teacher and the learning environment are seen as a resource;

Learning activities are negotiated and renegotiated and new and original ideas are welcomed, subject to disciplined evaluation and rigorous criticism;

There is recognition of the value of groupwork, where the strengths of different members of a team, as well as the talents of the individual, are drawn on;

There is an emphasis on problem-solving approaches, in which the processes of learning by doing, working and reworking, drafting and redrafting are valued as much as the finished product;

A creative curriculum is not only concerned with transmission of accumulated knowledge, but also with generation – with enabling students to take the initiative for their own self-development and to acquire the skills, understanding and flexibility to handle new situations with confidence.

This appears to me to be a very constructive framework for practical project work in GCSE Media Studies. It is not specifically designed for media education and in this respect can suggest ways in which common practice with other cross-curricular activities can be developed. In developing this argument, I propose to add my own observations relating to the specificities of video production.

'An environment which values experimentation' is precisely what is required where students are asked to study a range of media texts, to understand how narratives are constructed and coding systems are developed, and are then required to produce their own texts. I would contend that both the projects described above show evidence of students grappling with forms and techniques, not in slavish imitation of broadcast media, but in an attempt to find an appropriate means of making a statement. In both cases there is also a recognition of different individual skills and contributions.

'Self-directed learning' is only possible in some form of workshop environment where teachers are genuinely resources available to each student and not primarily agents who construct problems for students to solve. The extended nature of video production allows for groups of students to be engaged in different activities at different stages of the production process (providing, of course, that there is enough equipment available). Again, there is evidence in the projects described of a degree of self-direction, although it must be admitted that it is not a form of learning that young people who are used to a traditional relationship with a teacher-director find easy to handle. There was some evidence in my class that the traditional 'good' student found this more difficult than the student who found the formal classroom alienating. There is an opposite problem which I have encountered with adult students, where the teacher may be monopolised by a single student who fails to recognise that the teacher is a resource for everyone in the class.

'Negotiating and renegotiating learning activities' is an attractive ideal, 27
but one which may prove difficult to implement. For the GCSE project the
parameters are already set and in that sense the potential for renegotiation
is limited. However, I was happy that students changed their ideas as long
as they discussed the reasons for changes. As long as practical work includes
some formal process of self-evaluation and reflection it need never be simply
an 'expressive' act. It is possible to posit evaluation as the final stage in
video production, especially if it is directly related to screenings for the
target audience.

'The value of groupwork' in video production is of paramount impor- 28
tance. In the range of different types of skill and understanding required,
video and film production have few parallels. They require collaborative
work within which individuals might be expected to display communication, presentation, or performance skills in front of camera, technical
skills in operating equipment, social skills in organising a crew and per-
formers, and on top of that to develop ideas as to the form of the finished
product. It is no wonder that students of average ability find it a daunting
prospect – quite a few teachers find it difficult as well. Why then have
media educationists paid so little attention to this specific problem?

In a society which promotes the individual so assiduously and an edu- 29
cation system which remains based on individual achievement, it is not
surprising that some students find collective enterprise a bewildering
experience and 'let each other down'.

Notes

1. Len Masterman, *Teaching the Media*, London, Comedia, 1985.
2. City and Guilds of London Institute (CGLI) and Business and Technician
   Education Council (BTEC) are the two main vocational education examination
   and validation bodies. They both offer certification of media courses and in
   1984 they were jointly responsible for the launch of the Certificate in Pre-
   Vocational Education (CPVE).
3. Bob Ferguson, 'Practical Work and Pedagogy', *Screen Education*, no. 38,
   Spring 1981.
4. See Bob Ferguson, *Group Film Making*, London, Studio Vista, 1969.
5. Len Masterman, *Teaching About Television*, London, Macmillan, 1980, ch. 8.
6. Len Masterman, 1985, op. cit.
7. See David Buckingham, *Unit 27: Media Education (EH207 Communication
   and Education)*, Milton Keynes, Open University, 1987; Jenny Grahame, 'The
   production process', in David Lusted (ed.), *The Media Studies Book: A Guide
   for Teachers*, London, Routledge, 1991.
8. Jim Hornsby, *The Case for Practical Studies in Media Education*, London, BFI
   Education Department mimeograph, 1984.
9. J. Arthurs, 'Production projects for GCSE', *In The Picture*, Yorkshire Arts,
   Autumn 1987.
10. 'Vocational Preparation' is a generic term to describe the curriculum develop-
    ment of the late 1970s and early 1980s which attempted to create provision
    for young people unqualified for entry into traditional vocational education
    courses at a time of high youth unemployment. *Vocational Preparation* was the
    title of a Further Education Unit (FEU) publication of 1981. See also note 13
    below.

11. Roy Stafford, 'Media Studies or Manpower Services?', *Screen*, vol. 24, no. 3, May–June 1983.
12. See *A Basis For Choice*, London, FEU, 1979, a proposal for progressive educational initiative in Vocational Preparation which was effectively scuppered by the rapid implementation of the Youth Training Scheme. *Basic Skills*, London, FEU, 1982, is indicative of the impact of the Manpower Services Commission.
13. *Creative and Arts Activities in Further Education*, London, FEU, 1985. This document represents an intervention by the FEU in the debates surrounding the implementation of CPVE.

Pedagogy
Introduction

The place and significance of practice in media education is but one element (even if a particularly important element) in a broader debate about pedagogy. This is not the place to consider in any detail what may be meant by the term, but most people would concede that pedagogy has to do with formulating and implementing a rationale for what students should learn, how they should learn, and the proper role of the teacher in facilitating that process.

The development of any new subject or area of learning in education has a potential for pitting its proponents into combat with established orthodoxies. Curriculum space is a finite resource, and any attempt to seize a portion of that resource must inevitably disturb an existing balance. Additional factors, however, inflected the particular claims of media education as inherently oppositional. After all, this was a discipline which laid special store on the knowledge and skills required for the deconstruction of all manner of texts. How could it ignore and fail to question the role of authoritative texts in the construction of knowledge and representation of the world, and the prevailing models of knowledge transmission in education?

Given this essentially radical potential of media education, therefore, it is easy to understand why James Donald asked specifically what an 'oppositional pedagogy' should look like in the case of media studies. His answer emphasises forms of practice in the unfolding of ideology, perhaps especially of ideology as it operates in the process of representation. Ideology and representation are also the guiding priorities which inform Judith Williamson's contribution. Starting from a position not unlike that of Donald, Williamson poses a fundamental doubt: understanding of ideological operation in a particular text is not necessarily, nor even generally, translated by the student into a self-critical awareness of how ideologies operate upon all forms of his or her own mental processing and personal and social attitudes. How might the teacher help induce such a transformation? Rather than starting from the analysis of ideology as a means of accessing texts, Williamson offers the reverse: use of texts, or indeed of absolutely anything relevant at hand, to access and understand ideology.

David Lusted starts from the position that pedagogy is itself part of the process of the production of knowledge, a process in which theorists, teachers, and learners alike are engaged. The problem which he defines is that too often theorists take no account of their partners, the teachers and learners, in this enterprise. This failure is particularly galling when the theorists in question are radicals who want to promote a new vision of content yet who continue to work within a traditional transmission model of dissemination. Without much better interaction between theorists, teachers, and learners in the task of theory-development and understanding, there can be no radical transformation of pedagogy.

Lusted offers a history of the debate about pedagogy in media education, starting with Masterman (arguing for a pedagogy which starts with existing student preferences) through Manuel Alvarado (whose starting point is presented here as the delineation of really useful knowledge), through to Williamson (who is concerned not so much with content as with how to transform consciousness) and Ian Connell (critical of the autocratic character of much radical theory). Lusted concludes that the need for student-specific, contextualised pedagogy renders fruitless the search for a general pedagogy.

David Buckingham wonders whether the debate about pedagogy has been conducted at too rarefied a theoretical level, and too exclusively directed to higher education. He argues the case for much more attention to concrete practice – what actually happens in the classroom. While concrete practice was the particular merit of Williamson's contribution, Buckingham cautions against the assumptions about media studies on which Williamson's work was premised. As the subject itself develops (for example, away from an emphasis on conspiracy and a view of the 'reader' as passive towards an appreciation of media diversity, the fragility of consensus, and a view of the reader as 'active') there are implications for pedagogy. Likewise, there are political developments that affect educational provision, and these too have implications for pedagogy, sometimes (like TVEI) in directions that run counter to what radical theory itself might have predicted. Not least important are the micropolitics of the classroom itself: the dynamics of classroom relations may sometimes have more influence on what students say than on what they actually think or believe.

Media Studies:
Possibilities and Limitations

James Donald

From *Media Studies: Possibilities and Limitations*, London, BFI Occasional Paper, 1977.

Pedagogy

What would an 'oppositional pedagogy' look like? Clearly, a general theory of ideology would be rather daunting for fourth- and fifth-year students. It must therefore be in substantive (and substantial) issues that the mechanisms of ideology are studied – the way that racial images, images of women, or images of youth sub-cultures are typically presented in the media, for example, and how these images inform the consciousness of their audience(s). Oppositional teaching can thus be distinguished from 'progressive' teaching, on the one hand, and indoctrination, on the other. Progressive teachers are right to stress the importance of students being exposed to all points of view and formulating their own opinions. But this tends to lead to the conclusion that either all points of view are equally valid, or that truth is a matter of impartiality, balance, consensus, and common sense, or (in the social sciences) that there is an objective truth to be deduced from empirical evidence. All these, of course, reinforce that individualism which denies class interests.

One response to the mystifications of liberal ideology has been to assert that stereotypes are biased social products which should be rejected in favour of some alternative revealed truth. But as a teaching method, propaganda of any sort is ineffective. It can either be swallowed whole (without any need for analysis) or rejected out of hand as a distortion of common-sense reality. In either case, no real process of learning has taken place. This demands the development of the student's critical awareness – which means not just a general intellectual scepticism nor a refined discrimination in the supermarket of cultural consumer objects, but that active, analytical process which challenges the basic definitions and values perpetuated by the school's culture. How is this to be achieved? My answers at this stage can only be speculative.

Practice

The gamble at the heart of this course is that oppositional elements are contained in its stress on *practice*. It is thus that the students' relationship to both the media and education may be shifted from that of passive consumers to that of active, critical producers. This is not achieved by most practical work done in schools because it consists mainly of exercises that reproduce already existing knowledge – they are unproductive and (literally) use-less. To take just two examples: scientific 'experiments' are non-experimental in that they have a preordained outcome (any other is wrong), and most 'creative' writing consists of ill-digested pastiches of the dominant forms of narrative. Those subjects in which things are produced for use (woodwork, needlework, cookery, for example) are accorded low academic status.

In contrast, I hope to establish 'use' as the chief criterion of value on the course, both in the sense of the students' ability to use the available media to say something and also in the use of those products to have an effect in the school. Thus 'image boards' will decorate the classroom, radio tapes will be broadcast on the PA system, video tapes will be shown, and magazines distributed to parents and other students. This attempt to give the students a powerful channel of communication may reveal some contradictions both in the school and in the course. What would happen if genuinely oppositional messages by students were broadcast? Would they simply be suppressed or could they be incorporated into the liberal ethos of the school? Would media studies disappear as an unnecessary 'soft option' in an 'overcrowded' curriculum? Or would its funds dry up in the name of economy? The other (and perhaps greater) danger is that the students' messages will be affirmative, accepting and disseminating the forms and values of mass media.

Practice implies initially the production of useful messages. But it is also through the practice of learning (for example) how to use a video camera, record an interview, prepare a script, or reach a joint editorial decision that the first crucial step of revealing the human construction, the non-naturalness, of the products of the media will be achieved. This should make possible an investigation of the types of choices open to the 'professional' producers of mass communication, and the real determinants of their routine choices. Thus, the object is to reveal how the ideological messages of the mass media are put together, ('encoded', to use Stuart Hall's term), and to seek effective codes for the students' own messages.

Visual Literacy and Decoding
The method of productive practice is as important in studying the reception of media messages as in studying their production. The trouble is that here we are dealing with the production of *meaning*, with all the problems of such level of abstraction. So what can students actually do? Much valuable practice has been based on the work with images of Golay and Gauthier;[1] this field has generally come to be called 'visual literacy'. This is a clumsy and, I hope, provisional concept.

'Literacy' is a tricky analogy, not only because it remains largely opaque itself, but also because it is probably a quite different process from making sense of an image. The point is to find a way of making images 'strange' (often by presenting material derived from the psychology of perception, such as ambiguous images and visual tricks and illusions) and thus reveal their multi-layered significance (using concepts derived from semiology). The significance will depend not only on the content and internal form and style of the image (lighting, colour, angle of shot, etc.) but also on its context. This raises questions about the medium in which the image appears and the audience for which it is intended, as well as its relation to other images and any accompanying text. The activity of 'decoding' is thus seen to depend not just on cognitive processes and sets of conventional symbols, but crucially on the social position of the receiver. Any image may be interpreted in a number of different ways. The range of possible interpretations will reflect the economic, political, and cultural struggles and contradictions present in the audience. (Such considerations are at the heart of work on 'Images of Women' and 'Images of Blacks'.) . . .

Information

For all this practical work to make sense, students will need some quite straight-forward information about the organisation of the media. For example, the choices that will face them in the course of their own production will not of themselves reveal the determinants of professional choices – which are as much social as technical. To avoid this danger of 'technicism', they should learn about such things as the structures of the BBC and independent broadcasting organisations, the ownership of the press, the increasing power of industrial conglomerates, and the economic functions and effects of advertising. I do not see that teachers need be nervous of presenting such information quite didactically. It can, in fact, be oppositional if it unmasks such myths as 'the freedom of the press' or 'consumer choice'.

Note

1. Jean-Pierre Golay, 'Introduction to the Language of Image and Sound', *Screen Education Notes*, no. 1, Winter 1971; Guy Gauthier, *Initiation to the Semiology of the Image*, available from BFI Education.

How Does Girl Number Twenty Understand Ideology?

Judith Williamson

From 'How Does Girl Number Twenty Understand Ideology?', *Screen Education*, no. 40, Winter 1981–2, pp. 83–4.

The idea of ideology as something we *all* participate in underlies the first   1
possibility of critical thought, because it shows that no ideas are 'given' or
'absolute'. Without the notion of cultural relativism, truly questioning
thought is impossible, because our *own* premises are never questioned. The
more I have taught in further education, the more I think it hardly matters,
in a way, *what* you teach, as long as it leads to this questioning, which
itself is a prerequisite for social change. . . .

It was only after finding that I couldn't teach about gender without   2
students having personal crises that I stopped seeing a 'concept of ideology'
as the necessary prerequisite for teaching about images of gender, and
realised that it was the other way round. I was using those images, and
anything else I could lay my hands on, precisely to produce an understanding of ideology. I didn't really care if they learnt it through images of
women, or studying the history of TV, or just talking in class, which we
ended up doing most of all, about anything.

This was what happened with first-year Media and Communications. In   3
this class we studied TV and newspapers; again I was doing the standard
work (including history of broadcasting and the press) but they thought
people who watched *Coronation Street* or *Crossroads* must be dumb, and
assumed that the ignorance of the masses is *proved* rather than perhaps
encouraged by their readership of the *Sun*, *Star* and *Mirror*. I can't say too
often, *it is not enough just to analyse the media*. Students can know the history
of TV backwards and 'deconstruct' an entire TV programme but still think
the people who watch it are stupid. Unless you can find any analogous
situation in their own experience, and make it problematic for them, they
will never really grasp the ideological relation between 'text' and 'reader'.

I had had no luck in trying to show these first years how news-   4
presentation is biased (again, using classic teaching material, coverage of a
strike, of trade unionists, terrorism), because the view put over by the
headline or news item *was* their 'own' view, they *did* think strikes were
caused by troublemakers, and that the IRA should be shot. So I had trouble
making them 'see' bias in the news. . . .

I would say that students learn best to 'see' the 'invisible', ideology,   5
when it becomes in their own interest to – when they are actually caught
in a contradiction, believing things which are directly hindering their own
well-being or wishes, or which conflict with a change in experience. I don't

think people learn in the abstract, nor through moral purpose – like when some boys try to be feminist. I was asked to speak in a video some third years were making about violence to women: they were all boys but had a feminist teacher (not me). They were discussing violence in films, and sexist representations – but it meant nothing to *them*, it didn't *affect* them. I asked why they didn't do a video about men, or perhaps speak on this video themselves about sexism, instead of just filming me and other women. They were 'doing' images of women as an English student might 'do' medieval poetry, or a history student 'the Tudors'.

What is the point of an education like this? What kind of knowledge does it endorse? The value of ideas is ultimately in their use for changing things – not necessarily material things, but for changing ourselves. The only point I can see in teaching is to make this possible. And such change, if it takes place in any important sense, is really traumatic. So far I have tried to describe the kinds of ways I've found it possible to suggest to students that perhaps they themselves, yes them, actually think or feel things that they're not normally aware of, things which are part of a wider social system of ideas and values, things which they have not consciously controlled. As I've said, it's almost impossible to make anyone see this purely intellectually. And when they really do see it, when they grasp the idea that everything they took for granted is in fact relative, that everything they thought was natural is constructed, that everything they *are* can be deconstructed – they freak out. The idea that they participate in ideology undermines the sense of a 'free self' which they have hitherto taken as given. Their personal identity is called into question, there is no sure footing, no 'truth', only discourses and categories (poor souls, I protect them from those two particularly obnoxious words and talk instead about ideologies and stereotypes, old-fashioned stuff).

Why Pedagogy?

David Lusted

From 'Why Pedagogy?', *Screen*, vol. 27, no. 5, September–October 1986, pp. 7–10.

Why is pedagogy important? It is important since, as a concept, it draws attention to the *process* through which knowledge is produced. Pedagogy addresses the 'how' questions involved not only in the transmission or reproduction of knowledge but also in its production. Indeed, it enables us to question the validity of separating these activities so easily by asking under what conditions and through what means we 'come to know'. How one teaches is therefore of central interest but, through the prism of pedagogy, it becomes inseparable from what is being taught and, crucially, how one learns. In this perspective, to bring the issue of pedagogy in from the cold and on to the central stage of cultural production is to open up for questioning areas of enquiry generally repressed by conventional assumptions, as prevalent in critical as in dominant practices, about theory production and teaching, and about the nature of knowledge and learning. [1]

Pedagogy is desperately under-theorised. No loss, at one level; it's an ugly word in print and on the tongue. The problem is that what the concept addresses is crucial and the absence of its development has had material effects. One effect is a share in the failure to realise post-war aspirations towards a genuinely democratic and popular mandatory education system. Another effect is yet another failure; this time to connect radical cultural theory to popular movements whose interests that theory declares it represents. Big claims. . . . [2]

The history of successive waves of curriculum intervention in film studies, TV studies, and then media studies offers a key case in point. Shifts from one arena of study to the next have occurred in order better to take account of the changing cultural scene. But, throughout, there has been an implicit assertion that a revised subject constitutes in itself a radical intervention in education, somehow shifting the social relations of the classroom in more democratic directions, providing a site for dramatic changes of consciousness in and by itself. The emptiness of any such claim is surely now clear as these study areas begin to take firmer purchase on the curriculum, and it acts as a caution to making similar claims to the more expansive possibilities carried by the promotion of a new stage of 'media education'. [3]

Simply teaching about cinema or television (or, for that matter, Marxism or psychoanalysis) is no guarantee of a progressive educational and cultural intervention. There is a pattern of excellent, competent, and indifferent [4]

85

teaching every bit as evident as in the teaching of quite conventional disciplines. What is required is greater attention, not just to the development of criticism in the field, but to the pedagogies that need to be inscribed within the production of knowledge (remember, now rendered as theory/criticism/teaching/learning) in order to actually effect its radical/critical intentions.

So far, I have been writing as if pedagogy has never been addressed by cultural production, but this is not the case. There is a history.

A dispute over the pedagogy of media studies began in the pages of *Screen Education* when Manuel Alvarado[1] critiqued the pedagogy implied in Len Masterman's widely influential book, *Teaching about Television.*[2] Alvarado discerned a residual progressivism in Masterman's examples of classroom practice, a mixed economy of activities too reliant on pupils' expressed or presumed preferences. For him, this was a pedagogy of exclusion, denying learners the opportunity to engage in 'really useful knowledge' about the media which determined those preferences in the first place. This characterisation was subsequently denied by Masterman, who turned on the pedagogy he inferred from Alvarado: it amounted, he said, to an old transmission model in new clothes, the teacher defining what was to count as 'useful knowledge' and imposing a new academicism and a new autocracy over a potentially democratic mode of learning.

This was an important moment of debate, making explicit a generation of assumptions about the radical nature of media studies in education. But it was inconclusive. The dispute turned on different disciplinary emphases – for Masterman, textual analyses based on newly developing literary approaches; for Alvarado, institutional analyses based on media sociology – whose pedagogies were assumed rather than argued. It is not clear, for instance, that the study of a television game show bears any particular pedagogy more or less progressive or effective than a pedagogy borne by the study of the broadcasting structures in which the game show is produced. Although the critics were certainly disputing the *content* of knowledge, it became less clear how to understand the connections between that dispute and the claims they were making for different pedagogies.

It was Judith Williamson, however, who demonstrated some of the elisions in the debate so far, when she asserted,[3] contentiously, that although we all knew *what* the state of knowledge was pressing us to teach, there was, less contentiously, a resounding silence over the *how*. The debate had been inadequate so far, she argued, since it addressed only the teacher's role in the classroom. Her concern was with what was actually going on in the students' heads. Rather than seeing learners as abstractly active or passive, more or less informed, she turned her attention to how students in her own experience could ritually reproduce the knowledge she offered without fundamentally shifting their frames of thought. Boys could learn that romance magazines constructed girls as solely sexual objects, that the process was limiting and offensive, but it did not prevent them reproducing dominant patterns of behaviour towards girls in their own classroom, nor thinking of all girls outside it as complicit victims in that construction. What was, and remains, required was an effective pedagogy that precisely worked on *changing* the consciousness of the students.

Williamson's contribution can be understood as a founding moment of 'modern' media studies. It established the importance of the study of the media as a stage for connecting issues of personal identity with cultural activity and, even more importantly for this article, skilfully demonstrated the crying need for attention to an effective critical pedagogy.

Since then, only Ian Connell has taken the debate over media studies pedagogy a stage further. Connell[4] argued that Williamson appeared to be developing an effective general pedagogy that confronted students with knowledge of their own inscription in cultural activity. But what lay behind Williamson's pedagogy, he argued, was an assumption of the manipulative role of the media and a construction of students as inevitably positioned by the ideological meanings critics discerned in media texts.

Connell implied that it was the nature of this critical assumption that *produced* the statements from students that so little challenged what they believed, rather than what they said. What Williamson had skilfully discerned was the product of her teaching, but what she had misrecognised was its cause. At stake wasn't some independent pedagogy severed from a particular critical assumption but the necessary, arising pedagogy *of* that assumption. Connell asserted that what was required was a more agnostic model wherein students could openly explore what they actually discerned from their experience and readings of media texts (and, importantly, those critical positions on media texts and institutions), rather than the closed model within which students focused on the production of themselves by the media.

What Connell more generally discerned, in a moment of great insight, was the intimacy of the connection between the pedagogy of teaching and that of media criticism. Taking the cue from Connell, this connection would assert the implicitly autocratic pedagogy not only of the great swell of conventional teaching but also of the history of theory, both mainstream and critical. In Leavis's apparent appeal to consensus, 'This is so, is it not?', resides a blueprint for this state of affairs, a positioning of reader/learner inescapably within the terms of the theory/teaching. Like the mode of address of much critical theory, the maxim demands assent, suggesting that to be not so positioned is to be deviant – ignorant or foolish. The pedagogy, in other words, neither brooks dissent nor appeals to the possibility of debate within it. Critical theory often carries a contradiction in its address, calling for change in its content whilst reproducing the existing relations in its form. It appeals to the experience and understanding of its reader as supportive evidence of its argument, while at the same time denying the possibility of experience being a factor in its understanding. It is a pedagogy of closure and a politics, not of debate, but of direction.

No surprise, then, that in a teaching pedagogy conforming to the shape of the theory of which it is a product, the learner can only accept/reject the terms offered. Nor any surprise that teachers experience as much resistance to this form of critical education as others experience with forms of conventional education. In this scenario, my support is entirely with those who resist – they're learning a lot. Also, crucially, within the terms of acceptance lies a distancing between the learner as individual subject and as social subject.

Judith Williamson's student plainly cannot take on the identity of 14
another gender, but that does not explain the lack of fit between his learning
and the absence of change in consciousness. His learning, regardless of the
quality of the argument, operates in a realm of closure, unconnected to
transformations in his *own* experience, responses, argument, and sense of
self. The male student cannot learn, despite 'knowing' the feminist argument, not because, crassly, he is (only) a male, nor because his maleness
disenables him from transforming his knowledge into his social practice.
The male student cannot 'know' because his learning is not socialised,
operating only at a global level of structures and systems, disconnected
from the social realm to which he knowingly relates. To draw back from
the example, it could be said that for such relations to be worked towards
requires a constellation of pedagogies addressed to the complexity of experience constituting any learner's and learner group's gendered, raced,
classed, aged, and discrete biographical, social, and historical identity.

What is required, therefore, is attention to open-ended and specific peda- 15
gogies, sensitive to context and difference, addressed to the social position
of any learning group and the positions of the individuals within it.

The implication is that the search for a general pedagogy is fruitless, a 16
grasping at shadows. Pedagogy in general is always inevitably tied to a
historical moment defined within the then current state of knowledge. It
is consequently necessary to go on to clarify the nature of *particular* pedagogies in particular instances of theory and teaching. What is required
is productive distinctions between pedagogies of theory and teaching at
particular moments, pedagogies that release genuine engagement and trans-
formative understanding in the consciousness.

Notes

1. Manuel Alvarado, 'Television Studies and Pedagogy', *Screen Education*, no. 38,
   Spring 1981.
2. Len Masterman, *Teaching About Television*, London, Macmillan, 1980.
3. Judith Williamson, 'How Does Girl Number Twenty Understand Ideology?',
   Screen Education, no. 40, Autumn/Winter 1981–2.
4. Ian Connell, ' "Progressive" Pedagogy?', *Screen*, vol. 24, no. 3, May–June
   1983.

Media Education:
From Pedagogy to Practice

David Buckingham

From David Buckingham (ed.), *Watching Media Learning*, Brighton, Falmer, 1990, pp. 8–9.

To be sure, there has been an on-going debate about 'pedagogy' in media education – although, as the use of that term itself would suggest, this too has been conducted at a highly theoretical level, largely among teachers in higher education.[1] As a result, it has been a strangely abstract debate, in which there is a good deal of heated confrontation between one 'position' and another, yet little concrete reference to specific instances of teaching and learning. While it is somehow acceptable to theorise about other people's pedagogy, it remains very difficult to describe what actually takes place in real classrooms.

Nevertheless, there has been a growing recognition in these debates that the realities of teaching and learning are more complex than some academic theorists would lead us to suppose. The aggressively libertarian notions of media teaching which were advocated in the 1960s and 1970s have increasingly been questioned. The idea that teachers could simply provide students with a body of knowledge which would open their eyes to a previously hidden reality has come to seem like so much wishful thinking. Teachers may attempt to 'tell it like it is', but students aren't necessarily going to believe them.

Judith Williamson's article 'How Does Girl Number Twenty Understand Ideology?' was the first notable attempt to question this vanguardist approach towards media teaching.[2] As Williamson points out, however 'radical' the knowledge teachers offer, students can easily learn to play the teacher's game. Boys can learn to say the right anti-sexist things about images of women in the media, but this can end up simply reinforcing their belief that girls must be stupid to enjoy those images in the first place.

As Williamson argues, 'analysis' alone will not necessarily change students' attitudes. Unless the discussion of ideology in the media is related to students' own experience, to their sense of their own identity, it will remain a purely academic exercise: students will 'do' images of women in the same way that they 'do' medieval poetry or the history of the Tudors. As she suggests, there is a risk that ideology will be seen as 'what *other* people think, and the only possible explanation for why they believe such "lies" or "propaganda" is because they are stupid' – a risk which media teaching, perhaps particularly in higher education, has not always managed to avoid.

89

Although Williamson's article did represent a decisive – if very belated – acknowledgement of the complexities of classroom practice, there is a sense in which it remains tied to vanguardist notions of teaching. Williamson continues to assume that her students are victims of a monolithic 'dominant ideology', promoted by an omnipotent media, and that their only escape will be through a process of instantaneous conversion, provoked by their confrontation with the teacher – a kind of 'road to Damascus' version of media education.

Given the broader context of debate at this time, Williamson's article was clearly raising some uncomfortable questions, and it would perhaps be unrealistic to expect her to have answered these as well. Yet they are questions which have recurred in subsequent debate. For example, my own contribution to this debate[3] derives from a similar sense of the contradictions of classroom practice, and an acknowledgement that students will not automatically assent to the positions laid out by 'radical' teachers. While it is certainly possible that students will learn to play the teacher's game (as Williamson's students do), it is equally possible that they may resist it, not necessarily for profound ideological reasons, but simply because they enjoy challenging the teacher's power. Working-class students in particular are likely to resist the attempts of middle-class teachers to impose their own political beliefs, however surreptitiously this is done. 'Radical' teachers cannot easily step outside the institutionalised power relationships of the educational system, and the claim that they are acting on the students' behalf will not necessarily be accepted by the students themselves.[4]

There is, then a growing recognition in these debates that many of the prescriptions for media teaching developed in the 1970s do not actually work in practice – and that the social dynamics of classrooms, and the learning process itself, are much more complex and contradictory than has previously been assumed. Yet, as I have indicated, the debates themselves remain highly abstract. The accounts of classroom practice are limited and anecdotal, mere ammunition for broader theoretical arguments. Here too, theory has been privileged over practice.

Notes

1. Manuel Alvarado, 'Television Studies and Pedagogy', *Screen Education*, no. 38, Spring 1981; Len Masterman, 'TV Pedagogy', *Screen Education*, no. 40, Autumn 1981; Judith Williamson, 'How Does Girl Number Twenty Understand Ideology?', *Screen Education*, no. 40, Autumn 1981; Ian Connell, ' "Progressive" Pedagogy?', *Screen*, vol. 24, no. 3, May–June 1983; Judith Williamson, 'Is there anyone here from a classroom? And other Questions of Education', *Screen*, vol. 26, no. 1, January–February 1985; David Lusted, 'Why Pedagogy?', *Screen*, vol. 27, no. 5, September–October 1986; David Buckingham, 'Against Demystification', *Screen*, vol. 27, no. 5, September–October 1986; Len Masterman, 'Reply to David Buckingham', *Screen*, vol. 27, no. 5, September–October 1986; Cary Bazalgette, 'Making Sense for Whom?', *Screen*, vol. 27, no. 5, September–October 1986.
2. Judith Williamson, op. cit. 1981.
3. David Buckingham, op. cit.
4. For similar observations, see Paul Cohen, 'The Perversions of Inheritance' in

90

P. Cohen and H. S. Bains (eds), *Multi-Racist Britain*, London, Macmillan, 1988; Andrew Dewdney and Martin Lister, *Youth, Culture and Photography*, London, Macmillan, 1988.

Rationales and Principles

Introduction

On a broader level than either issues of practice or of pedagogy more generally, media teachers in recent years have returned to the struggle to justify their area of interest, provide a rationale for it, identify its guiding principles, and show how the application of such rationales and principles might influence content and student learning, yet also be responsive to the age and educational level of students.

Manuel Alvarado considers the broad rationale for teaching media studies in the classroom in two contributions included here. He argues that the purpose of media studies is justified in terms not only of knowledge that is useful or relevant for students to acquire, but also in terms of its potential for the radical critique of the educational process more generally as well as of the media industries themselves. His view of content allows a significant role for the study of large media institutions and their ideological role, in particular as this might be evident in a 'dominant mode of representation'. He dismisses worries about 'boring' the students, and considers that knowledge of media institutions provides a basis for informed future public scrutiny of the media.

The study of institutions also has a distinctive place on Nicholas Garnham's agenda. However, this broader agenda is an attempt to combat what Garnham considered to be the excessive emphasis on texts in the late 1970s, in favour of a stronger focus on contextual factors, and in particular on the historical development of institutions and modes of production as interpreted within an analytical framework of political economy. Without that kind of focus, he argues, any attempt to develop a concept of 'ideology' in communication studies is fatally flawed. The value of ideology as developed in Marxist thought resided precisely in that it offered a conceptual tool to relate the world of ideas to the material world.

Len Masterman's concern is much less with content and more with skills. The basic purpose of media studies, he says, is that it should encourage students to apply critical judgements to media texts. The emphasis on critical judgement, then, reduces the importance of content as an end in itself. His curriculum would focus on (*a*) particular texts, (*b*) relevant contextual factors that are necessary for students to know about in order to apply critical judgement, and (*c*) identification of general principles that are relevant to the analysis of similar texts and issues. Like Alvarado, Masterman is less interested in students' evaluation of media than in their ability to investigate media and media texts.

David Buckingham reviews the range of dominant approaches to teaching about media. Ideology is central to all of these, as it is for Buckingham, but he reminds us that a convincing theory of ideology must go beyond any simplistic notion of false consciousness. The most valuable asset of media study in this view is its generation of a questioning, problematising approach to media, one that is applicable both to the study of media and to the study of knowledge (and hence of education). It should not, therefore, be subject-bound, but is cross-curricular in its usefulness and relevance. He recognises a danger that such a cross-curricular media education might undermine subject specialist claims to media studies and promote the view that media is something anybody can teach. But Buckingham argues for a media education that is cross-curricular yet informed by specialist expertise. Such a wide-ranging approach to media would be particularly appropriate at the primary level. Buckingham looks with apprehension at trends towards greater centralisation of curriculum control.

The Question of 'Media Studies'

Manuel Alvarado

From 'The Question of "Media Studies" ', *Meridian*, no. 2, October 1983, pp. 182–4.

So far I have outlined the concerns and areas of work of media studies. But why should media studies be taught in the classroom? In one sense the answers to that question are disarmingly obvious – because [television] is there; because people watch it; because it is the major medium through which people learn about the world; because the government, teachers, parents, Mary Whitehouse *et al.* are worried about the effect it has on other people's lives (never their own, incidentally); and so on. However, I would suggest that there are much more important and polemical reasons which are rarely articulated, two of which I will enumerate.

The first is that it is important to study television because it is both an industry and a set of state institutions (despite the use of private capital in the 'independent' sector) whose purpose is to present itself, to expose itself continuously and conspicuously as no other set of institutions does, and yet which constantly effaces its own practices and methods, constantly denies its own materiality through the arguments of objectivity and neutrality. Furthermore, television institutions are extremely unwilling to make available for public observation and research their own 'production line'. As the Glasgow University Media Group discovered, it is far easier to visit most factories and places of work than it is to enter a TV studio (and copyright law, to some extent, makes analysis of the programmes themselves more difficult). So I would suggest that in studying television and television programmes we are studying not only a particular set of representations of the world and the language adopted to make those representations 'acceptable' and 'normal' but also a set of institutions, how they function, and how they function *ideologically*, thereby constituting an apparatus designed to maintain the status quo, to help reproduce the existing structure of society. Of course, that view of the importance of media studies does not help to make it an acceptable and respectable area of knowledge for study in school!

My second reason for studying the media is similarly problematic. The introduction of any new subject into the school curriculum is part of what is called 'curriculum development'. In engaging in the process of curriculum development, it is always possible to open up what I will term 'oppositional space', a space in which to do something very different, to pose different questions and problems than those which are raised in other subject areas, and to question our dominant conception of what constitutes 'knowledge'. This need not be the case, of course. If media studies is introduced into the curriculum for the reasons I listed earlier, I would argue that all that would be achieved would be the *modernising* of that curriculum – it would be made more 'relevant' (itself a highly dubious concept, in my opinion) for the child of the 1980s. I would be very distressed to see media studies appropriated by the education system in the way that television has appropriated the feminist movement, for example. What I wish to argue is that to introduce *any* new subject into the curriculum for the reason of creating oppositional space is to do something very important and something which, in the case of the media, is quite impossible to do from within the television institutions themselves. In the case of media studies, it means the exposing of both the actual and potential cracks, fissures, dislocations, and absences that exist within television and television programmes, and at the same time asking *how* could things be done differently. However, if we accept that the television institutions and the education system represent important and crucial elements within our social formation, then to pose those questions about television in schools is to make possible the posing of similar questions about the education system itself. And that, of course, is quite another matter.

I began by saying that I would deal with 'television' in its specificity, despite the substantial areas of overlap and mutual determination that exist between the various media (television presents films; shares an institutional space with radio; videotapes can be circulated like books; television news systems employ journalists drawn from Fleet Street, who operate within certain consensual paradigms about news values; similar news agencies are used, etc., etc.), and I did this for two main reasons. One is that the BBC and the ITV companies represent an extremely important and powerful set of institutions within our society – clearly defined, constructed, and controlled by the State, they are seen by the State to occupy a crucial position and to fulfil a vital function within the structure of our social formation. 4

The second reason is that television also operates within the ideological sphere of human existence, and that raises all sorts of questions and problems. To engage in an ideological analysis of television is to look at television programmes as part of a total television discourse which is constituted by a set of specific signifying practices. This 'language' of television – a system which involves simultaneous sound and image – is a highly sophisticated and complex culturally 'coded' system. Like our native tongue, it is normally successfully internalised and comprehensible to each and every member of our social formation but, as with language, we still have to engage in a sophisticated decoding process in order to understand the televisual code. This is not an immediately obvious fact because images possess an analogical relationship to the real world, unlike language which possesses an essentially arbitrary relationship (the fact that the French use the word 'chien' for 'dog' simply marks a different language – the object 'dog' remains the same, but an image of a 'table' would not substitute for the image of a 'dog'). However, this 'fact' becomes clearer if we see a programme which does not adopt the dominant aesthetic of television (which I have already called 'realist'), and which we have to struggle to understand rather as we sometimes have to struggle to understand an 5 unfamiliar dialect in spoken language. I am suggesting, therefore, that there is a *dominant mode of representation* adopted by television – as far as the programme-makers are concerned a right and a wrong way of making a programme and presenting a situation, which is determined by the dominant practices of making programmes.

The implications of this argument are serious because, if one accepts that there is a 'dominant mode' of representing the world, then it would suggest that there is also a 'dominant representation', a single view of the world offered by the media. If that dominant representation is in accord with our view of the world, then there is clearly no problem – we will simply enjoy the programmes that are offered. However, it is not easy to ask if other forms of television are possible or if other views of the world are available, in a situation where television is internationally dominated by a very few companies and countries;[1] when it is relatively rare for people to directly experience other country's television programmes or institutions; and when, to a large extent, our perceptions of the world have been formed by television, and when it is not easy for most people to gain access to the technology of television in order to make their own programmes.

It is in this situation that the concept of ideology is crucial to our understanding of the media. James Donald, in a Media Studies CSE syllabus, presented the argument extremely clearly when he wrote that the media are:

> ideological in that they present their consumers with structured images of themselves in relation to other people and to social institutions. They provide selective and fragmented knowledge in well-established (and therefore comprehensible) codes which are crucial in the formation of individual personality, imagination, and belief. They make particular social relations (those that exist here and now) seem natural and normal. They therefore inhibit the tendency to change those relations (between classes or the sexes, for example) in any radical way.[2]

However, just because there is a dominant mode of representation adopted by television does not mean that there is only one way of decoding or reading the programmes offered – there will always be the possibility of reading them alternatively or even oppositionally. It is this possibility – that of people being able to read and understand artefacts alternatively or even oppositionally to the way they were intended to be read – which offers, for me, the most positive, responsible, and fruitful position, and way forward, for the teacher interested in media studies to adopt.

Notes
1. See, for example, Jeremy Tunstall, *The Media Are American*, Constable, 1977, which is one of a number of books published in this field.
2. James Donald, *Media Studies – Possibilities and Limitations*, BFI Advisory Document, 1977.

Television Studies and Pedagogy

Manuel Alvarado

From 'Television Studies and Pedagogy', *Screen Education*, no. 38, Spring 1981, pp. 64–6.

Institutional Structures

Teaching about the film industry and about the structures of broadcasting has historically been recognised as an important area of work within film/TV/media studies courses. The rationale, at one level, has been clear, i.e., the mass media represent major institutions and industries and therefore should be taught about. The implications of work in this area do not, however, seem to have filtered through to other subject areas in the curriculum. For example, how many English teachers include in their syllabuses (in the teaching of all age groups) work on the production, circulation, and reading of texts, and on the organisation, ownership, and interrelationships of the various publishing houses? Or do work on book advertising and the retail distribution system? Or on copyright law and the interrelationship between authorship, ownership, and copyright?

Many teachers would no doubt respond to these questions by arguing that children would not be interested and would find the researching for, or provision of, such information boring. One response which can be made is to say that to have access to a publishing house is to have access to a certain power and, what is more, children know that they, in the main, don't enjoy such privilege. The questions then are, why not? who does? how? and why? In my experience, these are questions which interest children greatly. Another response one could make would be to question the notion of 'boredom' and the idea that it can define what work is done, what ground covered. The implication is that children are only prepared to engage in what provides fairly immediate gratifications, which is also fairly unlikely to have any relation to what might be considered hard work. The problem is that if one doesn't teach about the areas indicated above, it would seem to be impossible to introduce key concepts such as 'cultural hegemony' – key because without it it is unlikely that many children are going to recognise the importance and significance of engaging in cultural struggle in order that, for example, working-class/black/female/childrens' texts are distributed more widely and influentially.

Furthermore, is such work so boring? Is it boring to know why some people struggled to establish the 'alternative' bookshops which now exist across the country (like the Walter Rodney Bookshop, Sisterwrite, Centreprise)? Is it boring to know why 'alternative' publishing houses were similarly established (like Bogle L'Ouverture, Women's Press, Readers and Writers)? Is it boring to think through the implications of the policies

97

of the major publishing houses in relation to the hegemonic maintenance of a particular cultural heritage – one that is fed and reinforced by university English departments, book reviewers in the press, on radio and television, and by a bookshop chain like W. H. Smith? Is it boring to try to understand why certain authors and certain topics are extensively published and distributed and others hardly at all? Is it boring to analyse the inadequacy of the conventional response to these questions – which is that publishers and booksellers are merely responding to public demand? And finally, suppose that one accepted that such work was inherently boring. Why should work be easy, why do we kid 'kids' that they only need to do the pleasant and easy things at school when we know that life is unlikely to be easy for them when they leave?

An important point here, however, is that if children do find such work 4 boring it may be because the teacher has not located and contexted the material in the most pertinent way. If information about institutional structures is simply provided as a list of 'facts' then pupils will correctly find such information irrelevant – but if such information is placed within the broader context of children understanding more fully about *our* social formation, about *their* position within it, and about how it might be otherwise, then they are likely to be much more interested than Len Masterman would seem to believe. To ignore this area of work is implicitly to keep pupils in a position of ignorance, and ignorance is a form of powerlessness. If this seems merely a truism, I will relate a chilling anecdote. Recently, an Inner London teacher showed a racially mixed class of 15–16 year old boys and girls Programme 8 'Show Business' from the first series of *Viewpoint*. (This is the episode that both helped to get the series withdrawn[1] and which also prompted Masterman to write the following footnote – 'My own experience of the excellent *Viewpoint* series, for example, was that the programme dealing specifically with the business side of the media was one of the least popular with pupils.') One of the group was a white boy who openly declared his National Front membership, and whose response to the programme was that he knew all that stuff anyway but that what the programme didn't say was that it was all a Jewish conspiracy for it was they who controlled the media. The point is that he possessed a 'knowledge' – an odious and racist knowledge – and that it represented material which he could marshal and use in an argument. In order to combat that sort of response a teacher obviously needs to be well prepared and knowledgeable, but he or she also needs to be prepared to respond *directly* and not simply to suggest that the group has a discussion of that viewpoint.

It is not being suggested that the direct offering of information will 5 necessarily change this fascist view of the world, which is often clung to emotionally for 'students never take the teacher's messages straight but always submit them to resistances and transformations'.[2] Recognising the social relations in the classroom and the ideologies students bring with them to the classroom, we have to be aware that there can be no perfect pedagogy. However, it is important to recognise that the processes of teaching and learning should always be a struggle – and that the classroom is recognised as being a central, but not the only, site for that struggle, and that the provision of information is part of that struggle. Furthermore, whilst that provision won't necessarily change the attitudes of the young fascist mentioned above, it might, at the very least, provide useful information for the other members of the group who work with him. There is one final point I will make about media teaching in the area of institutional structures. If we, as teachers, avoid teaching about this area, who will teach it and to whom? Unless one believes in the early demise of the BBC, the IBA, and the ITV and ILR companies, then their maintenance will depend upon continuing recruitment *and* a public that accepts them as they are. If they are ever to change then a critical scrutiny of their structures and financing as well as of their programmes and practices will be required. Although this piece has concentrated upon teaching about the structures of broadcasting there are obviously many significant content areas with which a critical pedagogy must deal and which involve the consideration of abstract concepts, theoretical models, and modes of discourse.

Notes
1. See 'The *Viewpoint* Controversy', *Screen Education*, no. 19, Summer 1976.
2. 'Editorial', *Screen Education*, no. 34, Spring 1980, discussing Richard Johnson's important article 'Cultural Studies and Educational Practice' in that issue.

Film and Media Studies:
Reconstructing the Subject

Nicholas Garnham

From *Capitalism and Communication*, London, Sage, 1990, pp. 60–1
(originally published in Christine Gledhill (ed.), *Film and Media Studies in
Higher Education*, London, BFI, 1981).

What has been lost in this whole development of film studies, and now of communication studies as well, is the original reason for studying the subject in the first place. Leavis's work,[1] with its concern for the mass media, must not be seen in isolation. It was part of a general reaction on the part of western intellectuals to the phenomenon subsequently dubbed 'the industrialisation of culture' and of their various attempts to come to terms with that phenomenon. Shaped by the specific cultural contexts within which theorists were working, this produced mass society theory in its various guises. In particular it is striking now, with the benefit of historical perspective, to see the similarities between the contemporaneous analysis and concerns of Leavis and of the Frankfurt School.

But mass society theory is itself a development of that central strand of the western intellectual tradition stemming from Vico and Montesquieu in the eighteenth century, the tradition from which, in their damagingly separate ways, both modern history and sociology developed. Such inquiry took as its field the function of the symbolic realm in the maintenance, change, and differentiation of social formations. We see this central concern expressed in such a trio of classic texts as *The German Ideology*, *Elementary Forms of Religious Life*, and *The Protestant Ethic and the Spirit of Capitalism*. It is to this concern that, in my view, media studies has to address itself if it is to be a serious area of study, and in doing so at least as much emphasis will have to be placed upon history and economics as upon the subaltern discipline of aesthetics.

The mass media are concrete historical phenomena socially created as part of the general development of industrial capitalism, and their shifting function can only be understood within that context. If study of those media is to amount to anything more than the study of media artefacts in ways that merely reinforce by pandering to the particular cultural tastes of specific social groups (this is the tendency of the avant-gardism of *Screen*), then it needs to tackle the central historical questions surrounding the development of these phenomena.

The first conjunctural focus of such a study needs to be that period in Britain from about 1880 through to the First World War (and associated periods in the United States and Western Europe, although the exact temporalities will differ), when technologies of reproduction, the gramophone, film, high-speed printing, and photogravure, were mobilised and institutionalised as part of a shift in the general economic structure from competitive industrial capitalism to monopoly consumer capitalism. The actual forms of that development are rooted in the economic developments and classic struggles of the nineteenth century as a whole. To understand the continuing significance of that historical shift media studies students need to be familiar with the general theoretical problems concerning the development of capitalism; they need the appropriate intellectual tools with which to analyse a mode of production and distinguish between forces and relations of production, between production and exchange within the circuit of capital. An understanding of these historical processes would help such students to avoid conceptualising film in the narrow way that, in general and implicitly, film studies now does; namely, as a form that involves the projection of sounds and images reproduced on celluloid before an audience in a cinema, and which thus leads to the constitution of television studies as a separate field and media studies as yet another. Instead, the form at present studied by film studies would be seen as part of a historical continuum of the production and distribution of dramatic performances using different recording techniques, different modes of production and distribution, and differing associated modes of economic organisation, whether or not with significantly different social functions and effects remaining to be established.

Within this general process the shift from modes of production historically associated with film to those associated with broadcasting would serve as the second conjunctural focus for any study of the mass media, introducing the central theme of the role of the State in monopoly capitalism and leading both to problems surrounding international media and the analysis of media and cultural imperialism within the general context of an economic analysis of imperialism, as well as to debates over the so-called post-industrial society or information society and the role of new communication technologies.

Another focus of any media studies course needs to be the historical study of the development of the division of labour and of the division of mental and manual labour within that more general development, and such study needs to look closely at the problem of the labour process. Students need to be familiar with the debates concerning the social position and function of that social group variously referred to as intellectuals, as cultural workers, or as ideologists.

Note
1. F. R. Leavis, *Education and the University*, London, Chatto and Windus, 1948.

A Distinctive Mode of Enquiry:
Towards Critical Autonomy

Len Masterman

From *Teaching the Media*, London, Comedia, 1985, pp. 24–6.

It is scarcely possible to define an appropriate mode of enquiry for media education until we answer the question 'Appropriate for what?' What precisely are we trying to achieve with our pupils or students in a media education course? I would wish to argue that one of the primary objectives of media education should not be to produce in pupils the ability to reproduce faithfully ideas, critical insights, or information supplied by the teacher. Nor should it involve simply encouraging the students' own critical insights within the classroom, important though this may be. The really important and difficult task of the media teacher is to develop in pupils enough self-confidence and critical maturity to be able to apply critical judgements to media texts *which they will encounter in the future*. The acid test of any media education programme is the extent to which pupils are critical in their own use and understanding of the media *when the teacher is not there*. The primary objective is not simply critical awareness and understanding, it is critical *autonomy*. It is very important, then, that media education:

– does not degenerate into the stultifying and laborious accumulation of facts, ideas, and information about the media;
– should not consist of dehumanising exercises or 'busy work' on the media, designed primarily to keep students occupied;
– should not involve the dutiful reproduction by students of the teacher's ideas.

I would want to argue that the most satisfactory media education syllabuses will not be *essentialist* in terms of their content. Students may be freed, that is, of the oppressive load of content which *must* be covered. Syllabuses should seek, rather, to define the processes and principles which will enable students to stand as quickly as possible on their own two critical feet. Course content, teaching methodology, and questions of evaluation will need to be thought through in the light of this priority. Content, in particular, needs to be thought of, not as an end in itself, but as a means to developing critical autonomy, and not submerging it. A good deal of the content of an effective media course, then, will not be predictable. The teacher will generally find it a considerable advantage to maintain maximum flexibility, to be opportunistic, and not to plan too far ahead. The students' own interests and preferences ought certainly to be given due weight, as should programmes, articles, and issues which emerge as matters of topical concern amongst the group. The attractiveness and immediacy of this kind of content ought to be a powerful motivating factor within media education, and continuing dialogue and negotiation between teacher and students about course content will be necessary in order to guarantee this.

The critical act within media education should look three ways. First of all, it should pay the closest attention to a particular text or issue. Though media education attempts to develop *general* critical abilities and an understanding of general principles, they must always be grounded in 'local analysis' (to borrow a phrase from Leavis). Secondly, the development of a critical consciousness will be dependent on occasions upon the provision of relevant information from outside of the text. Access to such information and an ability to find one's way around it will need to be built into any media education course. The provision of information should always be judged by its relevance to the development of critical abilities. Thirdly, the act of criticism must look *beyond* the particularity of a specific text or issue towards those general principles which seem to have relevance to the analysis of similar texts and issues. It must work, that is, for critical transfer to new situations. That is the foundation upon which critical autonomy will be built. The objective is close to that outlined by Leavis in his essay 'How to teach Reading': 'The aim here is to insist on the essentials, the equipment, and the training that will enable the student to look after himself.'[1] I shall be parting company with Leavis, however, by arguing that within media education the aim of critical reading should not be primarily evaluative, but *investigative*.

Note
1. F. R. Leavis, 'How to teach Reading', in *Education and the University*, London, Chatto and Windus, 1948.

Media Studies and Media Education

David Buckingham

From *Communication and Education* Unit 27, Milton Keynes, Open University, 1987, pp. 36–8.

The definition of the role of media in education proposed by this unit is only one among many. There is a range of conflicting definitions, and these are likely to continue in uneasy coexistence. For example, the 'inoculation' approach to teaching about the media described by Masterman[1] is far from exhausted, and continues to inform varieties of English teaching that in other respects are very much opposed to it. The approach these days is more likely to be concerned either with 'discrimination *within*' (encouraging young people to like 'serious' television and despise popular 'trash') or with 'demystification' (attempting to expose the 'false' ideologies of the media and replace them with a 'true' account of the way things really are). If Masterman's account attempts to reject the implicit class bias of the former approach, the intention of my analysis has been to question the notion of 'demystification' with which he replaces it. At the same time, I hope I have indicated that my own account is far from proposing an uncritical celebration of 'the popular'. As well as acknowledging the pleasures the media provide, the approach I have outlined seeks to understand and also to *problematise* the processes by which they are produced. For this reason, I have argued for a theory of ideology that goes beyond notions of 'false consciousness' to consider the role of ideology in constituting the reading (or viewing) subject. This approach is informed by a number of disparate theories of discourse and ideology – certainly by versions of semiotics, but also by versions of psychoanalytic and Marxist theory. In attempting to avoid the theoretical quagmires such theories hold, I have certainly skated over many of their fundamental incompatibilities.

If media studies is perhaps unsure of its answers, then, it is probably clearer about its questions; and it is this questioning, or problematising, approach that I have argued should inform the use of media in other areas of the curriculum. Thus, I have opposed the 'instrumental' use of media as 'tools for learning', both in the case of educational television and in the case of students' practical media production. While I see educational television as an extremely valuable learning resource, it would clearly be far more valuable if students were encouraged to interrogate and analyse it, rather than merely to accept its claim to 'tell the truth'. Likewise, while I broadly support the claims by Lorac and Weiss[2] for the potential of practical media work as a method of learning, I believe that this potential would be far greater if it were informed by a questioning of established professional practices, rather than by an uncritical emulation of them. In both instances, it is important to demonstrate that these institutionalised definitions of what the media are and how they work are not neutral, but rather, as I have suggested, historically *produced*.

Some proponents of media studies have seen this questioning as a quality inherent in the subject itself. Manuel Alvarado and Bob Ferguson,[3] for example, extend theories of discourse that have been influential in media studies to a critique of the construction of knowledge within the curriculum as a whole. The school curriculum, they argue, is realist in the sense that it is based on an empiricist definition of knowledge: it does not problematise the way in which the world is represented to students, but rather sees knowledge as a transparent reflection of reality. Media studies, they suggest, challenges this dominant view by arguing that *all* knowledge is constituted through symbolic systems and discursive practices (i.e., institutions), which are in turn constituted by, and constitutive of, power relations. The forms of knowledge provided by specific disciplines should therefore be regarded, not as neutral representations, but as the products of specific symbolic systems or signifying practices.

However, this view of knowledge is not peculiar to media studies; such questioning can occur in other subject areas. Recent curriculum developments in history, for example, have been concerned to problematise the use of 'evidence', and to present history not as a body of facts but as a 'process of production'. Likewise, much of the potential of cross-curricular developments in areas such as integrated humanities or 'science and society' lies in their ability to question established subject divisions and the status quo of what counts as knowledge.

To some extent this may undermine the claim for media studies as a unique subject discipline. If, as I have argued, the perspectives developed within media studies should be informing the use of media in other curriculum subjects (and even the very processes by which those subjects are constituted), is it not contradictory or unnecessary to insist on media studies as a specialist activity? Defenders of media *studies* as a specialist discipline may well be correct in seeing the broader notion of media *education* as leading to a dilution of their specific concerns and expertise: it might well lead to a 'deskilling' of teachers, and the reduction of media studies to a 'servicing' role.

This distinction between media studies and media education has been increasingly debated in the wake of the 1983 Department of Education and Science report *Popular TV and Schoolchildren*.[4] The report itself, written by a group of fifteen teachers, examines 'the images of adult life and society made available to young people in a range of popular BBC and ITV television programmes'. It concludes that there is a need for teachers, parents, and broadcasters to explore more fully the influence of television on young people, and to ensure that it is 'positive and constructive'. In terms of education, it argues that 'specialist courses in media studies are not enough: all teachers should be involved in examining and discussing television programmes with young people'.

The report has been criticised – for example by Hartley *et al*.[5] – for relying on 'personal value judgements' and advocating an 'inoculation' approach: 'This approach to TV does not examine the criteria on which

105

TV is being studied and judged, and it takes for granted that it is the responsibility of teachers to provide an *antidote* to its influences.' These authors firmly reject the view, which they detect in the report's conclusions, that 'anyone' can teach about television. Media studies, they argue, 'is a better bet than media education – or at least a *prerequisite* of media education'.

My view is more tentative, for a number of reasons. Firstly, a good deal hinges on one's definition of 'media education'. If media education is merely a pretext for ill-informed discussion of last night's television programmes, it will serve little purpose. If it is seen as a covert means for teachers to control children's viewing and to attempt to mitigate what are presumed to be its harmful moral effects, it is likely, as Hartley *et al.* suggest, to be perceived by students as an invasion of privacy and a manifestation of teachers' prejudices, and may therefore prove counter-productive. Yet, as I have indicated in this section, there is also a potentially more radical definition of media education which seeks to extend the insights of media studies to inform the use of media in other curriculum areas. In the same way as the 'language across the curriculum' movement of the late 1970s emphasised the responsibility of teachers in all subject areas to develop a coherent policy on the role of language, so a 'media education across the curriculum' movement would argue that all teachers should understand and question the media they use. Such a broad-ranging approach would have significant implications for teacher training, given the relative lack of opportunities for initial and in-service training in the use of media.[6]

Secondly, an important aspect of the debate about media education has been the move to extend the study of the media from its traditional base in the upper years of the secondary school, and in further and higher education, into the lower secondary and primary sectors. The development of a co-ordinated and coherent media education curriculum for students from five to sixteen – a development that is being paralleled in other subject areas – inevitably involves a reconsideration not merely of what should be taught at different stages, but also of where on the timetable it should be located. James Learmonth, the HMI who initiated the *Popular TV and Schoolchildren* report, has suggested that media studies might continue to be offered as a subject specialism in the upper secondary school, but as a culmination of this more general media education curriculum.[7] In this sense it is false to regard media studies and media education as incompatible: the former is merely a specialist extension of the latter.

Finally, the future of media studies and media education is largely dependent on the broader educational and political context. At the time of writing, for example, there are considerable pressures on media studies teachers to accommodate themselves to the broader reformulation of the curriculum being initiated by central government under the auspices of the Manpower Services Commission. Yet here again, the portents of change may be read in contradictory ways. On the one hand, there is a broad attempt to divide the curriculum into vocational training for the 'non-academic' student and a traditional liberal education for the more 'academic'. Yet, at the same time, developments such as the Technical and Vocational Education Initiative (TVEI) appear – at least in certain schemes – to cut across such divisions, and to offer the possibility for an integration of practical and analytical work of the kind I argued for in the previous section. Nevertheless, if the drift towards centralisation and the erosion of teacher autonomy continues, it will clearly restrict the potential for innovation. Relatively new and vulnerable subjects such as media studies are at risk of being swept aside by such developments. At some point in the future, the claims for media studies may come to be seen not as an argument for a separate subject, but as an argument for the reconceptualisation of English, and media teachers may have to retreat to the fairly safe space that English currently occupies in the school curriculum. Whatever happens, the evolution of media education is likely to be less a matter of theoretical debate and more to do with questions of strategy.

Notes

1. Len Masterman, *Teaching About Television*, London, Macmillan, 1980, and Len Masterman, *Teaching the Media*, London, Comedia, 1985.
2. C. Lorac and M. Weiss, *Communications and Social Skills*, Exeter, Wheaton, 1981.
3. Manuel Alvarado and Bob Ferguson, 'The Curriculum, Media Studies and Discursivity', *Screen*, vol. 24, no. 3, May–June 1983.
4. Reprinted in David Lusted and Phillip Drummond, *TV and Schooling*, London, BFI 1985.
5. J. Hartley, H. Goulden, and T. O'Sullivan, *Making Sense of the Media*, London, Comedia, 1985.
6. U. C. Saunders, *Training for Effective Use of Schools Broadcasting*, Southampton, University of Southampton, 1980 (M.Ed. thesis).
7. James Learmonth, 'Media studies or media education?', *Secondary Education Journal*, vol. 15, no. 2, 1985.

The Politics of a Media Curriculum

Introduction

The promised introduction of the National Curriculum as a requirement of the 1988 Education Reform Act was at first feared by many proponents of media education, as it seemed not impossible that the subject be altogether excluded or emasculated. In the event, the National Curriculum has provided a niche for media education within the context of a core subject, English, from 5 to 16 (although there have been noises to suggest that it might also be considered as a cross-curricular theme). But the teaching of media education within the context of English has also been a matter of concern to those who regard that context as limiting.

Teaching about media had been advocated at national level within England and Wales for some time, and earlier references in this volume to Crowther, Newsom, and Bullock attest to this. The first extract in this section, however, is more recent: the 1983 Department of Education and Science (DES) enquiry, *Popular TV and Schoolchildren*. Criticised at the time for its dependence on a variety of personal viewpoints, it nevertheless testifies to the growing acceptance of popular television as a proper subject *for* education as well as sometimes constituting a vehicle *of* education. The report speaks as much to producers as to teachers and parents. It recognises that developments in technology and in the politics of regulation have an influence on children's use and experience of television. While this report may represent a broadly 'inoculative' approach to teaching about television, with an accent on parental control, there is also recognition of the opportunities for the study of representation and genre.

Hard on the heels of the 1988 Kingman report, the first of a series of reports addressed to the task of developing a national curriculum for English, came recommendations from the two Cox committees, the first, *English for Ages 5–11* (November 1988) being superseded in 1989 by the second Cox report, *English for ages 5–16* (June 1989). There are some differences in emphasis in the media sections of these two reports, yet both take a relatively broad view of media, both in terms of the range of media they include and in their incorporation of both textual and contextual analysis. The second Cox Report specifically regards media education 'largely as part of the exploration of contemporary culture alongside more traditional literary texts', thus building on the 1985 DES recognition of popular culture as a legitimate concern for education. Julian Bowker maps the extent to which the broad ambitions of Cox were translated into the National Curriculum guidelines for English, key stages 1–4. While he judges the result a matter for 'cautious celebration', he worries that not only is a distinction still drawn between 'literary' and 'non-literary' texts, but that 'non-literary' texts are defined as those which persuade or contain information, while images and audio-visual media are undervalued in relation to literary texts.

The incorporation of media education within the English National Curriculum does not in itself resolve some important differences in the approaches, subject cultures, pedagogies, and methodologies of the two subjects, and in the conceptions that each has of the other. These are examined by Buckingham, who defines the key differences in terms of their respective foci and treatment of texts, and their quite different assumptions about how texts are to be read. English is defined mainly in terms of practices, media studies mainly in terms of concepts. English privileges creativity, media studies privileges 'critical analysis'. Putting English and media studies together, argues Buckingham, will require a fundamental but potentially very productive rethinking of both areas.

The issue of the fusion of English and media studies within the English curriculum notwithstanding, there are many points of interrelationship of media education with other parts of the curriculum, which the BFI explores in its formal response to the second Cox Report. In particular the response notes that the framework for media education which the BFI had helped to generate is relevant to a wide variety of texts in different subject areas. The response usefully brings together references to media in a number of National Curriculum documents.

Issues raised by the fusion of media studies and English, on the one hand, or of media education across the curriculum, on the other, are also in part political issues, with important implications for what is fundamentally understood by media education. Cary Bazalgette begins her analysis with the traditionally radical vein of media studies. She suggests that the radical tradition in media education may have inhibited many of its proponents from appraising the real significance of developments promoted from a position of influence closer to the political centre. The radical tradition, with its distrust of the concepts of discrimination and aesthetics, may also have inhibited teachers from entering into any part of the debate posed by conservative government about issues of quality, values, and standards. Bazalgette thinks there has to be a way for media educators to describe, investigate, and justify what we enjoy and value in the media. Otherwise, she warns, we are saying we don't think they matter all that much. In the case of children, for example, progressive pedagogy requires us to find a place for children's own media choices and the pleasures which these represent, and the study of pleasure may offer one route of entry into the debate about quality, by questioning how terms such as quality and standards are defined in the first place and by whom.

Popular TV and Schoolchildren:
The Report of a Group of Teachers
Department of Education and Science Report

From *Popular TV and Schoolchildren*, London, DES, 1983 (reprinted in David Lusted and Phillip Drummond (eds), *TV and Schooling*, London, BFI, 1985, pp. 113–15).

Conclusion

a) In the programmes viewed there was a high level of professional and technical excellence and much of the output of BBC and ITV was interesting and entertaining. It is important to bear in mind the quality and acceptability of much of British television, particularly when concentrating on that which is controversial or anxiety-provoking. It is also important, particularly for teachers, to avoid falling into the trap of conferring greater value *per se* on programmes which set out to educate and inform than on those whose primary aim is to entertain.

b) It became clear in the course of discussions with producers and others working for the BBC and ITV companies that there was little agreement among them about the wider educational influence and possibilities of television. Producers often assumed that any discussion of the educational role of the programmes was an attempt to press them into taking a more didactic stance in their productions. This defensiveness militated against a thorough examination of how programmes of all kinds make available to young people images of the world and in this sense, and often more directly, disseminate information and opinions as well as relaying particular attitudes and values. For a minority of children the products of television may be the main source of significant influence on the way in which their images of certain groups develop: for example, the images of black people built up by those children who never meet blacks in real life.

c) Despite the work and efforts of the BBC's weekly Programme Review Boards, the regular studies of audience reaction carried out by both BBC and IBA, and of the various advisory groups, there was relatively little evidence among producers of a concerned awareness of just how powerful an influence their programmes may be on the lives of young people. In both the BBC and ITV companies too often it was assumed that if teachers were interested in the educational impact of television then schools programmes must be their main concern. It is not possible to separate the responsibilities to educate and to entertain into such self-contained boxes. Yet it seems that programme-makers often do so. As a consequence they fail to recognise or act upon the conflict and continuity between the duties to educate and to entertain. It is this failure to link the two that causes concern to teachers, parents, and others. For many outside the professional

110

world of television there is a worrying and obvious contradiction between, for example, the exploration of crime, violence, or the causes and consequences of war in programmes intended to educate and inform, and the treatment of these same themes in television drama and light entertainment. There is a desire for balance and some consistency that for most people falls far short of anything that could be described as censorship. But there should be at the least a clearer recognition among those in television at all levels that just as entertainment should not be missing from that which is primarily educational, education does not stop just because a programme is described as a play, a feature film, or light entertainment.

d) The arrival of Channel 4, the present video boom, and the potential of cable television all underline the urgency with which those working in television must consider their role with reference to children. Already through video clubs young people can have regular access to material which would be unacceptable to many adults; many young people now have access to video recorders which enable them to replay television material however often and at whatever time they choose; American research suggests that the more television channels that are available to young people, the more restricted becomes their taste as they become less likely to try something 'new'. How will broadcasters respond to these future developments, and how high a priority will their educational responsibilities have? In the past producers have too often used the lack of clear and consistent research evidence about the effects of television on young people as an excuse for their avoidance of such questions.

e) Schools, too, must review their responsibilities with reference to young people's experience of television. The fact that most children between five and fourteen spend more time watching television than they do working in a classroom underlines the magnitude of the part which television plays in their lives. There are few aspects of life about which television does not pass on messages to young people. Teachers now know what many of their pupils do in their leisure time, in so far as much of the evening is spent in the common experience of watching the same programmes on television. There are obvious opportunities for teachers to share some of this experience and to put it to constructive use in the classroom. It may be that the nature of the medium makes certain sorts of presentation almost inevitable: the drama series is drawn to 'soap opera', with social context and depth giving way to tortuous personal relationships; the complex industrial dispute is reduced to a personal confrontation between representatives of two extreme positions; previous success and public expectations lead comedy towards stereotypes of character and plot; the normal routine is ignored, the colourful, unusual, or controversial is highlighted. It must certainly be part of the educator's responsibility to explain these pressures to young people. In some schools, both primary and secondary, considerable attention has been given to the discussion of television programmes seen at home. Bodies such as the British Film Institute's Education Department and the Society for Education in Film and Television have been offering advice and in-service training to teachers for many years, and a small number of secondary schools have courses in media studies which may lead to public examination at CSE or O level. Both the BBC and ITV have themselves put on television programmes for schools which looked critically at their network programmes. But specialist courses in media studies are not enough: all teachers should be involved in examining and discussing television programmes with young people.

f) The vast majority of young people's viewing takes place at home and this lays considerable responsibility on parents to control the amount and nature of the viewing, and to discuss what young people have seen. This is no easy task because young people often have different interests from adults, and in quite properly seeking to cater for those different interests, specific programmes are aimed at particular age groups.

g) Parents and teachers have common concerns about the impact of television on the views and attitudes of young people. The debate about these matters tends to be confined to public confrontation between those taking up extreme positions in respect of particular programmes. There is an undoubted need for arrangements at appropriate levels to enable programme makers, teachers, and parents to explore together their different but related responsibilities in understanding better the impact of television upon the young and seeking to ensure that it is a positive and constructive influence.

Drama, Media Studies, and Information Technology

The First Cox Report

From *English for Ages 5–11* (the First Cox Report), London, DES, November 1988, pp. 61–3.

Introduction

14.1   Paragraph 17 of our supplementary guidance was headed 'Links   1
with other subjects' and said: 'There are a number of important subjects,
themes, and skills which can be taught and developed through the foundation subjects. You are expected to consider the place of these aspects within
the English curriculum and to cover them within your consideration of
attainment targets and programmes of study. English will provide one
appropriate context for the development of drama across the curriculum,
for an introduction to the classical world through its literature, for
developing information handling skills such as the use of libraries and
reference books, and for media studies. Time for covering such aspects
within English will need to be found within the overall time available for
English as indicated above. The links between English literature and drama
and the other expressive arts subjects are important. The practical use of
word processors in developing writing provides an introduction to information technology. You may have further suggestions for links with other
subjects, and about the contributions which these subjects can make to
learning English.'

14.2   We have already referred to the place of drama in our chapter on   2
the primary school. In the primary school, drama is most successful when
it emerges as a natural development from children's play. Successful learning often takes place when young children enjoy themselves in role-playing,
which can make an important contribution to their oral and aural experience, and we have sought to reflect this in our programmes of study.

14.3   We have considered media studies largely as part of the exploration   3
of contemporary culture, alongside more traditional literary texts. Television and film and video form substantial elements of children's experience
out of school which teachers must take into account. Our assumption is
that children should have the opportunity to apply their critical faculties
to these major parts of contemporary culture.

14.4   Both drama and media studies deal with fundamental questions of   4
language, interpretation, and meaning. These seem to us so central to the
traditional aims and concerns of English teaching that we would strongly
recommend that programmes of study in English should include exploration of both areas. We recognise, however, that drama and media studies
also have their own academic integrity: in the secondary school they may

113

exist separately elsewhere on the timetable as specialist subjects outside the National Curriculum. We believe that the English curriculum should prepare children for possible later study of these subjects as separate options. We would wish to stress, however, that we do not see the inclusion of drama and media studies activity within English programmes of study as in any way a replacement for specialist study.

Drama

14.5   Recommendations for attainment targets and programmes of study concerned with drama are to be found most particularly in the speaking and listening profile component. However, we see drama as central in developing all major aspects of English in the primary school because it:

- gives children the chance to practise varieties of language in different situations and to use a variety of functions of language which it is otherwise more difficult to practise: questioning, challenging, complaining, etc.;
- helps children to make sense of different situations and different points of view in role play and simulations, by allowing them to act out situations and formulate things in their own words;
- helps children to evaluate choices or dilemmas, to develop the logic of different situations, to make decisions that can be put into practice, tested, and reflected upon;
- accustoms children to take account of audience and purpose in undertaking an activity.

14.6   Drama makes an important contribution towards realising the overall aims of English set out in chapters 2 and 3 of this Report. For example, drama contributes to personal growth, by enabling children to express their emotions and by helping them to make sense of the world, and to preparation for adult life through such activities as the simulation of meetings. Role play activities can inform other areas of the curriculum, for example history, through children's pretending to be living in another age, or science, through their acting out a scientific discovery.

14.7   Drama is also of crucial importance as a learning medium, for example, in promoting collaborative talk, extending language skills and awareness of language in use, in assisting the development of voice skills in relation to reading aloud, and in extending both the form and the content of children's own writing. Drama is not simply a subject, but also – more importantly – a method; it is both a creative art form in its own right and also a learning tool. Furthermore, drama is one of the key ways in which children can gain an understanding of themselves and of others, can gain confidence in themselves as decision-makers and problem-solvers, can learn to function collaboratively, and can explore – within a supportive framework – not only a range of human feelings, but also a whole spectrum of social situations and/or moral dilemmas.

14.8   There is also still a place within drama activity for performance to a wide range of audiences, both within the school and in the wider community. However, most drama activity should not be seen as leading to a polished end product; even where this is the result, the most significant educational value of the activity will often have been found in the process that led to that end product.

14.9 Our terms of reference suggested that we should consider drama in the context of the great dramatic works of literature. We believe that all play should be approached through the dramatic medium; children should see or participate in the play being acted, and not just read the text. This approach will not only result in an appreciation of the literary merits, but will also foster an understanding of stagecraft. There is still an important place within drama activity for the exploration and study of scripted plays, and we address this aspect in our attainment targets and programmes of study. At primary level, the range of material for exploration by children needs to be more diverse: myth, legend, fairy stories, poems, and children's own writing can be explored through the medium of drama.

Media Studies

14.10 It may be helpful at this juncture to give a definition of 'media studies':

> Media education aims to develop a critical understanding of the media. It tends to be concerned with modern mass media such as television, cinema, and radio, but it can logically be extended to all public forms of expression and communication including books. It seeks to extend children's knowledge of the media through critical and practical work. It tries to produce more competent consumers who can understand and appreciate the contents of the media and the processes involved in their production and reception. It also aims to produce more active and critical media users who will demand, and perhaps contribute to, a wider range of media products.[1]

Our terms of reference used the term 'media studies'; we have, however, interpreted our remit here in the way described above as 'media education'.

14.11 Recommendations concerned with media studies are, as with drama, embodied within the three profile components.

14.12 Media studies are central in developing major aspects of English through:

- the understanding of how meanings are constructed in different media: literature, film and television, newspapers, etc.; and of how different interpretations of the same text are possible;
- concepts such as audience, convention, genre, author, editor, selection (of information, viewpoint, etc.), stereotype, etc.;
- the understanding of different genres: narrative, information, fiction, documentary, exposition, etc.;
- the understanding of stereotypes: questions of accuracy, realism, fiction, different points of view, persuasive and partial uses of language.

14.13   Television now provides a significant proportion of the language experience of many children. It is therefore important that they understand better how words and pictures are used on television.

Information Technology
14.14   There has been only limited national discussion of how the English curriculum should help to prepare children for life in an increasingly computer-oriented society. For example, the 1985 GCSE national criteria for English make no reference to new technologies. In the first paragraph of this chapter we refer to our terms of reference: the equation between information technology and word processing is common, but too narrow. This is clearly an important aspect of IT, but such an equation nevertheless represents an unfortunate reductionism.

14.15   Most interactions with computers are language experiences. 'Information technology' and 'communications technology' have to do with the storage, retrieval, processing, and transmission of 'information', much of it linguistic. This huge and expanding technology is therefore of great importance to teachers of English. And IT should be seen as a way of encouraging pupils' language development.

14.16   Education itself deals centrally with information, though not exclusively, of course: information has little directly to do with forms of aesthetic or literary education. There are profound differences between information, knowledge, and understanding. And, crucially, because of the power and limitations of computers, 'information' itself comes to be defined in particular (sometimes narrow) ways.

14.17   English teachers have always had special responsibilities for teaching children about forms of information: how to read, interpret, organise, and create it, so the development of a technology designed precisely to store, sort, search, and transmit huge amounts of information at high speed is potentially of great relevance to them and their pupils.

14.18   Pupils should be aware that voice recognition or synthesised voice production by a machine does not of itself indicate 'Artificial Intelligence'. Over the next decade it will be increasingly necessary to make more sophisticated distinctions between the present generation of 'user-friendly' machines on the one hand, and Intelligent Knowledge Based Systems on the other – particularly those which work with Natural Language input and output. We may return to this subject in our Report on the secondary stages.

14.19   English teachers have much to contribute to children's understanding of this technology and its uses: to the ways in which language and communication are developing in society. It is often simply assumed that IT is the province of mathematics and science, that these subjects are the natural arenas for the deployment of the new technologies in education, and that English (or other language) teachers could have nothing to contribute. In many schools computers are exclusively in the charge of mathematics or science departments. This is unfortunate if it restricts valuable cross-curricular collaboration in aspects of IT.

14.20   It is not appropriate to recommend specific attainment targets in IT. IT can help with language development, but the use of the hardware, or of specific software, could never in itself be central.

14.21   It is possible, however, to formulate areas of knowledge, skills, and understanding which are central to English teaching. The English classroom should be one place where pupils learn to:

- use IT to send and receive messages (e.g., by using electronic mail);
- use IT to help in the production and reception of written language for different audiences (e.g., by using desk top publishing, spelling checkers, style checkers, thesauruses, etc.);
- show a critical understanding of some of the ways in which information can be manipulated (e.g., by data bases, mail merge programs), and therefore show increasing discrimination in their interpretation of such information.

(Electronic mail, for example, can link classes elsewhere in the country or in other countries, and can furnish additional very powerful ways of providing children with real audiences for their writing. Such links have already been made and used by teachers.)

14.22   In general, English teachers should encourage children to study the ways in which language is used in the context of new technologies. And IT in English falls, perhaps, into four main broad categories:

- structuring and designing documents, with all the implications which this has for language in learning;
- manipulation of ideas;
- giving children access to a wider range of real audiences;
- developing study skills and information handling.

Conclusion

14.23   In this chapter we have concentrated on the three major cross- curricular themes referred to us. Others are mentioned in the course of the chapters on the individual profile components. But, as we have emphasised throughout the Report, the fact that in England English itself is the pre-eminent medium of teaching and learning gives it a unique cross-curricular role in addition to its own intrinsic worth. We have been conscious of this special responsibility of English when framing our recommendations and we refer especially in chapter 3 to the desirability of a school language policy.

Note
1.   Cary Bazalgette, *Teachers' Weekly*, 25 September 1987.

Media Education and Information Technology

The Second Cox Report

From *English for Ages 5 – 16* (the Second Cox Report), London, DES, June 1989, ch. 9.

Round the city of Caxton, the electronic suburbs are rising. To the language of books is added the language of television and radio, . . . the processed codes of the computer. As the shapes of literacy multiply, so our dependence on language increases.[1]

Introduction

9.1 The supplementary guidance to our terms of reference mentions both media studies and information technology (IT):

> English teaching will provide one appropriate context . . . for developing information handling skills, . . . and for media studies. . . . The practical use of word processors in developing writing provides an introduction to information technology.

9.2 Media education and information technology alike enlarge pupils' critical understanding of how messages are generated, conveyed, and interpreted in different media. First-hand use of media equipment (e.g., in making videos) and other technologies (such as desk top publishing) can contribute to children's practical understanding of how meanings are created.

9.3 We already have television, video tapes and disks, word processors, desk top publishing, electronic data bases, electronic mail, and experimentation in areas such as hypertext, natural language processing, and so on. Their use will become more widespread. New technologies and products will develop. For schools this also implies:

- an increase in data collection of all kinds and in the use of authentic language materials for teaching about the uses of language;
- an increase in accessibility to such collections via CD-ROM, video disk, satellite links, etc.;
- an increase in the diversity of learning materials geared to the needs of different learners;
- a proliferation of self-access teaching materials and study packages, including interactive materials;
- the development of new study skills to access and to make best use of such materials, and the reinforcement of existing skills in new contexts.

118

9.4 We have included in our proposals for programmes of study those 4
aspects of media education and information technology which contribute
most directly to the central aim of English: to widen the range of children's
understanding and use of language, and to develop their skills in it. Assessment of achievements in English should therefore be primarily concerned
with such understanding and skills, rather than with pupils' knowledge
about and competence in using IT and media facilities as such. Indeed,
media education and IT also have their own academic integrity, particularly
in the secondary school as specialised timetabled subjects outside the
National Curriculum. The English curriculum should prepare pupils for
possible study of these subjects as separate options, and not seek to supplant
them.

9.5 Many aspects of media education and IT involve the use of machines: 5
still cameras, video, computer terminals, etc. Our culture often regards
machines as a male preserve, and girls may need opportunities and encouragement to show that they can be just as expert as boys in such areas. It
may sometimes be necessary, for example, to arrange for girls to have access
to the technology in single-sex groups if they are to develop a confident and
active understanding of the media. New forms of technology often appear
to hold out the promise of increased access to knowledge but may then be
introduced or perceived in such a way as to reinforce traditional bias.
Similar points may also be made about the access of different social groups
to forms of educational technology. We wish all pupils to be able to benefit
from the opportunities that the new media and technologies offer, and we
have framed our proposals accordingly.

Media Education
9.6 Our terms of reference use the title 'media studies', which may be 6
best reserved for specialist study. We have interpreted our remit broadly
in accordance with the following description of 'media education':

> Media education . . . seeks to increase children's critical understand-
> ing of the media – namely, television, film, video, radio, photography,
> popular music, printed materials, and computer software. How they
> work, how they produce meaning, how they are organised and how
> audiences make sense of them, are the issues that media education
> addresses. [It] aims to develop systematically children's critical and
> creative powers through analysis and production of media artefacts.
> This also deepens their understanding of the pleasure and enjoyment
> provided by the media. Media education aims to create more active
> and critical media users who will demand, and could contribute to, a
> greater range and diversity of media products.[2]

9.7 Media education should be concerned not only with modern mass 7
media such as television, cinema, and radio, but also with all public forms
of communication including printed materials (books as well as newspapers) and computerised sources of information such as data bases.

9.8 We have considered media education largely as part of the exploration 8
of contemporary culture, alongside more traditional literary texts. And we

emphasise elsewhere that the concepts of text and genre should be broadly interpreted in English. Television and film form substantial parts of pupils' experience out of school and teachers need to take this into account. Pupils should have the opportunity to apply their critical faculties to these major parts of contemporary culture.

9.9 Media education, like drama, deals with fundamental aspects of language, interpretation, and meaning. It is therefore consonant with the aims of English teaching. In fact, media education has often developed in a very explicit way concepts which are of general importance in English. These include selection (of information, viewpoint, etc.), editing, author, audience, medium, genre, stereotype, etc.

9.10 We have drawn on these aspects in developing our recommendations for attainment targets and programmes of study. In particular, we have included the treatment of non-literary and media texts in the reading profile component.

Information Technology

9.11 The English class should be one setting where pupils learn to use IT to:

- help in the production and reception of written language for different audiences (e.g., by using desk top publishing, spelling checkers, thesauruses, etc.);
- send and receive messages: electronic mail can, for example, link classes elsewhere in the country or in other countries, and can provide very powerful ways of creating real audiences for children's writing;
- give and respond to precise and accurate instructions, upon which successful use of the technology depends, as does language competence more generally;
- comprehend systems of filing and classification, including alphabetic ordering, lists of contents, indexes, symbols etc.: the organisation, storage, and retrieval of information is, again, an important language skill generally;
- gain an understanding of some of the ways in which information can be manipulated (e.g., in data bases, mail merge programs), and therefore show increasing discrimination in their interpretation of such information.

9.12 The word processor extends opportunities for development and reflection on ideas and meanings, for example in designing, outlining, and re-structuring, and through the ability of writers to engage in dialogue with their own thoughts in the form of clean hard copy (printed text). The possibilities are analogous to those in graphics that are offered to the designer by computer-aided design (CAD). Since the information on a word processor or computer screen is visible to several children at once, it can be a vehicle for group discussion and exploration of the language. Word processors are regarded in the business world as productivity tools, but writers have come to see them also as tools of creativity.

9.13 In these ways English teachers have much to contribute to children's

120

familiarity with this technology and its uses, alongside the major aim of exploiting it to promote language knowledge and skills in themselves. This is reflected in our recommendations for programmes of study in both the reading and the writing profile components.

9.14 This will not, however, be achieved as long as IT is regarded as the province of mathematics, science, and technology in the curriculum, and English – or other language – teachers are seen as having little part to play. IT equipment and facilities are becoming increasingly common in schools. They can and should be made readily accessible to teachers and pupils in English as in other subjects. Our recommendations presuppose this. 14

Notes
1. Kingman Report, paragraph 2.7.
2. Cary Bazalgette (ed.), *Primary Media Education: A Curriculum Statement*, London, BFI Education, 1989.

Cautious Celebration

Julian Bowker

'Cautious Celebration', *Times Educational Supplement*, 1 June 1990, p. 18.

Compare this article with one in a tabloid paper and then with one in a broadsheet, and you have just started to fulfil attainment Level 8 in the Reading section of the Statutory Orders for English, Key Stages 2, 3 and 4, which were published in March.

The statement of attainment says that pupils should be able to 'show in discussion and writing an ability to form a considered opinion about features of presentation which are used to inform, regulate, reassure, or persuade, in non-literary and media texts'. This is an example of what English teaching could involve now that media education is established by statute, throughout the English curriculum 5–16 in England and Wales.

Few other countries in the world can make the same claim; cause for cautious celebration. If this were a reassuring tabloid, my headline would be *Media Classes in 'Neighbours'!* and if it were a persuasive broadsheet it would be *Media Matters in English.*

There are references to media in all three sections of the statutory orders – in reading, writing, and listening and speaking, but most detail is given in the section on reading. Here children are required at Level 5 'to show in discussion that they can recognise how subject matter in non-literary and media texts is presented as fact or opinion', and by Level 10 to 'show in discussion and writing an ability to evaluate techniques and conventions in non-literary and media texts'.

These requirements are statutory: markers of pupils' knowledge of skills and understanding, on which schools will have to report.

The examples in the orders focus on journalistic and advertising media texts and technologies, but for each level similar activities could be found for documentary, fictional, and entertainment texts such as film, radio, photographs, posters, and examples from press and publishing.

Last year's reports for English in 5–16 contained paragraphs of rhetoric about media education: 'Television and film [are] major parts of contemporary culture . . . media education . . . deals with fundamental aspects of language, interpretation, and meaning'. But the programmes of study gave little guidance to teachers looking for what this might mean in practice. The statutory orders outlined below have helped considerably, but there are still grounds for concern about the limits of the framework for media education.

Above all, 'non-literary texts' are still distinguished from 'literary texts'. Non-literary texts are defined as those which persuade or contain information. Any analysis of narrative structures, character, or genre is seen to be carried out only in 'literature' (stories and poems). Many examples for film and television which were in the National Curriculum Council report of November 1989 have been removed, with the result that images and audio-visual media are undervalued in relation to literary texts.

Following an outcry at the proposal to define media as 'non-literary', the statutory orders have been modified so that children can study character, narrative, rhetoric, and style in relation to 'literature and other texts'. But there needs to be greater recognition that the development of children's understanding of the media is just as important. 9

A good, broad-based media education ought to offer pupils opportunities to engage with the mythical and the hypothetical, the symbolic and the transactional, the imaginative and the scientific. We can no longer avoid asking whether the cultural changes represented by modern media can be reflected in the curriculum. Media education has a clearer conceptual framework and takes on areas such as representation and the production and circulation of texts that traditional English studies ignore. 10

Nor can English be viewed as the sole location of media education. If media education is deemed an essential part of every young person's curriculum, then every subject and cross-curricular theme should address its concerns. As all the working groups report on their respective subject areas in the national curriculum, numerous references to the media crop up, but there is no sense of coherence. 11

The Education Reform Act encourages schools to consider the place of media education in cross-curricular patterns of working. It is highly relevant to themes such as equal opportunities, personal and social education, or economic awareness. Now that there is a limited, but welcome, form of media education in the English curriculum, a fresh set of considerations about its place in the whole curriculum needs to be addressed. 12

English and Media Studies:
Making the Difference

David Buckingham

'English and Media Studies: Making the Difference', *The English Magazine*, 1990, pp. 8 – 12.

English teachers have been teaching about the media for many years. As early as the 1930s, work was being undertaken in schools on advertising and the press, and this interest has steadily extended to include film, television, radio, and popular music. By the 1960s, teaching about the media had become a staple part of most English teachers' repertoire, alongside fiction, poetry, creative writing, and the rest. Most English syllabuses now include at least one component dealing with 'mass media', and there is a wide range of teaching materials specifically designed for this purpose.

Separate courses in film studies, and subsequently media studies, are a more recent development, which began to gain ground in the 1970s. Media studies is now taught at GCSE and 'A' level, as well as in a variety of vocational and pre-vocational courses. Yet in many ways, these courses look quite different from mainstream English. It is not merely that they focus on different kinds of texts, or that they are more specialised: they also have a quite different conceptual and theoretical basis.

Furthermore, although most media studies teachers are primarily English teachers, the approaches they adopt in the two areas are often significantly different. These differences are not merely to do with the objects of study – the fact that one may be considering television programmes or magazines rather than books, for example. There are also fundamental differences in pedagogic practice. The way in which an English teacher approaches a poem or a class reader is likely to be very different from the way in which a media studies teacher approaches an advertisement or a television programme – even where, as is often the case, the English teacher and the media studies teacher are in fact the same person.

Challenge or Incorporation

The relationship between English and media studies is thus a paradoxical one. On the one hand, many English teachers regard media teaching as simply an element of English – as another string to their bow. Yet on the other hand, many advocates of media studies have been keen to emphasise its difference from English, and indeed its challenge to many of the fundamental principles and practices of English teaching.

This argument for the distinctiveness of media studies, and for its own viability as a unique and coherent subject discipline, is often mounted in historical terms.[1] According to this history, the primary enemy of media studies is that of 'Leavisism'. Len Masterman, for example, argues that this approach is essentially paternalistic: it seeks to impose middle-class tastes and values under the apparently neutral guise of a concern with artistic 'quality'. The Leavisite notion of 'discrimination', he suggests, is based on 'a naively transcendental notion of value', and fails to acknowledge 'the social and ideological bases of particular interpretations and judgements'. The application of such aesthetic criteria to media texts has been a largely negative exercise, which has inevitably involved attacking the personal preferences of students: as a result, it has generated little in the way of lasting or effective practice.[2]

In his most recent book, Masterman extends his attack on Leavisism to   6
an attack on English as a whole. He condemns English teachers for their exclusive concentration on texts, and their 'fatal neglect' of the contexts within which texts are distributed, circulated, and consumed. English, he argues, has historically failed to provide 'any adequate basis for making sense of the media' and has hence placed itself 'outside of the most progressive developments taking place within the field from the early 1970s onwards'. Only very recently, he suggests, has the interest of English teachers in the media been rekindled:

> . . . media studies is increasingly being seen by many English teachers as providing a long-awaited injection of critical and radical thinking into a field in which the liberal-humanist tradition has long since ceased to have either energy or much in the way of intellectual credibility.[3]

This kind of attack on English teaching is relatively common in media   7
studies,[4] yet it would seem to be at least partly misdirected. It is as if media studies need to construct an enemy, in the rather vague shape of 'liberal-humanism', against which it can define itself. The major problem with this argument is that it effectively ignores developments within English teaching itself over this period, and thus fails to acknowledge the progressive potential of contemporary English teaching. This is not to argue that English teachers have entirely cast off the legacy of Leavis, nor that the 'progressive' approaches to English which have gained ground since the 1960s are without their own problems – although they are scarcely as moribund as Masterman would like to believe. However, it is to question the implication that media studies somehow has the monopoly on 'critical and radical thinking', and that it has nothing to learn from English.

Perhaps for these reasons, the only direct responses to this attack have   8
come from latter-day Leavisites.[5] The predominant response to media studies among English teachers has been to welcome it on board, and to incorporate it in their work. Journals like *The English Magazine*, for example, regularly include articles and 'special issues' on media studies; while the National Association for the Teaching of English (NATE) has its own media education working party, alongside others on literature and drama.

While these are obviously positive and constructive developments, there   9

125

is nevertheless a danger that the broader challenge which media studies represents may simply be ignored. Media teaching may come to exist alongside other aspects of English, without significantly altering the ways in which poetry or fiction or indeed writing are taught.

The place of media education within the National Curriculum proposals for English raises many questions in this respect. To what extent will media education remain a 'bolt-on' component English? How far will it permeate the English curriculum, and promote a more fundamental rethinking of the subject area? In what ways will integrating media education within English encourage media teachers to change their approach? What difference will integration make?

Defining Differences

What then are the major differences between English and media studies? Obviously, one cannot avoid making some sweeping generalisations here. There is clearly no single definition of 'English' or 'media studies' to which all teachers of those subjects would subscribe. Classroom practice is inevitably much more ambiguous and contradictory than educational theory might lead us to suppose. Nevertheless, there are dominant definitions of English and media studies which are embodied, for example, in GCSE syllabuses, and which do exert a constraining influence on teachers' work. It is these definitions which will form the basis of my observations here.

1 Texts

To begin with, English and media studies are clearly concerned with different kinds of texts – although the basis on which the distinction is made is highly debatable. For example, we might make this distinction in terms of the medium which any given text uses. English is predominantly concerned with written texts, and particularly books. Media studies focuses primarily on visual and audio-visual texts – photographs, advertisements, television programmes, and films. Yet there is a considerable overlap here: both English and media studies teachers may consider radio, newspapers, magazines, popular music, and popular fiction, for example.

Nevertheless, the term 'media' is rarely seen to include books – although books, or written texts more broadly, clearly do 'mediate' the world in particular ways. 'The media' are conventionally understood as those media which use distinctively 'modern' technologies of mechanical or electronic reproduction. They are often seen (for example, in many English syllabuses) as 'mass media', in the sense that they often reach large popular audiences.

Yet in practice, these distinctions are arbitrary and difficult to sustain. Many 'older' media forms are increasingly reliant on 'modern' technology; and the audience for the 'modern' media is not always a 'mass' audience, nor is it always greater than that for more traditional media. Book publishing, for example, is obviously an industry which is heavily dependent upon mass reproduction and electronic technology; and many books reach much larger audiences than many television programmes or films.

In fact, of course, this distinction is neither objective nor neutral. What appears to be a division between media is in fact a division between approved forms of 'high culture' and forms of 'popular culture' which are often seen as intrinsically less valuable and worthwhile. This is a division which is obviously bound up with broader relationships of power within society, and in particular with social class. It is a division which enables certain people's tastes to be validated, while others' are merely dismissed.

Thus, English is not in fact concerned with all books, but almost exclusively with those it chooses to define as 'Literature'. The received canon of texts which are seen to merit the term 'Literature' has progressively widened, and is no longer so exclusively confined to the works of (preferably dead) white men. Nevertheless, the use or study of popular writing remains extremely rare in English teaching. While there are signs that more 'literary' genres such as romance or 'quality' crime fiction can be recuperated by English teachers, the chances of a Jackie Collins novel being chosen as a class reader, or of Jilly Cooper finding her way on to anybody's list of set books, remain highly remote.

For those teaching younger students, there is much more interest (and much more money to be made by publishers) in 'Children's Literature' – that is, texts produced by adults for children, rather than by children themselves. Yet here again, the term 'Literature' operates to exclude many genuinely popular texts in favour of those which appeal to adult notions of what children ought to be like. *Jackie* and *2000 A.D.* are clearly not Children's Literature, and English teachers are only ever likely to teach about them in an attempt to lead students on to 'better things'.[6]

Ultimately, then, the way in which the object of study in English is defined is itself deeply ideological. Yet while this has long been recognised by literary theorists,[7] its implications have yet to be fully realised either in higher education or in schools. The canon may have been slightly widened, but the very criteria by which it is constructed, the processes by which it is maintained, and the interests it serves, are rarely open to inspection or critical study. Even teachers committed to newer theoretical approaches seem strangely tied to Shakespeare and the 'Great Tradition'. Meanwhile, the processes whereby 'Good Books' arrive in English classrooms remain almost wholly invisible.

Perhaps more fundamentally, however, teachers in both areas are likely to approach these different objects of study with quite different assumptions about how they are, and should be, read. 'Literature' is seen to have broadly 'humanising' effects on the reader: it encourages the development of sensitivity to language, culture, and human relationships. The media, on the other hand, are often seen to have predominantly negative effects: they manipulate and deceive readers into accepting false values, in ways which readers themselves may be powerless to resist.

These assumptions lead to very different kinds of interventions in the reading process on the part of teachers. If Literature teaching is primarily about developing students' receptiveness to something which is seen as fundamentally good, a great deal of media teaching is encouraging students to resist or 'see through' something which is seen as fundamentally bad. In this respect, the ways in which the different objects of study are defined imply very different notions of the relationship between readers and texts, and thus result in very different pedagogic strategies.

2 Concepts and Practices

These pedagogic differences are immediately apparent when one examines the ways in which English and media studies are defined. In the case of English, both at GCSE and in the National Curriculum, the subject is defined in terms of a set of practices – reading, writing, speaking, and listening. In each case, there is some further division according to the range of different types of practice. Thus, for example, the SEG syllabus requires students to read 'whole works of literature (e.g., short stories, novels, autobiographies, poetry, and plays)' as well as what it terms 'non-literary material (e.g., newspapers, periodicals, brochures, reports, and advertisements)'; only in the case of Literature examinations are specific texts identified. Similarly, students are required to produce different kinds of writing – for example, 'expressive/imaginative', 'discursive/argumentative', and 'explanatory/instrumental'.[8]

In the case of media studies, by contrast, the subject is defined in terms of concepts. While there is some variation between the different GCSE syllabuses, four key concepts are found in all of them: 'forms and conventions' (or 'media language'), 'representation', 'institution' (or 'industry'), and 'audience'. Specific texts for study are not identified, although there is a requirement that students should study more than one medium: while there is a broad focus on film, television, the press, advertising, and radio, there is also some acknowledgement of areas like popular music and popular (or sometimes 'paperback'!) fiction.[9]

Perhaps more significantly, however, media studies students are not merely required to 'read' and 'write' – simply to respond to media texts, or to produce their own. They are also required to reflect theoretically on their own practice as readers and writers. Thus, for example, in assessing students' practical media production work, examiners are not primarily interested in technical abilities or in originality or creativity. On the contrary, students are expected to transfer the theoretical insights they have gained from analysing texts to their own production. The assessment of practical work relies heavily on the student's 'production log', which is expected to contain a clear rationale and evaluation of the work, describing the production process and the thinking behind the decisions which were made.

It would be false to imply that this process of theoretical reflection is always achieved or achievable: indeed, the relationship between 'theory' and 'practice' is one of the most problematic areas of media teaching.[10] Nevertheless, the difference between English and media studies in this respect is remarkable. While students are clearly expected to reflect upon their own writing in English – for example, in redrafting their work – this process is not expected to be as explicit, or as theoretically-informed, as it is in media studies.

On the surface, then, media studies appears much more overtly 'theoretical'. It is predominantly concerned with conceptual learning, rather than with the mastery of skills or processes, or with the expression of feeling or

128

the articulation of experience. This learning is seen to be manifested through the use of a specific 'technical' terminology. Beyond the 'key concepts', the syllabuses repeatedly use terms drawn from sociology and literary theory, such as stereotyping, narrative, genre, bias, ownership and control, ideology, and so on. While the English syllabuses also use 'technical' terms – discursive, expressive, instrumental – they do so to a much lesser degree. Of course, this is not to suggest that English is somehow atheoretical or even anti-theoretical, although it has historically tended to present itself in this way. The crucial difference is the extent to which these theories are made explicit, especially for students.

These differences have significant implications in terms of evaluation and assessment. Thus, the criteria by which teachers assess students' writing in English are notoriously vague and intuitive. In the SEG syllabus, for example, a Grade C candidate is expected to demonstrate competence in 'describing and reflecting upon experience and expressing effectively what is felt and what is imagined'; while a Grade A candidate should demonstrate competence in 'describing and reflecting upon experience and expressing vividly what is felt and what is imagined'. Just as students are expected to respond personally and sensitively to 'literature', so teachers are expected to respond personally and sensitively to students' work, and to distinguish the 'vivid' from the merely 'effective'. There clearly is a 'theory' underlying these judgements, yet it remains wholly invisible.[11]

In media studies, by contrast, there is the problem of what one takes as evidence of conceptual learning. As I have indicated, media studies syllabuses emphasise the importance of students being familiar with a specific academic discourse – to the extent of being required, in written examinations, to offer definitions of terms like 'genre' and 'representation'. Yet while the ability to use a theoretical discourse can assist the process of conceptual understanding, it cannot in itself be taken as evidence of it.[12]

3 Concepts

Clearly, it would be possible to define media studies in terms of practices, although one might wish to broaden the terminology – 'writing' might become 'production', or 'reading' become 'reading and looking', for example. However, it would probably be more difficult to define English in terms of concepts: while reading and writing clearly do involve students in considering 'forms and conventions' and (in some cases) 'audience', these are rarely addressed in abstract terms.

Perhaps more crucially, there are a number of concepts which feature in media studies which have no obvious equivalent in English teaching. For example, 'institution' (or 'industry') is one of the 'key concepts' in media studies syllabuses. Under this rubric, students are required to consider aspects such as the patterns of ownership and control of media industries, the economics of media production, the role of advertising, the processes by which media texts are distributed and circulated, and the relationships between the media and the State. Furthermore, these kinds of questions are related to other aspects of the media – to the forms and conventions of media texts, to the ways in which the media represent different social groups, and to the ways in which audiences make sense of them.

This is an area which English largely neglects.[13] Publishing is clearly a major industry, in which the financial profit motive plays a significant role. Publishers act as 'gatekeepers' who determine what we are able to read and – through advertising, marketing, and promotion – significantly influence the ways in which we read it. By neglecting these factors, English implicitly sustains the view of publishing as a genteel cultural activity, or indeed as a kind of charitable service for distressed authors. Yet book publishing is increasingly becoming a multinational, monopolistic enterprise, which is intimately connected with other media industries.

In neglecting these aspects, English implicitly adopts an idealised, asocial view of cultural production. The focus is on the individual author, abstracted from social, historical, and economic relationships. 'Culture' and 'commerce' are seen as fundamentally opposed, or as merely unrelated to each other.

A similar contrast may be observed in considering how English and media studies deal with the notion of 'audience'. In English Literature teaching, the focus is on the individual reader/student, 'understanding' and 'appreciating' literary texts, and developing a sensitive 'personal response' to what is read. In more traditional approaches, the text is predominantly defined as an object which 'contains' a meaning which is there to be recovered by the reader. The more recent influence of 'reader response criticism' assigns a more active role to the reader, yet the reader is still regarded as an isolated individual creating a purely personal meaning.[14]

Within English Language syllabuses, reference is often made to the writer's 'sense of audience', and 'the awareness that language is used in different ways in different circumstances'. Indeed, a good deal of research has been undertaken over the past twenty years with the aim of encouraging writing for 'real audiences' of various kinds. Yet in practice, these real audiences are often merely the writer's peer group, or perhaps younger children: they exist primarily within classrooms, and are rarely conceived in broader social terms.

In media studies, by contrast, the audience is regarded as a collection of diverse social groupings. The emphasis in teaching about media audiences is not merely on the students' own behaviour or responses, but on 'the social conditions of media consumption' and on the different ways in which different social groups will use and make sense of texts. In studying media texts, and in creating their own, students are required to consider the ways in which specific social audiences may be targeted and addressed.

In both respects, then, media studies would appear to be operating with a much more social account of the ways in which texts are produced and read. If English is concerned with the individual reader's personal response to the individual writer's personal vision, media studies is concerned with the social production of meaning, both on the part of social audiences, and on the part of media institutions.[15]

By contrast, English tends to abstract both reading and writing from the social contexts in which they are performed, and places them in a supposedly 'pure' personal space. Perhaps the clearest instance of this tendency in English teaching is in 'practical criticism'. Here, texts or extracts from texts are presented without reference to their authorship, their period or place of origin, as a kind of 'blindfold test' of the student's personal sensitivity. For I. A. Richards, the inventor of practical criticism, the truly sensitive reader was the one who had managed to cast away all 'stock responses' – who comes to the text effectively devoid of social experience.[16]

Yet again, however, it would be false to pretend that media studies offers   37
a developed and effective alternative practice. It remains the case that 'institution' and 'audience' are very much the most difficult aspects of media studies to teach, particularly to school students. Teaching about media institutions is too often seen as a matter of dumping information on students, or alternatively of encouraging them to subscribe to some mechanistic conspiracy theory about the evils of capitalism.[17] Teaching about media audiences is often confined to examining media texts in terms of the ways they target or 'position' hypothetical readers, and only rarely extends to looking at real readers.[18] The notion of 'the social' in media studies can often serve merely to exclude 'the personal': ideology becomes disconnected from pleasure, which must be disavowed at all costs. If English suffers from a celebration of untrammelled individual subjectivity, media studies suffers from the attempt simply to repress it.

4 Practices

If we examine the two subjects in terms of the practices they entail – and   38
in particular their notions of 'reading' and 'writing' – there are again some marked differences. This is clearly apparent in the terminology used in the respective syllabuses.

In the case of reading, English students are required to 'understand' and   39
'evaluate', to 'respond imaginatively', to 'enjoy' and 'appreciate' what they read. In the case of writing, they are expected to 'communicate effectively', to 'articulate experience and express what is felt and imagined'.

In media studies, while certain of the syllabuses do refer to 'aesthetic   40
awareness' and even 'creative work', the emphasis is very much on developing 'critical analysis' of the ways in which media texts are 'constructed'. In the NEA syllabus, for example, students are required, both in their theoretical coursework and in their practical projects, to demonstrate an understanding of 'the meaning and relevance of the basic concepts of media language, to include the concepts of denotation, connotation, signs, symbols, codes, signification, and structure'.

While English syllabuses do refer to knowledge of 'grammatical struc-   41
tures' and the 'conventions' of written language, these are primarily to be manifested through students' use of language, for example in their own writing. Language is not primarily an object of study, but a vehicle for understanding and communication. Students are assessed for their ability to 'exercise control' over the formal properties of language, but they are not expected to demonstrate any more abstract theoretical knowledge of them. Even within the National Curriculum, which places a much greater emphasis on language study, this kind of knowledge about language is located firmly within the context of students' own language use.

Ironically, perhaps, it is media studies which appears much more con-   42
cerned with the formal study of language. The list of 'concepts' above is derived from semiotics, and rests on a view of language as a rule-governed

system, which can be analysed into its component parts. This approach is manifested in many media studies teaching materials, which tend to adopt a highly mechanistic approach to analysing 'media language' – one which is in many respects reminiscent of traditional approaches to grammar teaching in English.[19] While media studies students are required to 'demonstrate an understanding of the technical and theoretical terminology of the subject', there is no such requirement even for English Literature syllabuses, where a specialist terminology clearly does exist.

At the same time, English would also appear to adopt a much more 'neutral' approach to reading. To be sure, students are expected to 'evaluate information in reading material and in other media, and select what is relevant to specific purposes'; but the primary emphasis is on understanding, enjoyment, and appreciation. Perhaps surprisingly, the word 'critical', which recurs almost obsessively in media studies syllabuses, is rarely featured in the aims and objectives for English Language or English Literature. 'Critical' is obviously a term which is subject to a variety of interpretations, yet the emphasis in media studies syllabuses on issues of 'representation', 'bias', and 'stereotyping' clearly suggests that students are expected to identify and question the ideological meanings they derive from texts. Again, this dimension of reading is conspicuously absent from English syllabuses.

Furthermore, it is important to note the relative weighting which the two subjects give to reading and writing – or, in the case of media studies, to 'theory' and 'practice'. In English, it is ultimately impossible to separate the two: while a certain proportion of students' writing is required to be 'in response to literature read during the course', the nature of that response is not clearly specified, and may well be in the form of 'creative' writing. Likewise, in oral communication, speaking and listening are seen as equal and interrelated. In the case of media studies, however, the emphasis is clearly on the critical and theoretical aspects: practical work is less important, and needs to be accompanied by written documentation which provides further evidence of the students' critical and analytical capabilities.

These differences reflect much more fundamental assumptions about reading and writing, and ultimately about language itself. English places a central emphasis on writing as a form of self-expression, whereas media studies is concerned to promote a much more self-conscious 'construction' of meaning. English values reading as personal response, whereas media studies values analytic deconstruction. In English, the student is implicitly seen as a free agent, whose relationship to language is purely 'personal'. In media studies, the student is seen as a potential victim of language, who must learn to resist through rational analysis.

Towards Integration
Given these broad differences, it is unlikely that any attempt to integrate English and media studies will be straightforward. It will not be simply a matter of applying existing approaches from English teaching to new objects of study, or extending media studies approaches to cover literary texts. As I have argued, the differences between the two subjects are not merely to do with their respective objects of study, nor are they merely

rhetorical. On the contrary, they reflect much more deep-rooted assumptions about the relationships between readers, writers, and texts.

At the same time, I would argue that both English and media studies 47 have a good deal to gain from this process. As I have implied, media studies offers a theoretical approach to cultural production which is in many (though not all) respects more rigorous and powerful than that provided by English. If media studies has tended to underestimate the extent to which 'reading' the media is an active process, its emphasis on the social production of meaning is one which has much to offer English teaching.

On the other hand, media studies has largely failed to develop an effective 48 pedagogy, which acknowledges and builds upon what children already know about the media. Books about media teaching typically offer potted versions of academic research, together with 'suggestions for teaching'. They rarely consider classroom practice in any detail, nor do they engage with questions about how students learn. It is as if the role of teachers were simply to transmit a given body of academic knowledge. While media studies has (perhaps despite itself) adopted many of the basic pedagogic practices of 'progressive' English teaching, it has tended to use them in more contradictory ways. Much of what students are expected to 'discover' in media studies is predetermined, and much of what passes for 'analysis' is simply a sophisticated exercise in guessing what's in teacher's mind.[20]

Yet content and pedagogy are obviously inextricably related. We cannot 49 simply add media studies theory to English pedagogy: both will need to be reconsidered. Putting English and media studies together will require a fundamental rethinking of both areas – a process which is both necessary and potentially very productive.

Notes

1. See, for example, Len Masterman, *Teaching About Television*, London, Macmillan, 1980; *Teaching the Media*, London, Comedia, 1985; Manuel Alvarado, Robin Gutch and Tana Wollen, *Learning the Media*, London, Macmillan, 1987.
2. Masterman, *Teaching the Media*, p. 59.
3. Ibid. p. 256.
4. For example, Andrew Bethell 'Media Studies', in Jane Miller (ed.), *Eccentric Propositions*, Routledge and Kegan Paul, 1984; Andrew Spicer, 'Necessary opposites? Media Studies and literature in secondary schools', in *Literature Teaching Politics*, no. 6, 1987.
5. For some particularly entertaining examples, see Roger Knight 'Understanding "discrimination": the case against "television studies" ', *English in Education*, vol. 16 no. 3, 1982; and Roger Knight, 'The teaching about television debate', *English in Education*, vol. 18 no. 3, 1984.
6. I would argue that this is apparent even in more 'radical' approaches to the area: for example, Jane Leggett and Judith Hemming's booklet *Comics and Magazines* (English Centre, undated).
7. For example, Terry Eagleton, *Literary Theory: An Introduction*, Oxford, Blackwell, 1983; Peter Widdowson (ed.), *Re-Reading English*, London, Methuen, 1982.
8. SEG (Southern Examining Group) English syllabus: quotations in the article are taken from the SEG, NEA (Northern Examining Association), and LEAG (London and East Anglia Group) syllabuses.

9. NEA Media Studies syllabus: quotations as above.
10. See Jenny Grahame, 'The Production Process', in David Lusted (ed.), *The Media Studies Book*, Routledge, 1991; David Buckingham, Unit 27: *Media Education*, Open University EH207 Communication and Education course unit, 1987; and David Buckingham (ed.), *Watching Media Learning: Making Sense of Media Education*, Brighton, Falmer Press, 1990.
11. See Gemma Moss, *Un/Popular Fictions*, London, Virago, 1989.
12. This issue is discussed in a number of contributions to *Watching Media Learning*, op. cit.
13. This point was made many years ago by Manuel Alvarado, in 'Television Studies and Pedagogy', *Screen Education*, no. 38, Spring 1981.
14. For a valuable critique, see Pam Gilbert, 'Post reader-response: the deconstructive critique', in B. Corcoran and E. Evans, *Readers, Texts, Teachers*, Open University Press, 1987.
15. See David Buckingham, 'Teaching about the media', in David Lusted (ed.), *The Media Studies Book*, Routledge, 1991.
16. I. A. Richards, *Practical Criticism*, Routledge and Kegan Paul, 1929.
17. For a critique of this approach, and a possible alternative, see Gill Branston, *Teaching Media Institutions*, London, BFI Education, 1987.
18. For example, Masterman, *Teaching the Media*; this approach is particularly apparent in the NEA Media Studies syllabus.
19. For example, in some parts of Andrew Bethell's *Eyeopeners* booklets, Cambridge University Press, 1981.
20. See David Buckingham, 'Against Demystification', *Screen*, vol. 27, no. 5, September–October 1986; and *Watching Media Learning*, op. cit.

Media Education and the National Curriculum

BFI Education

Media Education and the National Curriculum, London, BFI Discussion Document, 1989.

Media Education as a Cross-curricular Theme

The British Film Institute welcomes indications from the Secretary of State [1] and from the National Curriculum Council, that media education will be considered as a cross-curricular theme within the National Curriculum. In his Supplementary Guidance to the English Subject Working Group, the then Secretary of State, Kenneth Baker, stated that 'English will provide one appropriate context for the development of . . . media studies [*sic*]' (*English for Ages 5–11*, DES/Welsh Office, November 1988, p. 68). The National Curriculum Council's 'Interim Report to the Secretary of State on Cross-curricular Issues' (April 1989) states that the Council intends to consider media education as a cross-curricular theme (p. 8).

We endorse the proposal that media education be considered as a cross- [2] curricular *theme* (as opposed to a cross-curricular *dimension* or *skill*). Although we believe that media education can relate to all aspects of the curriculum, especially in the primary school (see our curriculum statement, *Primary Media Education*, BFI 1989), we acknowledge that at present it is more realistic to expect that media education will take place within a limited number of subject areas, as well as relating to other cross-curricular themes already identified by the NCC. It has a strong component of knowledge and understanding, in addition to skills, which the NCC has cited as a characteristic of cross-curricular themes. Teachers will need guidance and in-service training in order to be able to teach this knowledge and understanding with confidence.

The Role of Media Education in the Curriculum

Today, children gain much of their knowledge and understanding of the [3] world through media that in the past have not been seen as relevant to the school curriculum: television, cinema, video, radio, and the press – although the latter has gained some ground as a medium worth studying. It is often assumed – indeed argued – that the justification for media education is essentially a *quantitative* one: the media have proliferated and education therefore has to acknowledge this. But the arguments for media education are more complicated than this. Quantitative arguments have not sufficed in the past to guarantee the place of study objects in the curriculum: if they had, penny dreadfuls and the popular press would have been studied in schools in the 1890s. The reason they were not is that it was arguments about what is *worthy* of study that have prevailed in traditional constructions of the curriculum, and 'popular' or 'mass' cultural forms were not deemed worthy.

One of several influences on media education has been the field of Cultural Studies developed by people such as Raymond Williams, Richard Hoggart, and Stuart Hall in the 1950s and 60s. In this tradition, media educators have sought to move away from arguments about what is 'worthy of study', not in order to erect different canons of 'worthiness' but to address the question of what constitutes 'culture' and how children's cultural experience, both actual and potential, might properly be understood and developed. The basic proposition of media education is therefore that schooling can now no longer confine itself to dealing with selected aspects of culture (worthwhile literature, for example), but must address children's cultural experience as a totality. This proposition is not, of course, unique to media education. It reflects movements in many subjects towards recognising and validating children's experience and encouraging them to work towards intellectual autonomy.

In the particular context of media studies, however, this proposition had specific implications. The media seemed to necessitate different kinds of study because they are for the most part large industrial concerns, reaching larger audiences than have ever been reached by earlier cultural forms. Media education has thus developed a conceptual structure to handle questions about the production, circulation, and interpretation of media products (i.e., films, television and radio programmes, newspapers, etc.). But as this conceptual structure has developed into a more coherent and broadly agreed form, teachers have found that it is not necessarily completely specific to the study of the media. It generates questions that can legitimately be asked in many subject areas, such as 'who produced this text?' 'how?' 'why?' 'for whom?' and so on. Thus, media education can have a role to play in many parts of the curriculum.

There is a tendency, both among some media teachers themselves and among people trying to understand the area, that media education is essentially about *informational* and *persuasive* forms – news and advertising, for example. This allows media education to enter under the rubric of the 'worthwhile', because it can be argued that children must be taught to be critical of these forms in order to become good citizens and consumers. This is, of course, an important point. But we would argue that it is a limited view of media education that fails to take into account children's predominant media experience, which is with fictional and entertainment forms. These forms are contributing to children's understanding of fiction (narrative structure, character development, etc.) and to their range of aesthetic experience. But they are also contributing to their knowledge of, and ideas about, the world at large: the past, different parts of the world, social groups, moral issues, scientific concepts, economics, the environment – the possibilities are endless. Children are entitled to learn about how to handle the many ways in which knowledge and ideas are represented in the media.

It is also often assumed that media education is about the cultural *status quo*: about the dominant forms of cinema, television, and other media

136

which children are most likely to encounter outside school. This is true to a large extent, but it should not be the whole picture. Media education, like any other education, must play a part in extending children's imaginative capabilities. This can be done partly by ensuring that they get to experience media forms and products that they might not otherwise encounter. It can also be done by ensuring that children get the opportunity to make their own media products. This should not just entail copying professional practice, although this may have its place and value (and specialist media studies and pre-vocational courses in the upper secondary school certainly do involve the exploration of professional media production). It must also enable children to investigate the possibilities of media technologies appropriate to their own context and resources: single camera video, tape/slide, wall newspapers, etc.

Reference to the Media in National Curriculum Documents
The English Subject Working Group was specifically asked to consider media education and how it might be taught through English. We have contributed documentation to the Group and have assisted with the production of Non-Statutory Guidance. The emphasis in English is on extending the Reading profile component to include the study of media texts, although the Non-Statutory Guidance also suggests possibilities for media work under the Speaking and Listening profile component. We endorse the apparent tendency to ensure that media education has a clear presence within English, but we would not wish it to be the only part of the curriculum in which media education is undertaken. The English proposals also often mention the use of media such as film and video, in the teaching of literature, for example. Simply using media to illustrate or demonstrate a subject does not constitute media education, in our view, but it provides an opportunity for it to be undertaken if teachers have the knowledge and confidence to do so.

Attainment Target 12 in Science (the scientific aspects of information technology including microelectronics) includes many aspects of knowledge about media technologies, as do parts of Attainment Target 14 (sound and music) and Attainment Target 15 (using light and electromagnetic radiation). The Programmes of Study for Science make a number of references to work with media technologies themselves (e.g., in communication) and to work with aspects of these technologies (e.g. projection, sound waves, etc.). The Programme of Study for Key Stage 4, Model A, requires pupils to consider scientific ideas in their historical and cultural context, which would presumably include addressing the question of how ideas and information have circulated at a given time. The Programmes of Study also recommend the use of television and video as teaching aids, to which we would apply our comment in the previous paragraph.

The Design and Technology proposals (DES/Welsh Office, June 1989) make few specific references to the media themselves but cite a wide range of skills and understandings that would inevitably be called upon in any media production activity. The IT capability 'to develop ideas and to communicate information in a variety of forms, such as text, numbers, pictures, sound' could also be seen as a media capability. More details about our view of the relationship between media education and design and technology can be found in our proposals, sent to the Working Group in January 1989.

The History Interim Report (DES/Welsh Office, June 1989) has the only   11
National Curriculum documentary reference to classroom uses of the media that we have seen which does stress the importance of critical and imaginative uses of radio, TV, and films to illustrate or inform (p. 80). We believe that media education will help history teachers to understand the full connotations of this advice. It means effectively that media products should be treated like other historical evidence, and interrogated in terms of their authorship, provenance, purposes, etc. History proposes ways of handling evidence that are very close to the critical procedures of media education, and reminds us that media products of the past are themselves historical evidence that can be selected, assessed, and compared with other evidence. Further detail can be found in our paper 'History and Media Education in the National Curriculum', sent to the Working Group and to the NCC in October 1989.

We would like to supply evidence to future subject working parties and   12
cross-curricular task groups, and to respond to their reports, to show how media education can relate to other subject areas. A more detailed account of the role of media education in all the primary school subjects can be found in our curriculum statement, *Primary Media Education*.

Potential Points of Contact between Media Education and Foundation Subjects

As we have already pointed out in the previous section, media education   13
should help teachers and pupils use video, photographs, television, film, and radio – and, indeed, textbooks – in all subjects more critically and imaginatively than is always the case now. There are no neutral, totally reliable sources of information. Media education helps teachers and pupils assess the nature and extent of bias and selection, and to understand the reasons for them.

Media education activities offer particular ways of working towards cer-   14
tain attainment targets within specific subjects, and of integrating programmes of study across attainment targets and across subjects. But it is important to stress that the documentation produced so far also reveals many ways in which proposed programmes of study could simultaneously develop children's knowledge and understanding of the media. In our experience, teachers are usually ready to see how media work can enhance what they are already doing in their own subjects. But they need additional guidance and training to develop the knowledge and confidence that will enable them to perceive, and take advantage of, the opportunities that are constantly presented to them, of *systematically* developing children's media education.

The Role of the BFI in Media Education

The BFI as a whole receives its funding from the Office of Arts and Librar-   15
ies and its remit is to foster and develop public appreciation and understanding of film and television. The Education Department works across

138

the whole spectrum of education, from primary schools to continuing education, to encourage and develop the study of film and television, whether as specialist courses or as part of media education. We do not receive funding from the DES for this work and any extensions to our activities have to be supported by additional outside funding (see below). Within these constraints, we try to play a research, developmental, and lobbying role, and to encourage other agencies such as LEAs (Local Education Authorities), universities and polytechnics, or publishers, to take over and continue work that we have developed.

From 1987 to 1989 we convened a working party on primary media 16 education which produced, in February 1989, a curriculum statement, *Primary Media Education*. Copies of this have been sent to the NCC (National Curriculum Council), the DES (Department of Education and Science), HMI (Her Majesty's Inspectorate), and all primary advisers, and are also sold at cost price through our mail order department. This work was funded by the Calouste Gulbenkian Foundation, who have also given a pump-priming grant to a follow-up research and development project which is setting up classroom-based initiatives in a number of LEAs. Further funding is being sought to support this three-year project. Another project now coming to the end of its first year is researching media education across the lower secondary curriculum, with the aim of producing teaching units in eight subject areas by the end of 1991. These are likely to be produced in collaboration with a commercial publisher. The Nuffield Foundation is funding this project.

Since the publication of the DES report *Popular TV & Schoolchildren* in 17 1983, we have worked with HMI and the Regional Working Groups that were subsequently set up, to develop and disseminate good practice in media education. We work in a number of in-service training contexts, including our own annual residential course, to assist teachers' professional development in this area. We are currently negotiating with the Open University the terms of a contract to develop with them a distance learning package for teachers in primary and secondary schools who wish to get a basic understanding of media education. Our own teaching materials, documents, and listings play a key role in disseminating ideas about how media education may be taught.

Conclusion
We would be happy to discuss any ways in which we can help the NCC consider media education as a cross-curricular theme. It seems to us that the references to the media and to media education which are beginning to appear in National Curriculum documentation will eventually necessitate separate guidelines, as well as elements within subject-specific Non-Statutory Guidance.

The Politics of Media Education

Cary Bazalgette

The Politics of Media Education, Keynote Presentation at BFI Easter School 1989.

All education is political, but it is claimed that media education is more political than most. What I want to do this afternoon is to examine that claim, and relate it to the situation we are now in, and the legislative proposals that are before us. And, to offer the usual disclaimer, I shall be posing questions rather than answering them.

It has been said from time to time that media education is *essentially* radical. The people who argue this would say that in media education, unlike other subjects in the curriculum, we are asking children to examine how it is that they know what they know. In media education you have to look at where information and ideas come from, rather than accepting that they are just naturally there. You have to go through the classic litany of questions – Who is speaking here? To whom do they speak? For whom do they speak? – which lead into answers about media institutions, systems of circulation, representation, and power.

And, of course, many teachers would go on to claim – with a sort of masochistic pride – that media education 'leads them to challenge who I am, what right I have to speak, whose interests are served by the institution of schooling'.

Although there is more than one form of media education and they do not all share the same politics, I think it would be true to say that media education has always had a radical tendency. Most of the ideas that formed it came out of the impact of Marxism and structuralism on English teaching in particular. The net result of that (to cut a long story short) was to 'denaturalise' previous assumptions about what is worth studying and what critical work is for. Anything can be seen and analysed as a construct, as a product of specific histories and dispositions of power. Our ideas about what great literature is, about gender, or race, or childhood, are not natural but have been produced from somewhere, serve certain conditions and interests. We can examine them – and we can change them.

Coming to these sorts of understanding was a powerful liberating moment in my experience, and I am sure in many of yours as well. We should not underestimate their importance or become cynical about them. But neither should we sanctify them into a set of right-on propositions that cannot be examined.

The historical context of the things I have been talking about was, of course, the seventies, by which I mean something like 1974 to 1984, or, if you like, Callaghan to Thatcher's second term, or the winter of discontent

140

to the Falklands – add a gloss from your personal history. During that period, most media teaching (though that is a guess) became embroiled, along with other subjects, in what could be called the psychology of opposition. Media teachers saw themselves as chiselling away at the smug assumptions and neat certainties of capitalism. They were revealing the power networks that sustained media institutions. They were showing how images or films or programmes that just looked like light-hearted entertainment were really out to manipulate you ideologically.

It thus became possible to claim that media education was *naturally*   7
subversive, because it had to ask questions about power structures. And if it was doing that, then it would follow that those in power (whether they were in media institutions or in government) would not like it. This principle became reversible. If people in power did not like what you were doing, then it was probably subversive, and the consequence of that thinking was the notion that not having power gave you moral status. You were untainted. You had the freedom to maintain ideologically pure positions. You could be a martyr.

One of the worst results of this kind of thinking was a failure to distin-   8
guish between different kinds of power. Since, say, the chairman of a TV company, a chief education officer, and a member of the government are all powerful people, then it was tempting to see their common interests as more important than their differences. And one thing they would all particularly have in common from our point of view is that they would all be against us. Wouldn't they?

So when it was rumoured in 1982 that HMI were taking an interest in   9
media studies, this was seen as sinister. When media education did not figure in the national criteria for GCSE, this was seen as the beginning of the end. When TVEI was first set up, there were those who saw it as a portent of doom: media studies would be reduced to a mere technical training. When the first National Curriculum consultation document came out, there was an almost complacent despair about the absence of media studies as a foundation subject. To all these there was a sort of guerrilla warfare response: we must fight on the margins, we must defend what we have struggled so hard to achieve.

Those sorts of initial response have diversified as events have moved on.   10
The HMI 'interest' turned into the *Popular TV and Schoolchildren* report (DES 1983) and the subsequent initiatives that have probably done more than anything else to shift the status of media studies in the eyes of educational administrators and broadcasters. There are five GCSE syllabuses, taken by an increasing number of candidates each year. TVEI has enabled people to have the space, time, and money to relate practical and critical work in media studies in ways that just could not be done before. And media education is in the core curriculum, as a part of English, starting at the age of five, with the proviso that it should be a separate option at GCSE and above.

How should one respond to these developments? Has there been a real   11
'victory' for media educators? Should we be celebrating the fact that we have got what we wanted? Should we be wary because media education may still be only the flavour of the month, and once the core curriculum

141

testing requirements really take hold, media education will just get buried? Should we be warning each other that the widespread acceptance of media education must mean that it loses its radical edge? Should we be suspicious of anything this government approves of? Just what should be the politics of media education now?

I think that the correct strategy in trying to answer questions like that would be to look a little more broadly at the situation we find ourselves in now. After all, the Education Reform Act and other issues to do with schooling are not the only things that should concern us as media teachers. There are changes in the media that are also going to affect what we teach. James Donald is going to talk more about the relation between the Education Act and the Broadcasting White Paper, in his presentation later in the week, but I think it would be interesting to set the scene, as it were, by telling you about two recent pronouncements from government ministers.

The first was from Douglas Hurd, the Home Secretary, being interviewed at the National Film Theatre about the Broadcasting White Paper. As you might expect, he was full of optimism about the government's plans for broadcasting and at pains to explain to us that quality programming would be preserved – for those who want it – and that subscription TV would ensure that minority interests would continue to be catered for. When he was asked what he personally wished for most about the television of the future, he said that what he really hoped for was that people would begin to watch television more actively, that they would take a *critical* interest in what they watched. When he was asked whether he did not have a concern for the *universality* of public service provision as we have known it in the past (that provision that ensures there is always a *diversity* of programming available to everyone, whatever their personal tastes), his response was that 'that's telling people what to think'. So the underlying theme of everything he was saying was the idea of the viewers or listeners who think for themselves, who criticise what they watch, who go out and find – and if necessary pay for – the programming they really want.

Only a couple of weeks later Angela Rumbold, Minister of Education, was also speaking at the NFT, at the launch conference of British Action for Children's Television. Here is part of what she said:

> Schools have an important part to play in the relationship between children and television. They can develop a critical awareness in their pupils. . . . We at the DES think it important that all children are helped in school to develop their critical faculties, in the best sense of the word 'critical', so that they can assess and evaluate the presentation of both fact and fiction in the media. The ability to 'read' media texts – that is, to see them in the light of such a critical awareness and evaluation, and to have some understanding of the processes which produce them – is an important skill for contemporary and future citizens.

Let us consider for a moment the processes of thought from which those two pronouncements emerge. We need to remember that the Seventies

142

radicalisation I described earlier – the ways in which we came to see that the natural and the accepted could be questioned and analysed and changed – that radicalisation was not confined to the Left. As we have come to learn, perhaps painfully, over the last ten years, the Right has also come to question the natural and the accepted and to propose that they can be changed, and their analysis has not been tempered by any qualms about the exercise of power. So while the Left was busy getting its analysis correct, the Right was working out how change was to be brought about and how the new dispensation could be made to work. And as we know, the answer they came up with was that you can get anything to work if you invoke the principle of self-interest.

That is the principle you can see clearly at work in those two pronounce- 16
ments. On the one hand, Hurd is saying that broadcasting in Britain has to outgrow the 'nannying' of public service provision and come out into the cold hard world of the market-place. On the other hand, Rumbold is saying that education is going to provide the robust, individualistic con-sumers that this market-place is going to demand. Most of the criticism of Tory educational reforms that we have heard so far have concentrated on the 'training for jobs' aspect, but they are clearly going to be concerned with training for leisure consumption as well. You cannot leave that entirely to advertisers. So who else but teachers would get the job of ensuring that there will always be people who want to see *Blue Peter* and *World In Action*?

Well, in the end, how much does this matter? Are we not always in the 17
position of exploiting the gaps and contradictions in whatever system gets dumped on us? Will we not just get on with what we want to do anyway? Is it not a bit churlish, now we have media education on the national curriculum, to complain that we do not like the terms on which it is offered? And anyway, have teachers not always been seen as some sort of cultural conservationists?

These are not merely rhetorical questions, and you may well want to 18
address them in the seminar groups later. But you will infer that I do not think the heads-down, 'get on with it and we won't be noticed' position does form an entirely desirable politics for media education at the present time. That is not to say that I think we should do what media educators are so good at doing and say 'Aha! We know what you're *really* up to!' and dissociate ourselves from the new, core-curricular, standard-assessment-task media education that starts, apparently, in the nation's reception classes in September. I think we should get right in there and establish media education on our terms. But I would suggest that we do need to be a bit clearer about what those terms are. What do *we* think we are in this for? What are *our* aims as media educators? What is our area of concern?

I suspect that for most of us there is a contradiction between our concerns 19
as teachers about the media and our concerns as media consumers. My guess would be that in the latter role, most of us are alarmed about the new developments in broadcasting and the implications these may have for the public service principle. But how do we as media educators relate to the Broadcasting White Paper? What is our attitude to the 'quality thres-hold' that is going to be imposed on those who bid for the new ITV franchises? Do we care what happens to the BBC? If so, why? What do we

think ought to be the role of the Broadcasting Standards Council, the Independent Television Commission, the Advertising Standards Authority, the Press Council? What are we going to teach about them?

The trouble with questions like these is that they all relate, to a greater or lesser extent, to issues with which media teachers do not feel very comfortable: that is, questions about quality, values, standards. There have been good arguments for the avoidance of those issues in media education. Perhaps the best illustration of these comes from Len Masterman – here is part of what he said in a lecture in 1987:

> Is it *appropriate* to apply aesthetic criteria to most media output? Even if we could distinguish between good and bad advertisements, news bulletins, or sports coverage, would we want to do it? Is it so important to rank media texts into some kind of qualitative hierarchy? Or is it more important to *understand* some of the ways in which these texts are financed, produced, circulated, and consumed? Shouldn't we pay some attention, that is, to the ways in which the media function as industries? These questions were more frequently asked than satisfactorily answered throughout the 1970s. But it was evident that before any real progress could be made in the classroom English teachers would have to go beyond what were becoming increasingly attenuated definitions of discrimination. They would have to abandon the concept altogether.

Masterman's critique of aesthetics and discrimination rests on the problems that they entail for the democratic classroom teacher who respects children's own culture. He argues that they inevitably entail élitism and the imposition of middle-class preferences on children who would rather be reading the *Sun* and watching *The Price is Right*. In other words, such judgements are tainted with power. However, this does not necessarily mean that kids can go on happily reading the *Sun* and watching *The Price is Right*. Once they have analysed these in terms of the ways they are financed, produced, circulated, and consumed, the way they function as industries, and the ways they represent social groups, they will realise that they are not supposed to like them. But they will now know what are, according to Masterman, *the right reasons* for disliking them.

The trouble with this argument, though, is that I do not see how it avoids the very middle-class élitism that it is supposed to counteract. If we are democratic teachers and we do respect children's culture, then why are *their* reasons for their own media choices not on the agenda? The reason is – and it is not a bad reason – that this would get us into some very tricky and contentious areas: pleasure, taste, personal identity, class loyalty. The major difficulty here is one that Masterman defines well in his book *Teaching the Media*:

> We all, teachers and students alike, need to own up to the possibility that our media pleasures, which are actively produced for us, may be instrumental in engineering consent for forms of domination and oppression to which we are opposed.

144

Well, this is true. But is it true for all our pleasures? Is this an adequate reason for never talking about pleasure, about why we choose one text rather than another, about what we would want to defend as worth keeping under any future dispensation? The debate about the White Paper centres on the question of 'quality', and how, and by whom, that gets defined. Should we, as media teachers, be ignoring that debate?

I do not think we should, but what seems to me to be the dangerous 23
thing about the public image of media education, in so far as it has one, is that there is a general impression that media teachers disapprove of the media. Some more examples from Masterman: '[media education] involves the *deconstruction* of media texts by breaking through their surface to reveal the rhetorical techniques through which meanings are produced. It's an important step in moving from subordination to the text to critical liberation from it', and 'the ideological power of the media resides in the ability of those who control and work in them to pass off what are inevitably selective and partial representation as true, rational, authentic, and necessary'. Well, I can hear Thatcher and Hurd agreeing with that, wholeheartedly. Let media educators teach children how left-wing the BBC is! Let *them* produce an audience that objects to paying the licence fee!

So where does this argument get us? Does it force us back into the tired 24
old questions of taste and what counts as worthwhile and what is fit to be admitted to the canon of high culture? Those are certainly the terms on which much of the debate on broadcasting is going at the moment. But I think what that forces on us as media educators is a reassessment of how we would define, and teach about, quality, pleasure, value, aesthetics.

That is no easy task, and it is not just difficult because it is unfashionable 25
and embarrassing. Masterman's arguments about the dubiousness of pleasures is an important one and we should not abandon it. But there has to be a way of describing and investigating and justifying what we enjoy and value in the media. Because if we do not, then we are saying that they do not in the end matter all that much. Television, radio, video, cinema – even the press – are never going to matter as much as what now gets unproblematically counted as 'art'; they are never going to move us or challenge us or open up imaginative possibilities for us.

Unfortunately, there are plenty of people to whom that last point is not 26
at all remarkable. But if as media teachers we do not have some kind of long-term aim of teaching children to have high expectations of the media, then what *are* we doing it for? It seems to me that if we are to develop children's understanding of what the media might be like, as well as what they are like now, then we have to address these troublesome questions of – what should we call it? Quality? Value? Aesthetics? The trouble is that you cannot even start to address the area without using terms that for most of us reek with the smugness of high cultural judgements. For now, I shall use the term 'pleasure'.

It is no mean task to take on the question of how to investigate pleasure 27
in the classroom. I am massively intimidated by it, anyway. What I want to do now is to offer two possible starting points, possible ways of beginning to think about it, which you can follow up in subsequent sessions if you want to.

To get at the first one, I felt I should offer an example at this point, on which to hang my argument. But I precisely did not want to offer something worthy, something that would drop us back into the high culture/low culture debate. So what I have selected is something that should at one level introduce questions of pleasure in a very simple way – a bit of comedy. Our response to comedy is usually direct: if we like it we laugh, if we don't, we don't. It is often argued that you cannot talk about aesthetic judgements in relation to comedy in the same way as with other kinds of text, simply because it does produce that very particular, almost reflex, response. If you are going to talk about its value as art then you have to import issues such as realism, humanity, universality, and so on. But I do not see why you cannot regard the comic effect as a sort of condensation, a microcosm, of any response. So what I am going to show is a two-minute video clip of something that is taken from 'Nosenight' in *Comic Relief*, really quite a run-of-the-mill piece of comic business. If you laugh at it (and of course you might not) try to think: what is it you are actually laughing at?

[The extract used here was a comedy sketch by the British comedian Rowan Atkinson who pretended to chair a quiz game in which the participants were well-known politicians. Atkinson asked absurd questions to which the politicians appeared to give comically inappropriate answers; these were in fact edited fragments of news or current affairs programmes.]

I want to suggest that at least part of what you were laughing at was the *artifice* of that piece. You know perfectly well that Atkinson and the politicians are just edited together, but you laugh at the extent to which it looks as though they aren't. You are laughing in a sense at the narrowness of that gap between what really happened and what seems to have happened. The fact that it has been created through artifice is not a barrier to your pleasure but part of the source of it.

Is it possible, I wonder, to extend this principle to other kinds of text? I have recently been looking at art criticism, something that has not had a lot of influence on media teaching. I was struck by some observations that David Hockney was making in distinguishing between art and photography. This is part of what he said:

> Photographs are not exactly what we think they are. I realised that the camera is a lot older than photography; it has been in use in Europe for at least four hundred years. Canaletto used the camera – a *camera obscura*. This device was a box with a lens that projected the image of the exterior world on to a canvas, and his students traced the outlines. A problem of perception occurs because this is only one eye seeing, but to some extent this was hidden as the artist with his moving hand was layering time into the work. As your eye moves across the surface of a Canaletto, each area of the painting is a different time; it was done at a different moment. The hand making the marks moves through time and in viewing the picture you feel this, even though you might not be conscious of it.[1]

It is not hard to imagine the scoffing about assertions of the ineffable 32 with which a lot of media teachers would greet that account, and I am not at all sure how far I would want to go with Hockney's argument that it is this 'time factor' which distinguishes painting from photography. But at the same time I am interested in this suggestion that we perceive, and indeed take pleasure in, the *work* that produced the text. This seems to run completely counter to the realist aesthetic that is supposed to dominate 'quality' judgements about media texts which is, basically, that the less you can see the join, the better it is. Thus, dramatic performances are supposed to reach the heights of perfection when you forget that it is a performance and believe it totally. That may be true in relation to our involvement with the narrative, but in relation to our pleasure in the performance itself, surely it is the case that we never forget that it is artifice: our pleasure derives, again, from the narrowness of that gap between the performer and the illusion. We recognise the human activity, the work, that the performance consists of.

The second possibility I want to consider is not unrelated to Hockney's 33 argument. It goes back a long way in art criticism, but it might be worth reviewing some of that tradition and disentangling the parts of it that we might use from the dead hand of refined sensibility. For example, here is Roger Fry writing in 1909:

> . . . in our reaction to a work of art there is something more – there is a consciousness of purpose, the consciousness of a peculiar relation of sympathy with the man [*sic*] who made this thing in order to arouse precisely the sensations we experience. And when we come to the higher works of art, where sensations are so arranged that they arouse in us deep emotions, this feeling of a special tie with the man who expressed them becomes very strong. We feel that he has expressed something which was latent in us all the time, but which we never realised, that he has revealed us to ourselves in revealing himself. And this recognition of purpose is, I believe, an essential part of the aesthetic judgement proper.[2]

Doubtless Roger Fry would be somewhat taken aback at the thought of applying these arguments to popular media texts, and the high art rhetoric that surrounds it probably makes it seem a somewhat bizarre project for us, too. The point I am trying to make here is that, once you strip it down to its essentials, the argument itself is not élitist. It is the refusal to apply it to popular cultural forms that is élitist.

One person who has tried to do this is Richard Dyer. He is one of the 34 very few people in the media studies field who has really tried to confront questions of popular entertainment and the pleasures it affords. He suggests that we can understand entertainment through re-examining two terms commonly used about it in a derogatory way: escapism and confirmation. He argues that if we take the idea of 'escapism' seriously, we can see popular entertainment as offering what could be called Utopian ideas: a more plentiful, colourful, and happier world that we would like to aspire to. That is an important point, I think, but it relates specifically to entertainment forms. For a more general application, I am more interested in what he says about 'confirmation'. Media teachers often say that the sense of confirmation that the media offer us – the sense of belonging to a consensus – is spurious, if not actually dangerous; but Dyer argues that we nevertheless have to acknowledge that the sense of belonging to a consensus is a valid and identifiable pleasure that should not just be ignored, even if it is a pleasure in things we would want to disapprove of. And is not that feeling of consensus, of solidarity with the artist, close to what Fry was writing about? Why should it only be 'the higher works of art' that reveal us to ourselves?

So those are my two, tentatively offered, starting points for thinking about how we should approach pleasure in media education. Any text can offer us the pleasures of artifice, of recognising the *work* that produced it; any text can offer us a sense of confirmation, *solidarity* with those who produced it – and, of course, with others sharing the same response. But this is not to say that these pleasures can force aside the other issues that we confront as media educators. As Dyer says, 'we have to get at the issues and their consequences through the experience of entertainment, rather than inferring social implications beneath or despite the entertainment'. I would extend that argument beyond 'entertainment' to encompass the whole field of the media. We cop out if we do not acknowledge, articulate, and justify our own pleasures and values in the media, and encourage children to do the same. We also cop out if we confine children's media production work to copying professional practices or to critical exercises, and do not – or cannot – allow the space for them to imagine the possibilities of media languages. If media education is about empowering children – and I think it is – then it has to be about empowering them imaginatively as well as critically.

I want to conclude by bringing this argument back into relation to the politics of media education. Talking about pleasure and developing the scope of children's imaginative work seems to have more to do with personal development than with the wider political scene. There is still a relationship, though. One way of thinking it through is by using the concept of hegemony, that useful term for describing the way that those in power in society do not necessarily govern by force or intimidation, but by obtaining the consent of those who are governed. Hegemony is often thought of as the power to define the content of public debate: to define what gets said. But the real power of hegemony is to define the *agenda* of public debate: to define what it is *possible* to talk about, what it is possible to think. So Hurd can quite reasonably say he does not want to tell people what to think: in the new hegemony that is being created for us, that will not be necessary. The only way of beginning to resist this is to be able to rethink the agenda, to imagine different spaces, different ways of thinking, different ways of producing. When we teach children about what the media are and how they work now, then we are teaching within the set agenda. That is an important part of what we do, but it should not be *all* that we do.

Both as teachers and as citizens we are confronted now with more than

148

one set of possibilities. We could engage with the debate about the media on the terms that are being offered to us: what constitutes quality, standards, good taste? What do we want to defend – under the old rubric of middle-class approval and assumptions about what is worth studying? Or we could – and I think we should – attempt to shift the terms of that debate, to change the agenda. We have to address the question of how quality and standards and taste get defined – and by whom. Our own standard inquiries – who is speaking here, to whom, and in whose interests – can be applied to assertions about 'good television' and 'the quality press'. And I think children deserve to be in on those questions, too.

Notes

1. David Hockney, *On Photography* (V&A Lecture 1983), Bradford, National Museum of Photography, Film and Television, 1985.
2. Roger Fry, *New Quarterly*, 1909, reprinted in *Vision and Design*, 1920.

PART Iᴮ
Traditions

Traditions
Introduction

In the first section of this Reader we have offered extracts from key articles and documents in the formation of media education published over the last quarter of a century. These pieces arose out of a variety of working contexts and appeared in a wide range of publications. However, while media education may seem to have developed in a piecemeal fashion, it is possible to discern certain common threads through which to link and group many of the arguments and positions. In this section we have identified three of what we have termed, somewhat grandiosely, 'traditions'.

The three we focus on we have entitled the 'interpretive', 'social science', and 'creative' traditions. The 'interpretive' tradition is primarily text-based and concerned with analysis and critical evaluation. Thus Jim Cook concentrates on different approaches and methods that have been developed for analysing how meaning is generated, structured, and read in audiovisual texts. He contrasts the Leavisite approach, rather haphazardly dependent on the extent to which knowledge and beliefs happen to be shared between critics and their readers, with subsequent approaches which have sought to establish more systematic and accountable strategies for analysing textual forms of signification. Some of these latter pay attention not just to *readers* of texts but also to *audiences*, and as such these approaches overlap with the second tradition.

The 'social science' tradition offers contextual forms of analysis. The production and consumption of texts and their social, economic, and political interrelatedness with social structures, groups, and individuals provide the focus of much of this work. Audiences research and the 'effects' of television provide well-known examples of such 'extra-textual' information which has been used variously as evidence about people, about society, and sometimes about the substantive content of the texts themselves. In this chapter, Oliver Boyd-Barrett notes that many such studies converge on issues to do with the power of the media, and he traces changes in conceptualisation, focus, and emphasis through four discrete periods and between different centres of scholarship.

A quite different tradition is outlined by Manuel Alvarado and Wendy Bradshaw in their account of the teaching of film and television production. Deriving originally from the 'creative' impulse to undertake moving-image production largely within an 'art' tradition, this highly expensive activity was restricted to art schools and film schools and departments within the higher education sector. As Alvarado and Bradshaw note, there was often a tension, even a polarisation, between the study of media as a means of developing critical skills, and the study of media as a means of developing the creative and technical skills of media production.

However, this area of activity has changed dramatically (*a*) due to the development of increasingly sophisticated video cameras and editing suites, the prices of which are constantly dropping, and (*b*) due to the burgeoning of the television and video industry throughout the 1980s. Thus there has been a concomitant move to develop professional and vocational skills in the post-16 education sector and to introduce new training initiatives. At the same time, there has been an increasing determination to integrate critical/analytic activity with practical production at all age levels within the school curriculum.

In the overall selection and organisation of this Reader a central concern has been to offer contexts and avoid talking about the teaching of media in a rarified vacuum of pedagogical theory. As part of the contexting process, in this part of the Reader we have focused on the major features that constitute the field of media studies – that is to say, on the intellectual traditions which inform the study of the mass media.

At the same time, it is worth remembering that where and how each of these traditions is inflected within the educational system constitutes in itself a further context. In other words, each of these traditions has, in various ways, been adapted and transformed by incorporation within the school curriculum. While the interpretive tradition of media education has found a natural refuge within English, it has also perhaps suffered from this discipline's concentration on the verbal and relative neglect of the visual. The social science tradition has also been driven towards the English curriculum for uncomfortable refuge, sweetened only by the increasing necessity which the National Curriculum lays upon English teachers to incorporate at least parts of the social science agenda. The creative tradition, finally, finds itself either vocationally located within specifically technical post-16 courses, or scattered and dispersed across the school curriculum – at primary level by the Plowden emphasis on learning through doing, and at secondary level by the newer vocabulary of competence.

The Interpretive Tradition
Jim Cook

Introduction: The Meaning of Meaning

One of the basic aims of film, television, and media studies is to enable students to understand how audio-visual texts come to have a range of meanings or readings ascribed to them, and to be able to make their own warranted readings. The intellectual activity through which this aim is realised is traditionally known as criticism although, as the rest of this essay will argue, it is specifically forms of *interpretive* criticism which are deployed.

Any type of criticism which is concerned with interpretation poses some kind of relationship between the artefact (book, play, film, etc.) and the culture within which it is produced. The problem is both that there are different ways of posing the relationship from complete independence of the one from the other (art is autonomous) to total dependence of the one upon the other (art directly reflects society), and that often these differences are not made explicit. Mainstream cultural commentators like Malcolm Bragg, Phillip French, and Sarah Kent regularly ricochet from one or other of these positions in their literary, movie, and art criticism. The problem is not so much that they do this, even though it does not make for especially logical or rigorous writing, but that they do it seemingly unconsciously and without any perception of the logical inconsistencies.

It is with the aim, therefore, of trying to make explicit what is often implicit that this essay offers an outline history of how and why over the past twenty years audio-visual productions have been read in particular ways.

Our starting point must be F. R. Leavis and the writers about film who were influenced by him. For Leavis there were two very different discernible relations between artefacts and the containing cultures:

(1) As far as 'great art' was concerned his critical brilliance was to synthesise, through readings of a highly selective set of novels and poetry, three critical emphases which dated back at least to John Dryden at the end of the seventeenth century if not to Aristotle's *Poetics*. In general terms these characterised art as either: mimetic/realist (i.e., art imitates life and experience); or pragmatic/legislative (i.e., art at its best is a moral exemplar); or expressive/creative (i.e., only special creators can produce the profundities of great art).

(2) All other works (the vast majority of English literature which did not offer Leavis a 'great tradition' of profound moral visions of aspects of

155

social experience) were not considered to be 'art', and were designated as of sociological interest only: mass-produced material lacking either challenges or real gratifications.

It is worth stressing that the challenges and gratifications of great literature were emphatically not just those of a fine critical intelligence formally understanding the text, but also involved those of a fine moral intelligence gaining a deeper understanding of the human condition. 'The study of it [literature] is, or should be, an intimate study of the complexities, potentialities, and essential conditions of human nature.'[1]

Within film criticism these positions were influentially taken up and developed by Robin Wood, a former student of Leavis. Although Wood's concerns were with popular film, a mass medium Leavis considered to be barely of even sociological interest, the closeness of his approach to that of the master can be gauged from the following quotations chosen (almost) at random:

> . . . the only essential factor that distinguishes art from non-art is the artist's personal involvement in his material. . . . When a masterpiece emerges it is because Hawks was suddenly completely engaged by his material.[2]

> One can easily demonstrate that most of Bergman's films deal with themes and concerns absolutely central to human experience.[3]

Film debates were rather more lively in the 1960s and 70s than now, and Alan Lovell went into print challenging Wood. Conceding Wood's seriousness and rigour, Lovell none the less expressed 'a dissatisfaction at two important cultural levels, that of value judgements and that of interpretation'.[4]

Lovell argued that absolute value judgements are both impossible and undesirable in societies characterised by differing value systems and ideologies. As for interpretation, he felt that Wood rushed into it, asserting meanings rather than demonstrating the analytic procedures whereby he had reached them.

Wood replied in the issue of *Screen* that also carried Paddy Whannel's article, 'Film Education and Film Culture', reprinted in part in 'Dominant Attitudes to Mass Media' above. Wood's position was that Lovell was pushing towards an almost scientific objectivity:

> I get the impression that Mr Lovell thinks a critic should only write down what other people will be forced to acknowledge as the truth. The 'assertions' to which he objects are always, I think, supported by reasoned argument but by their nature they can't be proven. A critic who restricted himself to that kind of truth would be crippling himself.[5]

He concluded combatively by endorsing a remark of F. R. Leavis that 'the judgements the literary critic is concerned with are judgements about life'.

In the final exchange[6] Lovell argued equally firmly that it is criticism and not the critic which is important, and that the function of the critical activity is less to establish or endorse values than to describe as convincingly as possible the structures and mechanisms in any work which enable meanings:

> Just as bodies can be studied in terms of such common characteristics as their bone structure, blood circulation, nervous systems, etc., fiction films can be studied in terms of such common characteristics as editing devices, narrative structures, character relations etc. . . . Robin Wood seems not to understand that an essential point of any human study is to produce generalisations that make it possible to study particular objects.

It is worth pointing out that these debates around the meanings of meaning (i.e., what is being read and interpreted from what perspective and for what reason) still have enormous relevance today both for the ways in which we elect to understand texts ourselves and for the ways in which we elect to 'open' them to our students. The only difference between now and twenty years ago is that today no one is conducting the debates as explicitly – hence this potted history.

During the 1970s there were a number of applications of these first principle debates. Most influentially, interpretive approaches were applied to:

(1)   Auteur studies, derived from Leavis, which located the most important sources of meaning in individual directors' (creators') deployment of conventional narrative or generic elements;

(2)   Genre studies which focused more centrally on conventions, such as on what groups of Westerns, gangster films, musicals, and so on, had in common visually, narratively, and thematically;

(3)   Industry studies which, recognising the capital intensive and technological nature of cinema and television, sought to locate the determinations of meaning in the conditions of production of films and television programmes.

Useful examples of each of these approaches in operation, and in tension, can be found in two special issues of *Screen Education*, one devoted to John Ford's *The Searchers*, and the other devoted to Euston Films' television police series *The Sweeney*.[7] The most successful articles in these two issues are those which deploy notions of genre to demonstrate how 'we', the audiences, are actively involved in reading texts and (via our recognition of conventions) in the reproduction of conventionally shared meanings. Between the authorship and industry pieces, however, it is now possible to see not just alternative approaches but real differences between articles which locate *The Searchers'* tragic contradictions around racism and masculinity within the director John Ford, and those which see *The Sweeney's* particular construction of a police/crime/society nexus as generated from an interaction between textual conventions, conditions of production, and the 'world view' of the production team.

157

These problems of interpretation remain, and are not resolvable in the sense of a single answer being possible – 'by their nature they can't be proven', as Robin Wood said. What can be further elaborated, however, is the procedural clarity which Alan Lovell was calling for along with some rethinking of the terms of value judgements. As a reminder that these elaborations are still needed, one only has to turn to the book and film review pages of most quality papers where, thirty years later, a crude and simplified version of the 'great tradition' still holds power and sway.

Reading Conventions
Fundamental to any positing of a relation between the artefact and the culture out of which it is produced are assumptions that elements (signs) in texts have attributable meanings (semiotics) and that these elements taken together constitute a relationship to socially experienced realities (representation).

There is no space in an overview article for an adequately detailed account of these terms, but in order to understand developments in the interpretive tradition the following points are relevant.

Realism
In the 1970s it was the formal properties of realism as much as the politics of representation which were stressed. As in the examples offered below from David Bordwell and Kristin Thompson, it was progressively recognised throughout the 1970s that narrative realist stories follow logical sequences appropriately framed, thereby constructing worlds which we are invited to find both plausible and coherent.

However, along with attending to the pleasures of identification and recognition of the conventions at work, a number of critiques of the realistic effects of coherence and plausibility were also mounted. The forms these took derived especially from a reading of Bertolt Brecht's critical writing, and the argument was made that narrative realism's concentration on the surface detail of a particular situation always masks the underlying social, cultural, political, and often contradictory, causes which have brought about that situation. At a formal level it was argued that narrative's illusion of realism always draws attention away from the fact that a text is artificial and constructed, and that there is nothing natural or inevitable or immutable about its structure. The solution proposed was the production of anti-realist, self-reflexive texts which would draw attention to their own constructedness and hence become resistant to easy identification with character, freeing the reader to reflect on the underlying causes of, for example, a character's situation.

Counter-positions argued that Brecht was never as proscriptive in his own practice regarding the construction of a progressive text, and that anyway self-reflexivity, contradiction, and underlying causes could be found in any text (see the notes on the *Cahiers du Cinéma* 1969 editorial below). In other words, what was at stake was reading strategies rather than texts' constructions. In *Pictures of Reality*[8] Terry Lovell offers a way out of this argument by distinguishing between realist intention and realist

158

effect. Realist intentions, she argues, are realised through aesthetic strategies which are entireiy conventional and can thus range from stylised
tableaux through naturalistic details to cinéma vérité. The extent to which
they are recognised as realistic depends on the extent to which any particular work or genre variously 'realistically' represented meshes with any particular audience group's assumptions about what life is like and how it
should be represented. Beyond its intellectual clarity in general a distinction
like this is particularly useful in that it allows for consideration of the
constructed nature of all representations, that is, those of 'documentary'
material (news, current affairs, sport, and so forth) as much as those of
more overtly fictional material.

Semiotics

In its concern to demonstrate the constructed nature of what seems natural,   19
semiotics draws on the insights of structural linguistics which assert that
language is arbitrary in its relationship to the realities to which it refers:
neither 'cat' nor 'chat' have any natural relationship to a four-legged feline
living in London or Paris, for example. It is also a term whose applicability
is so widespread that there is a danger of losing sight of the purchase which
particular applications of it can offer.

In relation to audio-visual texts, the key points to grasp are the insistence   20
on the fact that meanings are generated through two sets of interaction.
Firstly, there is an interplay of specific cinematic and televisual codes of
lighting, editing, framing, and the like, and non-specific ones deriving from
the culture in which the text is produced: the types of story it tells, the
language people use, the way they dress, the lives they lead, and so on.
This interplay lays out the possibilities for the production of meanings.
What particular meanings are in fact produced then depends on readers'
abilities to recognise what is being constructed by the specific and non-
specific codes, that is, from their own classed, gendered, ideological experiences, to recognise both what the codes *denote* and then to read meanings
into them to assess what they *connote*. This stress on the production of
meanings is explicit in the gloss below on *S/Z* and implicit in all the
subsequent accounts of the interpretive tradition.

An interesting debate around meanings, which drew on realism and   21
semiotics, occurred in exchanges between Colin McArthur and Colin Mac-
Cabe about the TV drama series *Days of Hope*.[9] In considering the progressive nature of the plays from a left-wing perspective, each reads the same
signs of realism quite differently. For McArthur the plays are capable of
revealing social contradictions (a veneer of constitutional rule masks military repression), while for MacCabe the realism works rather to render one
aspect truer than the other (for the authors of *Days of Hope* the reality is
military repression), and this is not to reveal a contradiction but to resolve
it.

Interesting as such a debate is it cannot be resolved or progressed any   22
further without more attention being paid to notions of the reader and
audience, and subsequent sections of this essay address these. Before turning to them, however, it is useful to describe some of the elaborations of
the 'common characteristics' of texts which Alan Lovell called for, along

with Roland Barthes's account of the reading process derived from *S/Z*.

David Bordwell and Kristin Thompson[10] listed the following rhetorical devices as being constitutive of a plausible and coherent visual world:

– space within the frame organised to forward the drama;
– editing cuts to emphasise continuity of space; cuts 'are always motivated by the ongoing cause/effect chain of narrative';
– objects and décor are functional to narrative or character traits;
– action is centred in the frame and attention drawn away from the screen as a construction.

Regarding the processes of reading in *S/Z*, Roland Barthes[11] proposed that meanings are produced through five 'codes of intelligibility' which the reader recognises and in the deployment of which she or he makes sense. Although elaborated for literary fiction the codes also have an applicability in relation to audio-visual texts.[12] The five codes are:

(1)   The *hermeneutic* code, which is the sets of cues that initiate, develop, and resolve the narrative; when we want to know what happens next or react to suspense we are working with the hermeneutic code.

(2)   The *proairetic* code, which is the sets of basic actions which take the narrative forward; depending on how action-packed the text is, these can range from walking across a room to chasing the bad guys.

(3)   The *cultural* code, which invokes common sense or social knowledge to enhance the plausibility of the narrative. Ideological positions frequently masquerade behind the common sense, as in film noir's assumption that women are ambiguously motivated.

(4)   The *semic* code, which organises all the cues relating to characters and places and our attitude towards them; in literature it is organised through language (nouns, verbs, adverbs, etc.) and in cinema through non-specific codes (physical appearance, clothing, movement) realised through the specific codes of lighting, framing, angle, and so forth.

(5)   The *symbolic* code, which is a more extended version of the cultural code, organising themes so that we are able to perceive that behind overt content a particular text may be 'about' male anxieties, imperial guilt, cultural identity crises, and so on.

The Reader

Although concerns with realism, semiotics, and reading conventions can usefully provide a description of structural constants (what is needed to enable meanings), increasingly generic identification by skilled readers of visual and thematic conventions was understood not as yielding fixed meanings but as offering the conditions for the possibility of a limited variety of meanings, a limited *polysemie*. Crudely: the Western can be set in North America or Mexico between about 1840 and 1910 and be about masculinity, genocide, or myths of history, or be evidence of particular sets of creative and technical collaboration, depending on who is reading, what they are reading for, and where they are reading from. However, a reader who insists that typically a Western is set in the future, features bug-eyed monsters, and is about 'science', has placed her/himself outside any consensual interpretive group or community. This is an important point to grasp: texts can mean many things to many readers but they cannot mean *anything*.

In thinking through more fully the terms of this consensus, the mid-1970s saw attention turn to the conditions under which 'we', readers, make readings:

> The 'competence' of individuals to read is not a social constant but is dependent on the distribution of that 'competence' in class society. . . . Language is a skill not given but acquired in the educative sites of class, family, schools, workplace, sub-group, etc., and the 'competence' and ensuing pleasure is produced in these various social configurations. The 'truth' of a reading is not an essentialist one but produced in the interaction between the reader's 'competence' and the text.[13]

The concerns here have important implications for teaching, and indeed parallel quite closely theories about language acquisition:

> At each stage, the child endeavours to communicate using the resources currently available to him (*sic*). The adult with whom he is interacting interprets his behaviour in terms of his own cultural and linguistic framework and responds in a way that both reflects to the child the perceived significance of his behaviour and, in the form and context of that response, provides information about the communication system and its relation to the world that enables the child to supplement and modify his communicative resources.[14]

A concern with competence moves consideration away from the positions so far summarised, which broadly are all concerned with the *text* and with attempts to describe the meanings which it might yield. Now the concern is as much with the reader who may need to be skilled (i.e., made competent) in modes of reading different from those which come 'naturally' to her/him, and who may read differently for different reasons in different cultural and political contexts.

As with the Reading Conventions section above, the rest of the interpretive traditions summarised below are also framed around differing notions of the reader.

Reading Activity

Once the point is made that people deploying their various competences in working through the reading conventions actually produce quite different readings (even within the bounds of consensus as to what a text is about), then the issue of what readings are made under what circumstances becomes important.

These points were developed and elaborated in the late 1960s and into the 1970s. What was at stake now was not only to insist on the activity of the reader but to argue also for a politicisation of reading and interpretation,

161

and in so doing to rethink absolute value judgements. Once it is recognised that particular meanings are produced (that is, selected from a range of possible ones), in particular circumstances by particular groups of people, it follows that it becomes possible to read against the grain of a text's dominant meanings, to contest them, and perhaps to think of and produce other differently conventional forms which will generate in turn their own conventional readings.

Among the most influential texts arguing through these positions are the three which are summarised below for the purposes of this sketch history. The summaries do not pretend to represent fully the sophistications of the arguments made, which can only be gained from reading the articles themselves.

Cahiers du Cinéma[15]

Here it was argued that, although most mainstream movies reproduce dominant ideologies, a number of them:

> throw up obstacles in the way of ideology causing it to swerve off course. . . . If one reads the film obliquely, looking for symptoms; if one looks beyond its apparent formal coherence, one can see that it is riddled with cracks. An internal criticism is taking place which cracks the film apart at the seams.

The kinds of film the *Cahiers* writers had in mind were ones where the narrative's attempts to resolve neatly all the issues it has unleashed seem to meet with resistances either at the level of sudden shifts in our sympathies for characters and/or at the level of a kind of stylistic excess whereby the way in which the film is made seems at variance with, if not actually critical of, its overt subject matter. Examples of the former would be the films of John Ford, especially *Young Mr Lincoln*, and of the latter films of Douglas Sirk.

For *Cahiers* it was important to understand the formal narrative realistic mechanisms whereby ideology can be subverted so that 'it no longer has an independent existence but rather is presented by the film', since such understanding could potentially give rise to the production of popular texts which would also be subversively critical of dominant ideologies.

Encoding and Decoding in the Television Discourse[16]

Here, Stuart Hall shifted the emphasis from the text to the readers of it. Hall's argument is that in relation to any piece of television (especially but not exclusively 'factual' programmes) the reader always actively reads by negotiating meanings. He identifies three broad types of reading:

(*a*) *dominant*, in which the reader recognises what a programme is saying and broadly agrees with it;

(*b*) *oppositional*, in which she or he recognises the dominant meaning but rejects it for cultural, political, or ideological reasons;

(*c*) *negotiated*, in which elements of the programmes are subjected to acceptance, rejection, and/or refinement in the light of previously held views and assumptions.

In other words, for Hall it is both the culturally acquired competences of formal reading skills and also those of ideological assessment which determine how a text is understood. At the time of writing, media coverage of the war in the Gulf is being filtered through complex sets of readings on the part of both the encoders and decoders of these 'messages'.

Visual Pleasure and Narrative Cinema[17]

Here, in this highly influential expression of the anti-realist position described above, Laura Mulvey argues that not only narrative contents but also their structured visual organisation systematically construct women as passive objects serving the purpose of patriarchal male story-telling. To sustain such a comprehensive critique Mulvey draws upon the insights of psychoanalysis to show how the very way in which we watch films fixes us all, men and women alike, in positions of superiority vis-à-vis woman. 34

This psychoanalytic underpinning has been subsequently criticised for being a-historical, that is, it ignores readings made in specific cultures and contexts by particular groups of men and women. Similarly, Mulvey's conclusion calling for the destruction of these traditional cinematic pleasures of identification and for their replacement by the new pleasures of a political avant-garde has increasingly been seen as polemical rather than pragmatic. Indeed, it is a measure of the article's originality and productivity that it has been susceptible to so much revision. Its lasting achievement is to explode for all time any lingering notions that gender representations are in any way innocent or natural in filmic narrative. The task of media studies is to ensure that the explosion resonates above the cacophony of reviewing practices which still, for the most part, precisely construct their analyses on such assumptions. 35

It follows from all of this that readers read conventions in a number of overlapping ways, and the most important of these are summarised below. 36

Ideological readings: One of the most influential examples here has been the development of feminist analyses concerned to demonstrate the ideological work of textual conventions in relation to representations of women. 37

> If meaning is a production then the reader/critic plays a part in this production by bringing to bear on the work her/his own cultural knowledge and perspective. A feminist reading re-works the text and produces meanings that would have been impossible prior to the development of the conceptual framework of feminism.[18]

In other words, a feminist politics applied to an understanding of how films work produces re-readings. Through its reconsideration of the ambiguities surrounding the presentation of the stereotypical figure of the *femme fatale* and a recasting of it as a projection of male anxieties rather than a figure with any significant reality status, *Women in Film Noir* lucidly demonstrates how it is possible to generate a range of meanings hitherto unformulated and therefore unrecognised in the pictures under consideration. Subsequently, there has been a great deal of feminist scholarship and writing on cinema, and the recently published *Feminist Companion to Cinema*[19] both usefully summarises this work and itself makes an important contribution to the field.

Cultural historical readings: If feminism-driven issues around the representation of women have been one of the most culturally and politically important sets of interpretive activity over the past fifteen years, another more diffuse perspective has investigated further the term 'cultural production' which is sometimes ascribed to texts. Looking at the culture out of which they were produced, this perspective offers history-driven speculations about the relations that might obtain between the artefacts and the containing cultures. 38

This has resulted in a series of studies (of, for example, British Cinema)[20] in which contexts have been considered as important as texts in grounding any interpretation. This concern with history/audiences/institutions indicates a productive convergence between the interpretive and social science traditions. More broadly, it is indicative of the interdisciplinarity which to date has characterised film and television studies at their best and will hopefully do so for media studies in the future. 39

Critical radical readings: In addition to the concern with audiences and their cultures, there has more recently been a consideration of the links between cinema and national identity. This arises in part as a corrective to an implicitly assumed ethnic homogeneity in some of the above studies which are otherwise careful to stress differences of class, age, gender (less so sexual preference) within the 'nation'. Thus, while many of the movies and the studies of them show sophisticated readings of many tensions and differences, overall Britishness is still most often reduced to Caucasian English. Such a reductiveness brings with it many entailments for resentment and bitterness from the marginalisation of linguistic communities (such as native Welsh speakers and writers) to a wilful ignorance of ideologies (for example, the dominant response to some British Asians' 'fundamentalist' response to the 'Rushdie affair'). 40

In this context a number of black British independent practitioners (Sankofa, Black Audio Film Collective, Ceddo, Retake) have been reading/decoding oppositionally and challenging earlier 'race relations' representations of blacks as problems or victims. Linked to an urgent need to extend the range of representations there is also a desire on the part of some film- and video-makers to challenge and change the forms of representation – in other words, they display a commitment to a version of the anti-realist position described above. In so doing they are unfixing notions of national identity (for example, whatever reading you make watching a Second World War British movie now it is impossible not to notice the absence of any representation of the considerable black and Asian presence within the fighting forces), reworking forms, and, through the connections they are developing with other non-British black film-makers, posing the possibility of a new international or transnational cinema which is not 'national/industrial Euro/American'. 41

Such work, a powerful combination of theory and practice, 42 highlights the way image-making has become an important arena of cultural contestation – contestation over what it means to be British today; contestation over what Britishness itself means as a national or cultural identity; and contestation over the values that underpin the Britishness of British cinema as a national film culture.[21]

In 1991 *Young Soul Rebels* (Isaac Julian, director), the first popularly conceived picture to emerge from this critical practice, received a Critics Prize at the Cannes Film Festival and generally mixed reviews on its subsequent UK release.

Conclusion

In some ways we have come a long way from the Wood/Lovell debate,   43
having traced how the move from an assumption of fixed immanent meanings has introduced variously author's meaning, psyche's meaning, history's meaning, and culture's meaning as guarantors of whatever reading is made.

That it is possible to trace these various meanings is due in principle to   44
a commitment within film and television studies to intellectual enquiry and the positing of relations (theory) which goes back to Paddy Whannel (see 'Film Education and Film Culture' above.) In practice, it is due in large part to the existence in the 1970s of *Screen* magazine with its frequently intimidating, occasionally inaccessible, nearly always (finally) invigorating explorations of texts, institutions, readers, and of the relations between them.

Indeed, it is a nice irony that, while setting itself resolutely against   45
'Leavis', *Screen* formed and influenced a generation of 'interpreters' through policies and practices very similar to those deployed by Leavis's journal *Scrutiny* in the 1930s and 40s: both were intellectually austere, presented new and challenging ideas, engaged in polemic, and addressed a broadly educational constituency from the margins. This is not to argue anything as naive as 'the wheel's come full circle', but rather to underline the fact that all texts (including *Scrutiny* and *Screen* articles) are never just words on a page, or images and sounds on and behind a screen. They are always potential sets of meaning in circulation, susceptible to a range of interpretations between readers inhabiting a variety of specific institutional, cultural, intellectual, social, and historical circumstances. Such meanings can range from being narrowly focused and specific to broadly referential and post-modern.

Greater precision and clarity about why a reading and from which per-   46
spective is therefore clearly always important, and indeed returns us to the starting point where the problem of the circulation of confused and vague readings was offered as one of the reasons for attempting this ground-clearing essay. In order that this does not become too grand a conclusion, however, it may be salutary to end on a note of pedagogic caution. This centres on the caveat that in order to interpret at all a prior requirement is basic comprehension. As David Bordwell points out in *Making Meaning*,[22] 'teaching cinema furnishes plenty of occasions to watch people plunge into interpretations of shots whose diegetic status has not yet been established'.

In other words, precisely because the interpretive activity is such a funda-   47
mental critical one, it is imperative that we proceed accurately and attentively and, both in our own meaning-making and in that in which we
participate with our students, avoid rushing to make interpretive judgements before deciding what type of meaning it is we want to make, and
why, and what are the demonstrable warrants for our making them.

Notes

1. F. R Leavis, *The Common Pursuit*, London, Chatto and Windus, 1952.
2. Robin Wood, *Howard Hawks*, London, BFI/Secker and Warburg, 1968.
3. Robin Wood, *Ingmar Bergman*, London, Studio Vista, 1969.
4. Alan Lovell, 'Robin Wood – A dissenting view', *Screen*, vol. 10, no. 2, March –
   April 1969.
5. Robin Wood, 'Ghostly Paradigm and HCF: An Answer to Alan Lovell',
   Screen, vol. 10, no. 3, May–June 1969.
6. Alan Lovell, 'The Common Pursuit of True Judgement', *Screen*, vol. 11, nos.
   4, 5, July–October 1970. See also: John C. Murray, 'Robin Wood and the
   Structural Critics', *Screen*, vol. 12, no. 3, Autumn 1971, and the 'Note' from
   Ted Welch in the same issue.
7. *Screen Education*, no. 17, Autumn 1976, and *Screen Education*, no. 20, Autumn
   1977.
8. Terry Lovell, *Pictures of Reality*, London, BFI, 1980.
9. See Colin MacCabe, 'Realism and the Cinema: Notes on some Brechtian
   Theses', *Screen*, vol. 15, no. 2, Summer 1976; Colin McArthur, 'Days of
   Hope', *Screen*, vol. 17, no. 1, Spring 1976; Colin MacCabe, 'Principles of
   Realism and Pleasure', *Screen*, vol. 17, no. 3, Autumn 1976; Colin McArthur,
   Television and History, London, BFI, 1978.
10. David Bordwell and Kristin Thompson, 'Space and Narrative in the Films of
    Ozu', *Screen*, vol. 17, no. 2, Summer 1976.
11. Roland Barthes, *S/Z*, London, Cape, 1974.
12. See, for example, Sarah Turvey, *Barthes' 'S/Z' and the analysis of film narrative:
    'The Searchers'*, University of London, 1982.
13. Iain Chambers, 'Roland Barthes: Structuralism/Semiotics', *Working Papers in
    Cultural Studies*, no. 6, 1974.
14. C. G. Wells, 'Language Development in the Pre-School Years', *Language at
    Home and at School*, vol. 2, Cambridge University Press, 1985.
15. *Cahiers du Cinéma*, Editorial 'Cinema/Ideology/Criticism', *Screen*, vol. 12, no.
    1, Spring 1971.
16. Stuart Hall, 'Encoding/Decoding', in Stuart Hall *et al.* (eds), *Culture, Media,
    Language*, London, Hutchinson, 1980.
17. Laura Mulvey, 'Visual Pleasure and Narrative Cinema', *Screen*, vol. 16, no.
    3, Autumn 1975.
18. Christine Gledhill, '*Klute*: A contemporary film noir and feminist criticism',
    in E. Ann Kaplan (ed.), *Women in Film Noir*, London, BFI, 1978.
19. Annette Kuhn and Susannah Radstone (eds), *Feminist Companion to Cinema*,
    London, Virago, 1990.
20. In relation to British cinema and culture the most interesting work produced
    has been: Charles Barr, *Ealing Studios*, Newton Abbot, David and Charles,
    1977, a study of an interpretive community's organisational structures, values,
    and products; Geoff Hurd (ed.), *National Fictions*, London, BFI, 1984, a
    series of essays considering the way in which the Second World War was
    represented in both films of the time and has subsequently been represented
    in both films and television programmes; John Hill, *Sex, Class, and Realism*

in British Cinema, 1956–63, London, BFI, 1986, a study of the links between British cinema's penchant for realism and how this affected its capacity to adequately represent Britain during a period of rapid social and cultural change; Charles Barr (ed.), *All Our Yesterdays*, London, BFI, 1986, a series of essays ranging across British cinema history, forms, and influences.

21. Kobena Mercer, 'Decoding Narratives of Race and Nation', *Black Film, British Cinema*, ICA Documents 7, 1987.

22. David Bordwell, *Making Meaning*, Cambridge, Mass., University of Harvard, 1989.

The Social Science Tradition

Oliver Boyd-Barrett

Is there a distinctive 'social science' approach to the study of media? I believe the answer is 'yes' when comparing, in very broad terms, the work of many social scientists in media research to that of intellectuals working within the literature or arts traditions. Over the area of media research as a whole, social scientists have typically concerned themselves either with the *context* of media production (who made this programme, in what environment and circumstances, with what motives, using what techniques and procedures?) or with the *consequences* of media production (for individuals, groups, or for the wider society). This is not to say that the interpretive tradition is uninterested in context – far from it, as you have seen in the previous chapter. But within much of that tradition, the central focus of intellectual activity has been the text itself. The social science treatment of media *content*, by contrast, has traditionally been rather crude, even absent, and rarely has media content been examined by social scientists on its own terms in the light of internal aesthetic or creative criteria. The purpose of the study of media content in social science invariably has had to do with shedding light on the manner in which a media message gets to be made, how it represents social groups and social issues, and what the broader social implications of this might be.

In the past decade or so there has been a coming together of the two major traditions of 'interpretive' and 'social science' approaches, the two finding considerable common ground in conceptual and theoretical approaches such as structuralism (see note 2), psycho-analysis (see note 54), discourse theory (see notes 91, 93), and semiotics (see notes 4, 24), which they find useful as tools for exploring the meanings of texts, how and why texts 'work' for their various readers and audiences, and for indications, therefore, of how media relate to broader social issues (e.g., notes 26, 32, 38, 40, 43).

Within social science, different disciplines have their own particular inflections. Psychologists have been among those most closely involved in attempts to analyse the impact of particular given media programmes or programme stimuli on particular individuals, drawing on social psychology to show how these 'individual effects' of media may be mediated by gender, family, group, and occupational and social class membership, as well as variables relating to an individual's previous experiences and personality. More than any other discipline within social science, psychologists have tested the limits of laboratory research, experimental design, and quantitative methods generally with respect to media.

168

Educationalists, either as teachers or as educational psychologists, have   4
paid particular attention to the role of media in the lives of children, how
children's exposure to and use of media is related to such aspects as their
stage of development, intelligence, educational attainment, and social
adjustment. They have looked to see how media can and do contribute to
children's learning, as well as exploring alleged detrimental effects of certain kinds of media output. They have studied the variables that may
account for children's acquisition of a range of encoding and decoding
skills, whether of print or audio-visual media. They have asked whether
different media relate in distinctive ways to different physical and cognitive
capacities (for example, the impact of television on visual skills in detecting
properties of spatial domain). In recent years there has been considerable
research into ways in which children use computers in the classroom, and
the place of computers in the dynamics of relationships between teachers
and children and between children themselves (see notes 12, 15, 23, 36,
47, 65, 77, 78, 94).

Political scientists have explored the part that media play in the electoral   5
process, or their contribution to major political goals, such as that of 'nation
building' in the newly independent regimes of the ex-colonies in the 1960s
and 1970s. They have shown how political groups and interests vie for
control over or access to the media. They have looked at the impact of
media on the presentation of political issues and the understanding of such
issues among readers or viewers (see notes 8, 53, 63, 83, 84, 87, 89, 90).
Economists have helped identify particular features of the economics of
media production, developing concepts such as that of 'first-copy costs'
(the total costs required in order to be able to produce the first copy of,
say, a newspaper) which then become useful for other social scientists in
seeking explanations of, for example, the persistence of oligopoly conditions in many media markets (i.e., where a few firms enjoy an entrenched
hegemony that effectively bars newcomers from gaining entry to a market;
see notes 20, 44).

The contributions of sociologists have been in three broad areas. Firstly,   6
they have told us how media organisations and their employees actually
work, their structures and working practices, how these are informed by
certain values and norms, and the relationship of these things to criteria of
profitability and effectiveness (e.g. notes 3, 10, 13, 81, 89, 90). Secondly,
they have looked at a very broad range of ways in which the media may be
said to contribute to social cohesiveness or to social conflict. They have
demonstrated the relevance of the concept of ideologies to media study:
sets of values which explicitly or more often implicitly are embedded both
within media practices and media products or texts (see notes 2, 4, 5, 24,
38, 39, 42, 88). Thirdly, they have broadened our understanding of the
ways in which people respond to these media texts, and of the interaction
between what is presented and the meanings that are read into media texts
(see notes 40, 45, 46, 67, 68, 71).

There are two points I would like to emphasise in this extremely cursory   7
sketch of some of the inflections of different disciplines. I think it could
be agreed that a prevailing, if not a dominant, preoccupation of social
science approaches has been to do with the 'power of the media', whether

that power is thought of in relation to whether, for example, media can 'win elections' or whether they 'depress reading standards' (more of such things in a moment). Following from that dominant preoccupation one can begin to understand why the concept of 'ideology' has been so influential, and why it has cropped up so often in the debates on media education (see Part 1A of this Reader, 'Dominant Attitudes to Mass Media'), because ideology is related to meaning, and everyone can agree that media generate meanings and that from meanings they derive their power. On the other hand, one may suspect that the preoccupation with power and ideology in part depends on their usefulness as tools serving to unify a very broad range of different discourses. I say this because I am sometimes uneasy that the preoccupation with power and ideology may tend to marginalise issues which are also important, either in themselves or in relation to some rather different kind of discourse (see the examples I have just given about computers in education), and that the net effect of this on the media education curriculum can be somewhat reductionist.

I have said that social science has concentrated rather more on the context of media products than on their internal content as such, though this is a rough and ready distinction which I would not want to press too far. In my own field of interest (international news flow), for example, much of the *raison d'être* for looking at the political economy of news flow is to gain a better understanding of the consistent patterns that studies have detected in content. Let me digress for a moment to examine how content and context are brought together in this area of interest.

Contextual features help to explain the high measure of consistency over time and across different media institutions in the kinds of international news, and the locations and sources of such news that are disseminated through major news media. Important features include:

(1) historical factors (the emergence in the nineteenth century of profitable mass media organisations, financed by a mixture of advertising, subscription, and state revenues, in a handful of western industrialised countries which also had extensive political and economic interests in other countries);

(2) ideologies of news: these are informed in part by major clients (advertisers wanting a suitable media environment in which to sell their products; financiers and governments needing up-to-the-minute news of financial and political developments across the world which could affect their investment and foreign policy interests; and of course the various and segmented populations of readers);

(3) general ideologies, which stem from the cultural and geographical location of the world's major news media and the nationalities of those who exercise most influence in them. Such ideologies were evident in the framework of cold war and superpower conflict within which so many international events were interpreted and analysed over many decades;

(4) organisational and working practices, which include the 'routinisation' of news: for example, the stationing of correspondents in particular locations thought likely to generate a continuous and reliable flow of news. Such 'news nets' tend to privilege news centres thought to be in 'crisis'

over stable centres, powerful over non-powerful, urban over rural, news sources associated with the political apparatus of the national state over non-state sources (see notes 34, 41, 80, 88).

The 'Everydayness' of Media

In later sections I am going to talk about how social science in general has contributed to our understanding of media power. Let me say, first of all, that this preoccupation with power among social scientists does little more than reflect a deep prejudice among so many members of the citizenry that the media are powerful. Let me ask you a few questions: do you think it is acceptable if very young children are exposed to horror videos? Would it worry you if Parliament allowed the ruling political party to make all senior appointments of, say, at least one major broadcasting institution? Do you think that the BBC should allocate slots unconditionally to nations or political movements with which the UK government currently has poor relations, so that such parties have a chance to put across their point of view (e.g., in 1991: Iraq, Libya, the PLO, the IRA)? Do you consider it would be appropriate for media producers to set quotas for (negative or positive) dramatic representations of women as wives or mothers, or of minority and ethnic groups? Do you think pornography and press accounts of cases of criminal sexual assault should be banned from circulation in prisons? Do you think the broadcasting institutions should lift controls on swearing and portrayals of sexual behaviour?

I suspect that the answers many of you give to those questions, and the reasons you have for them, will reveal quite strong beliefs about the power of the media to influence thought and behaviour, if not of yourselves, then of other people. You may take the view that society has to maintain certain 'standards', regardless of whether specific categories of media content have an 'effect' or not, but I think even this view is premised on assumptions about what then becomes of a society in which such standards are not maintained.

Regrettably, you will find that the sum total of so much social science research is not always of great assistance in helping you make up your mind on such issues. On many of the most 'serious' issues of media power (e.g. influence on political attitudes, effect of pornography and violence, etc.), research has often given an equivocal answer at best, engagingly subtle in its identification of interrelating variables, but only irritating as a basis for action.

Take violence on television, for example. What effect does it have? Does violent TV cause aggression? How do you define aggression? Can you distinguish between inclination towards aggression and a generalised state of arousal (which can be triggered by a wide variety of different stimuli)? How do you measure aggression once you have defined it? Do you set up a controlled experiment? Can you do this in a way which is not so unreal for the participants that the results tell us absolutely nothing about how those same people would behave in real life? Does it make any difference if the subjects are viewing in a group, with their spouses or parents? Is it aggression we should be worried about – how about an alternative theory that watching violent acts on television is more likely to create a general state of *fear*? And how are we going to define and measure that? Or, yet again, perhaps watching violence on television has a cathartic effect in the manner identified so long ago by Aristotle, namely, that in allowing for the vicarious experience of violence or of being violent it drains an individual's desire for such experience in real life. Indeed, could there be a mixture of effects?

Besides, what exactly *is* violence on TV? Does it include cartoon viol- 14 ence? Is watching violence in news programmes different from dramatised simulations of violence? If A kills B because A wants to rob B, is that different from when A kills B in order to stop B killing C? Does it really matter if on television A kills B, when what is really interesting about the programme is the camaraderie of C and D as they set about trying to capture A? What is the role of 'media forms' in all this: that is to say, can the addition of high-tempo music, fast pace of movement, or editing, affect how people react to dramatised violence? (See notes 16, 31, 38, 48, 96.)

When people talk about the effects of television violence what they often 15 have in mind is violence in the context of lawlessness, not so much violence in terms of, for example, war reporting and war documentary. David Morrison and Howard Tumber (note 70) refer to the widespread belief at the time of the Falklands War (often justified by unproven reference to the experience of the Vietnam war coverage) that unsanitised television pictures of war injury and destruction would tend to promote anti-war sentiment among viewers (a view running in a direction counter to concerns about dramatised violence). They argue that the most relevant factors in influencing how people would react to war coverage were most likely to do with, not the news coverage in itself, but the way in which that news coverage was assimilated within documentary programmes (which often adopt a structure of anti-war sentiment almost as a genre form), and with whether government explanations for war were perceived as credible or justifiable. Government policy in the Vietnam war was not perceived to be credible or justifiable in the same way, for example, as Allied involvement in the 1991 Gulf War. These comments indicate first of all that there is a wider range of beliefs about the effects of media violence than might seem to be the case if one looks only at the research addressing dramatic violence, and that speculation about actual effects at the very least needs to be set against much broader contextual factors.

Another example: does television depress reading standards? How much 16 time do children spend watching television, has it increased, and do children read as much as they used to? If not, is it significant if what they used to read was mainly comics or the sort of literature not regarded very favourably by schools? How do you measure reading standards? There are many different measurements available, and it is difficult to assess changes over time, given the variety of measurements that have been used and in the light of doubts about their validity and reliability. Are there other factors which might account for falling reading standards, if these could be measured (e.g., new methods of teaching reading, lack of interest of parents, under-resourced school libraries)? How are we going to relate viewing behaviour with reading behaviour? In terms of the overall number of hours spent on either activity? Or are we going to look at which particular programmes were looked at, or the kinds of books that were read? Have we allowed for the possibility that television might also stimulate reading? Or that many children read things while they sit in front of the television? If television could be shown to improve children's understanding of a wide variety of different oral registers of speech, improve their overall listening and oral communication skills, and their general knowledge about such subjects as current affairs or Africa, how would this knowledge affect our interpretation of any answers we got to our original question about reading standards?

Before I say a little more about the equivocation of a great deal of 'effects' research, I think it is useful to bear in mind some of the things which social anthropology is telling us about the role of media in our lives. It may not be what the media *do* to us that is significant, but rather the ways in which we *use* the media, how we often organise our personal timetables around media and, indeed, the inseparability of media from our everyday lives. This approach suggests both that the power of media is in part its ubiquitous *ordinariness*, and that it is extremely difficult to disentangle any particular 'effect' of the media out of all the contradictory media-derived stimuli which fill an average day and which interact intimately with all the other factors that impinge on our consciousness and which help explain our behaviour.

Here I want to draw attention to recent work by people like Sue Van Noort (note 92) who offer good examples of how media interweave into our lives, and of the relationship between media and culture. This is not a theme that has been entirely absent from the study of media (and we are well supplied with statistics about the amount of time people engage with media), but it is one which receives much more considered attention today and which usefully puts into perspective some of the more traditional concerns about the 'power' of the media which I shall be going on to consider in later parts of this chapter.

Concluding her account for the Primary Media Education Project (Sheffield Initiative), Sue Van Noort talks about the major influence on media in the lives of the nursery-age children whom she studied. The media influenced their clothing: Mutant Turtle T-shirts and sunglasses, Ghostbuster sweat shirts, He Man and Batman T-shirts, My Little Pony bags and hairslides. The media influenced their imaginative play (Turtle, Ghostbuster, and A Team games), they influenced the toys they or their parents bought (cuddly Spots, Postman Pat bags, Thomas the Tank Engine bath toys). She constantly heard the singing of theme songs. The media influenced the children's drawings and paintings, their choice of storybooks. The children said that watching television or videos was their preferred way of spending their leisure time, and they exhibited wide knowledge of programme content. Most could skilfully operate a video recorder. The programmes they watched included some that were directly addressed to their own age group, but their favourite programmes were those targeted at older children or adults.

Dorothy Hobson (note 46) gives an account of discussions about television among women telephone sales representatives of a large pharmaceutical and feminine hygiene company. These women used television programmes as part of their general discussion on their own lives and the lives of their families and friends, and to add interest to their working lives. Work was fitted in and around conversations which were sometimes triggered by television programmes or newspaper articles; sometimes the conversations led on to discussions about the media. Once the people in the office were talking about a television programme, they quickly adapted the conversation to include topics which were about their own lives and interests. Hobson notes that the use of events within fiction to explore experiences which were perhaps too personal or painful to talk about to a complete work group is a beneficial and creative way of extending the value of the programme into their own lives.

The media figure, therefore, as a substantial component of day-to-day 21 living, even outside specific viewing or reading contexts. Many accounts testify to this from a variety of countries and cultures, as provided by James Lull, for example (note 60).

These recent examples suggest that the most significant feature of our 22 media experiences is how we interweave them so *naturally*, so *ordinarily*, through so many areas of our day-to-day existence. Secondly, the fact that children wear My Little Pony hairslides, or that women telephone sales representatives organise their work around discussion of media, does not necessarily mean that media are 'powerful' in the traditional 'serious' sense (in determining political and social attitudes, for example), but what it does suggest is that people draw on media narratives as a *resource* (not, I hasten to add, a neutral, value-free resource) both to express meaning, to explore the meaning of their own lives, and as a way of relating to others. People also organise at least part of their lives, the temporal and spatial organisation of their lives, around media, and in so doing they express cultural values. Even the physical location of a television has cultural significance. Which rooms have television sets, or which rooms have the *best* television sets, who has access to those sets at what times of day, who tends to use, or has the authority to use, the remote control device, or who knows how to set the video timer – these are questions the answers to which vary across social class, age, gender, and ethnic groups (see note 60).

At another level, and as a departure from focusing on the effects of media 23 on, say political attitudes, we can concentrate on how political parties and groups, trades unions, and individual politicians adjust their own organisational strategies in jockeying for the attention of media. In the 1991 Gulf War we were able to see, more clearly than ever before, perhaps, how political and military strategies on both sides were influenced by constant second-guessing of media reaction (assumed both to represent and to inform public opinion) in a large number of countries.

How are the Media Powerful?
The answers to this question vary, among other things, according to (*a*) 24 period, (*b*) theory, and (*c*) research methodology. Denis McQuail (note 63) has categorised attempts to identify the relationship of media to social change in three different ways.

Interdependence
This broad approach sees the media as interactive with changes in society, but without there being one dominant direction of media effect.

25

Idealism
This category sees media as primary moulders of society as well as reflectors of it. Media have a variety of different kinds of influence: (*a*) individual value change, through influence on attitudes favourable to innovation, mobility, achievement, and consumption (see note 59); (*b*) media are used in a planned way to bring about change by applying them to large-scale programmes of development (see note 82); (*c*) technological determinism, wherein civilisations are characterised in terms of their dominant modes of communication (consider the terms the 'global village' or 'information society' – see notes 49, 63); (*d*) cultivation theory sees the media as creators of shared ways of selecting and viewing events, delivering technologically produced and mediated message systems (see notes 19, 73); (*e*) the cultural imperialism approach emphasises the role of media as destroyers of traditional cultures in the developing world (see notes 9, 61, 80, 88).

26

Materialism
Materialist perspectives are primarily Marxist: (*a*) classical Marxist approaches consider that the media, as a form of property, must be an instrument of the dominant, capitalist class; (*b*) the political economy approach is concerned to uncover just how the economic forces in capitalist media favour resistance to fundamental social changes (see note 29); (*c*) hegemonic theory emphasises the role of ruling ideas in achieving subordination to the interests of the dominant classes (see note 35); (*d*) dependency theory is interested in the functions (e.g., promoting consumerism, advertising western goods and life-styles, reporting world events through the prism of western political interests) which the transnational media perform in contributing to the economic dependency of poorer nations on the wealthier nations (see notes 9, 28, 33); (*e*) the Frankfurt School was especially concerned with the capacity of the 'superstructure' to subvert the historical processes of economic change, by making people and classes dependent on mediated images and terms of debate common to the system as a whole (see note 1); (*f*) the socio-cultural approach seeks to understand the meaning and place assigned to popular culture in the experience of particular groups in society, and also to explain how mass culture plays a part in integrating and subordinating potentially deviant or oppositional elements in society (see notes 14, 38).

27

McQuail also addresses the different kinds of media power by summarising the range of 'effects' commonly attributed to media. These include: changes to individual behaviour and attitudes; collective reactions; the public response to media 'campaigns'; diffusion of innovations; distribution of knowledge (e.g., including issues of agenda-setting and 'knowledge-gaps' between information 'haves' and 'have-nots'); long-term change in the form of the media's role in socialisation of children to social culture, media definitions of reality, and the structuring of reality through the ways in which countries, people, and interests come to be covered and represented;

28

cultivation theory; social control and consciousness formation; effects on other social institutions (e.g., effect on democratic process).

I shall be returning to some of these ideas and perspectives in talking about the history of research into the power of the media.

Two Broad Approaches to the Issue of Power

I shall draw a crude distinction between studies which are concerned primarily with individual reactions to media (individualist), and those which are primarily concerned with the society-wide role and significance of media (societal).

In the first category of 'individualist' studies, some are 'unfavourable' to media – for example, where they provide evidence to suggest that the behaviour of certain individuals is affected by exposure to media in what is deemed a negative way. I have already suggested that the methodological issues surrounding such claims are extremely complex. Other studies may be more reassuring because they purport to demonstrate either that the media can have 'pro-social' effects (such as greater respect for democratic procedures, learning about world events), or that there is such a great diversity of response, of different readings, among audiences that it is impossible to speak unambiguously or globally about 'effects' at all.

The second, 'societal', approach focuses on how the media relate to the broader society. Some studies in this category are very unfavourable in their depiction of the media: they suggest that media are agents of systematic ideological reinforcement at the service of capitalism. Others, more positively, suggest that media are a form of countervailing power, that they act as watchdogs on behalf of the public (as in 'the fourth estate' model of the role of the press) and are important sources of information on which democratic process must depend.

Over the course of the twentieth century, either one of these two approaches has tended to prevail over the other in an alternating pattern. However, each generation of research adds its own particular nuances, foci, and insights. I identify four main periods. The first, the 'mass society' period, brings us up to and perhaps includes the Second World War. Here, the negative, 'societal' model prevails. The second, 'reinforcement', period is marked pre-eminently by publication in 1960 of Joseph Klapper's summary of post-war research, *The Effects of the Mass Media* (note 52). During this time, it is largely a positive, 'individualist' view that prevails. The third period is the neo-Marxist period which can be dated from 1968 up to the early 1980s. This returns us to a negative, 'societal' view. This is followed, finally, by what Curran (note 20) has called the 'revisionist' period, or perhaps which could be called more neutrally the period of the 'critical reader', again, a period of positive 'individualism'.

The Mass Society Period, up to 1945

In this period, then, concern about the media is often posited on the basis of an implicit *mass society thesis* in which the individual is regarded as urbanised, typically alienated, subjected to manipulation through the media by commercial and political interests, deprived of meaningful support from intermediary institutions such as political parties or trade unions, and surrounded by an artificial culture that is constructed in the service of power and profitability, and which exploits aspects of traditional community culture and values without authentic concern for their nourishment and preservation. There is a prevailing belief that individuals are easy prey to media influences. These conclusions are based more on critical analysis than on empirical research. They are fed in part by growing conviction in and concern about the increasingly sophisticated uses of media for propaganda, as in the First World War, in helping to establish the rise of the Nazi party, and in advertising.

The Reinforcement Period, 1945–1968

Post-war empirical research, as summarised in Klapper's 1960 book, suggests on the whole that media do not generally account for major changes of attitude; they more often reinforce people's attitudes than change them, through people's exercise of selective attention, perception, and retention. People choose what they want to watch, which tends to be what they already agree with; they tend only to 'see' what they already know or believe, or only to remember that with which they feel most comfortable. These processes of selection are often mediated by the membership of an individual within the family, community, or social class: the values which lead people to be selective, in other words, are the values of the groups to which they belong. Where the media bring about change it is in the context of new knowledge and information. This 'limited effects' model was influential on how researchers thought of the audience: it helped generate the 'uses and gratifications' approach to the study of audiences, one that asked how and for what purposes people used the media rather than what was done to them by the media. (See notes 6, 7, 11, 25 and 56 for key empirical researchers in this period.) 35

A broad concern with how the media relate to the rest of society is rarely in evidence at this stage, and then only within a 'pluralist' model which considers that societies function organically through the competition for power, status, and wealth among groups which possess roughly equivalent (but different) chances in this competition. While they erred very much on the side of caution in attributing effects to media at home, researchers were far less inhibited in attributing power to media in the developing world, where they expected media to shape national consciousness (note 74), to diffuse agricultural and other important innovations (note 75), to deliver effective mass education programmes (note 82), or simply to bring about a more 'modern' psyche (note 59) – although such claims were modified substantially over time. 36

Neo-Marxism of the 1970s: 1968–1982

In social science generally, neo-Marxism developed as a reaction against Parsonian 'functionalist' models of society which seemed unable to come to terms with the genesis of social conflict. Talcott Parsons was the single most influential sociologist of his generation (note 73). His position was 37

177

succeeded both by the intellectual reactions of fellow-American social scientists like C. Wright Mills (note 66), and also by the drift to student radicalism which in itself was associated with reaction to the Vietnam war. Sociologists rediscovered social conflict, and Marxist theory seemed to provide some of the most insightful explanations.

Neo-Marxism brings media study back to the macro level. Just as in the period before the Second World War, the mood is critical and pessimistic. It is no longer posited on the same mass society model but rather on a model of capitalism and class conflict (not altogether absent, admittedly, in the pre-war work of Leavis (note 58)), within which subordinate classes are implicated in their own suppression through the workings of ideology. Like its pre-war mass society predecessor, neo-Marxism is not particularly impressed with empirical study for its own sake, and much more concerned with the development of theory. The Marxists are both able to live with the idea that media have 'limited effects' (because this confirms their view that media have an essentially reinforcement role, supporting a suppressive *status quo*) and at the same time to regard the media as infinitely subtle and variable in how they achieve their function of 'social reproduction' – in other words, the preservation over generations of the hegemony of certain social classes. The process of social reproduction is studied through analysis of representation – for example, of political coverage (trade unions, Cold War) or of social groups (ethnic minorities, women) – with a view to unmasking underlying ideologies, as well as through the study of political economy to reveal how the media are used to generate profits in conditions of very imperfect competition.

There are several major variants of neo-Marxist analysis of media. As a group these have been contrasted with the dominant non-Marxist tradition of this period, namely pluralism. Analysis of media within a theoretical framework which pits pluralists against Marxists, and vice versa, exerted a major influence on media study in the 1970s and 1980s and may be traced back to the Open University course, Mass Communication and Society, which first appeared in 1977, and in later work by Curran (see notes 17, 18).

The post-Klapper pluralist tradition regards the media as rather more than agents of reinforcement: it stresses the contexts within which the empirical evidence has suggested that media are influential. Curran *et al.* (note 17) summarise the most likely forms or occasions of influence: when audience attention is casual, when the media source is prestigious, trusted, or liked, when monopoly conditions are more complete, when the issue at stake is remote from the perceiver's experience or concern, when personal contacts are not opposed to the direction of the message, or when the recipient of the message is cross-pressured. The media are not seen as all-powerful, but they are seen as one of the social arenas to which different centres of power have access, and within which they contest one another.

Marxist and neo-Marxist political tradition is impatient of empiricism (although not entirely rejecting of it, as evidenced by the political economy school). It stresses the influence of media as agents of reinforcement, but in quite a different way and at quite a different level than the reinforcement message of Klapper.

These separate traditions influence which aspects of media are studied.

Curran *et al.* (note 17) give the following illustrations: Marxists look at media portrayals of violence in terms of whether these legitimise forces of law and order, build consent for the extension of coercive state regulation, or delegitimise outsiders and dissidents. Liberals asked whether media portrayals of violence promote and encourage violence in everyday life. When they are looking at voting practices, Marxists look on election coverage as dramatised ritual to legitimise power in liberal democracies, while liberals are interested in whether or not media actually changed the way people voted.

There are several traditions within neo-Marxism. All these approaches highlight the importance of ideology, but they differ in their conceptualisation of ideology. The most important include the following. 43

Structuralism
As represented in the work of Louis Althusser (note 2) this is primarily an approach to media texts which views ideology as a representation of the *imaginary* relationship of individuals with the real conditions of their existence. It has a material existence, inscribed within 'an apparatus and its practices'. Structuralism moves away from traditional Marxist preoccupation with economic and social determinants to 'the internal relations of signifying practices'. It shows that ideology is not simply a superstructural phenomenon that merely reflects the material conditions of existence. It is itself a part of those material conditions and can exhibit a degree of autonomy with respect to them. Jacques Lacan (note 54) helped show how this work could be linked with psychoanalysis, and has helped theorise the relationship of texts to readers. Here the reader (or 'subject') is no longer posited as a unique, unified being (as in Althusser) but as a decentred psychic entity, rooted in a range of discourses. 44

Political Economy
This approach criticises structuralism for preferring the theorised unconscious (idealism) to historical materialism (economism). Here the role of the media is to conceal and misrepresent the fundamental tensions between social classes. Ideology becomes the route through which struggle is obliterated rather than the site of struggle. The media seek to legitimate through the production of false consciousness. The main concern in this tradition is with the increasing monopolisation of the culture industry. For example, in the study of international news flow, the political economy approach focuses on the factors such as heavy first-copy costs, vertical integration (alliances between producers and consumers) on domestic news markets, and opportunities for market diversification, to help explain why the dominant news agencies are so strong and why it is so difficult for newcomers to establish themselves on world markets (note 79). Issues of ownership and control, and relations of media with other major corporations, the state, and the ruling classes (and in particular the ruling classes of the dominant nations) are central to political-economy analysis (note 77). However, this approach sees the economic base not only as a necessary but also as a *sufficient* explanation of cultural and ideological effects. In doing so it returns to the 'distorting mirror' model of media power. 45

179

Culturalist
This tradition rejects economism. It sees the cultural dimension not as   4(
residual but as inter-woven with all social practice (see notes 14, 40, and
more generally, the work of the Birmingham Centre for Cultural Studies).
Culturalist studies seek to place the media and other practices within a
society conceived of as a complex expressive totality. The role of 'moral
panics' ('teddy boys', 'mods and rockers', 'skinheads') have been studied
as examples of the manipulation of popular culture to engineer consent at
a time when the prevailing hegemony is said to be under threat from
Britain's declining economic world role. In news, however, media are not
the primary definers, but secondary (to political and the like).

Period of the 'Critical Reader'
This period returns us in some ways to the 1945–1968 period: there is   4:
renewed emphasis on the space that exists for different readings of media
texts and for varieties of production, but many fresh insights are generated
into how meanings are produced and the pleasures they provide. It is
stressed that people are active rather than passive consumers of media,
even if they have little direct influence over the media 'products' which
they are offered. (See notes 21, 22, 40, 67, 68, and 76 for some of the key
references.)

James Curran (note 18) has offered an analysis of the erosion of the older   4(
pluralist/Marxist dichotomy which he had helped to formulate. I have
adapted his account here as a framework to illustrate features of this new
period. A number of explanations are offered which reveal both a loss of
confidence within each of the two camps, but also elements of convergence
between their respective traditions.

(1)   Disenchantment with the class conflict model of society was perhaps   4!
stimulated by the entrepreneurial political philosophy of the Thatcher
years, and by the collapse of socialism in the Soviet Union and Eastern
Europe. Michel Foucault (note 27) offered a contrasting ('neo-pluralist'?)
model of a complex and multi-faceted conspectus of society in which mani-
fold relationships of power are said to be in play in different situations.
Patriarchal rather than class exploitation was a further alternative approach
to conflict analysis for some of those who applied Foucault's insights.
Marxism has been found considerably wanting by many feminist writers
in the process of identifying the genesis of gender divisions. This legacy,
Curran claims, has promoted a 'decentring of cultural and media research':
in other words, it is no longer considered necessary to relate particular
aspects of media or media-related activity to their broader political-
economic context. Hence, for example, it is possible to offer reader-text
discourse analysis which makes no reference to power relationships, or
which is situated within a model of society in which power is assumed to
be widely diffused.

(2)   The liberal tradition, meanwhile, has entered new areas, like study   5(
of the media impact on the structures and functioning of the political

system, socio-cultural integration, and the relationship between media and social change.

(3) Marxism in its most totalising form has been rejected, as in the breakdown of the assumption of total correspondence between the economic and the political. This had already been encouraged by the writing of Althusser (note 2), who emphasised the autonomy of social practice. 51

(4) The concept of 'dominant ideology' has also collapsed, often shown to crumble into a miscellany of themes and ideas not accepted by the subordinate classes. Social cohesion has been shown to owe more to resignation and routine rather than ideological incorporation. This disillusion was 'anticipated' by Antonio Gramsci (note 35), for whom the ruling class was a shifting and often precarious alliance of different social strata. Dominant ideology has been redefined as a field of dominant discourses, with the media viewed as a site of contest. 52

The Marxist or critical tradition had adopted an increasingly defensive posture in the face of these developments, conceding more space to the influence of such factors as individualist values, source availability, and available discourses. Philip Schlesinger (note 81), for example, has argued within the context of analysis of 'agenda setting', that 'primary definers' of media agendas sometimes offer conflicting frames of reference to the media, that the concept is simplistic, that primary definers change over time, and that the concept of agenda-setting overstates the passivity of the media. 53

Such considerations, then, bring the Marxist tradition close to the traditional pluralist approach, but for two arguments: that for Marxists the balance of power is still uneven, and that they attach special weight to the factor of media ownership (for instance, because of its influence over or control of senior appointments). 54

In illustration of the collapse of the old pluralist-Marxist dichotomy, Curran (note 18) refers to recent work on media production and reception which tends to stress (i) inconsistencies and ambivalences in texts, and 'producerly' texts that delegate the production of meaning to the viewer-producer, and (ii) the reconceptualisation of the audience as an active producer of meaning. This encourages a more cautious assessment of media influence. It also encourages a refocus, away from the political to the popular: an interest not so much in how media can retard political struggle but how and why they are popular, how they create pleasure. 55

There are three distinctive tendencies in what Curran calls the new revisionism: 56

(a) the radical tendency. This continues to situate cultural consumption in the broader context of social struggle;

(b) another approach sees popular culture as providing the raw material for experimenting with and exploring social identities in the context of a postmodernist society where the walls of tradition are crumbling;

(c) rejection of élitist pessimism. From Bourdieu comes the insight that cultural and aesthetic judgements have no absolute, universal validity but are merely ways of defining, fixing, and legitimating social differences. 'High' and 'popular' culture are related terms; because meaning is defined in the process of consumption, audiences can create quality in popular culture. Valorisation is less about application of literary norms, more about audience pleasure. But there is caution about the focus on pleasure – such a shift runs the risk of seeming to validate Hollywood domination of the worldwide television market, and even the most 'creative' audiences can be confined.

Beyond Power

Is an emphasis on the power of media enough? Does it tell us enough about the media to adequately understand them? While the history of media research certainly does tell us a great deal about their power and influence, it is notable that within this research there are a number of very different kinds of discourse. The kind of discourses within and across which, for example, the variety of Marxist traditions have engaged battle is very different from that in which educators argue about the influence of television on cognitive skills, or that in which a more recent generation of scholars have engaged in studying state-wide policies for media control and development (stimulated considerably by the fashion for deregulation of media industries in the 1980s and into the 1990s). In the literature, certain fashions of theory and focus seem to dominate particular periods, and unfashionable issues to find themselves marginalised. In the context of media education I would argue that this is something to be guarded against, on the following grounds. Firstly, media education claims to be cross-curricular in scope, and therefore cannot afford to identify itself solely with one particular intellectual tradition or preoccupation if it wishes this claim to be taken seriously. Secondly, over-cultivation of particular traditions can and does sometimes lead to jargon-ridden sterility; more equitable distribution of attention to the different discourses of media education is more likely to lead to creative new discoveries and experimentation in teaching.

Notes

1. Theodor Adorno and Max Horkheimer, 'The Culture Industry: Enlightenment as Mass Deception', in *The Dialectics of Enlightenment*, New York, Herder and Herder, 1972.
2. Louis Althusser, 'Ideology and Ideological State Apparatuses', in *Lenin and Philosophy and Other Essays*, London, New Left Books, 1971.
3. Manuel Alvarado and Edward Buscombe, *Hazell: The Making of a TV Series*, London, BFI/Latimer, 1978.
4. Roland Barthes, *Mythologies*, London, Jonathan Cape, 1971.
5. Tony Bennett, Graham Martin, Colin Mercer, and Janet Woollacott, *Culture, Ideology and Social Process*, London, Batsford and the Open University, 1981.
6. B. Berelson, 'What Missing the Newspaper Means', in Paul Lazarsfeld and F. M. Stanton, *Communications Research 1948–9*, New York, Harper, 1949, pp. 111–29.
7. B. Berelson, 'The State of Communication Research', *Public Opinion Quarterly*, vol. 23, no. 1, 1959, pp. 1–6.
8. Jay Blumler and Denis McQuail, *Television in Politics: Its Uses and Influence*, London, Faber and Faber, 1968.
9. Oliver Boyd-Barrett, 'Media Imperialism', in James Curran *et al.*, *Mass Communication and Society*, London, Arnold, 1977.

10. Oliver Boyd-Barrett, *The International News Agencies*, London, Constable, 1980.

11. Warren Breed, 'Social Control in a Newsroom: A Functional Analysis', *Social Forces*, vol. 33, 1955, pp. 467–77.

12. J. Bryant and D. Anderson, *Children's Understanding of Television*, London, Academic Press, 1983, pp. 221–43.

13. Tom Burns, *The BBC: Public Institution and Private World*, London, Macmillan, 1977.

14. Stan Cohen and Jock Young, *The Manufacture of News*, London, Constable, 1973.

15. Cedric Cullingford, *Children and Television*, Farnborough, Gower, 1984.

16. Guy Cumberbatch and Denis Howitt, *A Measure of Uncertainty: The Effects of the Mass Media*, London, John Libbey, 1989.

17. James Curran, Michael Gurevitch, and Janet Woollacott, 'The Study of the Media: Theoretical Approaches', in Michael Gurevitch *et al.*, *Culture, Society and the Media*, London, Methuen, 1982.

18. James Curran, 'The New Revisionism in Mass Communication Research: A Reappraisal', *European Journal of Communication*, vol. 5, 1990, pp. 135–64.

19. James Curran, Michael Gurevitch, and Janet Woollacott (eds), *Mass Communication and Society*, London, Arnold, 1977.

20. James Curran and Jean Seaton, *Power without Responsibility*, London, Fontana, 1981.

21. Ariel Dorfman and Armand Mattelart, *How to Read Donald Duck*, International General, 1975.

22. Ariel Dorfman, *The Empire's Old Clothes*, London, Pluto Press, 1983.

23. Aimée Dorr, *Television and Children*, London, Sage, 1986.

24. Umberto Eco, *A Theory of Semiotics*, London, Macmillan, 1977.

25. L. Festinger, *A Theory of Cognitive Dissonance*, New York, Row Peterson, 1957.

26. John Fiske and John Hartley, *Reading Television*, London, Methuen, 1978.

27. Michel Foucault, *The History of Sexuality*, Harmondsworth, Penguin, 1983.

28. Andre G. Frank, *Capitalism and Underdevelopment*, Harmondsworth, Penguin, 1971.

29. Nicholas Garnham, 'Contribution to a Political Economy of Mass Communication', *Media, Culture and Society*, vol. 1, no. 2, 1975, pp. 123–46.

30. George Gerbner, 'Cultural Indicators – The Third Voice' in George Gerbner, Larry Gross, and William Melody (eds), *Communications Technology and Social Policy*, New York, Wiley, pp. 553–73.

31. George Gerbner and Larry Gross, 'Living with Television: The Violence Profile', *Journal of Communication*, vol. 26, no. 2, 1976, pp. 173–99.

32. Glasgow University Media Group, *Bad News*, London, Routledge, 1977.

33. Peter Golding, 'Media Professionalism in the Third World: The Transfer of an Ideology', in James Curran *et al.*, *Mass Communication and Society*, London, Arnold, 1977.

34. Peter Golding and Philip Elliot, *Making the News*, London, Longman, 1979.

35. Antonio Gramsci, *Selections from the Prison Notebooks*, London, Lawrence and Wishart, 1971.

36. Patricia Greenfield, *Mind and Media*, London, Fontana, 1984.

37. Michael Gurevitch, Tony Bennett, James Curran, and Janet Woollacott, *Culture, Society and the Media*, London, Methuen, 1982.

38. Stuart Hall, 'The Determination of News Photographs', in Stan Cohen and Jock Young, *The Manufacture of News*, London, Constable, 1973.

39. Stuart Hall, 'The Rediscovery of Ideology: Return of the Repressed in Media

Studies', in Michael Gurevitch *et al.*, *Culture, Society and the Media*, London, Methuen, 1982, pp. 56–90.

40. Stuart Hall, Dorothy Hobson, Andrew Lowe, and Paul Willis, *Culture, Media and Language*, London, Heinemann, 1980.

41. Phil Harris, *News Dependence: The Case for a New World Information Order* (final report to UNESCO of a study of the international news media), Paris, UNESCO, 1977.

42. John Hartley, *Understanding News*, London, Methuen, 1982.

43. Terence Hawkes, *Structuralism and Semiology*, London, Methuen, 1977.

44. Fred Hirsch and D. Gordon, *Newspaper Money*, London, Hutchinson, 1975.

45. Dorothy Hobson, *Crossroads: The Drama of a Soap Opera*, London, Methuen, 1982.

46. Dorothy Hobson, 'Women Audiences and the Workplace' in M. E. Brown (ed.), *Television and Women's Culture*, Sydney, Currency Press, 1989.

47. Bob Hodge and David Tripp, *Children and Television*, Cambridge, Polity Press, 1986.

48. Denis Howitt and Guy Cumberbatch, *Mass Media, Violence and Society*, New York, John Wiley, 1975.

49. Harold Innis, *Empire and Communication*, Oxford, Clarendon Press, 1950.

50. Morris Janowitz, *The Community Press in an Urban Setting*, Glencoe, Ill., Free Press, 1952.

51. Elihu Katz and Paul F. Lazarsfeld, *Personal Influence*, Glencoe, Ill., Free Press, 1955.

52. Joseph Klapper, *The Effects of the Mass Media*, Glencoe, Ill., Free Press, 1960.

53. S. Kraus and D. Davis, *The Effects of Mass Communication on Political Behaviour*, University Park, Pennsylvania State University Press, 1976.

54. Jacques Lacan, *Language of the Self*, Baltimore, John Hopkins University Press, 1968.

55. Kurt Lang and Gladys Lang, 'The Mass Media and Voting', in E. Burdick and A. J. Brodbeck (eds), *American Voting Behaviour*, New York, Free Press, 1959.

56. Paul Lazarsfeld, B. Berelson, and H. Gaudet, *The People's Choice*, New York, Duell, Sloan and Pearce, 1944.

57. Paul Lazarsfeld and F. M. Stanton, *Communications Research 1948–9*, New York, Harper, 1949.

58. F. R. Leavis and Denys Thompson, *Culture and Environment*, London, Chatto and Windus, 1948.

59. David Lerner, *The Passing of Traditional Society*, New York, Free Press, 1958.

60. James Lull, *Families Watching Television*, London, Sage, 1988.

61. Armand Mattelart, *Multinational Corporations and the Control of Culture*, Brighton, Harvester Press, 1979.

62. J. McGinnis, *The Selling of the President*, New York, Trident Press, 1969.

63. Marshall McLuhan, *Understanding Media*, London, Sphere, 1968.

64. Denis McQuail, *Mass Communication Theory: An Introduction*, London, Sage, 1982.

65. Máire Messenger Davies, *Television is Good for Your Kids*, London, Hilary Shipman, 1989.

66. C. Wright Mills, *The Power Elite*, New York, Oxford University Press, 1956.

67. David Morley, 'Cultural Transformations: the politics of resistance', in Howard Davis and Paul Walton (eds), *Language, Image, Media*, Oxford, Basil Blackwell, pp. 104–19.

68. David Morley, *The 'Nationwide' Audience*, London, British Film Institute, 1980.

69. David Morrison and Howard Tumber, *Journalists at War*, London, Sage, 1988.
70. Hamid Mowlana, *International Flow of Information: A Global Report and Analysis*, Paris, UNESCO Reports and Papers on Mass Communication, 1985.
71. Laura Mulvey, 'Visual pleasure and narrative cinema', *Screen*, vol. 16, no. 4, Autumn 1975.
72. Graham Murdock, 'Large Corporations and the Control of the Communications Industries', in Michael Gurevitch *et al.*, *Culture, Society and the Media*, London, Methuen, 1982, pp. 118–50.
73. Talcott Parsons, *The Social System*, Glencoe, Ill., Free Press, 1949.
74. Lucien Pye, *Communications and Political Development*, Princeton, NJ, Princeton University Press, 1963.
75. Everett Rogers, *The Diffusion of Innovations*, Glencoe, Ill., Free Press, 1962.
76. Nicholas Ryder, *Science, Television and the Adolescent*, London, IBA Report, 1982.
77. G. Saloman, *The Interaction of Media, Cognition and Learning*, San Francisco, Jossey-Bass, 1979.
78. G. Saloman and T. Leigh, 'Predispositions about learning from print and television', *Journal of Communication*, Spring 1984, pp. 119–35.
79. Rohan Samarajiwa, 'Third World Entry to the World Market in News: Problems and Possible Solutions', *Media, Culture and Society*, vol. 6, 1984, pp. 119–36.
80. Herbert Schiller, *Mass Communication and American Empire*, New York, Augustus M. Kelly, 1969.
81. Philip Schlesinger, 'Rethinking the Sociology of Journalism', in Margaret Ferguson (ed.), *Public Communication*, London, Sage, 1989.
82. Wilbur Schramm, *Mass Media and National Development*, Stanford, Stanford University Press, 1964.
83. Colin Seymour-Ure, *The Political Impact of the Mass Media*, London, Constable, 1974.
84. Colin Seymour-Ure, *The British Press and Broadcasting since 1945*, London, Basil Blackwell, 1991.
85. Anthony Smith, *The Geopolitics of Information*, Faber and Faber, 1980.
86. Surgeon General's Scientific Advisory Committee, *Television and Growing Up: The Impact of Televised Violence*, Washington, DC, GPO, 1972.
87. Michael Tracey, *The Production of Political Television*, London, Routledge, 1977.
88. John Tulloch and Manuel Alvarado, *Doctor Who: The Unfolding Text*, London, Macmillan, 1983.
89. Jeremy Tunstall, *The Westminster Lobby Correspondents*, London, Routledge, 1970.
90. Jeremy Tunstall, *Journalists at Work*, London, Constable, 1971.
91. T. A. Van Dijk, *News as Discourse*, Hillstock, NJ, Lawrence Erlbaum, 1988.
92. Sue Van Noort, Research Report for the BFI Primary Media Education Project (grant aided by the Calouste Gulbenkian Foundation) unpublished manuscript, 1990.
93. L. S. Vygotsky, *Thought and Language*, Cambridge, Mass., MIT Press, 1962.
94. M. Winick and C. Winick, *The Television Experiment: what children see*, London, Sage, 1979.
95. Mallory Wober and Barrie Gunter, *Television and Social Control*, Aldershot, Avebury, 1988.

The Creative Tradition:
Teaching Film and TV Production
Manuel Alvarado and Wendy Bradshaw

Introduction
There has been a tradition of film-making that stretches almost as far back as teaching film analysis. It has taken place at all levels of the education system, using 8 mm and 16 mm equipment, whenever teachers had access to the necessary resources – equipment, money, small class size, and time (both curricular and non-curricular).

However, the most systematic courses have been developed in the further education/technical college and art school sectors. These were the sectors where examination and curricular pressures were the lightest in the 1960s and 1970s, and as a result offered the institutional space for innovation and imaginative syllabus experimentation. Some of this work is well documented in BFI and SEFT (Society for Education in Film and Television) publications, but the absence of institutional requirements for such courses meant that such innovation rarely lasted beyond the period the lecturer(s) responsible remained in the college.

Important as much of the further education experimentation in film studies undoubtedly was – and many of these innovations influenced teaching in all other areas of the education system (cf. Jim Kitses and Ann Mercer's influential *Talking About the Cinema*[1]) – the imperatives involved with the creation of the new technical qualifications and pre-vocational courses during the 1980s have removed many of the possibilities for such experimentation. These developments will be returned to later in this section. First, we shall provide a short account of the history of such work in colleges of art and the film schools.

Colleges of Art
The range of film studies courses offered in art schools over the decades is, with one or two exceptions, poorly documented. The best-known courses established in the early 1960s were those at Hornsey, Kingston, Bradford, Birmingham, Bournemouth, Sheffield, the Royal College of Art, and the Slade School of Fine Art. Broadly speaking, this work evolved in liberal studies departments and largely coincided with the establishment of the Dip.AD (Diploma in Art and Design) in 1963. The Dip.AD was created as a result of the recommendations of the Coldstream Report 1960[2] (and confirmed by the Report of the Summerson Committee 1964[3]) which found that previous NDD (National Diploma in Design) courses were too vocational, too short, and too uneven in quality.

186

The fine art practical traditions of the art schools provided an ideal location for taking film studies seriously, but the general ethos meant that particular areas of work were favoured over others. Where film analysis took place student preference focused on the auteurist and avant-garde traditions of European, non-Hollywood cinema, but it was the practical activity of film-making which was most in accord with the individualist, anti-critical ideologies of art schools.

One significant factor in the increase of film studies, both critical and practical, was the Dip.AD requirement (a diploma which some defined as a 'liberal education in art' and not a full professional qualification) that 15 per cent of the entire three-year course should be spent on the 'History of Art and Complementary Studies'. Seen in the early stages of the new qualification as a key element in the introduction of structured film teaching (cf. Peter Kneebone[4]), within a decade Gerry Coubro' was to attack the 'nebulous and diffident' thinking of the Coldstream Committee for allocating so small a proportion of course time to Complementary Studies, which resulted in students' general lack of interest in such non-studio activities as film studies. Coubro' wrote:

> As such, the notion of Complementary Studies stands more as a wish fulfilment than as a reality because it both ignores the fact that there are problems and methods peculiar to them as disciplines in their own right, and also reduces the issue of critical methodology and the essential difference between the criticism of products, whether a film or painting, and the making of them to the practical issue of teaching and teachers.[5]

Coubro' here refers to the oft-debated dichotomy in art schools between an ideology 'based on practice, vocationalism and the acquisition and development of technical skills', and the encouragement of analytic and critical skills based on linguistic abilities. Despite this division, the work in the teacher training section of the Hornsey College of Art pioneered important work encouraging future art teachers to relate analytic to practical production work in the classroom (three lecturers – Douglas Lowndes, Bob Ferguson, and Keith Kennedy – all published books based on work undertaken in that department[6]).

Some students from that period managed to find employment in the film and TV industries, but the significant development of courses more recently at colleges such as West Surrey College of Art and Design and Harrow College have fed students increasingly into the industry. However, it is the film schools which appeared to offer more directly vocationally oriented courses.

Film Schools

Many countries have long-established national film schools, but the National Film and Television School in Britain, established as a result of the findings of the Lloyd Report in 1967, did not open until 1971.[7] Prior to that there were four institutions, offering different professional courses at different levels. There was the private and non-subsidised London

School of Film Technique (now the London International Film School);[8] the Cinematographic Department of the London Polytechnic (now the Polytechnic of Central London); the Department of Film and Television at the Royal College of Art; and the Department of Drama at Bristol University. None of these courses, however, could provide any guarantee or assurance that students would gain entry to the film or TV industries on graduation.

One general curricular attitude that did connect these institutions and courses (including the National Film and Television School) was a general lack of interest in locating the technical and craft-based skills of a production course within the context of extensive structured screenings and systematic classes on the analysis and criticism of world cinema and television.[9] Although the course at the PCL has changed significantly since the early 1970s (and now includes substantial historical, theoretical, and critical elements in its degrees) and one hopes that the other courses at least include 'master classes' at the Steenbeck, the anxiety of many British cultural critics is that our training courses still make little provision for increasing students' knowledge and 'visual image store' of world cinema, which they discern in the films of so many young film-makers from other countries.

Nevertheless, there have been two major developments in this sector since the 1970s. The first is the increase in such courses, with the London Institute, Sheffield Polytechnic, and Christchurch College, Canterbury, among others, now offering exciting training possibilities. The second is the increasing number of graduates from these schools managing to find employment in the burgeoning media industries. The next stage in this development are the moves to bring education, training, and employment more closely together through the establishment of nationally approved industrial qualifications at both pre-vocational and vocational levels.

The Shift to Vocationalism

The relationship between education and training, theory and practice, and employment, is high on the agenda, motivated by current government trends in education and training. Various measures are in place and are being introduced which herald a new age of vocationalism. Government policies and practices reveal an overall strategy to link education, training, and employment. This is central to the government's reports: *Working Together – Education and Training* (1986); *Review of Vocational Qualifications* (1986); and *Education and Training for the Twenty-first Century* (1991).[10]

A perceived mismatch between education and employment, between the school and college curriculum and the skill requirements of employers and industries, forms the basis for the changes that are taking place. The Training and Enterprise Councils (TECs) and the Scottish Local Enterprise Companies (LECs) are central to these changes. The TECs, which were formally launched in April 1989, will eventually take over the local work of the Training, Enterprise and Education Directorate (TEED). Central to the philosophy of TECs is employer involvement in the education system, and central to the remit is the development and strengthening of education/

188

industry links. The functions of TECs include Work-Related Further Education, the Technical and Vocational Education Initiative (TVEI), Education–Business Partnerships and Compacts.

The aim of TVEI, introduced in 1983, is the reshaping of the education 13 curriculum to include vocational elements of a technical bias in order to make education more relevant to the world of work and to ease the transition from school to work. Work placements for students form a central part of the initiative. In the words of TEED, the aim is that of 'helping to educate young people who will be able to take their place . . . in a more highly skilled workforce and in the wider community in which they live'. Aimed at the 14–19 age group, the intention of TVEI is to increase and enhance students' technological awareness and knowledge. TVEI is not in itself a course, but it can be part of all existing provision, including GCSE (General Certificate of Secondary Education). A large proportion of TVEI schemes include media studies. In itself, the initiative allows for the possibility of combining the more theoretical side of media studies with a technical skills learning component. This is especially so as funding for the scheme can be used to build up or complement existing technical resources.

Compact is concerned with forging links between industries/employers 14 and schools. Within this scheme students attend work placements, teachers are involved in work-shadowing exercises, and employers are given the opportunity to engage with the educational curriculum. The overall aim is to heighten employment opportunities for school-leavers through their gaining direct knowledge of working environments and the skills associated with particular jobs. Compacts are run by local education authorities and, while covering all industries, can allow media education students to gain experience of what is involved in working in the media industries. Kensington and Chelsea Local Education Authority (LEA) have, for example, forged links with the BBC in their Compact scheme.

Other initiatives designed to forge education/industry links include the 15 Certificate in Pre-Vocational Education (CPVE), Professional, Industrial, and Commercial Updating (PICKUP), Enterprise in Higher Education, and the reshaping of the qualifications and certification system through the National Curriculum, the Schools Examination and Assessment Council (SEAC), GCSE, and National Vocational Qualifications (NVQs). All these initiatives have a bearing on media education.

Most of these initiatives are funded by the Training Enterprise and 16 Education Directorate, others by the Department of Education and Science (DES), while the Department of Trade and Industry (DTI) is also involved in, and has resources for, education/training/industry link initiatives.

The government's *Review of Vocational Qualifications* has as its central 17 aim a change in the whole qualifications system from schooling to further and higher education, to incorporate all education and training provision wherever it occurs, whether in the workplace or in education, into a coherent pattern. One of the major concerns of the *Review of Vocational Qualifications* was the perceived gap between education and employment and the need to bridge 'the unhelpful divide between so-called academic and so-called vocational qualifications'.

With these concerns to the forefront, the government established the 18

National Council for Vocational Qualifications (NCVQ) to oversee, administer, and develop National Vocational Qualifications (NVQs). The qualifications comprise units based on levels and areas of competences which relate to the functions and skills required to perform particular occupational areas. Overall, these signify the occupational standards. While they are predominantly skill-based, relating to occupational competencies, they also embody a theoretical dimension, known as 'underpinning' or 'inherent' knowledge relating to the industry. Each qualification is awarded on the basis of the ability of the individual to perform the key tasks set out in each of the units associated with a particular occupational area. The individuals hold and present the qualifications gained in their own 'National Record of Achievement' or portfolio. The qualifications signify 'a guarantee of competence to do a job not just in theory but in practice',[11] and can be seen as an attempt to bring together academic and vocational learning.

These standards are primarily defined by employers and are drawn up by groupings called 'Industry Lead Bodies'. These include representatives from the employer organisations, trade unions, and professional groups. Within the area of media studies several Industry Lead Bodies have been established. The Industry Lead Body dealing with film and broadcasting has been set up with the title 'Skill-Set'. Other Industry Lead Bodies deal with the different aspects of media education, for example, the Arts and Entertainment Training Council, the Design Council, the Photography Lead Body, and the Arts and Entertainment Technical Training Council. The Industry Lead Bodies will eventually be subsumed into the newly-formed Industry Training Organisations which will have NVQ developments as part of their remit.

Once the Industry Lead Bodies have set the standards they are submitted to awarding bodies, such as the Business and Technician Education Council (BTEC), the Royal Society of Arts (RSA), and the City and Guilds of London Institute. The qualifications are then presented to the National Council for Vocational Qualifications for approval and endorsement.

The aim is to have most NVQs, apart from the higher professional level, in place by the end of 1992. The government's intention is that by 1992, levels 1–4 of NVQs will be in place, affecting 80 per cent of the working population.[12]

The aim of the NVQ structure is to set in place a system of flexible qualifications which are available at any time whatever the individual's age, which are transferable, and which will improve progression routes through training and employment. NVQs can be acquired in the workplace, in the education context, and at home. Open learning and distance learning are part of the move towards flexible delivery systems.

While NVQs are industry-led in terms of the definition of occupational areas, competences, and standards, they link in a wider sense with the reshaping and redefinition of skills and qualifications within education and with the overall move towards vocationalism.

Linkages between the NVQ framework, GCSE and 'A' level, BTEC courses, and the work of the National Council for Vocational Qualifications and the Schools Examination and Assessment Council are encouraged. Various measures are being introduced and proposed to bring together academic and vocational studies and qualifications. BTEC First Diploma courses are now open to 16- to 19-year-olds in schools, City and Guilds have responsibility for CPVE, and the government proposes setting up a new system of qualifications, namely, Ordinary and Advanced Diplomas. These will be awarded on the basis of gaining academic and/or vocational qualifications. All these measures, including NVQs, as set out in the White Paper *Education and Training for the Twenty-first Century*, are an attempt 'to remove the remaining barriers to equal status between the so-called academic and vocational routes'.

In addition, the government proposes establishing a general NVQ as well 25 as occupationally specific NVQs. The general NVQ will be education based, for full-time students in colleges and, when appropriate, schools. The qualifications will provide a basis for progression to occupationally specific NVQs, offering a preparation for work in broad occupational areas and/or preparation for entry into higher education.

Within the NVQ framework there are five levels, from the basic level 26 up to and including professional standards. Broadly speaking, the framework for equivalences between NVQs and educational qualifications is:

Level 1 – pre-academic, foundation vocational level, national curriculum;
Level 2 – GCSE;
Level 3 – A/AS level, university entrance;
Level 4 – degree, professional qualifications;
Level 5 – higher professional qualifications, and post-graduate vocational qualifications.

The relationship between the general NVQ and the occupationally-specific NVQ within the five levels is:[13]

General NVQs:
Level 1 – pre-vocational certificate;
Level 2 – broad-based craftsmen foundation;
Level 3 – vocationally-related national diploma, advanced craft preparation;
Level 4 – vocationally-related degree/higher national diploma.

Occupationally-specific NVQs:
Level 1 – semi-skilled;
Level 2 – basic craft certificate;
Level 3 – technician, advanced craft, supervisor;
Level 4 – higher technician, junior management;
Level 5 – professional qualification, middle management.

The overall aim is the establishment of 'an integrated programme' of certification in education, training, and work experience, to make education more relevant to the adult world of work, and to break the disparities between academic and vocational qualifications.

The NVQ initiative, together with the initiatives mentioned above, are 27 grounded in an attempt to redress what is perceived as a major skills problem, a lack of cohesion between education and employment, and the inability of employers to provide for, and produce, systematic training. These concerns were expressed in the government-commissioned report *Competence and Competition* (1984).[14] One of the major findings of the report was the lack of training and skills within the UK compared with other European countries.

NVQs are an attempt to bring our qualifications system in line with other   28
European countries in preparation for the lifting of the trade barriers in 1992. The European Community has set up an organisation called CEDE-FOP, the European Centre for the Development of Vocational Training (Centre européen pour le développement de la formation professionelle) with the express purpose of examining comparability of qualifications in order to enhance the mobility of labour. Qualifications are currently being assessed on a sector-by-sector basis, relating to industries, the professions, and so on.

Theory v. Practice?

These initiatives have fed into what is perceived as a gap between education   29
and the world of work, and within education between the academic and the vocational. In the area of media studies the academic and the vocational have often coexisted in an uneasy relationship. This division clearly operated in film courses in arts schools, as referenced earlier. Within media studies, the technical and vocational aspects of the curriculum have often taken second place, overridden by notions of a liberal education associated with media studies. Critical awareness has taken precedence over practical applications. This rests on a humanistic/individualistic approach associated with creativity and self-expression which technology, in its associations with mass culture, mass society, and control, is somehow deemed to destroy. This is evident in the concept of 'technicism' and the notion of 'the technicist trap' (cf. Len Masterman) which is grounded in the fear that concentration on technical skills will supersede and displace critical practice, and restrict knowledge and awareness.

Where engagement with the practical occurred it often took the form   30
of practical exercises geared towards gaining greater understanding in an immediate sense of the meaning of images and representations. In engagement with the technologies associated with production, it was often the terrain of the so-called 'low achievers', those who were deemed unable to grasp the conceptual framework of academic and theoretical study. As Tim Blanchard writes, 'Technicism has . . . held the less hidden agenda that courses with an ostensible practical and vocational bent are most suitable for those "less intellectually able" '.[15] This again serves to privilege the academic and reify theory over practice – there is, after all, no 'theoreticist trap' on the agenda. Again, this is grounded in traditional divisions with all their class resonances between mental and manual labour, education and training, the former belonging more to intellectual activity and to education with its notions of enlightenment, the latter to vocationalism and training, with its culture of labourism and preparing the masses for work.

A greater awareness of the media industries for both students and   31

192

teachers cannot go amiss. It is necessary to equip young people with skills for the labour market, in the same way as the acquisition of those skills enhance opportunities for those young people, and increases awareness of what is involved in working in the industry. Technical training and knowledge of technologies has the capacity to place students in a more powerful position in gaining employment or further training or both. With the constant and rapid change in technologies associated with the mass media this is ever more critical. Technical skills themselves are, on the one hand, becoming more specialised, for example, with computerisation, on the other, with the trend towards multi-skilling and flexibility, opening up to incorporate more occupational activities and skills. Developments in technology mean that a film-maker, for example, could need to know the skills of film and electronic operations. In the area of post-production, it is not so much a case of acquiring traditional film skills; as Mark Bishop states, 'In my view, the post-production business has more in common with the computer industry of the 90s than the British film industry of the 50s, and its training and recruitment should reflect that.'[16]

This also points to the further fact that when it comes to technical jobs in the industry, media technical training, whether in film or art college or gained in further education, does not necessarily bear a one-to-one relationship. Physics and maths are qualifications looked for in gaining certain jobs associated with television and engineering degrees or HND. These qualifications certainly apply for entry to many of the BBC's training schemes. However, with jobs in the industry becoming more multi-skilled, media studies, in its widest sense and with its cross-curricula activities, seems an appropriate grounding. TVEI with its modular approach is an added example of where students can gain a variety of skills associated with media.

At the same time, education is also, and should be, about more than pure vocationalism. Media studies can involve critical practice or technical skills acquisition but does not have to be one thing or the other, or placed in a position of warring opposition with the vocational as subservient to the academic. Indeed, media studies is in the unique position, as a curriculum subject, of combining theory and practice, of utilising theory in the widest sense to do with critical understanding and awareness and a knowledge of the media industries.

Certainly the trade union, the Broadcasting, Entertainment and Cinematograph Technicians Union (BECTU) recognises this combination as a crucial component when accrediting courses. Central to their criteria is, firstly, that courses should be as relevant as possible to the demands and requirements of the industry, and secondly, that courses show in their curriculum a combination of theoretical and practical study. The theoretical component should include, for example, both an understanding of the media industries' technological developments, industry trends, and current and future practices on the one hand, and an understanding of the 'social', 'cultural and political context of the media' on the other. This should incorporate 'a critical understanding of the influence the media have on public attitudes to issues of race, gender, sexuality, class, disability, and political beliefs'. The BECTU currently accredits seven colleges: the

National Film and Television School; the Polytechnic of Central London; Bristol University; Bournemouth and Poole College of Art and Design; West Surrey College of Art and Design; the London International Film School; and the London College of Printing (part of the London Institute).

What initiatives such as TVEI, Compact, and NVQs can do is help overcome what Carol Varlaam calls 'the discrepancies between the objectives of courses, the expectations of students, and the reality of the industry'.[17] This is not to say that the aim of media studies should be preparation for the industry, but to acknowledge, as Hilary Coote says, 'a big gap between media studies graduates and skilled people of immediate use to the industry'.[18] Neither is it to say that theory has no place in the process – media studies is welcomed by others as a grounding in critical awareness of immediate use to the industry. As Professor Desmond Bell maintains, 'if media studies students are favoured in recruitment to the media industries – which they are – it is primarily because they represent a pool of very bright and creative young people and not because they possess some specific set of technical skills in media production'.[19]

At the same time, while initiatives in the field of education and training, and the move towards vocationalism, are designed to provide students with the skills and qualifications relevant to the workplace, it is a matter for conjecture whether recruitment practices will radically alter. It is not simply that the possession of appropriate skills will guarantee a job, it is also a question of creative tendencies, attitude, and personality, including such things as motivation and ability to work hard. These, in themselves, are difficult to measure within the NVQ structure. However, such qualities are often sought, especially in the area of broadcasting. Within ITV companies and the BBC, while qualifications are seen as important, the main criteria for entry are often such qualities as 'flair for the job', 'single-minded determination', 'lively interest to work in the industry', an imaginative and enquiring mind, and evidence of creativity. The 'right' attitude can often be the determining feature in gaining a position in broadcasting.

In certain ways it is not sufficient to merely possess technical skills and assume that this will help gain employment. Film school graduates who have received a thorough training in film techniques, film theory, and so on, are often seen by the industry as having the wrong attitude, as 'arrogant', and lacking in the knowledge required to work in the industry, specifically when it comes to working within strict time limits and given budgets. Thus, while undertaking a film course (depending on the slant of the particular film school) allows students the freedom to experiment and make mistakes and not to be constrained by financial considerations, such educative experiences can be detrimental if not informed by the realities of the working environment. In a further sense, business acumen is ever more important, given the current economic and labour trends in the industry. With the move towards freelance and independent production, education and training in film and television may need to be reshaped to incorporate such skills as finance, management, and marketing, in addition to technical and creative skills.

For individuals, including those leaving higher education, one way of entering the broadcasting and film industries (excluding the BBC, which

194

has its own pattern of recruitment) is as a 'runner'. This involves long hours, low pay, and hard work. However, this is not just a time to gain some knowledge of the industry for the participant – it is also a time when employers can assess the individual's general character and aptitude. At the same time, it is not so much skills that guarantee a job but chance and contacts; as Cecilia Garnett writes, 'success is as much the product of patronage and luck as it is of real merit'.[20]

Notes

1. Jim Kitses with Ann Mercer, *Talking About the Cinema – Film Studies for Young People*, London, BFI, 1966 (reprinted in an expanded edition, 1972). See also: Roger Hill, 'In a Technical College', in Peter Harcourt and Peter Theobald (eds), *Film Making in Schools and Colleges*, London, BFI, 1966; Jane Corbett, 'A College of Further Education', in Roy Knight (ed.), *Film in English Teaching*, London, Hutchinson/BFI, 1972; Chris Mottershead, 'Film Making in a College of Further Education', *Screen Education Notes*, no. 2, Spring 1972.
2. *The First Report of the National Advisory Committee on Art Education*, (the Coldstream Report), London, HMSO, 1960.
3. *The First Report of the National Council for Diplomas in Art and Design*, (the Summerson Committee Report), London, NCDAD, 1964.
4. Peter Kneebone, 'At an Art School', in Peter Harcourt and Peter Theobalds (eds), *Film Making in Schools and Colleges*, London, BFI, 1966.
5. Gerry Coubro', 'Art History and Film Studies in Art Colleges', *Screen*, vol. 12, no. 3, Summer 1971.
6. Douglas Lowndes, *Film Making in Schools*, London, Batsford, 1968; Robert Ferguson, *Group Film-making*, London, Studio Vista, 1969; Keith Kennedy, *Film in Teaching*, London, Batsford, 1972.
7. See H. R. Willis, 'The Need for a School', *Screen Education*, no. 33, March – April 1966; Paul Alexander, 'Towards a National Film School', *Screen Education*, no. 33, March–April 1966; Paddy Whannel, Cedric Blackman, Ray Wills, Douglas Lowndes, and Alan Lovell, 'Evidence to the Lloyd Committee', *Screen Education*, no. 36, September–October 1966; *On the Need for a National Film School* (the Lloyd Report), London, HMSO, 1967.
8. Tim Horrocks, 'Film Making as Training for the Professional', *Screen Education Notes*, no. 2, Spring 1972.
9. Stephen Crofts, 'Film Education in England and Wales', *Screen*, vol. 11, no. 6, Winter 1970.
10. *Working Together – Education and Training*, London, HMSO, Cmnd 9823, July 1986; *Review of Vocational Qualifications*, London, HMSO, Working Party report, April 1986; *Education and Training for the Twenty-first Century*, London, DES, Cm 1536, May 1991.
11. DES: Ibid. p. 16.
12. Ibid. p. 17.
13. Ibid. p. 18.
14. *Competence and Competition: Training and education in the Federal Republic of Germany, the United States and Japan*, a report prepared by the Institute of Manpower Studies for the National Economic Development Council and the Manpower Services Commission, 1984.
15. Tim Blanchard, 'TVEI and Media Studies/Skills For All', *In The Picture*, Autumn 1987.
16. Mark Bishop, 'An absolute beginner', *Televisual*, June 1990.

17. Carol Varlaam, 'Skills Shortages Will Hit Production', *IPPA Bulletin*, Spring 1990.
18. Hilary Coote, cited in Rachel Murrell,'The business of learning the business', *Televisual*, June 1990.
19. Desmond Bell, 'On The Box, On The Course . . . And On The Case', *Times Higher Education Supplement*, no. 922, 6 July 1990.
20. Cecilia Garnett, cited in Rachel Murrell, op. cit.

PART II
Key Aspects of Media Education

VICTORY PROCESSION... Liz McColgan leading from the front last night.

Key Aspects of Media Education

Cary Bazalgette

What is Media Education?

As the texts in Part IA of this Reader show, this apparently innocuous 1
question rarely receives a simple answer. Sometimes it is treated as a
demand for rationales ('why teach about the media?'); sometimes as a
demand for content ('what do you teach about?'); sometimes for pedagogy
('how do you teach about the media?'). Indeed, many existing publications
and training courses offer this appealing trio, 'the Why, What, and How
of media education', which implies that these elements will explain each
other and will comprehensively cover all you need to know. Furthermore,
existing pressures on the curriculum and teachers' time require that all
explanations be simple and accessible (thus countering any lingering anxieties that media education is abstruse, jargon-ridden, and esoteric), as well
as rational and uncontroversial (thus anticipating any surviving suspicions
that media education is radical, subversive, and probably Marxist).

However, the end result of these demands and pressures to make media 2
education easily assimilable can often be that other important questions go
unanswered. Is media education a separately definable subject, or a broader
thematic or pedagogical approach? What difference would it make to the
pupils who learn it? What are its basic principles? In the absence of answers
to questions such as these, teachers are likely to assume that on a conceptual
level it will fit in with their own subject expertise and that they can use
their common sense and general knowledge to formulate their objectives
in media teaching. Versions of media education are thus developed which
are effectively part of English, or art, or social studies, and where the
existing curricula in those subjects take priority over any specifically 'media
education' objectives. Enthusiasm for it then takes the form of describing
how you can 'use media education' to promote close observation, or talk,
or collaboration. This may be true, but it is avoiding any statement of what
children might also be learning *about the media*. Another problem with
'common sense' and 'general knowledge' as aids to curriculum planning
for media education is that they tend to derive from current public debate
and may thus prioritise 'manipulation and bias', 'trivialisation', or 'violence' as key issues.

Likewise in course planning, 'common sense' often leads to teaching 3
about one medium at a time, such as 'television', or 'newspapers', placing
the emphasis solely on the characteristics of only one set of practices. This
prioritises specialist investigation into one medium over the knowledge and

understanding of elements which recur across the media, and ignores the fact that people usually experience media as a set of interrelated and interacting systems.

Alternatively, teachers who have encountered academic texts expounding critical theories about the media may be excessively daunted by the mass of esoteric theory they assume they ought to teach. They are likely to pick up issues such as stereotyping, institutions, genre, or ideology, whose 'teachability' has apparently been proved by the existence of published material, without enquiring too far into how each of these relates to pupils' existing knowledge, how they expect their pupils' learning to progress, and how the different components might logically fit together. Attempts on these lines can be seen in Part IA of this Reader, in 'The "Field" of Film Study' by the editorial board of *Screen Education* (pp. 32–38), and in the section 'Core Concepts and Principles' in Len Masterman's 'The Case for Television Studies' (pp. 45–51).

Such explorations are an inevitable and often an ultimately useful part of the process by which a new aspect of the curriculum gets developed. However, they compound the piecemeal institutional development of media education, and make it hard for teachers in different subject areas to share media teaching and develop it systematically across the curriculum. They can also very easily lead to what has been called 'the Lego curriculum'. In a paper written for a working party set up by the BFI to investigate primary media education, Richard Eke described how this tendency manifested itself in many existing teaching materials on media education, as:

> the tendency to break down media issues/theory into smaller 'logical' components. In other words, there seems to be an idea of syllabus construction which breaks down the holistic event of being a viewer [of television] into a list of component parts that can be reasonably derived from an analysis of the activity. Once a way of communicating has been fragmented it is difficult to avoid the temptation to sequence the fragments logically in terms of difficulty, with progress carefully mapped from the easiest to the most difficult, and to teach on this basis. An understanding of mass media appropriate to the child can then be glossed over in favour of an understanding of the child's performance on a particular course component.[1]

The working party attempted to respond to this critique by trying to identify the basic principles that they felt did differentiate media education from the rest of the curriculum. This involved more than simply identifying areas of 'content' that were thought to be important. It also entailed a process of analysing typical comments, questions, and responses by young children that seemed to be crucial in the development of understanding about the media. Through this process, the working party tried to arrive at some of the constructs or generalisations which seemed to constitute the most basic, initial understanding of any given area of content. For example, most media courses, at any age, usually propose to teach something about media production, and would state this in terms such as 'media education should enable young people to understand how media messages are created'.[2]

Thinking about this further in relation to very young children suggested 6
to the working party that there is a basic construct which needs to be
understood even before children can begin the most elementary exploration
of 'how media messages are created'. The very first idea children need to
get hold of in relation to media production is 'knowing *that* media texts are
made by people'. Four- and five-year-olds need time to think about this.
In their world they are still finding out the differences between things that
are made by people (like bread, or cars, or television programmes) and
things that aren't, like rain, or flies, or stones. It is on the basis of that
distinction that they are motivated to find out why, and how, it takes many
people to make a car or a television programme but that a loaf of bread can
be made by one person – and then to find out how, and by whom, the
ingredients of the loaf are made.

The working party tried to at least begin thinking in this way about all 7
of the conventionally accepted 'key concepts' of media education, and to
identify those for which it seemed there had to be *initial* constructs or
generalisations which anyone would need to start with before their learning
could develop, and which teachers would need to be clear about before
they could build upon them in classroom situations. This resulted in six
headings which have variously been called 'key issues', 'key concepts', 'key
areas of knowledge and understanding'.[3] These six headings have been
widely adopted as a useful conceptual framework, and form the basis of
the Open University/BFI distance learning pack of which this Reader forms
a part. There, and in this Reader, they are called key aspects of media
education.

Why 'Key Aspects'?

The word 'aspects', rather than 'concepts' or 'issues', has been chosen 8
deliberately to indicate clusters of concepts without hard and fast boundaries. If you look at one aspect of a building and then another, you may
be able to see the same feature of the building each time, although it will
not look the same. Each aspect will also reveal things that could not be
seen from anywhere else, and if you really want to get a sense of the whole
building, you need to look at several different aspects.

So using the term 'aspects' I am trying to signal that the key aspects 9
are not meant to constitute a list of contents that media teaching is supposed
to 'deliver', but rather an initial way of organising one's *thinking* about the
media. Whether you are a pupil or a teacher, and whether you are making
a media text or analysing one made by someone else, it is useful to be able
to think systematically about what you are doing at every stage: planning,
teaching, learning, making, analysing, and reflecting upon it afterwards.
By using the term 'key' I am proposing that, although these are not the
only ways in which the media can be thought about, these six may be able
to function as the ones carrying the most influence in determining what,
and how, meanings are made.

For example, if you were producing a media text (taking a photograph, 10
perhaps) there are several questions that you could ask yourself if you

201

wanted to make a really thorough investigation of what you were doing. Of course, in many circumstances you would not want to bother with such a detailed analysis, but in a teaching/learning situation some or all of the following could be important:

- Why am I taking this photograph?
  What is my (real or pretended) role here (e.g., expert, learner, teacher, reporter, spy, family archivist, etc.)?
  How much control do I have over what I am doing?
  Who else is involved in the production of this photograph (e.g., film manufacturers and processors; teacher trainers, pupils or family members offering instruction or advice, etc.)?

- What sort of photograph is this going to be (e.g., family snapshot, a record of a school or other professional event, an illustration for teaching materials or a book, or an imitation of a type of 'professional' photograph: news, advertisement, photostory, etc.)?
  What difference does this categorisation make to the way I think about the photograph and how I set about taking it?

- What sort of technology am I using (e.g., type of camera, type of film)?
  How much control do I have over it (e.g., am I confident with the camera and how to use it; where and by whom will the processing and printing be done)?
  What technological choices are available to me (e.g., focus, aperture, exposure times, filters, type of film, type of paper)?

- What choices can I make about what the photograph will look like (e.g., framing, distance, angle, lighting, sharpness of image, contrast and tone)?

- Who is going to see this photograph?
  In what circumstances or context will they see it?
  Do I want to add things to it before, or when, I show it to people (e.g., mounting, framing, adding written or spoken words, showing it together with other photographs, etc.)?
  What kind(s) of response am I anticipating or hoping for?

- What do I want to show in this photograph (e.g., person(s), place, event, object, etc.)?
  What attitude or idea do I want to convey about the subject of the photograph (e.g., accurate record, illustration of an issue or state of affairs, fantasy or puzzle, expression of mood or feelings, polemical message, etc.)?

These questions have been grouped into sets which correspond to the six key aspects: Agency, Category, Technology, Language, Audience, and Representation. It will probably be immediately apparent that these groupings are not watertight. For each set of questions, your answers would have to relate to other questions: your choices about what the photograph is going to look like, for example, cannot be separated from the technology available to you and the amount of control you have over it. Your ideas about what you want to 'say' in the photograph are likely to be closely related to your chosen or imposed role as photographer.

Devising and grouping questions in relation to a production activity is only one way of using the key aspects. It is possible to turn all these questions round in order to redeploy them as questions you could ask of an existing text. In relation to the photograph on page 198, for example, it would be possible to ask: 11

- Who took this photograph and why? (Agency)
- What sort of photograph is it? (Category)
- How was it produced? (Technology)
- How do I make sense of it? (Language)
- Who is its intended audience? (Audience)
- What does it say about athletics/women? (Representation)

The answers to some of these questions can be relatively easily 'read off' from the printed image: the photographer is credited by name, and in its original newspaper context readers would already know it was from the *Guardian*; they would also be able to categorise it as a 'news' photograph on the sports page. Reprinted with its caption, as it is here, the 'news' and 'sport' categories are also clear. Seen in isolation, plausible arguments for other types of categorisation could be made: an advertisement, perhaps, or an illustration for a documentary feature on sponsorship. These identifications will also help to suggest the intended audience: *Guardian* readers, and those with an interest in sport. The technology question is more dependent on the knowledge brought to the image by the 'reader': that it is a black and white photograph may be obvious enough, but the graininess caused by the dot-screen process used for newspaper printing, or the foreshortening caused by the use of a telephoto lens, may not be identifiable by everyone.

The 'language' of the photograph relates interestingly to the caption: among the group of runners it is not so much McColgan who attracts attention but the second runner (number 1) whose eyes are looking ahead and whose head is closer to the centre of the frame. Without the caption, the awkward bunching of the figures and the range of expressions could suggest a variety of meanings; however, the tight framing, absence of extraneous detail, inclusion of complete figures (head to toe), the blurred elements and the angle and position of the runners are likely to combine to produce a fairly close consensus of interpretations relating to speed, athletics, effort, winning, and losing. 12

Representation is, as often happens, the aspect most likely to invoke divergent ideas. For some readers this could be a powerful and encouraging image of women; for others it could seem disturbing and at odds with ideas about 'normal femininity'. The way the photograph is taken and presented could be judged as a realistic and informative image of 'athletics'; but it might also be judged unrealistic or confusing in its exclusion of context 13 and the choice of angle which privileges the lead runners and fails to show the positions of the rest of the field. These judgements all relate to, and could feed back into, the other aspects.

What is New about the Key Aspects?

In many ways these key aspects will be seen as analogous to the lists of concepts and curricular frameworks that are described in some of the papers in Part IA, but it would be a mistake to think of them as a ready-made curriculum, in which you do 'Agency' one week, 'Category' the next, and so on. It is crucial that they are not seen as a fixed and permanent framework to be imposed upon the learning process, but as a way of provisionally grouping useful concepts in order to link pupils' existing understanding with the learning objectives of a media education curriculum.   14

The term 'provisionally' should not, however, be taken to indicate that the key aspects can be seen as casual or arbitrary; it is also crucial that they are described and accounted for as rigorously as current states of knowledge will allow. They cannot operate as a basis for planning or evaluation unless the elements that underpin them – hypotheses about pupils' understanding, and critical theories about the media – are clearly understood.   15

Nevertheless, the key aspects are intended to be enabling rather than prescriptive. They should offer ways of thinking about how to evaluate and respond to pupils' activities (these could include informal talk as well as production planning or critical analysis); they should open up possibilities for envisaging how learning could develop. The assumptions behind this are similar to those described in Neil Mercer's paper 'Teaching, Talk, and Learning about the Media' (pp. 235–241): the key aspects could function as ways of supporting and progressing learning, and would not exclude the possibility that teacher and pupils can learn together and from each other. A central concern here is with the important, if problematic, notion invoked by Richard Eke: 'an understanding of mass media appropriate to the child'. There is no certain and simple answer to the question of what such an understanding might be, but media teachers nevertheless have to develop working hypotheses about it: the key aspects may assist this process.   16

They exist, therefore, to be developed and modified in the light of teaching experience. Although their interdependence has been stressed so far, the rest of this part of the Reader will deal with each of them separately, offering ways of tracing their relationship to existing ideas about the media and about learning. This, of course, has meant that they are presented one after the other: this should not be taken to mean that their order here represents their order of importance. They can all be regarded as of equal importance, or certain aspects might be emphasised at certain points in a course or topic, depending on context. It could happen that one aspect becomes an appropriate starting-point because of the way a teacher identifies and evaluates pupils' existing knowledge: any of them can function as a way in to all the others. They should therefore certainly not be seen as ready-made topics which offer a hierarchised course structure. At the beginning of each account, I have included one or two of the basic constructs that the primary working party thought could be seen as starting-points for each aspect.   17

Agency

Media texts are produced by people: some by individuals, some by groups.

Film study, one of the major early influences on media education, has always had a concern with the individual or collective originators of a text. By analogy with literary study, 'authorship' (relating usually to film directors) was an important concept, but its validity was never universally accepted, and by the late 1960s the idea of studying films (and later, television) as industrial products, emerging from a complex process of collaborative work, was gradually gaining ground. Since then, either 'industry' or 'institutions' has almost always featured as a component of media studies courses, and at most levels media teachers have felt it important to stress the industrial/commercial nature of media production. At the same time, this aspect of media education has become notorious as the most problematic to teach. The difficulties of, firstly, obtaining and making sense of the economic and institutional information that forms the background of every media text, and secondly, figuring out how to motivate pupils to imbibe this information, have daunted many teachers.   *Pedagogic problems*   18

In the circumstances, it is interesting that teachers have continued to insist upon the importance of this area. Other parts of the curriculum that deal with culture and communication have not attempted it: literary studies rarely include the economics of publishing or the law of copyright, and critical studies in art tend not to deal with the gallery system or the economics of international art markets. The origins of this difference between media education and other curricular areas go back to the anxieties about 'commercialism' that have from time to time fuelled interest in media education (see, for instance, James Halloran and Marsha Jones, pp. 10–13). Yet it is hard to see how such a difference in approaches to cultural products can logically be sustained: most texts, whether print or audio-visual, are produced industrially for profit, and either it is or is not of interest and importance for the consumers of such products to understand something about how this works and what it means.   19

Media educators would argue for its importance, frequently on the somewhat simplistic grounds that the power and profit motives of industrial producers will necessarily have a direct influence on texts. Undoubtedly this can often be true, and there are numerous studies available which show how corporate power and control operate in media industries. However, it is not the whole story. Although ownership patterns, market forces, and political allegiances can affect (sometimes dramatically) the content of media texts, both in terms of what is included and what is excluded, they can never ultimately control how audiences make sense of those texts; nor can they always completely control the processes of production. The more complicated these processes are, the harder it is to identify dissenting or subversive voices, and the history of media is in large part the history of contesting and negotiating change.   *how is that essential?*   20

So although it is important for pupils, as citizens and as members of a culture, to develop their understanding of the processes through which texts are constructed and circulated, it is perhaps even more important that   21 this understanding is developed in ways that enable them to see where the possibilities for change (regressive as well as progressive) may lie.

Such understandings are unlikely to develop solely through critical analysis. Although practical exercises and production in the classroom may be very different from professional and industrial production, they share conceptual features: the constraints of time and technology, for example; the demands of collective work and decision-making hierarchies; the limitations on what can and cannot be said or shown. It is also important to realise that large-scale industrial production is not the only way in which texts can be produced and circulated: small production companies, workshops, and publishing houses can be more closely analogous to school productions. Pupils need to learn that media texts can originate in a range of different ways and that this may account for differences between texts.

It is for this reason that the term 'industry' seems inappropriate as a term to indicate all the issues that relate to how media texts get made and reach audiences. If this area is to include consideration of individual roles as can occur in pupils' own productions, as well as macro-issues such as economics and legal frameworks, then a broader term is needed. 'Institution' is a valuable concept here, and for older pupils it can be introduced as a necessary underpinning of even the most individual production (because technologies like cameras or tape recorders are locked into institutional practices like 'family photography'). But a more abstract term is necessary if we are trying to envisage a conceptual grouping that will apply at any age level, and therefore has to be capable of accounting for the learning that goes on at age five when children think about how they decided where to set up a camera, as well as seeing how that can link forward to the learning that goes on at age fifteen when pupils consider whether press monopolisation matters. This is why 'Agency' seems a better term for accommodating such a broad range of concepts, while indicating at the same time that they are intrinsically linked.

A five-year-old's understanding of Agency may seem far removed from a sixteen-year-old's, but it is important to see the connections between them. Everyone is conscious that texts of any kind do not just appear but get made, even if they do not know by whom, or why. Children's talk about the media often uses phrases such as 'they did it that way because . . .' or 'they never show you the bit where . . .', using the portmanteau term 'they' to indicate the spheres of influence behind media texts, of which they are usually aware even if they cannot explain them in any detailed way. In contrast, they will usually be absolutely clear about exactly who did what in their own productions. Older pupils should be able to gain an understanding of more abstract issues, such as the institutional constraints regulating broadcast 'repeats', and the different censorship rules governing cinema and video releases. Their increased experience of production should have taught them the problems as well as the possibilities of making their own texts.

Learning about media agencies inevitably involves accumulating information about production roles, professional practices, institutional hierarchies, sources of finance, systems of circulation, and so on. But the key

22

23

24

25

issue here is the development of an understanding about what *difference* it might make to the meaning, significance, or authenticity of a text if it is made by, say, Disney rather than by the Black Audio Film Collective, or financed by Macdonalds rather than by the Calouste Gulbenkian Foundation.

Evidence of learning about media agencies would be clearer in pupils who are able to ask key questions about the production and circulation of texts, like 'is that publisher owned by another company?', than in the pupils who can reel off facts and figures. Progression in learning about Agency is likely to be indicated by a growing sophistication of understanding that many variables can affect the final shape and status of a media text, and that these variables affect each other in ways which can sometimes be so complex they can never be fully understood.

Pupils' understanding of Agency and their confidence in using it themselves as an organising concept is likely to take place best in the context of their own practical productions, especially where these are for real audiences and have to confront real issues of cost, appropriateness for the audience, time constraints, and so on. It can also take place in the context of simulations that encourage them to explore the decisions available to people such as schedulers, editors, or financiers; or in case studies, which can be quite small scale, but which open up the detail of a production history or an issue such as censorship.

Pupils can also study the roles of other people and institutions in the production of media texts. Although this can involve daunting questions of tracing and accessing information, it can be done on a limited scale through analysing short texts like credit sequences, trailers, and other promotional material where professional and corporate identities are signalled particularly strongly, and attention can be given to both how and why this is done.

As will become clear in each of the following sections, no key aspect is really separable from the others. For example, it is debatable where issues about the circulation of texts ought to be located. The Agency aspect can include things like broadcasting policy, or distribution practices in the film industry, but these are also crucial in the area of Audience, where it makes a big difference if a programme is scheduled late night rather than peak time, or if a film is released only on video rather than in cinemas. There is no hard and fast answer here, and many other such 'overlaps' will occur in the processes of planning, teaching, and learning. Teachers will work out the most appropriate way to organise such learning, using the key aspects as guidelines but not as dividing walls.

Category

Any categorisation makes a difference to interpretation.
Any media text can be categorised in a number of different ways.

Another concept that was well established in film study before it was adapted to media education is genre, and theoretical writing accumulated about Hollywood genres such as the Western and the Musical while they continued to be potent marketing formulae. Genre continues to be seen as a comparatively accessible 'way in' to critical theories about cinema, because most people can recognise the typical features of, say, horror or gangster films, and find it interesting to think about how far the 'rules' of each genre are fixed, and how far they can be broken or even combined with one another. It also offers a useful approach to combining textual analysis with studies of production and exhibition. More recently, the genre approach has been adapted to television, not without some difficulty, since television tends to combine different genres more easily. Even so, soap opera, situation comedy, game shows, and perhaps news and sport, can be studied as genres.

However, generic analysis is only one feature of a more basic conceptual process, that of categorisation. An initial and often almost unconscious response to any text is to categorise it: if we cannot ascribe a category to a text it can be difficult to make sense of it. We identify a television programme as 'the news' before we start to take in its information, but even before we do that we have already set up certain expectations about 'watching television' which are different from seeing a film or reading a newspaper. Categorisation provides the initial understandings of which audiences become able to recognise typical features such as the forms and conventions of a particular medium. But the point of Category as an aspect of media education is not merely to identify texts in different ways. It is to understand how media categories produce expectations about texts and hence affect how they are understood.

Because most children already have knowledge and experience of a wide range of media texts they inevitably also operate their own personal or peer group categories, which may be highly idiosyncratic. Most individuals probably retain personal categories that relate to their own cultural biographies (as in 'I hate happy endings!'), but by secondary age most children have also acquired a working understanding of how media texts get categorised, since categories are a key factor in marketing as well as in everyday talk about the media. When children encounter a category with which they are unfamiliar – art cinema, for example – they may have negative reactions which are not necessarily because the texts are intrinsically difficult, but because they cannot recognise the texts' generic characteristics, and are trying to impose expectations derived from other categories: hence comments like 'It's so boring! Nothing happens!'

Categories themselves are never hard and fast, and are continually developing. For example, the BBC television series *Blackadder* could be identified as a television programme, a drama series, and generically, as a situation comedy. But it could also be described as a satire that refers to other historical drama. None of these categories by itself satisfactorily invokes the particular appeal of the programme: much of the comedy comes from the tension *between* categories and the ways in which this is played upon. But once a particular combination of categories has worked successfully, it becomes an instrument of categorisation in itself. Both audiences and producers can now describe subsequent comedies in relation to *Blackadder*, if they want to invoke a similar mixture of genres.

Categorisation of media texts can thus be a way of developing children's

208

ideas about how texts are understood and how (and why) they are produced. The identification and discussion of categories reveals the framework of rules and conventions that support them: for example, how a science fiction comedy like *Red Dwarf* can differ in subject matter and special effects from science fiction like *Dr Who*; how the blurring of genre boundaries as in drama-documentary can lead to moral or political controversy; or how and why classifications of film and video into PG, 12, 15, and 18 are made. These considerations in turn can give rise to experiments in altering conventions, and shifting category boundaries. Pupils can select, use, and perhaps break, the formal elements and conventions which characterise particular categories. In both analysis and production, therefore, Category is a powerful way of organising thought, and therefore of developing ideas.

But Category also, inevitably, overlaps with other aspects of media education. The processes of setting up and funding media productions depend heavily on the shared understandings of category held by media professionals (as in 'the programme's going to be a mix of vox pops, talking heads, and a sofa show'). So any work on the aspect of Agency has to involve at least some thought about Category as well. Because audience understandings are heavily inflected by Category, and because audiences themselves may be targeted in terms of Category (as in 'this will appeal to the people who liked *Twin Peaks*'), work on the aspect of Audience is bound to include consideration of how audiences are assumed to operate categories. Likewise, Category is an important element of understanding Technology and Language. Indeed, its permeation of other aspects leads some people to argue that it cannot be sustained separately: in some syllabuses it is subsumed under 'Forms and Conventions', for example. I would suggest that its validity as a separate aspect lies in the importance of its role in the construction of meaning: the ascription of Category to a text *makes a difference* to the way that text is understood. This is important at the production stage as well as in the reading and analysis of texts: categories are invoked and used in the collective processes of production and are a significant means by which understandings are shared. Although it plays an important role in the other key aspects, it cannot be satisfactorily contained in any one of them; it therefore seems practicable, for now, to attempt to work with it as a separate key aspect.

Technology

Any technological choice makes a difference.

Looked at in one way, the technological characteristics of a media text can be thought of as simply one of the ways of categorising it. We note that a photograph is in black and white or in colour, or that a film is in CinemaScope, and these features can then contribute to the ways in which we process the meanings of the texts or have expectations about them. But most people's capacity for making technological observations about media texts is fairly limited. It tends to depend upon their media production experience: most people have taken photographs and are thus reasonably

209

confident about discussing framing and perhaps the characteristics of different lenses; most people have not done multi-track audio recording or video editing and are less likely to notice the roles of these technologies in a text.

The traditions of critical analysis and teaching about the media have reflected these limitations. The texts in Part IA of this Reader demonstrate the lack of analytical emphasis on the technological aspects of texts, and the tendency to separate, and place different values upon, critical and practical work in media education (see, for example, David Buckingham, pp. 63–68). Paying attention to the technical aspects of analysis or practical work has often been sneered at as 'technicist'. Even where practical work is a valued part of media education, it has tended to be technologically limited: for example, it is probably a reasonable assumption that the vast majority of video tapes made in schools are unedited.

Nevertheless, even the most basic experience of media production can reveal to both teachers and pupils the immense significance of technological equipment and processes. Media technologies can play a major role in determining not only the meaning of a text, but to whom it can be made available. Technological possibilities, constraints, and choices are always capable of opening up questions such as: What kinds of technology are available to whom? How are they used? What difference do these technologies make to the final product?

'Technology' can include any tools and materials used in the processes of producing meaning, from crayon and paint to video cameras and mixing desks. The essential conceptual point about technologies in media education is that technologies affect *meaning*, not just 'quality' or 'finish'. Therefore, any technological choice, constraint, or opportunity involves a decision about the meaning, not simply the appearance, of a text. They can also lead into other key aspects: some technologies can reach more people than others (Audience); any technology involves questions of cost and perhaps also of legality (Agency); technological choices affect the processes of selection, exclusion, and juxtaposition that are crucial in Representation.

Shifting the main focus of this aspect away from the acquisition of technical skills and towards the development of conceptual understanding may help to dispel the idea that media education is necessarily dependent on complex technology. Although I would argue that, in an ideal world, all pupils are just as much entitled to learn about the potential of media technologies as they are to learn about any other medium of expression or communication, it is nevertheless true that much understanding of the principles of technological choices can be gained through the use of 'low-tech' materials. Drawing or drafting storyboards and cartoons, using a photocopier to reproduce, enlarge, or produce images, exploring the use of translucent and opaque materials in slide mounts – all these open up a huge range of representational possibilities. This is not to suggest that teachers should be satisfied with cheap ways of resourcing their media equipment needs, but that where it is appropriate children are able to learn about the processes of production by adapting available resources, materials, and equipment.

210

Progression in Technology does not, of course, just constitute the acquisition of skills. However, the importance of skills should not be underrated, and nor should the time it takes to acquire them. It also has to be recognised that, given the right equipment and enough time, the acquisition of technological skills has nothing to do with age. Many teachers are already familiar with the experience of discovering that five-year-olds know more about video recording and playback than they do, and may be very disdainful of the low-quality equipment found in school compared to what is available at home. Although it may take young children a little time to get used to using viewfinders or tripods, there is no physical or intellectual developmental reason why they should not be able to do so, and every reason, in terms of their imaginative and communicative potential, why they should.

However, progression in Technology is equally related to the growth of understanding about how technological choices can affect meaning. This is closely tied to the acquisition of skills and experiences with different technologies, and should make possible an increasing flexibility and imaginativeness in problem-solving. As with all the key aspects, progression in learning would also be shown by an increasing ability to integrate any one aspect with others. There is hardly ever such a thing as a purely technological problem. For instance, working out how to set a camera at the desired angle is likely to entail making decisions that relate technical feasibility (Technology) and the potential meanings of the image (Language).

Language

Everything in a media text has meaning.

One of the fundamental assumptions of any version of media education is that every medium has, to some extent, its own 'language' through which its meanings are constructed. It is asserted that media texts are actively 'read' by audiences: that people hardly ever just passively view television programmes or look at photographs in the same way as they look at things in real life. It is a basic premise of media education that even the most idle glance through a magazine or flip through the television channels must draw upon skills that have been learned, as does taking holiday snaps or playing with a video camera.

Media education seeks to develop awareness of the ways in which meaning is made in media texts, and to build on this awareness by developing skills of textual analysis which can be applied to still or moving images, recorded sounds, or any combination of these. In critical work this is typically done through analysis of single images or short segments of an audio-visual text, giving a very detailed account of what exactly is seen and heard, before moving on to interpretative comments and expressions of response. Although making sense of a photograph is in many ways not the same process as making sense of a written text, media educators often use the word 'reading' in relation to both, in order to stress the idea that any text must in some way be using a 'language' which has to be learned before you can understand it. The types of question used in classroom practice and the kinds of response preferred are very much influenced by semiology (see 'The Interpretive Tradition', pp. 155–167). The stress is thus on techniques of analysis that can be applied to any kind of text, from a frozen-food package to an eighteenth-century oil painting, although it is noticeable that these techniques are better developed in relation to visual images than they are in relation to aural texts.

In the early years of schooling, analysis of media texts is likely to concentrate on close observation of an image or sounds, encouraging children to notice and think about all the features that are present, rather than moving directly into interpretation and evaluation. Of course, many teachers already do this, and the ability to observe closely and accurately, and to talk about what is seen and heard, is rightly valued as a worthwhile skill in itself. But within the Language aspect of media education, it becomes important to lay the foundations for more sophisticated analyses of the codes and conventions used in the media. This can mean paying attention to aspects which are often ignored in the usual approaches to close observation and discussion.

'Convention' means any agreed, established way in which elements of a media text can be made to refer to, symbolise, or summarise particular meanings or sets of ideas. For example, when we see a character in cinema or television fiction look off-screen, and then see another shot which does not include that character, we assume that the second shot shows us the character's point of view. Another example of a convention is the way that little lines and puffs of 'smoke' are used in cartoon images to indicate 'speed'.

A 'code' is a set of conventions fixed in a predictable pattern of usage. News broadcasts, comedy cartoons, or horror films are examples of highly coded texts. Our knowledge of media categories may lead us into expecting certain codes and conventions in particular texts. If we see what appears to be a news broadcast in which an interviewee speaks direct to camera, we are instantly aware that the codes of 'news' are being broken through the challenging of the conventional 'interviewee' role. A great deal of comedy in cinema, television and radio depends on audience knowledge of generic codes when it subverts these for comic effect.

Looking at codes and conventions, then, often means examining what is usually taken for granted, especially by older pupils and adults who have internalised them. This is an aspect of media education that may well be easier with younger children, who can be more open to asking, and thinking about, questions concerning media languages. For example, very young children may not be clear about the relationship between, say, a medium shot and a close-up: they may think that a bird seen in close-up is not the same as the one seen in the previous shot, but a different, bigger bird. It may be possible to clarify this through discussion and slow replay, but play and experimentation with cameras, frames, and lenses are far more likely to open up their understanding of the different kinds of shot that are possible.

Where critical and practical work can be integrated fully and systematically, the value of experiencing critical analysis of media languages should become apparent as children become more able to deploy purposefully the codes and conventions of a medium and to use them in group planning (as in, for example, 'it would be good if we had a close-up before we see the whole room'). This in turn enriches children's understanding of how these codes and conventions are used by other people. But the constraints upon practical work in classrooms have meant that work on the Language aspect of media education has tended to overemphasise critical work and to separate it from the practical.

Although financial constraints are even greater in the primary school than at secondary level, it is here that the balance between critical and practical media work is beginning to change, given primary teachers' commitment to practical and creative work in the classroom. Play with cameras or even cardboard frames, masking and cutting up photographs, looking at things from different distances and angles, can all be valued for the way they extend a number of skills and a range of understanding in several subject areas; but at the same time they extend children's abilities to predict, control, and talk about the way framing and editing can be made to affect meaning. Similar activities can encourage thought about how words, sounds, and music affect the meaning of visual images, and vice versa, and about how images, on their own or together with sounds or words, can be selected and sequenced or grouped in order to emphasise one meaning rather than another.

Ideally, children should have opportunities to develop familiarity and confidence with many different media, both through informal play and experimentation and through more structured exercises. Such activities should precede more formal media production for other audiences, although of course this is often impossible when teachers have to seize what opportunities they can to give children access to media production equipment. Limitations on access to equipment also often mean that children tend to have 'one-off' experiences of media production, which are usually only enough to give them the imaginative scope and confidence to start again, by which time the equipment is no longer available. The arguments have to be made that Language is a significant aspect of media education, and that time has to be spent on enabling children to gain basic practical expertise which will enrich their critical understanding as well as their creative potential.

Progression in learning about Language in media would be signalled by an increasing ability to identify, reflect upon, and discuss the ways in which meanings are derived from all kinds of texts. As pupils' understanding of media languages develops, we can expect it to incorporate more complex ideas about how certain sets of meanings can be coded: how changes of time or place can be signalled in visual, audio, and written texts respectively, for example, or how typical characters or situations can be introduced (villains, suspense). Through both critical and practical work, children can explore the ways in which media languages are used conventionally (links here to Category), but we should not underestimate the extent to which, even in everyday television viewing, these conventions are continually broken, subverted, and reworked in new ways; as a consequence, children's awareness of conventional forms as conventions may often be more sophisticated than teachers at first suppose. Such awareness is likely to find expression through parody, but it should not be forgotten that, in the post-modernist era, parody is often not particularly subversive but merely follows one of the most established comic formats of mainstream media.

Media educators have a responsibility to ensure that children encounter experimental and alternative media texts, and are themselves encouraged to explore the limits of media languages in their own productions. One of the ways in which media work in schools has been unnecessarily limited is through an overconcentration of the analysis of dominant media forms and a use of textual analysis techniques solely to reveal manipulation and bias. Although such work is undoubtedly important, it sells children short if it does not also encourage them to explore the imaginative and communicative possibilities of media languages, and thus to be able to evaluate existing changes in media production practice and to envisage others.

Audience

You can make a media text for people you don't know.

How are audiences identified, constructed, addressed, and reached? How do audiences consume and respond to texts? Who receives a text, and what sense do they make of it? When and how do they receive it? What pleasures might audiences derive from it?

It is very striking that questions like these, which nowadays seem pressing and significant to most people who have an interest in media, did not figure at all in media curricula during the 1970s and early 1980s (see, for example, 'The "Field" of Film Study' in Part IA). Indeed, entire bodies of theory were constructed on the premise that meanings were completely contained within texts and all audiences had to do was read them off. The more pervasive model, however, was that audiences read texts naively, while the 'media-educated' read them knowledgeably, perceiving the thematic patterns or ideological projects at work in each text ('The Social Science Tradition' in Part IB, pp. 168–185, covers the background to these and other concepts of audience). For many people, including many teachers, oversimple assumptions that the media have direct effects on ideas and behaviour are still broadly accepted and may, indeed, be part of the motivation to undertake media teaching. Of course, if you assume that when you find bias and ideological manipulation in a text audiences are inevitably going to be taken in by it, then teaching about audience is hardly necessary. By concentrating on areas of the media where bias and manipulation can most easily be demonstrated, as in advertising and perhaps news, discrete and manageable courses can be constructed. However, such teaching commits the double error of omitting the areas of the media that usually interest pupils most, such as fiction and entertainment, and of ignoring pupils' actual experiences as members of audiences.

It is by now a widely accepted premise of media education that audiences bring meanings to audio-visual texts in broadly the same ways that they are assumed to do with print texts. The audio-visual literacy/print literacy analogy can be pushed too far, overlooking the significant differences between the ways we experience different kinds of text, but the assumption that audiences are passive and gullible is fast losing ground to the idea that

214

audiences *make* meanings from texts, rather than having meanings thrust upon them. This opens up a broad area of informational and conceptual investigation that is immensely significant for media education and can in some ways be seen as pivotal within the six key aspects: audiences learn media languages, operate categories, and make judgements about represen-tations.

Clearly, if media education takes on board the complex and shifting ideas 57 about audience that the newer research and critical theories are producing, then it sets itself a difficult task pedagogically. On the other hand, the constituents of audience study are more readily to hand in schools than are the texts and hardware that form its other study objects. After all, a class of children constitutes, in its own way, a kind of 'audience'. Schools group individuals by age, but each class includes a range of interests and back-grounds. Furthermore, each child is a member of several 'audience' group-ings at any one time.

Looking at a media text in a classroom entails, like any moment of 58 consumption, specific conditions which can be compared with others. Viewing a television programme in school means that certain expectations are already raised about the educational nature and value of the activity (Will it be boring? Will we have to write about it?) which are quite different from the conditions of home viewing (You never let me watch the pro-grammes I like! I'll come and eat when 'Home and Away' has finished). Watching a programme with one's peer group may involve quite different responses than with parents, and reflections upon Audience can begin with considerations of what these differences are and how to account for them.

It can also begin with pupils' responses to each others' productions. 59 Because media practical work and production are usually collective, there is a sense in which a text's first audience is the members of the production team.[4] These experiences can open up initial issues and problems in developing an understanding of Audience, such as the fact that different classes, races, ages, cultural backgrounds, and personal histories can all affect the interpretation of texts and the kinds of pleasures people may derive from them. This perception has to be balanced against the fact that audience groupings *can* appear to have more or less uniform collective responses in some circumstances, laughter being one of the most obvious signals of this, as well as one of the most complicated to investigate. It is through investigating the relationship between these two ideas that pupils can begin to perceive the problems and possibilities of seeing audiences simply as 'markets' for products. Advertisers, and newspaper or broadcast-ing producers hoping to sell space or time to advertisers, spend enormous amounts of time and money trying to identify new audience groupings and segments, or even construct them, and to predict their responses and behaviour. Not only advertisements themselves, but also fictional, enter-tainment, or informational texts, can be analysed in terms of how they are designed to appeal to specific audiences, and the problems of actually achieving such appeals can be reflected upon through production as well as through analysis.

Progression in learning about Audience will be seen as pupils become 60 able to discuss the range and variety of audience responses, and the issues of taste, appropriateness, codes of practice, censorship, and legislation which relate to them. These can be investigated through both critical and practical work. At more advanced levels pupils can study theories about 'effects' of media on audiences and how audiences accept, negotiate, or reject what producers circulate. Studying Audience should help pupils to interrogate assumptions about media effects that are commonly found in public discourse about the media. Through sharing responses to their own and other people's media texts they should become able to explore and develop their own values and attitudes more confidently.

Representation

Media texts relate to reality in different ways.

Teachers, theorists, and critics agree that media texts do not replicate or mirror reality, but construct their own versions of it. There is less of a consensus, however, about the significance of this observation. In spite of the fact that it is true not only for what are conventionally called media texts (films, television programmes, newspapers, etc.) but also for more traditional types of text such as novels, plays, and poems, and, for that matter, paintings and at least some music, it is only in relation to media texts that it continues to attract the kind of anxiety and opprobrium exemplified by the Newsom Report in 1963: 'children . . . must learn to realise that many makers of films and of television programmes present false or distorted views of people, relationships, and experience in general' (quoted in James Halloran and Marsha Jones in Part IA). It is perhaps worth remembering that all the other media I have cited have in their time attracted the same opprobrium; we happen to be living in a phase when it is television, rather than the novel, or the Bible in English, which is considered the most serious threat to the innocent and gullible.

When media education is motivated by anxieties about how texts may distort or manipulate reality, teaching plans tend to have at their centre key issues such as 'ideology', 'stereotyping', or 'bias'. They thus have a built-in emphasis on the negative aspects of the media and on teaching pupils to recognise and resist them. While it is certainly important to look at how texts manage their ideological work, it is problematic to place this at the centre of media education (see in Part IA, for example, Judith Williamson, pp. 83–84, and David Buckingham, pp. 89–91). To do so places to one side pupils' own experiences in negotiating the meanings of media texts and in making their own judgements about Representation – how texts relate to reality.

A central focus of the primary working party's discussions about the key aspects was how they might get closer to understanding these experiences of Representation. By using transcripts of children's talk and by drawing upon the concept of 'modality' described in *Children and Television*,[5] they realised the importance of shifting to a new way of conceptualising Representation. It had previously been thought of as essentially to do with a two-way relationship, between texts and reality. Thus texts could be characterised as 'stereotyped' or 'biased' or 'objective', even when it was

216

acknowledged that 'reality' was in itself a problematic term. The working party proposed that it was rethought as a three-way relationship, as follows:

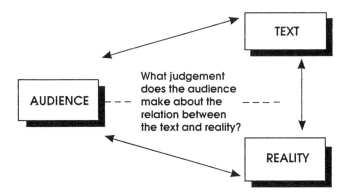

This formulation was later revised, on the basis that it related only to the analysis of texts and not to processes of production, and became a four-way relationship:

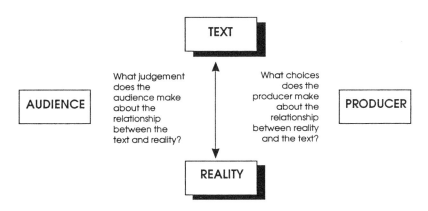

The key term in thinking about this set of relationships is 'modality'. Bob Hodge and David Tripp derive it from linguistics, and describe it as 'not a fixed property of a message: it is a subjective, variable, relative, and negotiable judgement'. Their project here is not to make concepts such as stereotyping and manipulation disappear into relativity, but to set them in a wider context.

It has become a commonplace to assert that 'children can't tell the difference between television and reality', but anyone who actually investigates children's understanding of television (see, for example, Sue Van Noort's account on pp. 274–291) quickly discovers that, far from accepting television as reality, children constantly make judgements about *how real it is*. The problem for adults in assessing these judgements is that, because children are busy learning about television and about reality in the course

64

of their everyday lives, their 'modality judgements' about the relationship between the two tend to be variable. Describing a study of his own, Tripp comments:

> It is a world in which things are more or less real according to how you look at them. Nothing is real or unreal in a global sense. To an adult, such a world would be confusing, but that's only because we tend to operate with more and higher order concepts and classificatory systems which make us think of classes of things, and hierarchies of classes of things. . . . Natalie doesn't have such organising concepts, which is why she is an agnostic in the sense that she is saying. 'Well, you can call them real if you look at them like this. But if you look at them like that they're not.'[6]

Although there is a greater consensus about modality judgements as people get older, the idea of centring Representation on the relationship between texts and reality, and how this is judged, rather than simply on the texts themselves, is still pertinent. It enables us to make powerful links between Representation and each of the other key aspects. At every level of production decision (Agency), choices are made about selection, exclusion, and inclusion, and about Category and Technology. These choices affect how a text makes sense (Language) and how we make sense of it (Audience). Each of these has a bearing on what a text may be said to represent.

It does not lessen the significance of issues such as stereotyping, bias, ideology, and manipulation if they are considered within the broader context of Representation. It is in order that they may be more effectively understood, analysed, and, where appropriate, subverted and changed.

Progression in understanding and using the concepts that relate to Representation as I have described it would be dependent upon an increasing ability to comprehend the range of issues that it can cover. At one extreme there are more or less metaphysical questions about relative realities; at the other, tightly focused issues like the law of libel. At a more advanced level pupils would begin to investigate the kinds of issues described by Jim Cook in Part IB ('The Interpretive Tradition', pp. 155–167). Representation is, perhaps more than any other aspect, dependent for its full realisation on people's ability to integrate the key aspects, to see how each of them can generate questions that affect, or lead into, some or all of the others.

Conclusion

Although I have so far described the key aspects one by one, I hope it has been indicated already that learning about the media should enable pupils to develop an increasing ability to draw upon all the key aspects and to combine them in flexible and appropriate ways: to be able to use them imaginatively, rather than as filler for model answers or standard exercises.

But by this point a further question may be presenting itself, which relates back to my initial questions about whether media education is a separately definable subject, or a broader thematic or pedagogical approach. The key aspects have been developed because teachers have found they work well in thinking about and planning media education curricula, but the way they have been developed means that they include propositions which are extremely basic and general and which therefore cannot be confined to media teaching. This may be another way of saying that media teaching cannot be confined to one subject or topic, and it is certainly true that many primary teachers who have been able to internalise these or similar aspects and use them confidently in their teaching, have found that in teaching across the whole curriculum, their media education approaches have begun to underpin everything. This may not mean that there is something special about media education that argues for it having a central place in the curriculum, although there are people who would make that argument. It may simply mean that media education, because of its relative novelty and marginality, has come to be conceptualised more systematically and more rigorously than other subjects and that teachers welcome this.

Notes

1. Richard Eke, 'Media Education Issues', in *Working Papers Two*, BFI/DES National Working Party on Primary Media Education, London, BFI, October 1986.
2. 'Key Areas of Knowledge and Understanding' is the term used in *Primary Media Education: A Curriculum Statement*, London, BFI, 1989, and *Secondary Media Education: A Curriculum Statement*, London, BFI, 1991.
3. *Media Education Curriculum Guidelines*, Glasgow, Scottish Film Council, 1988.
4. 'Any future audience can only be approached through the first audience for the film – the cast and crew who produced it.' Colin MacCabe, in Isaac Julian and Colin MacCabe (eds), *Diary of a Young Soul Rebel*, London, BFI, 1991.
5. Bob Hodge and David Tripp, *Children and Television*, London, Polity, 1986.
6. David Tripp, 'Television as Educator', paper given to the BHP Australian Television Festival, Perth, 1988, an extract from which is reprinted in Part III of this Reader.

PART III
Analysing Classroom Practice

BBC crew working in the classroom

Analysing Classroom Practice
Introduction

The five articles which appear in this section make, to some extent, diverse reading. They vary considerably in content, complexity, and direction, reflecting the different institutional positions and areas of expertise of each writer. Most of them effectively offer an approach to classroom practice which either looks back to Part II, offering a link between the six key aspects and their application in the classroom, or looks ahead to Part IV, making sense of the accounts of classroom practice therein. However, all the articles, whether explicitly or implicitly, offer strategies and conceptual tools for analysing readers' own classroom practice.

Although Julian Bowker's 'Classroom Practice' is ostensibly less concerned with evaluating classroom practice than in pinpointing the types of activity which teachers will need to deploy if they are to engage in recognisable media education, we have placed it before the other articles in this section since it offers a systematic 'how to' guide of what classroom practice should look like – a foundation from which evaluation could proceed. Bowker lists six types of observable classroom activity: practical activities, content analysis, textual analysis, case study, simulation, and production, giving examples of how these activities might be structured and approached in the classroom. He contends that the aim of media teaching should be to integrate practical skills with analytical, critical, and creative approaches into an amalgam of 'practice'. Furthermore, he argues for a progressive media education pedagogy which raises questions about both how the subject should be taught and how the classroom environment should be organised. Finally, Bowker makes a plea for pupils to practise self-evaluation and evaluation of their peers' work in simulation exercises in particular, which can form the basis of teacher evaluation. In so doing, he broadens the scope of approaches to evaluation offered in the companion articles.

In contrast, Neil Mercer's 'Teaching, Talk, and Learning about the Media' is a piece grounded in theoretical work, originated by the psychologist Vygotsky, in which insights into the relationship between teachers and learners are explored and which provide a basis for analysing and evaluating both teaching and learning in classrooms. Although applicable to all learning, this model is of particular relevance to media education as the neo-Vygotskian belief is that learning is built on a social and interactive process, a sharing of cultural resources between teacher and learner, as opposed to the Piagetian emphasis on individual cognitive development. Central to this belief is the conceptual metaphor of 'scaffolding', which describes the intervention and learning support a teacher gives to a pupil. Mercer exemplifies the concept in practice with reference to one of the case studies in Part IV (Sue Van Noort's 'Nursery School Children Talking about Television'). In terms of the application of 'scaffolding' to wider media education practices and with reference to the preceding Part of the Reader, it would seem that, with the kind of learning support frame and potential for progression that the six key aspects offer media education teachers, the key aspects themselves could be considered a prime example of 'scaffolding'.

Peter Scrimshaw's 'Evaluating Media Education through Action Research' is central to gaining an understanding of the why's and how's of analysing classroom practice. Although posited upon theoretical research, it offers a common-sense approach which offers step-by-step guidance to the uninitiated. He begins by defining the meaning of action research, how it operates, how its research problems are formulated and planned, and how its interpretations are checked. Its relevance to readers lies in the fact that it is a self-reflective operation, carried out by teachers on their own educational practices and with a view to enhancing the curriculum. Furthermore, he draws an interesting parallel between a teacher's position vis-à-vis action research and that of a student of media education through the respective subjects' predication upon active learning and critical reflection, both of which are contextualised by the social and institutional environment. Drawing on some of the case study examples from Part IV to illustrate his theory, Scrimshaw details a plethora of useful ways in which information for action research can be collected and how the focus for the research should be chosen, explaining the difference between reactive and non-reactive methods. Flexibility in developing a research plan is stressed, and he suggests how to transform interpretation of results into action. If readers feel inspired and feel they have the time to initiate an action research project, then Scrimshaw's comprehensive guide makes essential reading.

The benefits of documenting classroom practice, as expounded by Scrimshaw, through using video or audio tape or both, are further explored in Paul Manner's 'Filming in the Classroom', which provides a useful manual. Indeed, this piece serves two purposes in that it contextualises the filmed case study extracts of classroom practice, which can be seen in the video which relates to this Reader while suggesting a rationale for an approach to video recording. He clearly talks through the choices available, offering his professional guidance as a producer of BBC/OU video and schools' broadcasts. In the first part of the paper he explores the practicalities of recording in classrooms: the need to have a clear sense of what you hope to achieve which will, in turn, dictate the method and approach adopted; the ethical considerations and technical problems inherent in filming (or taping) in classrooms in terms of background noise, positioning and moving the camera, lighting, and so on. He then offers practical suggestions as to how to overcome or at least live with the problems. Like Scrimshaw, he considers the way that recorded material can serve as a basis for reflection and evaluation.

Finally, turning to 'Television as Educator' by David Tripp, we are again in a different domain. Unlike the other articles, Tripp's was prepared for a public talk at which he presented a polemic, based on experiential research findings, asserting the rightful place of television in the classroom and the paramount importance of allowing children to verbalise their televisual experiences. Using the example of questions asked to a six-year-old about the reality of television characters compared with people the child knew in real life, Tripp expounds a theory of children's perception of reality and their ability to make relatively sophisticated modality judgements precisely through watching television programmes. Unlike Scrimshaw and Manners, Tripp offers no explicit approaches to analysing what goes on in the classroom, but he does make an implicit plea for teachers to make space in their classrooms for children to talk through their own televisual experiences and, like Mercer, is implicitly arguing for their knowledge to be treated as a cultural resource to be shared between pupil and pupil, and between pupil and teacher in the classroom.

In assembling articles for this section we feel the variance with which the respective writers approach the analysis of classroom practice is precisely their strength, since they offer readers a rich and wide framework upon which to reflect upon both their own classroom practice and that illustrated in the case studies in Part IV of the Reader.

Classroom Practice

Julian Bowker

From *Secondary Media Education: A Curriculum Statement*, London, BFI, 1991, pp. 18–26.

Approaches to Media Work

There are six types of classroom activity commonly used in media education: practical activities, content analysis, textual analysis, case study, simulation, and production. These methods should be seen as elements of a developmental approach to learning about the media, and they should naturally be part of thematic or topic work which may include several other types of learning skills, experiences, and activities. Also, they need to be handled sensitively, with awareness of the possible problems involved in the relationship between private and public.

General Principles

There is a useful distinction between practical activity and full-scale media production. The former describes a range of small-scale exercises and activities undertaken regularly as an integral part of media education; the latter refers to intensive, usually collaborative work on a complete text aimed at an audience. In either case, the process of production is of central importance, but production work is likely to entail more emphasis on the finished product. Practical activities should not be used just to demonstrate a grasp of theoretical concepts, like warming-up exercises, but should be a fundamental way in which media learning takes place. It is through participation in the practical process, and reflecting on that process, that pupils gain insights into the ways media products are constructed. The process model of production described in the Statutory Orders for Technology, rather than the idea of writing derived from the English Statutory Orders, may be relevant here.

'Practice' suggests different things to different people in terms of scale, focus, or method. But the main aim of media teaching should be to integrate practical skills with critical, analytical, and creative approaches, and ideally these should all be thought of as 'practice'. Teachers will need to balance the introduction of technical skills with the analysis of the processes and the products of media. It is important for pupils to see that their learning is part of a structured reflective process. A systematically developed approach will distinguish valuable learning about media from the type of mechanical or busy activity where media are used simply as resources.

Just watching a schools' television broadcast is not media education unless children use the critical tools of media education to make sense of

226

their own understandings and investigate how meanings have been produced. Such an approach can be introduced through structured discussion which encourages children to reflect *collectively* on their responses and understandings and upon how these inevitably vary. Practical activities also frequently involve group work. Both types of practice thus highlight the social nature of media production and consumption, and accentuate the need to talk, compromise, and negotiate. These skills are part of a broader curriculum but are often difficult to manage in the classroom. For this reason, pupils often need a formal induction to the technical aspects of practical and production work and carefully structured activities to make group work productive and enjoyable. Arranging exercises that allow the pupils to experience a collaborative process can motivate learning about complex areas such as agency and audience.

Classroom Organisation

An ordinary classroom can be organised to meet the needs of media education if the space is used flexibly to allow groups of pupils access to different facilities as they need them. Rigid and traditional desk arrangements serve little purpose if pupils are to spend time engaged in different activities at the same time, and can be restored if necessary. The following will be needed at different times: thinking/quiet area, talk/discussion space, viewing/listening areas, mess/cutting/pasting space, sorting/spreading out space, writing surfaces, display space, 'hands on' space, and storage for teachers' and pupils' work.

Pupils may not be used to working in a classroom which is organised in this way. The teacher will need to create an atmosphere which fosters purposeful work and movement within this organisation. Pupils should be introduced to and encouraged to develop a sense of personal responsibility for the success of the following activities:

- research and investigation (print/visual/audio texts);
- drafting/evaluating/redrafting in a variety of media;
- sharing/showing/displaying work;
- collaborating in groups of varying sizes;
- discussion/talk for a purpose;
- experimenting/testing hypotheses;
- using media technologies;
- producing texts for specified audiences.

Pupils will need to know where things are kept, where to return things, and why they should be returned after use; how to make the most of available facilities; which things they may use unsupervised; acceptable levels of movement and noise; rules for leaving the classroom (for example, to visit the library, to conduct interviews, to take photographs or shoot video). It is also important that they deal with evaluating each other's work from a standpoint of helpful support and sharing; they should be encouraged to accept the responsibility which is inherent in the use of critical powers.

In working with the media it is crucial that the model of teachers providing the knowledge for their pupils is adjusted. By drawing on their own experiences pupils are able to develop an understanding of media forms and conventions. The teacher's role, as a consequence, is more complex; she or he must be convener, manager, and facilitator. 7

Media education raises questions about how teachers should teach as well as about how pupils develop the ability to understand, create, and produce from what they already know about media. This involves learning to develop the conditions to bring together the media product, the knowledge of pupils, and the means to understand and produce it. 8

Practical Activity

The technical difficulties of media work often deter the hard-pressed teacher, but it must be borne in mind that children's understanding of media processes and products can be developed through 'low-tech' work. Transforming a written story into a visual form through storyboarding or making a photo-story; making an image collage by selecting and redesigning images taken from magazines; dubbing new sound effects, music, or narration on to a television extract, using a domestic VCR; these are all relatively straightforward practical assignments which can be as effective as the more complicated video or simulation. Arranging for pupils to manipulate visual elements, to frame and sequence shots for themselves, to add sounds, to select and edit, should develop their general critical awareness of how the media work. Where more sophisticated technology is involved, gradual familiarisation through small-scale practical activities in preferable, but may often be impossible if equipment is only available for a limited time. 9

Learning to use a video camera, or introducing the idea of a storyboard, will often require didactic teaching. But where time allows, learning how to handle the technical aspects of equipment can also be introduced through autonomous play, and through experimentation in the context of learning about the roles of a production team. Practice and theory can be combined in an enjoyable way at the same time as giving pupils the chance to familiarise themselves with the workings of the equipment. In this way, learning about the technology is purposeful and contextualised. It is important not to minimise the logistical problems posed by practical work, but media education without practical work is rather like trying to take experiments out of science. It reduces the subject to an academic, highly theoretical body of knowledge and subtracts a particular way of thinking and learning from the curriculum. 10

Pupils need to evaluate their learning from what can often be absorbing activities, and to extrapolate general principles from particular examples. They need to connect their experiences as consumers with the ones teachers can provide as producers and to relate received knowledge to the understanding they produce in practical work. 11

Content Analysis

Content analysis is a quantitative method of study leading to an evaluation of the formal aspects of a medium. For example, pupils may gauge how 12 much of a newspaper is devoted to pictures compared with text. Or they may count the number of advertisements matched against the number of news stories. The reasons for their conclusions have to be set against what type of paper it is, whether it is local or national, etc. Other standard exercises are to define a magazine's representation of women by counting the number of pictures of women in passive roles compared to those seen in active roles, or to count the number of shots in a short piece of television news. This type of activity involves the ability to read selectively and to summarise findings in and through media texts.

Textual Analysis

Children need to be introduced to ways of 'reading' the language of sound 13 and vision in media texts, as well as the language of other media texts such as comics, just as they are asked to learn how to make sense of literary texts. Children can explore how meaning is produced both through their own productions and through analysis of media products.

Any media text, whether it be a painting from the eighteenth century 14 or a comic from the late twentieth century, can be analysed using the interdependent areas of knowledge and understanding as the basis for practical work. Close textual analysis will steer pupils away from making judgements too quickly about what it is they think they can see or hear. For example, a typical exercise often used is to introduce a short piece of television and ask pupils to identify and describe what they see and hear. By turning down the sound pupils can concentrate on aspects of visual meaning. They can then listen to the sound without the picture and describe and identify what they can hear. With both sound and vision turned on pupils can share individual interpretations of the combined meaning of sound and vision. A second stage involves pupils saying what they think it means, and explaining why they have made those assumptions. Finally, they move on to making judgements about how effectively the producers have conveyed their meaning to them or to the targeted audience. The aim is to draw attention to the joins and to various formal elements such as how lighting, camera movement, framing, close-up, and medium shot contribute to the meaning of a piece of television.

Unless children perceive how textual analysis fits into the study of a 15 medium or theme the exercise runs the risk of being overly schematic and dry. Reflecting back on their own productions will also enable them to make more sense of their analytical studies. Conversely, a production-led approach where pupils are simply launched into producing a newspaper or video may result in some laudable facsimiles of newspapers. But these will not necessarily provide knowledge and understanding about forms and conventions unless attention is drawn to them by themselves, others, or the teacher. Knowledge of how products are constructed does not automatically imply that pupils can talk about what they mean.

Case Study

Media education often tends to focus on texts – single images, extracts
from film or television, etc. – for analysis. This may make sense experienti-
ally and pedagogically at first, but as such work develops it becomes important to know about and understand the historical, industrial, and political
context in which texts are produced and circulated.

Questions about production decisions, censorship, political controversy,
and the popularity or notoriety of particular texts cannot be answered
through textual analysis alone, but may be of crucial importance in understanding a text. Undertaking the research necessary to answer some of
these questions can pose insuperable problems for the classroom teacher.
Some published materials, such as *Bookmaking* (Scottish Film Council) or
Hammer Horror (BFI), attempt to fill this gap by offering a wealth of
contextual information, but present problems about how to handle it pedagogically.

It is thus a useful strategy for the media teacher to be constantly aware
of current media issues, including the coverage of major events, and to
look for opportunities to encourage case studies by pupils on the coverage
of these issues and events. This not only helps to build up school resources
to back up contextual analysis, but develops pupils' own understanding of
the range of issues that may affect the meaning and significance of individual texts. Investigating the reasons for a television programme being
pulled off the air will usually involve research into a range of other media,
including print. Local events and institutions may provide opportunities
to interview real people to find out more about how producers relate to
their audiences. Typical subjects include the study of advertisements and
how the Advertising Standards Authority (ASA) monitors and makes
judgements on specific cases. Both advertisements and the ASA documentation are quite easy to obtain. Children can also investigate materials
and texts relating to a local event, such as the building of a road or the
drama created when a personality is reported by press and television. When
pupils include media producers in their own investigation of a subject, their
sense of the complexity of the issues involved is likely to be heightened.

Where case studies can take place in parallel with pupils' own practical
activities and production work, pupils should be able to get a good sense
of what are the key questions to ask about context.

Simulation

Simulations are sometimes understood in a limited sense as packaged, preselected materials through which children follow a set of predetermined
activities. We mean simulation here in a broader sense – the idea of creative
and analytical activity which allows not only approximation of real media
practice but also reflective space. Simulations start from the question 'What
if?' and can range from looking at a photograph from the point of view of
another person to sophisticated desktop publishing in the style of a well-
known magazine. They do not, as is sometimes assumed, demand acting
skills, but usually group work will involve a presentation or exhibition of
ideas and outcomes, sometimes in 'role', for example, as a media producer
or editor.

Teachers can use simulations to explore a range of media processes, 21
systems, and practices. In turn simulations can help to illustrate institutional, technological, and economic aspects of media. If well constructed
they provide staged learning experiences, which can be assessed and used
for self-evaluation and evaluation by teachers. Pupils can learn through
simulations that professional products involve finance, materials, and technology, as well as the combined work of professional producers in the
construction of a real product. There are several packs and materials available for simulation work and teachers can adapt these or invent new ones.

One type of simulation is the scheduling exercise which requires pupils 22
to timetable a list of real or given programmes into an evening's viewing
for a television channel, sometimes set up in competition with another
channel's listings which have already been fixed. The aim of this exercise
is to draw on pupils' ability to target certain programmes to specific audiences who may be watching programmes at particular times of day. Pupils
learn about different broadcasting institutional styles as well as focusing on
understanding the area of audience.

Variants on this type of simulation require pupils to produce researched 23
programme proposals. For example, they have to take on the brief of a
programme-maker tendering to a television broadcaster for a new children's
series. Pupils have to produce draft materials, outline scripts, character
profiles, series plot lines, audience profiles, and costings of a production to
present to a commissioning programme editor.

Other simulation activities are programmed to work under strict time 24
constraints and deadlines. One typical tried and well-tested simulation was
Radio Covingham (no longer available), upon which many other simulations
have been modelled. This required pupils to place themselves in the role
of copy editors and technical producers in a radio station who receive a
memo from their executive manager to 'improve their ratings performance'.
Over a period of two hours, or two lessons, letters, bulletins, memos,
and in-tray material flood in throughout the 'day', and pupils prepare a
ten-minute news programme by selecting, writing, linking, reading, and
recording the material as a 'live' broadcast. Production constraints are
introduced such as news updates and last-minute news items. This type of
exercise encourages pupils to think about working to real deadlines to
produce material in a form which is recognisable to a specified audience of
listeners. Pupils also have to consider the organisation of their roles as a
group. This enables them to consider how media products are the result
of many producers. Teachers should bear in mind that the agenda of any
pack like this has been 'set' already in its selection of the raw material.

In planning, teachers will need to decide which elements of the process 25
they wish to emphasise. If, for example, a secondary age group aimed to
address an infant audience through a radio weather report, then their ability
to link the bits of narrative together might not be given as much prominence
as the ability to find a language and format to engage with that age group
audience. Technical and theoretical elements of assignments need to be
carefully balanced; expected outcomes should be carefully identified and
agreed, supported and evaluated.

Simulations can be devised for other media such as books, newspapers, 26 or television, where pupils produce proposals in the form of class presentations to 'newspaper editorial boards', 'book publishers', or to 'commissioning editors' for new television programmes. The content of these presentations can include plot synopses, cover and package design, schedule breakdowns, and film treatments.

Another, much simpler, type of simulation requires pupils to act in the role of film editor by putting a number of specially designed photographs in an order appropriate for a particular category of film. Packs such as *The Visit* (English and Media Centre, London), where the images have to be sequenced to create the maximum suspense effect, as for a thriller, are basic staples of media teaching. These can be annotated with comments about shot changes, camera angle, movement, atmospheric effects, dialogue, and music. Pupils can explore different kinds of narrative and often experiment with other categories of film and television such as comedy, horror, or advertising. The function of this activity is to enable pupils to understand selection, ordering, and construction. From this exercise pupils are able to use storyboards more effectively.

A third and more sophisticated kind of simulation takes pupils through the processes of film script development, including outline scripts, genre and narrative, marketable stars and producers, and budgets. Tendering production companies present their 'treatment' proposal to their sponsors, one group in role, briefed by the teacher. Such exercises, when skilfully handled, help pupils to understand that selling an idea for a film also means producing a marketable product which has several spin-offs in other media and marketing contexts. Some pupils display previously unrevealed skills in persuading the other side to change their mind, and the exercise can demonstrate some sleights of hand and shifts of principle and motivation. Pupils can explore the process by which institutional determinants influence the content of the text. They also learn how social dynamics can shift and change decisions and attitudes.

Production

Through systematic development of their knowledge, understanding, and technical skills, pupils are prepared for more extensive projects such as the production of whole publications or videos. The different elements of the production require careful structuring to balance theoretical issues and practical execution. It is important to start with small-scale activities which develop all the aspects of technical, theoretical, and group skills so that larger productions are successful.

There are a number of general principles about the organisation of any practical media activity, including production. Firstly, in setting up assignments it is important to monitor the allocation of roles of pupils and to review it regularly. It is worth ensuring that groups are not divided up along self-selected gender lines – sports page for boys and fashion page for girls, or low-ability pupils into word-searches, or someone appoints themself director and never a technical operator or processor of materials. It is also worth intervening, if necessary, to ask questions of principle or theory. Would disabled people feel happy about receiving that birthday card? What difference would a close-up shot make here instead of a medium shot?

When setting up practical work, it is useful to determine the appropriate form of written and spoken record-keeping for evaluation purposes. Finished videos may not reveal valuable work in the process of making them. Conversely, written logs of what happened may not provide evidence of practical work achieved. The problem can be more complicated if small artefacts are produced as part of the production process. For example, pupils may produce a set of written proposals and story outlines, a draft storyboard, a book jacket, and a newspaper front page, all as part of a video project culminating in a title sequence for a new soap opera. 31

Pupils will need to be encouraged to value the media forms they are using, given the normally high status of written work. Audio or visual texts need to be given as much status as written ones as evidence of understanding, especially where they show exemplary demonstration of forms and conventions and other areas of understanding. While errors of spelling and grammatical weaknesses in pupils' written work should not be ignored, pupils should be encouraged to develop their ability to explore the possibilities of other media. Where the media artefact's technical aspects are likely to be deemed by pupils to be of inferior quality to that produced by professionals, any sense of failure should be pre-empted by agreeing likely outcomes and realistic standards beforehand. 32

It is usually worth considering whether the technical competence required to operate equipment (learning time and ease of use) is worth the learning outcomes anticipated. In other words, is there a low-tech way of achieving the same knowledge and understanding? 33

To formalise a structure for projects over a period of time, there need to be meetings to review, update, assess, and evaluate work in progress. Particular note should be made of progress, allocation of tasks and roles, and group dynamics. These meetings could all be done formally, in role with the teacher, or an appointed group as editor, producer etc. Allowing 'cooling-off' time or space to reflect in pre-exhibition, post-production periods may provide better, different opportunities to evaluate learning about the process of production. 34

In an article in *Initiatives* (no. 10, Autumn, 1988), Alistair Smith, a teacher of media studies, recommends a 'contract' approach to large-scale practical project work. He suggests a diversity of approaches to prevent difficulties of managing practical work. To avoid bottlenecks for the use of the same equipment and to ensure full use of every pupil's potential he recommends a contract sheet which is designed to meet teachers' needs but ideally should include space for, or encourage the recording elsewhere of, review and appraisal by both pupil and tutor. 35

The contract is the mechanism for driving the tutorial process; the tutorial guarantees review and negotiation and does so whilst encouraging open, non-hierarchical relations. It serves as a reminder to group members of their shared aims, individual responsibilities, and as a focus for their thinking. The rest of the contract includes what tasks will be completed by the next stages and lists what requirements will be needed. Both teacher and pupil sign the contract. 36

Private and Public

In addressing the media, teachers are venturing into an arena which may represent a private and pleasurable space for pupils, one which teachers might be tempted to keep separate from the formal school curriculum. This raises several questions which a progressive pedagogy must address:

- How far might media education be perceived as an intrusion by the public institution of the school into the personal space of the pupil?
- How far does work on the media foreground emotions and experiences, for example around romance, relationships, and the family, in which young people might feel vulnerable, and which they would prefer to keep private?
- How far and in what ways should it encourage young people to question their own cultural identity, which may be particularly fragile, i.e., in the process of being formed? Would this process alienate, anger and increase the insecurity of pupils?
- Is there a danger of a hierarchy being constructed in which certain media texts or genres are prioritised over others? For example, are action and adventure – the genres often identified with male pleasures – prioritised to the exclusion of texts which address a specifically female audience, for example, romance, beauty, fashion?
- How far can – and should – media education encourage a shift in the 'private' as well as the 'public' consciousness? Should we be seeking a transformation of consciousness? Does the delivery of 'correct' answers and attitudes in the classroom merely serve as a mask behind which sexist and racist perspectives continue to thrive?
- How censorial an approach should teachers take to racist and sexist attitudes? Teachers can exclude racist behaviour or modify it, but can they and should they expect to do so? How far will such approaches be resisted by pupils who may perceive them as overstepping the boundaries of school?
- How do schools manage the pupils' relationship with media professionals, organisations, or institutions? What mediating influence should the teacher have and what experiences and understandings would we expect pupils to have out of learning through mechanisms and institutions designed for adult working practices? What degree of participation can children have in learning and training through outside agencies and what are the best ways of achieving the most appropriate opportunities?

234

Teaching, Talk, and Learning about the Media

Neil Mercer

Introduction

In this article, I shall begin by briefly describing an approach to the analysis of communications between teachers and children which has become influential in Europe and the USA in very recent years, but which is based on the much earlier work of the Russian psychologist L. S. Vygotsky. I think it is an approach of particular interest to teachers involved in media education and communications studies, because it attempts to do two things. First it offers a theoretical account of the development of human thought and knowledge which is 'socio-cultural'. That is, it is based on a conception of human knowledge and human learning which takes account of the fact that we are essentially social creatures, and not the 'lone organisms' which seem to populate so much psychological research into cognitive development. Secondly, it is not just a theory of learning, but one of 'teaching-and-learning'. It offers insights into the relationship between teachers and learners, and provides a basis for analysing and evaluating teaching and learning which goes on in real classrooms. I will begin by describing some elements of the approach, and will then go on to consider some of its implications for our understanding of communication in the classroom, with special relevance to media education. (Limits on space do not allow me to go into much detail about theoretical issues. Interested readers might like to look also at other publications: see notes 1, 2.)

Vygotsky and a 'Communicative' Approach to the Analysis of Teaching and Learning

When the Russian psychologist L. S. Vygotsky died in 1934 at the age of 37, his ideas on child development and learning had already had a profound influence on those around him. However, because those ideas were so at odds with the official, state-sanctioned psychology of Pavlov, his publications were banned, and little of what he had done filtered through to the West. What did get through made some impact, and most British teachers who trained since about 1968 will remember Vygotsky's inclusion in student reading lists (see note 3). But it is really only since the easing of East-West relations in the last decade, and the resultant emergence and discussion of much more of his work (for example, the collection of essays in Wertsch, note 4), that Vygotsky's ideas have been used to construct the basis for a whole new approach to the study of learning in educational

235

settings. This 'neo-Vygotskian' approach is one which emphasises the social, interactive nature of human learning: within it, education is represented as an activity more concerned with the sharing of cultural resources rather than with the cognitive development of individuals (in contrast with Piagetian theory, for example).

The Concept of 'Scaffolding'

I believe I can best convey the essence of the neo-Vygotskian approach here   3 by discussing one concept which was not actually formulated by Vygotsky himself, but by some psychologists who were among the earliest Western researchers to appreciate the essence of Vygotsky's socio-cultural approach to learning. As early as 1971, the American developmental psychologist Jerome Bruner was pointing out that 'One of the most crucial ways in which a culture provides aid in intellectual growth is through a dialogue between the more experienced and the less experienced' (note 5), and thirteen years later he was saying 'the process of learning how to negotiate communicatively is the very process by which one enters the culture' (note 6). But theories of learning did not seem to take 'culture' and 'communication' into account.

In their research on interactions between parents and very young chil-   4 dren, Bruner and his colleagues developed a concept they called 'scaffolding' (note 7). It is a conceptual metaphor used to describe the form and quality of the effective intervention by a 'learned' person in the learning of another person. It was originally used to describe how children were learning language and being 'tutored' in problem-solving tasks by their parents. However, it seems to me a concept whose relevance to all kinds of teaching is worth exploring. Bruner described the concept as follows:

> If the child is enabled to advance by being under the tutelage of an adult or a more competent peer, then the tutor or the aiding peer serves the learner as a vicarious form of consciousness until such a time as the learner is able to master his own action through his own consciousness and control. When the child achieves that conscious control over a new function or conceptual system, it is then that he is able to use it as a tool. Up to that point, the tutor in effect performs the critical function of 'scaffolding' the learning task to make it possible for the child, in Vygotsky's word, to internalize external knowledge and convert it into a tool for conscious control. (note 8)

The concept of 'scaffolding' is closely related to the original Vygotskian   5 concept of the 'zone of proximal development' (note 9). This zone is 'the distance between the actual developmental level as determined by independent problem-solving and the level of potential development as determined through problem-solving under adult guidance or in collaboration with more able peers' (note 9). Although the term and its definition sound complex and abstract, I believe that the concept of the 'zone' represents a very basic, straightforward, and yet essential aspect of human development. On the journey from being ignorant to being able to understand something, or do something, on your own, you may go through a phase when you are able to succeed at that enterprise with a bit of help. The point that Vygotsky makes is that this phase is a normal, common, and important feature of human mental development, and 'scaffolding' such development is exactly what teachers are supposed to do.

The appeal of the concept of 'scaffolding' for anyone concerned with 6 educational practice is, therefore, obvious: it directs attention to the quality of the participation of a teacher in the learning process, and does so in a way which emphasises that good teaching strategies are necessarily predicated on and responsive to the state of understanding achieved by particular learners. Moreover, I believe that there is much receptiveness among teachers to the model of teaching-and-learning within which the 'scaffolding' metaphor is presented. I say this on the basis of considerable recent involvement with teacher in-service education. The concept of 'scaffolding' seems to elicit an intuitive, positive response among practitioners. Teachers appreciate a model of the learning process which can accommodate the teacher as active participant, and which, moreover, offers teachers a possible ideological escape from the tired debate about 'traditional' versus 'progressive' pedagogies.

Scaffolding

Some educational researchers, notably sociologists and linguists, have 7 shown much interest in classroom talk as a medium through which teachers attempt to control children's behaviour, and through which roles and identities are defined and maintained. They have shown less interest in it as a medium for sharing knowledge, and one through which adults influence the representations of reality, the interpretations of experience, which children eventually adopt. This is what seems to me to be a crucial area of interest for media education. The emergence of the concept of 'media literacy' reflects a growing awareness that children need to be helped to interpret, as well as to appreciate, the products of the mass communications industries.

Notwithstanding the seemingly obvious relevance of the concept of 'scaf- 8 folding' to educational practice, it must be admitted that, like most of the concepts of neo-Vygotskian psychology, it still lacks a very firm basis in classroom research. Apart from some research with which I have been associated (see, for example, notes 2, 10, 11), I know of no other attempts to incorporate Vygotsky's and Bruner's ideas into a systematic analysis of teacher–pupil discourse, and we did not look specifically at the teaching of media studies. I therefore see the rest of this article as no more than a preliminary attempt to test the value and relevance of the neo-Vygotskian approach, and of the concept of 'scaffolding' in particular, to the field of media education.

Watching a Video with the Teacher

The dialogue transcribed below comes from a recording made in a nursery 9 class in a Sheffield school, in which a teacher, Susan Van Noort (see note 14), was engaged in a research project on media education. As part of this project, she watched some selected videotapes of television programmes with the children, and then talked with the children about what they had seen. She devised a special set of 'trigger questions' to elicit the children's views about the programme. One of the programmes they watched was about an animal cartoon character, Henry the kangaroo. In it, live actors appear alongside the cartoon figures.

In the programme, Henry appears initially as a viewer of television, watching TV with a family. But then he jumps into the programme they are watching, becoming self-evidently to the children a television performer. One of the 'trigger questions' Van Noort asked the children about Henry was about this shift, as in this sequence (note: T = Van Noort; S, C, and F are children):

T You remember when Henry jumped into the television. How did he do it?
S He might press the button and that video may and then he might want to jump and then his tail [tape becomes unclear].
T You think his tail is magic? It might be.
F I don't know how he jumped in that telly.
T Do you think that there is any way at all that Ellie [the girl actor in the programme] could have jumped into the television?
S No – she hasn't got a tail!
T She hasn't got a tail?
S If you had got a tail, Mrs Van, you could jump in it, but you haven't got a tail.
T So you think it was the magic tail and that was how Henry did it?
S Yeah.
[S then went on to discuss Henry the character in the soap opera *Neighbours*.]
S I like Henry in *Neighbours* – I kiss him.
T You kiss him?
C She goes out with him.
S Yeah [agreeing, pleased with this idea].
T She goes out with him – but could she go out with him? Henry in *Neighbours*?
S Yeah [changing to 'no' as the other children are chorusing 'no'].
T Why not?
S Because I haven't got a tail.
T What, do you mean because you couldn't get into the television?
S No, I haven't got a tail – if I did I would be magic.
T I see, and then you could jump into the television and go out with Henry?

Although van Noort was on this occasion a teacher-researcher, the episode above has many features which are typical of 'classroom talk'. For example, the teacher directs the flow of discourse, asks all the questions, and comments on most of the children's answers. These features are well-known findings of sociolinguistics research (see notes 12, 13). Here, however, I want to focus more on the content, rather than the structure, of the talk. The talk is very heavily contextualized – it depends for its meanings on the recent shared experience of the teacher and children in watching the video. Moreover, this recent shared experience and the talk about it

238

is made meaningful to the children by its relationship to other cultural experiences in their lives – at home, watching different types of TV programmes, talking about them with their friends; at school, engaging in talk with teachers which has qualities similar to this episode. Anything they learn here will be built upon these cultural foundations.

The important point is that what they learn, what they take away from this educational activity, may depend almost entirely upon how the teacher 'scaffolds' their experience. This is where the neo-Vygotskian identification of a process of 'teaching-and-learning', rather than just 'learning', is most helpful. As Sheeran and Barnes (note 15) succinctly put it: 'Left entirely to their own devices, groups of children may do little more than pool their ignorance; though the teacher's guidance can be subtle and indirect, it must none the less be there.'

The dialogue above shows some of the ways that a teacher uses talk to structure the experience of a group of children. We can see that the teacher is able to:

(a) use the shared experience of the TV programme to explore children's understanding of what they saw (so that they are encouraged to consider and reflect upon their experience);
(b) help children focus on what she considers educationally significant aspects of events by recapping past experience ('You remember when . . .');
(c) paraphrasing or reformulating what children say to check understanding and make meanings clearer ('So you think it was the magic tail . . .');
(d) eliciting children's responses to their experiences so that individual perspectives are brought into the realm of the shared, 'common knowledge' of the group;
(e) help learners perceive continuity in their learning by relating things said and done in earlier events;
(f) relate classroom activities to other cultural reference points outside the classroom (those of television viewing at home).

Although not apparent in the piece of discourse above, teachers will also commonly do the following:

(g) evaluate and legitimise children's responses and contributions in terms of their relevance to the curriculum;
(h) introduce concepts, terms, and styles of discourse which might serve as models for pupils' own work.

The teacher may thus provide a supportive, socially-dynamic framework for the development of pupils' understanding of the media. Of course, teachers may, on any particular occasion, do this well or badly. The effectiveness of such 'scaffolding' would, of course, need to be judged in terms of how well the pupils came to be able eventually to make sense of media experiences on their own.

Conclusion

The neo-Vygotskian approach encourages us to treat knowledge as cultural resource, rather than as individual attribute. It reminds us that the essence of, the unique quality of, human learning is that it is facilitated by social interaction and grounded in culture. The approach is potentially of more than theoretical interest to teachers in media education and communication studies because it provides a possible framework for examining how knowledge is shared, how cultural perspectives are formed, and how social practices are transmitted, through talk and joint activity in the classroom.

Good teachers contextualise new experiences for children by relating them to other experiences, past and present. They 'scaffold' learning through communication and interaction, and in so doing they offer children access to conceptual frameworks which are part of the cultural knowledge of their society, frameworks through which children can make more sense of the world. Of course, teaching can be done well or badly; but we should be able to assert that one important function of education is to assist the creation and continuity of culture, without feeling that this necessarily supports a 'traditional' rather than a 'progressive' educational philosophy. It is through the process of communication that children come to understand culture, and it is through understanding that they may come to own, to possess, what they have learnt. They are then enabled to be active participants in, and creators and critics of, the culture of their society. I believe that it is in dealing with these matters that the neo-Vygotskian framework offers us the best starting-point for making a practical, applied analysis.

Notes

1. N. Mercer, 'Context, continuity and communication in learning', in F. Potter (ed.), *Reading, Learning and Media Education*, London, Blackwell, 1990.
2. N. Mercer, 'Accounting for what goes on in classrooms: what do the neo-Vygotskians have to offer?', *BPS Education Section Review*, no. 15, 1991.
3. L. S. Vygotsky, *Thought and Language*, Cambridge, Mass., MIT Press, 1962.
4. J. V. Wertsch, *Culture, Communication and Cognition: Vygotskian perspectives*, Cambridge, Cambridge University Press, 1985.
5. J. S. Bruner, *The Relevance of Education*, Harmondsworth, Penguin, 1971, p. 20.
6. J. S. Bruner, 'Interaction, communication and self', *Journal of the American Academy of Child Psychiatry*, vol. 23, no. 1, 1984, pp. 1–7.
7. D. Wood, J. Bruner, and G. Ross, 'The role of tutoring in problem-solving, *Journal of Child Psychology and Child Psychiatry*, vol. 17, 1976, pp. 89–100.
8. J. Bruner, 'Vygotsky: a historical and conceptual perspective', in J. V. Wertsch, op. cit. pp. 24–5.
9. L. S. Vygotsky, *Mind in Society*, London, Harvard University Press, 1978.
10. D. Edwards and N. Mercer, *Common Knowledge: the development of understanding in the classroom*, London, Methuen, 1987.
11. D. Edwards, N. Mercer, and J. Maybin, *The Development of Joint Understanding in the Classroom*, Final Report of ESRC-funded project C00232236, 1987.
12. M. Stubbs, *Language, Schools and Classrooms*, London, Methuen, 1976.
13. A. D. Edwards and V. Furlong, *The Language of Teaching*, London, Heinemann, 1978.

14. Sue Van Noort, 'Nursery School Children Talking about Television' in Part IV of this Reader.
15. Y. Sheeran and D. Barnes, *School Writing*, Milton Keynes, Open University Press, 1991, p. 80.

Evaluating Media Education through Action Research

Peter Scrimshaw

Introduction

From one point of view it could be argued that media education is too new an activity to be evaluated at all. If the purpose of evaluation is to establish levels of success against well-established benchmarks, there may be something in this. Given the current preoccupation with the National Curriculum, such a perception of evaluation is the one that may come most easily to mind. Yet it is arguable that what media education needs at present is a form of evaluation that enables teachers to explore and test out a variety of possibilities, aiming at expanding understanding rather than checking current practice against already fixed standards.

Media education, as a relatively new curriculum area, is one with which few curriculum theorists are very familiar. But as the classroom accounts in this Reader show, interesting and thought-provoking ways of introducing the area are beginning to emerge. These accounts provide a resource for teachers, suggesting ideas and approaches that can be tried out and modified for different situations. Some of them, referred to below, go beyond this, however, and indicate what kind of evaluations of media education will be needed in the future. The question is how evaluations of sufficient variety and quality can be generated. Classroom action research offers one important way of achieving this.

Action Research and Media Education

A detailed discussion of the methodology of action research cannot be provided in a single article; for that you will need to go to the sources mentioned below. Nor is it possible to convey briefly the internal divergences and ideological tensions subsumed under this general label. There are disagreements between those who favour a broadly objectivist perspective, seeing research as providing a progressively more accurate approximation to 'how things are', and those who see all knowledge as socially and culturally relative. Among the relativists there are degrees of difference in the extent to which they see knowledge as an individual or a group construction. Another major tension is between those who favour a pragmatic approach based upon teachers' common-sense categories, and those who believe that action research must generate its own theory, and the specialised vocabulary to go with this. All these differences (and there are others) affect both how and why action research is carried out. Something of the range of positions can be seen by contrasting the views of Stenhouse (note

17), McNiff (note 11), and Stronach (note 18). To attempt to discuss these positions would take us far beyond a single article. Instead I shall try to indicate in broad terms what action research is, the ways in which information is collected by action researchers, research problems formulated, the research planned, and interpretations checked.

Action research is quite widely used in the social sciences. Cohen and Manion (note 6) define it as 'a small-scale intervention in the functioning of the real world and a close examination of the effects of such intervention'. In education in particular it has developed in a more specific way, and is usually defined more closely; as Carr and Kemmis (note 4) put it:

4

> Action research is a form of self-reflective enquiry undertaken by participants (teachers, students or principals, for example) in social (including educational) situations in order to improve the rationality and justice of (*a*) their own social or educational practices, (*b*) their understanding of these practices, and (*c*) the situations (and institutions) in which these practices are carried out.

I have characterised action research as a form of educational evaluation, but not all evaluation involves action research. In educational contexts, evaluations can be carried out by outsiders rather than teachers, and may not be directed to understanding educational practices at all. They may, for instance, be concerned with grading pupils or checking the extent to which teachers or schools are conforming to an externally defined set of requirements. Such evaluations do not involve action research, which is a distinctive type of curriculum evaluation, carried out by one or more participants, and emphasising increased understanding as a means to curriculum improvement. This kind of evaluation is, I believe, highly compatible with the stance towards media education taken in this Reader. As Robin Bower (note 2) points out in his study:

5

> Asking pupils to articulate their views is a vital step to their own understanding of issues and their position. Giving them the means to communicate those views is a liberating process which will hopefully empower them to influence others.

Thoroughly researching an aspect of their own practice and disseminating the results empowers teachers in a very similar way, and for the same reasons.

When evaluating media education, simple checklists and multiple-choice questionnaires have only a limited role. By contrast, the usual action research methods of personal observation and detailed recording fit the requirements well. On a pragmatic level it is also important that media education can, at least in secondary schools, expect to get some priority in the provision of, for instance, cameras, word processors, and video and audio equipment, and that staff using them should get a chance to learn how to handle these effectively. The same equipment and skills are well suited to action research, too; indeed, where more equipment is needed the combined case for its provision for media work and staff self-development is surely a strong one.

6

Both media education and action research emphasise active learning, see critical reflection as a precondition for changing practices, and set these practices in their social and institutional context. They differ in that in media education it is the student whose autonomy and self-awareness is to be increased by critical reflection, whereas in action research the teacher is the immediate beneficiary. Naturally they also differ in their objects of study: the media in the one case, educational activities in the other. Nevertheless, many of the basic techniques of study and analysis are common to both.

Collecting Information

Information for action research purposes can be collected in many ways. Details of most of these can be found in standard books on educational and social science research methods (notes 1, 6), and their employment in evaluation contexts is clearly and carefully discussed in McCormick and James (note 12). Within the range, however, there is an important difference between reactive and nonreactive methods, although variants of many research methods can be used in either way.

A great deal can be learned about classroom life without affecting what goes on. Such nonreactive approaches are convenient for action research and avoid the collection of information itself affecting what is collected (note 22).

One method is to look for available sets (or archives) of material (note 22) that can be collected and studied without disturbing the normal processes of the classroom. Pupils' work can provide some of this information. Their own texts are a significant source of evidence: assignments, project work, and exam papers are obvious examples. Jenny Grahame, for instance, used written evaluations produced for GCSE coursework as one source (note 9) but group-produced videos (note 2), photographs, drawings, and graffiti are equally valuable.

Material chosen by pupils are another reservoir of information, although their precise significance for the pupil is less easy to establish without enquiring. T-shirts, clothes, choices of records or tapes, videos hired, TV programmes watched, magazines, papers, and comics bought, can all be relevant. Sue Van Noort, for instance, documented one effect of media on nursery children by recording the clothes and toys that they brought to school which had media connections (note 20).

A third set of archives are those produced by the school. Many are about the pupils individually or as a group; classroom records, school records, results of tests or exams all tell much about the school as well as the pupils. Selections of purchased artwork displayed in school (or its absence), the characteristics of the pupils' work shown in public spaces in the school, and within their own classroom, may also tell a story.

A quite different way of gathering information without affecting what is observed is to use concealed audio or video recording equipment. Similarly, where computers are being used it is often possible to modify the program so that it unobtrusively records and saves all the pupil's keyboard entries for later analysis. As this emphasises, all nonreactive methods are, by definition, covert. They therefore raise ethical issues that you need to consider (note 12).

Participant observation offers yet another possibility, although whether 14 it is a covert method or not depends upon precisely how it is carried out. When working with pupils it is often possible to observe them without doing anything obviously different from your usual activities (note 8). Many of the classroom accounts in this Reader rest very heavily upon this one method. If accounts based on such observations are to be reliable they need writing up quickly afterwards outside the classroom, perhaps in the form of a teaching diary. Later these descriptive entries can be reviewed, and possible interpretations and questions for further study added.

Observations can cover a selected phase of an activity, focusing upon a 15 particular concern. What is involved in encouraging the learning of media languages, categories, agencies, technologies, audiences, and representations offer obvious targets for research in media education, but how pupils learn about the interrelationships between two or more of these are probably even more important. This implies that studies, if they are to be of any depth, will need to concentrate upon quite short sequences. Part of David Sudbery's classroom account, for instance, concentrates upon how teacher and pupils analysed a single brief continuity sequence (note 19).

Because nonreactive methods do not create any new interference effects, 16 they are less vulnerable to the preconceptions that you bring to the situation, because these cannot directly affect what is available. On the other hand, these preconceptions will still influence your decision about what to observe or collect, and how to interpret it. Finally, nonreactive data always has the potential to surprise; because they are not in the control of evaluators and were not intended to answer the questions they have in mind they often force a productive reconceptualisation of the original problem, as well as suggesting quite new ways of handling it. This is particularly helpful at the start of an evaluation, and where a major aim is to help evaluators become more reflective about what is going on. This has obvious benefits for action research on media education.

The limitations of nonreactive methods are the converse of their advantages. Because they cannot be changed by the evaluator they have a take-it-or-leave-it quality; what is not there has to be done without. However, they actually contain far more information than is immediately obvious, and much can be inferred from such data. Indeed, as archaeology, history, and astronomy illustrate, whole disciplines are based upon the collection and analysis of nonreactive data. Nonreactive data is also non-selective, so picking out what is relevant from the pile of material available can be time-consuming. Furthermore, much of this material will not be in standardised form, so that simple comparisons between individuals or subgroups are not easy to make.

The obvious way to avoid these problems is for you to intervene directly 18 to collect the information you need, in the form that you want it. Direct non-participant observation is one option. This may involve someone else taking the class while you watch a group at work, or arranging the programme so that you can be free to observe key parts of the lesson uninterrupted. Notes and photographs can provide an immediate record of such observations, and polaroid pictures are particularly useful as a focus for discussion with pupils immediately after a lesson (note 21).

Where observation is difficult to arrange, video and audio recording is an alternative. A clear idea of who and what you need to record is essential, and the positioning and effective functioning of the equipment must always be checked beforehand, preferably with a complete dummy run. This also reduces the pupils' reaction to being recorded. Using a zoom lens and an external microphone limits the effects of the camera's presence somewhat, and records non-verbal communication better. Analysing the techniques and camera positions used in, for instance, BBC/OU classroom programmes will suggest ideas that can be adapted to your own equipment and purposes.

Interviews can be used together with observation, either as a preliminary or a follow-up method, or as an independent source of information (note 24). As well as individual or group interviews by you, pupils can interview each other, using questions provided by you, or indeed discuss a general topic together without a formal interview structure. These discussions can be recorded on audio or videotape, with the equipment being set up and operated by the pupils. Like most methods of collecting information, interviews are not as simple to carry out and report as they may seem (note 16).

Questionnaires are another possibility. These can be more or less open-ended, but in either case need to be designed and interpreted carefully (note 25).

Pupil and/or staff diaries are useful, but need to be written within an agreed framework if you expect to make comparisons across them. The topics to be covered can be negotiated with the pupils, or structured logs with agreed topic headings might be provided. In either case, a very realistic assessment is needed about how much work you expect others to do for your evaluation. Because the completion of such diaries are outside your control, the success of the evaluation should not be totally dependent upon their successful completion.

The strengths of these more direct methods are that they allow you to begin to formulate assumptions about what is happening and why, to test these out, and then to revise them and repeat the process. If you know before you start what you are trying to find out, these approaches allow you to go directly to the information you need. Unfortunately, the direct approach necessarily affects what information you get. You need to try to minimise this effect, or at least to get some idea of how strong it is, so that you can make due allowances for it in interpreting the information obtained.

Formulating the Problem

Action research typically involves the study of a specific case, rather than a comparison across a large number. So one classroom, one department, or one school are likely sites. Even with that restriction, to research your own practice cannot ever be to research all of it. It is sometimes claimed that to analyse a single hour of classroom activity takes something like ten hours, so selection is essential.

It is also difficult. Despite the formal divisions into periods and courses of study, classroom events and processes interrelate, and all have links with

246

events back in time and outwards into the school and beyond. It is seldom obvious quite where the boundary of a particular case should be drawn. Angela McEwan's account (note 10) of the implementation of media education in the Renfrew Division of Strathclyde Regional Council is a study of one innovation involving 180 English teachers in 29 schools; it is therefore both the study of a single case and an account of what happened in a range of different situations, as seen by one of the innovators.

Similarly, the precise issue that you are interested in is often hard to define, and in any situation all sorts of combinations of focus are viable. So how should the focus for the research be chosen? 26

If you have started with a clear picture of the problem you wish to research, a fairly structured approach is possible. If not, a more open strategy is needed, in which an understanding of the nature of the problem and of how it can be researched can evolve in step as the work goes forward. This choice between structured and open approaches is an important one, affecting problem formulation, the research plan, and how evidence is collected and processed. It is also a choice that you may well revise as you go along. Often what starts as an apparently simple question unravels into a more difficult set of underlying problems as you proceed. Conversely, you may want to close down an initially broad area of concern as the research progresses, until you are focusing attention upon a specific and central issue within it. 27

One way of seeing where you stand on this is to try to write down your problem in three different ways: as a statement of the topic, as a set of questions, and as a set of hypotheses. How far you can work down this sequence at the outset gives an indication of how far you can use structured methods straight away. The research project described by Eddie Dick (note 7), for example, addressed two questions: what counted as media education and what counted as policy for media education. Cathy Pompe, by contrast, started work on one of the two projects she analyses (note 15) from an interrelated set of hypotheses: 28

> The idea of combining science with media work arose from the conviction that children's interest in science is kindled by the attractive ways science is packaged and presented in the media, and that science is itself a constructed discourse with its own set of communication and persuasive devices: a programme in media awareness might help children become more skilled at assessing and communicating scientific information . . . by making room for the powerful narratives and other media texts in which science and technology play star parts, children might be given the imaginative space within which scientific notions could be meaningfully explored and absorbed.

If no questions or hypotheses come to mind, a preliminary period of open-ended observation and reflection will be needed to allow the reasons for your concern with the topic to begin to surface. Jenny Grahame's experience in researching the role of practical work (note 9) illustrates this:

. . . somewhere along the line my focus changed – not once, but several times. At various stages I found myself shifting from an evaluation of simulation as a methodology to an examination of the significance of social interaction, to an analysis of gender differences and, ultimately, to reflections on the process of students' own self-evaluation.

An easy mistake to make at this initial stage is to want to decide what research methods to use before having any questions or hypotheses in mind. Making informal notes of important points and possible questions is helpful at this point, as on later rereading an implicit pattern often appears from which you can draw out your concerns more clearly. If, on the other hand, a set of questions or hypotheses can be formulated at the outset they will often indicate how to proceed. Of the two, hypotheses tend to be more constraining, but both can be more or less tightly specified.

Developing a Research Plan
The degree of openness built into the plan affects how the problem is formulated, the methods used, and possibly the form of any account that is later given of the research. Another issue is the relative importance given to quantitative and qualitative methods of collecting information and presenting findings. These two aspects can be combined or counterpointed in several ways.

A design often used by social scientists is to begin with an exploratory qualitative pilot study to provisionally identify the key issues, then to plan a relatively closed main study, using largely quantitative methods.

Another is to use qualitative methods throughout, starting with a broadly defined area of concern, and moving steadily towards a clearer and more specific definition of the central concern of the study as you work on it. Jenny Grahame's study (note 9) illustrates this general approach. This technique is often called progressive focusing, and is compatible with retaining qualitative methods throughout.

A third is to start with a quantitative preliminary study, in which you are looking for thought-provoking or unexpected patterns, and then to move to qualitative methods to explore the possible reasons for these patterns. The role of the quantitative element here, then, is not to answer questions so much as to provoke them, by giving the researcher something unusual to explain.

David Brockie's investigation (note 3) into ways of using fragrances to explore gender images illustrates a particular variant of this approach on a small scale. Pupils were first asked to decide whether they thought each of eight fragrances was designed for men or women. The results of this clearcut task were recorded, and subsequently used to confront pupils with the difference between what they claimed they knew about the connection between fragrances and gender and what they had actually been able to tell in the absence of other cues of the sort provided by TV advertisements. When they were later asked to analyse such advertisements Brockie noted that

the activity of 'content analysis' which I have used previously
number of occasions seemed to have bite and relevance here, in ι
the fragrance activity had made the students sharply aware of hι
their senses could be manipulated.

From Information to Evidence

Action research is a guide to what to do next; it therefore has to come up
with some conclusions that indicate what would constitute a more rational
and just course of action. These conclusions are not obvious from the
information that you collect, although they often appear so. It is a natural
thing to get new information, map it intuitively upon our current beliefs
and values, and then allow the course of action to emerge as self-evident.
This, however, ignores the need for reflection, and limits the possible value
of the work to finding better means of achieving unexamined ends. It also
assumes that all the information collected is both internally consistent and
correct. These assumptions need checking, and in the process your original
beliefs may need revising. So how can such checks be carried out?

All the information collected is gained either from texts (e.g., video,
audio, photographs, pupils' work, observation notes, etc.) or from direct
observation. In the case of direct observation you can only gain access to
this for analysis either by referring to a text that records all or part of it,
or completely from memory. The latter is particularly vulnerable to selec-
tivity and bias, so I would say that even direct observation needs to be
permanently recorded in some form if it is to be really useful.

One way of interpreting texts is through content analysis. This involves
creating a set of categories and allocating segments of text to them. From
this, patterns of relative frequencies and frequent sequences of segments
can be identified. Although this is sometimes dismissed by action
researchers as too mechanical an approach, I think it has a place in a
preliminary quantitative analysis. Deciding upon a limited number of categories and allocating items to them forces us to make our conceptualisation
of the problem explicit and simple. It also tests that conceptualisation hard,
against direct pressure from the details of the data. Finally, it may well
reveal unexpected patterns.

Content analysis, however, goes only so far. While it can be used to
establish patterns, it cannot in itself suggest explanations for those patterns.
It also assumes a rather simple atomistic structure for elements in a text
that fails to bring out underlying themes and their interrelationships. Some
form of structural analysis is required to do this, and David Sudbery's
deconstruction of the BBC continuity sequence (note 19) provides an
example of this kind of analysis.

Interpretations and explanations need to be validated by more than reference to a specific observation or comment in an interview. One way of
doing this is to accumulate a range of evidence for the claim from, say,
different points in an interview. This can establish internal coherence, but
does not establish that the beliefs held are defensible.

To do this you need to cross-check (or triangulate) different sources of
information. If interviews with pupils, your observation notes, and the

35

36

37

38

39

40

pupils' written work all support the same interpretation, that greatly strengthens the case for it. Tony Carroll's study of his photomontage project (note 5) illustrates this. To interpret one pupil's development, Carroll refers to her drawing observation exercises, to the classroom scene she finally produced, and to her own record of the oral work that the creation of the picture involved. Later he also draws upon pupils' taped discussions to get another perspective upon the montages they have created.

This sort of triangulation also partly compensates for the limitations of particular kinds of information; a group's joint written summary of their conclusions shows detail that is not picked up on a videotape of their discussion, but the latter allows you to see something of the process by which those conclusions were reached. Participant observation will include information on relevant classroom events out of range of a tape recorder but, as Cathy Pompe points out (note 15), even when listening directly to a pupil you can miss much that you would notice on later listening to a recording of the same conversation.

It is a basic assumption throughout that your own current interpretation is itself treated as open to revision. Indeed, at every stage you should be searching out new information to challenge your present views. A particularly important form of triangulation is one which involves preparing preliminary drafts of your reading of the situation and circulating this to other participants. They then comment upon its accuracy and relevance from their perspective, and in the process provide information which can be used to improve the accuracy and sensitivity of the account. At an earlier stage you may want to circulate a first draft to people who may have experience of similar situations, to see if they can suggest new topics or point out questions or problems you have not anticipated. Written classroom accounts by others, such as those in this Reader, serve the same purpose.

From Interpretation to Action

In theory, the action element of action research need involve only a personal decision to make whatever changes seem best. If so, why bother to write up anything at all about what you have found out?

One reason is that some action research (note 14) is a joint enterprise anyway, where a final response needs to be formulated and agreed. Another is that even where you are dealing only with your own classroom the changes that are required often need agreement from others outside it, or indeed from the pupils. Providing a written account that makes clear the information upon which it is based is one way of giving everyone involved an external point of reference around which discussion can take place. Finally, even if you can introduce change on your own, writing out the account both during and at the end of the process can be an invaluable way of both crystallising and distancing yourself from your own prior beliefs; in other words, you become a critical reader for your own account (note 23).

Written accounts are the usual form that such summaries take, but media education teachers could assist action researchers generally by loosening up the conventions about how evaluations are presented. Although researchers often talk about using other media, in practice a conventional text is nearly always what appears at the end of the day. Video, tape/slide shows, photo and text-based collage are all possibilities, as is the use of computer-based hypertext and hypermedia packages. Quite how we need to rethink the procedures of action research to allow the collection and display of findings in these ways is an interesting question, as is the likely effects of different forms of presentation on the audiences for whom such accounts are prepared. Here, as at many other points, media educators and action researchers could have a lot to learn from each other.

Notes

1. Walter Borg and Meredith Gall, *Educational Research: An Introduction* (3rd ed.), New York, Longman, 1979.
2. Robin Bower, 'Media Education as an Essential Ingredient in Issue-based Environmental Education', p. 312 in this Reader.
3. David Brockie, 'Sniffing out Stereotypes: Using Fragrances to Explore Gender Images in Advertising', p. 350 in this Reader.
4. W. Carr and S. Kemmiss, *Becoming critical: knowledge, action and research*, Brighton, Falmer, 1986.
5. Tony Carroll, 'Photomontage: Image and Meaning', p. 359 in this Reader.
6. Louis Cohen and Lawrence Manion, *Research Methods in Education*, London, Croom Helm, 1980.
7. Eddie Dick, 'Developing Broad Strategies and Interventions', p. 408 in this Reader.
8. Dot Froggatt, 'Representation', p. 292 in this Reader.
9. Jenny Grahame, '*Playtime*: Learning about Media Institutions through Practical Work', p. 369 in this Reader.
10. Angela McEwan, 'Renfrew Raises the Media Standard', p. 414 in this Reader.
11. Jean McNiff, *Action Research: Principles and Practice*, Basingstoke, Macmillan, 1988.
12. Robert McCormick and Mary James, *Curriculum Evaluation in Schools* (2nd edn), Beckenham, Croom Helm, 1988.
13. Roger Murphy and Harry Torrance, *Evaluating Education: Issues and Methods*, London, Harper and Row, 1987.
14. Sharon Nodie Oja and Lisa Smulyan, *Collaborative Action Research: A Developmental Approach*, Brighton, Falmer, 1989.
15. Cathy Pompe, ' "He Quickly Changes into his Bikini": Models for Teacher – Pupil Collaboration', p. 303 in this Reader.
16. Janet Powney and Mike Watts, 'Reporting Interviews: A Code of Good Practice', *Research Intelligence*, no. 17, September 1984. (Reprinted in Murphy and Torrance, *Evaluating Education: Issues and Methods*, 1987.)
17. Lawrence Stenhouse, 'The Conduct, Analysis and Reporting of Case Study in Educational Research and Evaluation'. Reprinted in Murphy and Torrance, *Evaluating Education: Issues and Methods*, 1987.
18. Ian Stronach, 'Practical Evaluation', in David Hopkins (ed.), *Evaluating TVEI: Some Methodological Issues*, Cambridge, Cambridge Institute of Education, 1986. (Reprinted in Murphy and Torrance, *Evaluating Education: Issues and Methods*, 1987.)
19. David Sudbery, ' "What Does it Mean?" Deconstructing a Continuity Sequence with 9G', p. 328 in this Reader.
20. Sue Van Noort, 'Nursery School Children Talking about Television', p. 274 in this Reader.

21. Rob Walker and Clem Adelman, *A Guide to Classroom Observation*, London, Methuen, 1975.
22. Eugene Webb, Donald Campbell, Richard Schwartz, and Lee Sechrest, *Unobtrusive Measures: Nonreactive Research in the Social Sciences*, Chicago, Rand McNally, 1966.
23. Harry Wolcott, *Writing up Qualitative Research*, California, Sage, 1990.
24. Edward Wragg, *Conducting and Analysing Interviews*, Nottingham, Nottingham University School of Education, 1978.
25. Michael Youngman, *Designing and Analysing Questionnaires*, Nottingham, Nottingham University School of Education, 1978.

Representing Classrooms:
Using Video to Record and Represent Practice
Paul Manners

Evaluating teaching and learning involves interpretation: looking at what happens in classrooms and reflecting on it. One way of doing this is to tape-record or video classroom interaction, creating a record which can then be used as a basis for analysis and discussion. What are the choices facing anyone choosing to video classroom practice, and represent it televisually? And what are the problems and possibilities opened up by the use of video for this end? 1

To answer these questions I want to draw on the experience of producing three classroom accounts of media education, included on the video accompanying the pack *Media Education: an Introduction*. These accounts were produced using BBC crews and post-production facilities, but they do raise issues relevant to anyone planning to use their own video equipment to record classroom practice. 2

I want to explore two areas: firstly, the practicalities of planning to record in classrooms, which are likely to be crowded, busy, and noisy, and secondly, the way that the recorded information can serve as a basis for evaluation and reflection. 3

Planning to Record
Before even beginning to record it is likely that you will have some idea of the kind of end product you hope to achieve. This will inevitably influence the way you go about the recording and the amount of preparation you put in. In the case of the Media Education Pack, we were keen to show what media education can actually look like, assuming that a significant proportion of our audience might be new to the area. We also wanted to support the 'theoretical' drive of the Workbook and Reader, exemplifying general principles in actual classroom interactions. 4

In planning the sequences we discussed three distinct options. We toyed with the idea of a documentary-style approach, which attempted to place the child's experience in school in a wider context: watching television at home, choosing comics at the newsagent, perhaps. Conventional televisual devices here might include a zoom out from the school and a pan taking in some of the manifestations of 'media' in the community around school. 5

Another idea concerned the use of classroom material as observational 'data'. This would involve recording 'real time' sequences in which children were engaged in media education work, and trying to capture as faithfully as we could the content and quality of the interaction. We would then be 6 in a position to present this as evidence. Any editing would be clearly signalled to the viewer.

Another possibility concerned something of a half-way house: not attempting to offer 'data', but to capture something of the flavour of media education work through carefully edited sequences. These sequences would be shaped within a narrative framework organised tightly around themes or issues pertinent to media education; it would not pretend to be a classroom in 'real time', and would use fairly extensive teacher voice over. 7

In electing for the third option it was clear that we needed to look for classrooms where we could capture interesting work in progress, and for teachers who could articulate clearly what they were doing and why they were doing it. At the same time, we anticipated a considerable amount of post-production work, editing, scripting, and shaping the sequences so that they would work as distance learning material, communicating points clearly and raising issues that could be expanded in the accompanying workbook. A quite different scenario might see a teacher planning to use video simply for her or his own personal use, almost like a notebook to record observations. These would be compiled on a tape, but not edited. There might be no audience other than the teacher. 8

Being clear about the purpose of the recording, and the expectations of its intended audience, means that you can then approach the actual recording knowing where to focus and how far to compromise. Inevitably, trying to record in classrooms is fraught with difficulty. The presence of a camera tends to transform what is going on, and the recording technology itself struggles to capture the dynamic process of learning. 9

A final point to bear in mind before recording concerns copyright. Whether you are recording your own class or relative strangers, it is clear that the act of recording involves copying something that does not belong to you, and so is subject to the ethical and legal restraints enshrined in copyright law. For informal purposes it is more the spirit of the law that counts – ensuring you have people's permission and that they are clear about what the recording is for. In the case of the Media Education Pack, because we were intending to sell the material, we needed to ensure we had written permission from the schools and teachers involved, who were acting on the students' behalf. Parents also needed to be informed, and given the option to withdraw their children; this was done by a letter home. 10

Finally, Local Education Authorities are justifiably anxious about publicity that can be generated by recordings of their schools, and if you are intending to go 'public' with the material then they like to know about it. 11

Whatever the circumstances of the recording, you are likely to be asked by the people you have filmed whether you will show them the end result (and if you are intending to show it to a larger audience, whether you will allow them to veto the use of any sequences they are unhappy with). As this kind of recording depends so much on trust, it is important that clear answers are given to these kinds of concerns. 12

Recording in Classrooms

Walking into a class, our senses quickly adjust to the noise level and the 13 variety of interactions. Following a whole-class discussion is easy – our eyes flick from teacher to child, and our ears respond to the geography of the room and its natural acoustic, adjusting automatically between the different 'levels' of sound. Following a small group, we can fairly unobtrusively eavesdrop on their shared discourse and pick up the quality of interaction between them. With a camera and microphone, however, the situation is very different. Sound itself can be an immense problem: for the voice to be reproduced so that it sounds 'natural' and is audible, the microphone needs to be near the speaker. But if someone is answering from the back of the class, how quickly can you get the microphone near them? Are you prepared to have someone in shot holding the microphone, or are you willing to wait while the camera frames the shot carefully to exclude the microphone? Furthermore, while the human ear and brain can 'process' sound so that we focus on one feature and ignore the background noise, a microphone will not be able to differentiate, so how much control over noise levels in the class do you wish to exert?

While the microphone is struggling to reach the speaker, the camera has the same kind of problem. Imagine the class discussion again – the teacher is talking and the camera is on her or him. A child responds, but by the time the camera has swivelled, the teacher is talking again and you end up missing both responses. Likewise, in a small group, the children's utterances are likely to be short, overlapping each others'. They are likely to be noting ideas down on paper, or may be discussing objects laid down on the desk. The human eye would naturally flick between these, but if the camera did the same the recorded information would be made up largely of wobbles and blurs. Another scenario might involve some children seated against a window, but if you shoot towards them their faces will be in darkness or heavy shadow. Shooting in the room as a whole it is unlikely that you will be able to record clean and clear pictures unless some kind of lighting is used. So how can some of these difficulties be overcome? 14

One option is to accept that recording quality need not dominate, and that you can live with the whip pans, variations in light and colour quality, and in sound. However, it is often the sound that is most troublesome; wonderful things might have been happening, but if the viewer is struggling to pick up every other word then the piece will not work at all. This is particularly critical if you intend to make copies of your original tape, as this will cause further deterioration in quality. At the same time, the implications of keeping in all the whip pans and wobbles rather than trying to edit around them means that the viewer will be confronted by an uncomfortable and distracting amount of 'noise': the technology will be constantly announcing its presence and interrupting the 'flow' of the sequence. 15

A second option is to pursue the technical quality while attempting to interfere with the way the room is organised as little as possible. Paradoxically, this involves more equipment and personnel in the room: a doubling-up of cameras and sound operators, and a set-up approximating to a mobile television studio. Inevitably, this option is very expensive and technically complex. The director will sit outside the classroom at a mixing desk and will be able to communicate with the crew via talkback. One camera might be directed to focus on the teacher, and the other to cover the class. The 16 two sound-recordists can between them cover a large room. Something of the cut and thrust of discussion can be captured by skilful direction and camera work, and 'real time' sequences can be recorded with ease as you cut between the cameras, allowing the 'free' camera to reposition and re-frame in response to the developing situation.

However, the price you pay is the complexity of the operation in terms of operators and equipment. A small classroom can easily be swamped, and the director/producer will be outside the classroom and unable to 'tune' into the interactions or relate to the children and teachers being filmed.

A third option involves keeping the 'crew' to a minimum, and so using only one camera, but adopting a more interventionist approach to ensure that picture and sound quality is of a high standard. A list of interventions includes:

- sometimes asking children to repeat answers, or to start again if they have started just before the camera reaches them;
- arranging that some groups work outside the classroom, to ensure that there is room to breathe and that the sound levels are manageable;
- recording cut-aways or 'listening shots' at the end of a discussion to allow bridges to be built in at the editing stage;
- asking groups to pause while the crew change tapes or reposition the camera.

Other strategies which try to alleviate the interference are:

- talking to the children and teacher about what is happening and why, so they at least feel involved in the process;
- trying to cover class discussions in such a way that it is the teacher who needs to repeat their questions, rather than the children. This would be done at the end, after following the children's responses and noting down what the teacher actually asked. Another solution is to try to avoid using whole-class discussion altogether because of the time it takes to set up and its awkwardness to shoot;
- trying to position groups before starting filming so that they can be covered from one position: for instance, placing them around two or three sides of a table, but not on all four sides;
- using fairly gentle pans and zooms to follow the action, impersonating an eye following events, rather than attempting to whip the camera into position to capture each fresh utterance and running the risk of missing it, and asking for it to be repeated;
- editing on the spot: knowing when something is really important, and so taking steps to ensure it is captured in picture and sound (and knowing when to let something go, if it is unlikely to be used anyway);
- having realistic expectations about what it is possible to achieve in one day, allowing for the time it takes a crew to set up in a new setting and the time the children will need to get used to them and to relax. At the same time, trying to keep the class informed of what is happening, and how long it will take, allows them to feel a measure of control over the events;

256

- finally, not trying to achieve all of this at one attempt, but to spend several sessions with the group, allowing them to get used to the presence of the camera and to begin to ignore it.

Reflecting on the Material

So what is the value of using video recordings of classroom practice? The answer to this very much depends on what your purposes were in the first place, and how the material you collect allows you to realise these.

At its simplest, the process of recording and then viewing the material involves looking and listening in a focused way, and so seeing or hearing things that would normally pass unnoticed.

The ability to replay the material means that complex understandings can be generated from interactions that are at first sight uncomplicated. Such analysis, done in groups and with a particular focus (say, looking for evidence of pupils' grasp of a particular key aspect), can allow discussion of theory and practice to overlap productively.

If you have access to editing facilities (other than the fast-forward and rewind buttons) then the material can form the basis for compilations or presentations. Selecting sequences and organising them into a larger text allows arguments to be shaped or evidence to be accumulated.

In our own case, the Media Education Pack offered particular opportunities as well as specific constraints. The resources available to us were far greater than would normally be the case in a school, but at the same time our large and diverse audience meant that we had to think very hard about how we represented practice to them. A video made for use within a school department could depend on a great deal of shared understandings and knowledge, and trust within that department would be likely to mean that embarrassing or unflattering sequences need not be excluded. In our case, we could not ethically set up teachers or pupils to be seen as failing. Instead, we chose a fairly up-beat and positive note for each account. Each was premised on the notion that this is *interesting* teaching and that pupils are learning as a result.

We all know that such is likely to be the case for only part of the time in any classroom, but given that we only had thirty minutes to fill, we wanted to ensure that that time was densely packed. What this meant in practice was that large chunks of discussion were edited down so that progress was clearly seen. If boys were dominating a class discussion then the unrepresentative number of replies from girls were sometimes used. In addition, a number of 'televisual' techniques were exploited when their use was appropriate – most obviously here the use of 'voice over', edited from interviews with the teachers, and laid over the action, interpreting and evaluating what was going on.

This re-working of the material resulted in a condensed and heavily mediated representation of the featured classrooms, which is clearly a long way from the showing of a 'home-made' video at a department meeting, but then its purposes were very different. Its design as distance learning material meant that it needed to be closely linked to the accompanying workbook, illustrating or providing evidence of key points in the design of the pack as a whole.

In conclusion, representing faithfully what happens in any classroom poses technical, ethical, and strategic difficulties. Knowing what your own aims are (and knowing your audience's expectations) is important. It also helps to understand how these intentions can be frustrated or realised through a lens, a microphone, and a finished text. It takes time to feel confident with the necessary techniques and to find a style or format that matches your purposes. However, whatever the end result, the process of planning, recording, and shaping the material is a valuable way of focusing on teaching and learning, and acting on these understandings.

Television as Educator

David H. Tripp

From a paper given to the BHP Australian Television Festival, Perth, 1988.

Some Characteristics of the Child as a Learner

I have to come clean on my assumptions about children and their cognition [1] before I can legitimately suggest ways in which they might be more formally educated about television in school.

One can never articulate all one's assumptions, of course, but both what [2] I am going to say now, and my media education talk, are recognisably premised on the following view:

- children are active in the interrogation of their televisual experience (and therefore in making their own sense of the world);
- that televisual experience is socially constructed (and therefore heavily mediated by other individuals, social structures, and experiences);
- children construct a reality which is just as logical and coherent as an adult view (thought very different from it); and
- children have mental processes which are essentially the same in kind as an adult's (though more limited in some respects, and, more importantly, usually premised quite differently and put to quite different uses).

In that view, children's 'errors' of judgement and perception do not demonstrate that the child is necessarily confused in the same way that adults are confused by, for instance, contradiction, but is, to use Piaget's term, in a state of disequilibrium. And that state of disequilibrium is not the precursor of some pathology (as favourite 'horror stories' about children blindly obeying the box might suggest), but rather is a precondition necessary for meaningful learning to occur. It is a view of children which suggests that for a programme to be educative, for instance, it must not only have things in it which the child cannot understand, but it must also have things in it which signal to the child that there is something in it which they might not have understood. Very often the signals of that disequilibrium are the powerful images which we dream about as we work through to an understanding.

Furthermore, it is a view of children as emergent adults in a relative [3] world. Contrary to a popular myth of schooling, and though experimenters may mark responses right or wrong, people, neither adults nor children, simply do not understand or misunderstand something in any absolute sense: they have an understanding that is more or less consonant with their world view at the time. That means that our understandings are constantly being developed, revised, embellished, and connected to other understandings. In children, these processes are much more active, volatile, and extreme, so that their understanding of anything is more fluid. Because they have so few established understandings, they are more actively engaged in making understandings than they are in recalling them. For this reason, perhaps, they have a more powerful ability to generalise than adults, but less ability for certain kinds of memory. It is so easy to convince children to believe in Father Christmas or magic because of the fact that they have no explanation for, or understanding of, much of what happens in their world. But what parent worries over such beliefs? They know that they will change through the normal course of development as the child grows up. We trust children about such things.

Parents, psychologists, and educators do not trust their children about television in the same way, however, and I would be the first to agree that they have very good grounds for not doing so. A reality constructed mainly from television programmes is quite different from one in which things can happen by magic. If for no other reason, televisual reality is far more interconnected and holistic. I would not trust my children to be able to counteract an early brainwashing in religion, or all later negative peer group pressures, either. But my reasons for my lack of trust in my children about such matters is social, not psychological. Though I often fail to admit it, it is because I want to be active in bringing my children up to be particular kinds of people with respect to certain values, attitudes, knowledge, and abilities. It is not because I think their minds cannot process the data. There are no cognitive reasons for not trusting them to come up with an answer that makes sense to them in their world, but there are good personal and social reasons for wanting them to come up with particular answers which will thereby construct a particular kind of world. And because I see the world in a particular kind of way, if we are all going to live together, it helps if their world approximates to (or at least intersects with) mine in certain basic respects.

Children and Reality

No one could argue that much of our concern over television is with the child's developing sense of reality, what the child treats as real and what as unreal. So I want to present some of the responses of a just above average in ability, middle-class, six-year-old child, to some questions about what is real and unreal to her. The questions were put as part of an experiment using a technique known as Kelly's repertory grid. I won't go into details of the method or results here as these are available in more detail in an earlier paper.[1] But all the television and real life characters were chosen by the child (Natalie) herself, and were in that respect 'significant others'. Here are some examples of what the child came up with. The numbers refer to the order of response, and are important because there were powerful serial effects.

1.	Pet dog	is more real than	Mr Ed
2.	Natalie	is more real than	Tweety Bird
3.	Mummy	is as real as	Monkey
4.	Sister	is more real than	Daffy Duck
6.	Friend	is as real as	Mr Ed
8.	Sister	is as real as	Tweety Bird
9.	Natalie	is as real as	Monkey
14.	Mr Ed	is more real than	Monkey
15.	Monkey	is more real than	Tom and Jerry

And there we have it. Who could ask for stronger evidence of the mind-warping role of television in the creation of a chronic pathology of cognition? In Natalie's fevered misunderstanding of reality, her pet dog is more real than a talking horse, who is both as real as her friend and more real than a monkey who flies around learning religion, who is as real as both her mother and sister. People have objected at this point that, as the neo-Piagetians have shown, what the experimenter thinks they are asking the child and what the child thinks they are being asked, often bear no relation to each other. But quite what the child meant by 'more real' was problematised as part of the experiment, and the evidence which follows strongly suggests that children of this age do have a good understanding of the general meaning of the term, though they apply it rather differently. The question, then, is why Natalie made these responses, and the reason for using Kelly's technique, was, of course, precisely because it can give some insight into the reasons behind such reality judgements. So I want to briefly examine six of Natalie's responses in more detail, drawing out the 'constructs' that Natalie appeared to be using. First, we'll look at responses (1) and (6).

1.   Misty (Pet Dog)
          Mr Ed

Natalie: Misty's 'realer', like we've got him, that's our dog and Mr Ed's only on television.

6.   Nichole (Friend)
          Mr Ed

Natalie: They're both the same.
Interviewer: Mm. Why is that?
Natalie: Because Mr Ed's a horse, and like he lives in where the horses – lives in a barn, and Nicole's here.

It is mainly in the analysis of data that our view of children becomes crucial. If we believe a six-year-old child is not confused by such contradictions, and credit her with being logical in her processing of data although she is not yet always integrating one response with another, then we can make sense of this by suggesting that she is shifting the basis of her judgement. That is to say that, when Natalie compares her own pet dog (Misty) with Mr Ed in (1), she is considering Mr Ed as the television character and her dog as a dog, but when she considers Mr Ed in (6) she sees him as the real horse that he is, not as a talking horse character on television. That is, she can separate the basis of the character from the character, and switches from seeing it one way to the other in different responses. So although she recognises that Mr Ed is a horse and must live in the real world, yet she also recognises that Mr Ed the talking horse character is something which only exists on television. He is thus 'less real' according to the aspect upon which she bases her first judgement, 'more real' according to the second. Although she makes this apparently arbitrary switch in the bases of her judgement, Natalie is nevertheless making a subtle distinction which is supported by two other responses.

14.   Mr Ed
           Monkey

Natalie: Mr Ed.
Interviewer: Is what?
Natalie: 'Realer.' Like Monkey's just in Japan. They've just made him, someone's dressed up as him and Mr Ed's a horse.

15.   Monkey
          Tom and Jerry

Natalie: Um . . . Monkey's more real.
Interviewer: Why is that?
Natalie: Like Monkey's dressed up and Tom and Jerry are just a photo of people dressed up.

Here she recognises that Monkey and Mr Ed have a real existence as a horse and a person inside a suit, but that a person dressed up is less real (or more 'pretend') than a horse which is not dressed up. One might object that horses don't talk, but we have already shown that it is characteristic of this six-year-old child to fasten on a single dimension at one time, and, after all, monkeys don't talk either.

A further development of the notion of continued existence as held by Natalie is the genesis of existence, or the origin of the character. We have already seen that she is aware that a character which has a continued existence independent of television is more real than one which has existence only on the television, but this six-year-old is also aware that something which exists has, at some stage, to come into existence. It is interesting to compare responses (9) and (4) in this respect.

9.   Self
          Monkey

Natalie: Just as real.
Interviewer: Monkey's just as real as you?
Natalie: Yeah, like Monkey's in Japan and I'm here.
Interviewer: Why are you real, how do you know you're real?
Natalie: Like, I was born in Mum's tummy and I'm here. I was a baby and now I came here.
Interviewer: And how do you know Monkey is real?
Natalie: Like, he came out of an egg, like what chickens do.

Interviewer:	Really?
Natalie:	Yeah, that came out of this mud and went right on top of the mountain and then became a monkey.

4.   Katy (Sister)

Daffy Duck

Natalie:	Katy is more real because she's grade 3, she's my sister, she's at school and Daffy Duck, they just make him, they just put him on television. See they get the cameras and they put some stuff in it to make them come.

Again, what seems at first a very surprising and 'incorrect' judgement, that she is as real as Monkey because she was born and Monkey hatched out of an egg, may be seen to be a reasonable response in terms of the nature of the character: she is real because she is a human and she was born after the fashion of humankind; Monkey is real, because Monkey is a magic monkey, and he had a miraculous birth entirely in keeping with the nature of his character. His birth is true to the world in which he lives as Monkey. Daffy Duck, by comparison, is a cartoon character and is thus seen to have a different origin, an origin which is not a part of the existence of the character. Whereas Monkey's birth is seen to be integral with and essential to his abilities and behaviour, Daffy Duck's origin is fundamentally irrelevant in contrast: Daffy was not born into the world in which she exists, she came to exist there only by artificial manufacture by humans which was not part of the story, and as such she is considered 'less real'.

Thus we have at least two major dimensions of this child's construction of television reality: first and foremost, she characterises things as being more real if they, or parts of them, can continue to exist in some respects off television (and this must include the way in which the characters have originated), and secondly, she is aware that the way in which actuality is represented is also a criterion of reality. 9

What these results tell us is not that Natalie is 'confused', but 'confusing'. The ease with which Natalie replies suggests that there is no need in her mind for her to think about the questions: she can produce an answer which will apparently satisfy the experimenter straight off the top of her head. She isn't confused because she occupies a different kind of a world to the normal adult. It is a world in which things are more or less real according to how you look at them. Nothing is real or unreal in a definitive and global sense. To an adult, such a world would be confusing, but that is only because we tend to operate with more and higher-order concepts and classificatory systems which makes us think of classes of things, and hierarchies of classes of things, such as fiction and non-fiction, historical non-fiction and history. But even adults would get into difficulties if asked whether the hero of *Dune* was as real as the heroine of *Jamaica Inn*. We would probably think it an impossible question put in those terms, because we would wish to invoke ideas of genre and characterisation. Natalie doesn't have such overall organising concepts, which is why she is an agnostic in the sense that she is saying, 'Well, you can call them real if you look at them like this. But if you look at them like that, they're not.' Her judgements are 10 conditional, fluid, even capricious, and they indicate that she does not hold the verbal conceptual term 'real' in the same way that an adult does, though that does not mean that she is unclear about the reality of things. But the constructs upon which she makes those judgements are anything but capricious. Here are the five constructs that Natalie used to answer the questions in that interview:

(1) things are more real if they continue to exist in places other than on television;

(2) things are more real if they are representations of things which exist in places other than on television;

(3) things are more real if they behave in ways similar to the things being represented;

(4) things are more real if the manner of their representation is more like that of their other-than-on-television appearance;

(5) things are more real if their behaviour is consistent with the system of reality in the world in which they are represented as existing.

What is notably missing from these criteria is the crude 'other than on television is real: on television is unreal' criterion, which prior to the data was my expectation. But this absence also turns out to be entirely reasonable: it is not a useful distinction, because much of what is on television is known to be real. Hence the only clues to the reality status of an on-television character versus a not-on-television character is that while the latter is real, the former may or may not be real. In a deep sense, everything on television is a two-dimensional representation. It would require logical processing of a formal operational nature to recognise that this criterion should be applied *first* to eliminate judgement of one or more element(s) of the diad or triad. Without this conceptual grasp of the judging process criteria, the crude distinction is in fact less heuristically helpful than the criteria she actually applies.

With regard to the question as to the likely effects of these judgements upon behaviour, the answer suggested by this analysis is that Natalie's judgements are so fluid that maintained physical action based upon them becomes unlikely and difficult, if not actually impossible. What is clear is that Natalie will, through natural maturation, continue to apply and develop these thoroughly appropriate judgemental criteria until the concept 'real' accords with adult usage. At present, it is not helpful to suggest she is 'deceived' by the distinction, for the distinction is simply not held.

From this data I would postulate that Natalie is not making a qualitatively different order of judgements about the reality of the on-television world from that of adults, but that the television world is a part of her 'real' world and as such is subject to the same criteria. It is difficult to see how Natalie's television judgements could be other than subject to her natural and ongoing construction of reality, and as such not causal of some unseen malformation of that process, but an appropriate and beneficial dimension in which to exercise and accelerate her development. This is to say that the fact that the substantive content of her answers are bizarre and

264

constantly changing cannot be held to be the result of the way in which the characters are presented on television, but as symptomatic of her developmental stage, of which her judgements about television are mere indications.

So the first picture we had of a child confused by television which has 13 retarded, warped, or redirected her natural development turns out to be quite the reverse. What we have is an agnostic, a child who isn't yet sure, one who always seems to be saying, 'on the other hand . . .' as she brings a number of subtle and appropriate criteria to bear upon different dimensions of the characters she is presented with. The strategies she is using are leading to the accretion of anomalies and hence a state of disequilibrium, which in time she will attempt to resolve, and in so doing move towards consistent dichotomisation as she gains experience and cognitive maturity.

In more general terms, she is a child who appears to be working towards 14 an appropriate answer from all possible answers, which is typical of all knowing. Knowledge is always incremental, and we all have to work with what we currently know, however inadequate that may be, until we can improve it, or until we believe we have the whole picture. Natalie does not yet have any complete answers, but she is patiently and intelligently working towards a deeper and more comprehensive understanding of her world. What may appear to researchers asking simplistic questions and accepting simplistic 'yes/no', 'correct/incorrect' answers as a child's confusion, is revealed by another method of interpretation to be a rationally pursued, highly complex, multi-dimensional intellectual affair, in which the positive educational benefit of television is very obvious.

Note
1. David H. Tripp, *Television and Reality: One Child's Constructs*. Active Eye Project Working Paper, presented at the Third National Child Development Conference, Perth, August 1984.

265

PART IVa
Accounts of Practice

monday

BBC-1

7.00 Wogan
7.35 Best of British
8.00 In Sickness and in Health
8.30 Joint Account
9.00 Nine O'Clock News
9.30 Panorama
10.10 Golf: US Masters
10.50 Miami Vice
11.35 The Rock 'n' Roll Years
12.05 Advice Shop
12.35 Mother Teresa

TEXTUAL ANALYSIS - David Sudbery

PHOTOMONTAGE - Tony Carroll

Simon Pattenden, aged 15

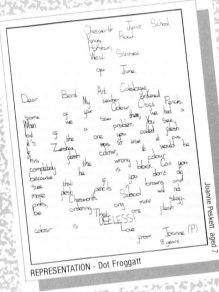

REPRESENTATION - Dot Froggatt

Joanne Peskett, aged 7

He quickly changed into his bikini - Cathy Pompe

Lisa Waterson, Michelle Tabor, Nicola Saunders

Accounts of Practice
Introduction

These accounts of classroom practice show how teachers have engaged with media education in practice. The accounts have been selected not because they conform to an editorial view (many do not fit into the framework of the key aspects), but because they reflect the diverse and different starting points of teachers at both primary and secondary level. Writers were commissioned at the outset to write reflective commentaries about work in progress rather than to carry out any specific scientific evaluation. For this reason the subjective mode in the accounts distinguishes them from a case study approach, with the exception of Sue Van Noort's piece. We believe that teachers will not only enjoy reading these articles but will also want to compare, affirm, or contend with, and extend their own practices through, the vicarious experience documented by other professionals.

To extend the picture of how media education is developed we have felt that it is also important to include the perspectives of teacher trainers, curriculum developers, and policy-makers. Together with the teachers' accounts these offer a prospectus, albeit speculative, of how to move media education from the position of institutional marginality towards a place where it engages at the centre of all children's learning.

The reader will note the diverse contexts of experience and modes of expression in these accounts. Careful attention needs to be paid when comparing and contrasting them as the pieces work in different ways. Readers might also make comparisons between the different age levels and the range and type of activities described. It is important to explore and identify issues of progression and evaluation but, as teachers will vouchsafe, age level is not itself a sufficient indication of the performance level expected or achieved. The reader is therefore invited to elicit from these accounts the particular context and starting-point for each of these writers. This section is as much about how teachers imply or explicitly define the terms of issues such as evaluation and progression as about the pedagogic strategies they describe for carrying out media education work.

Finally, it is worth noting that beneath the surface of these accounts is discussion about the role of the teacher or the image of the teacher. Cathy Pompe's and Tony Carroll's accounts, for example, suggest the complexity of this representation in the context of media education.

In the first account, 'Nursery School Children Talking about Television', Sue Van Noort studies the knowledge and understanding that two groups of pre-school children bring to their home experience of watching television

269

and video. This piece is adapted from a research project and for this reason should be read as a formal case study. It is included here because it provides a valuable insight into pre-school knowledge and experience of media, and provides the reader with some reference point in comparing pre-school and school experiences. In particular, she highlights the importance of culture, class, and social conditions in evaluating television viewing. She also unveils good examples of children's 'modality judgements' as described by Bob Hodge and David Tripp.[1]

Dot Froggatt argues in 'Representation' that work on the key aspects of representation and agency (she uses the term institution) is well within the grasp of seven-year-old (year 3) children. In order to develop language and art work she integrates aspects of representation and agency within cross-curricular projects. Two contrasting approaches to representation are among those described. In one project Dot Froggatt describes how children can draw on their own knowledge and experience to explore representation; by contrast, in another project developed through technology and drama, children look outwards to the local community at the representation of Romanies.

Kate Dewar's 'Nature Park' continues the integrated approach advocated by Dot Froggatt. She outlines a topic approach to media education which embraces several subject areas: if media education work like this acts as an enhancement of *all* learning it is less likely to be viewed by primary teachers as an 'extra' activity taking up time and curriculum space. It is also worth noting that seven-year-olds use the video camera for animation, which begs the question of what we might expect from older children.

In ' "He Quickly Changes into his Bikini" ', Cathy Pompe unpicks modality judgements which 11-year-old children make in talking about film and television and other media texts. She highlights the difficulty of engaging in productive educative activity when linguistic and cultural differences are constrained by classic teacher–pupil relationships. The piece is also interesting as science and media work are combined.

Robin Bower approached media education through a video project on the environment as a cross-curricular theme: 'Media Education as an Essential Ingredient in an Issue-based Environmental Education'. In Robin's view, the project produced confident technicians who could transfer their experience of production to an increased understanding of mainstream broadcast material. It is worth speculating on whether the learning of the principles governing the science curriculum in this project through media production enhances children's ability to understand the principles of other subject curriculum methods and content.

In 'Clash of the Titans', Jude Brigley uses a range of texts, including literature, to develop media education skills. Her work is directed to meeting the requirements of English and Welsh in the National Curriculum, but the media outcomes exceed these. The notion of writing, for example, is extended to producing photo-collages. Fictional media representations are not emphasised in the statutory orders, yet here these are explored through photography.

David Sudbery describes how textual analysis can be used as part of a study of television in ' "What does it mean?" ' He borrows and introduces, from his media pupilsteaching, the concept of institution (agency) to the English lesson, and recommends a contextualising activity to prepare pupils for the idea of institutional branding of a television product. Simulation activities, in scheduling and creating a corporate image through product branding, then provide the real context for textual analysis of programme output. Teacher-led discussion is used for the textual analysis, and team work is the mode of working for the production company simulation.

Julian Sefton-Green, in 'Comics and Magazines', directs the focus of a familiar English classroom activity towards the aspects of audience and agency in comic and magazine production. By investigating a magazine's economic and readership profiles pupils are led towards an understanding of the agencies which shape media content and forms. Pupils also reflect on the production processes and the job roles they have undertaken in order to evaluate the aspects of agency which they have experienced. The project involves both individual and team activity, practical and analytical work, and the production of an artefact for an audience. In the context of English language work it extends the range and scope of pupils' critical vocabulary and social awareness.

In his introduction to three teachers writing about 'Newspapers in Education', Ben Moore describes aspects of the liaison with newspaper companies. The accounts all share a different approach to news-gathering from that often used in English lessons, where textual analysis about bias in newspapers provides the main teaching focus.

The aim of the Newspapers in Education Project is to raise circulation figures in the short and the long term. Teachers are often interested in links with newspapers because they offer a chance to find out more about the processes and systems of production. However, one drawback of producing newspapers in this context is that teachers can find they are reduced to a heavily product-oriented schedule without understanding the forms, conventions, and values of newspapers. Ben Moore warns against this, and one lesson that can be learnt from this project is the importance of bearing in mind the analytical aspects of media education. Readers might consider how the work described here might be further developed, away from concerns about persuasion and bias, to exploring the complex relationship between ideological representations, audiences, and producers.

The project also raises the question of industrial liaisons and the relationship of the adult world of work to education. Ideally, pupils will discover aspects of technology and agency which they would not know about within the context of their own resources and institution. However, educational agendas do not always match up with market-place agendas, especially when the papers are donated free, but teachers can determine how they will best mediate between the world of journalism and the school.

In 'Sniffing out Stereotypes', David Brockie conducted an experiment into perceptions of gender difference through perfume advertising. The method he uses avoids the common 'spot-the-stereotype' approach, but by directly drawing on students' raw responses he touches upon delicate issues of sexuality. Though recognising the unresolved pedagogic implications of exposing children to such questions of identity he manages to tap behind the safe and pre-emptive responses often made in more distanced

approaches. The work forms part of a personal and health education programme but could easily be applied in various subject areas.

Peter Frazer, in 'Teaching TV Cartoons', introduced a long-established
popular American cartoon, *The Flintstones*, into his English lesson as a
way of comparing representations of the family with present-day popular
animated sitcoms such as *The Simpsons*. The concerns of his media teaching
are naturally integrated into his English teaching, although he still suffers
the odd pang of conscience. However, he notes that, after studying cartoons, pupils conclude that both literary texts and television cartoons can
be subsumed under the same title of 'the media'.

Tony Carroll, in 'Photomontage', explores the relationship between
experimental form in art education and the media education key aspect of
representation. The development of critical studies in art education has
some place in Tony Carroll's background but, as a media studies teacher,
he also has knowledge and experience of critical aspects such as representation. In addition, he describes the role of oracy in the project in enabling
a formalised reflective element to come into pupils' learning processes. He
believes that pupils come to a greater understanding of themselves and
society through a critical consideration of form and content.

Julian Sefton-Green, in 'Publishing', describes work carried out in an
examined year group of fifteen-year-olds. He integrates the study of the
form and genre of various literary texts into the programme of English
language work. Questions of institution and publishing are related to personal consumption and audience. The choice of texts reflects the ethnic
and gender mix in his class.

In '*Playtime*', Jenny Grahame problematises 'the text-based literary criticism approach' against 'the concept-based experiential model' in terms of
evaluation. The account is in two parts. The first part is the introduction
and the second is the final section of a longer account taken from *Watching
Media Learning*.[2] In this piece Jenny Grahame offers a challenging perspective of the complexity of pedagogical issues in media teaching. There are
the teacher's changing aims, competing pupil and teacher agendas, and
gender differences in approaches to given assignments. In one important
respect this account makes demands of the reader to review the previous
accounts and determine exactly what terms of reference teachers make in
their evaluation of teaching styles, and learning outcomes and processes.

Angela Devas is concerned about issues of manipulation and bias in 'Pop
Music and Newspapers', particularly the sexism and the 'trivialisation' of
events in some tabloids. She openly explores her limited success in finding
pedagogical solutions to negotiating a pathway between her ideological
reservations about these newspapers and the populist agendas found in
pupils' media consumption. But she finds that there are some notable
surprises during the course of the project. When pupils debate the issues
which they know about from their own experience (for example, of press
controls from having lived in Iran or Pakistan), or from their own eclectic
knowledge of the music business, aspects of agency are more easy to draw
out. This piece is, therefore, a companion to 'Newspapers in Education'
and contrasts practical and analytical approaches to understanding agency
and languages, though the reader should bear in mind the different social

contexts and age levels. The accounts are ordered in terms of the age of the children described in the classroom, starting with 4-year-old infants and finishing with 16-year-old students.

Notes
1. Bob Hodge and David Tripp, *Children and Television*, Cambridge, Polity, 1986.
2. David Buckingham (ed.), *Watching Media Learning*, Brighton, Falmer, 1990.

Nursery School Children Talking about Television

Sue Van Noort

Background

As part of the Primary Media Education Project[1] I set up an initiative to explore the knowledge and understanding that two groups of pre-school children, in two different nurseries, brought from their home experience of watching television and video. In particular, I wanted to look at the children's judgements about different levels of reality in media texts, so I was mainly concerned with the area of media representation.

I have had an interest in media education for a long time and was previously a member of the BFI National Working Party for Primary Media Education. I was released from teaching for ten working days to plan, execute, and write up this project in liaison with the nursery teacher at another school.

The two schools are inner-city Sheffield schools, approximately three miles apart, with nursery classes situated in the main school building close to the reception classes they feed.

School A (where I work) has a thirty-place nursery unit staffed with one teacher, two nursery nurses, and a bilingual child-care assistant funded through Section 11. [Section 11 is a system whereby the Government provides funding to Local Education Authorities for the provision of bi-lingual staff in schools where there are large numbers of ethnic minority children.] The children are predominantly Asian of Bangladeshi and Pakistani origin, and are learning to speak English as a second language (ESL). They live in a mixture of council housing and privately owned terraced housing, and all have access to a garden or small yard.

School B has a thirty-nine-place nursery unit staffed with one teacher and two nursery nurses. The children are mostly white, though the nursery has two Asian children currently on roll while they are temporarily fostered in a local white home. The children all live on the council estate surrounding the school, and all have access to gardens.

In both schools, watching television is an established part of the nursery curriculum. School A shares a portable television and video which is transported into the nursery to a carpeted story area by means of a trolley when required. The nursery children watch television once a week, and the programme they watch is always pre-recorded by the nursery teacher and is shown as a video. School B has separate television resources for the nursery and the first school. The video recorder is sited in the first school and not easily moved. The nursery has its own television sited in a pleasant carpeted area, and the children daily watch a live pre-school programme broadcast by the BBC. In both nurseries the children were already accustomed to talking with the nursery staff about the programmes they had watched.

Research Method

For the purposes of this project questions were targeted at children in the 'rising five' groups, that is, children who were four years of age and in their last term at nursery and who were due to have their fifth birthday during their first term in the reception class. In nursery A this group consisted of eight children; in nursery B the group initially included thirteen children, but I later reduced this to a group of four. 7

My research took place in three stages. Firstly, I engaged in conversations with the children about their experiences of, and pleasure in, watching TV and video in their homes. Secondly, at different times, I watched three specially chosen video tapes with the children. Thirdly, I talked with the children about these tapes, using specifically devised trigger questions, and then recorded the children's responses, either on tape or in note form. I also noted instances of imaginative play based on television or video, and clothing worn depicting media characters, for example, Teenage Mutant Hero Turtles. 8

Finally, I examined the tapes and notes for evidence of the children's judgements about different levels of reality. I looked for evidence that the trigger questions helped the children to focus their thoughts, and I looked for evidence that dialogue with an interested and informed adult may extend children's knowledge and understanding of what they are seeing. I examined the language the children used when talking about the three video extracts. I considered what this revealed about their understanding of what they had seen, what it revealed about the pleasure they may have experienced watching them, and how the experience had, or had not, touched their imagination. 9

I spent two days planning the project, looking at research methodology, making a breakdown of the three chosen video tapes, compiling trigger questions, and looking at language to be used or avoided. I also drew up an observation sheet to record the children's attention while watching the short films. 10

For five days I observed imaginative play in the two nurseries, talking with the children, showing the selected video tapes at each school, recording, and then considering and reflecting on the children's responses. I then spent three days looking at the material evidence that had been collected of the children's responses, transcribing some sections of audio tapes, and writing up the project. 11

Video Extracts

The three short videos were all aimed at the pre-school age group and were chosen for specific reasons. One was a short clip from a BBC *You and Me* programme which showed children dressing up in a nursery and singing a dressing-up song. The film includes lots of close-ups of children wearing 12 different hats, shoes, belts, and so on, thus giving the teacher the opportunity to introduce simple technical language concerned with camera work. The film then moves on to show a little boy dressing up as a wizard and then apparently performing magic tricks as a consequence. With a flick of either his wand or his fingers he produces a meal on the table, washes the pots, and changes old toys to new.

This film was chosen in order to find out whether the children thought the little boy was actually performing the magic or thought it was some kind of television trick that made him look as if he was performing magic.

The second video was also from the *You and Me* series. The film mixes live actors and animation, showing them on screen together. The cartoon character is a kangaroo called Henry who joins a little girl, her friend, and her father in their home where they are watching television, and who then appears to jump into the television set and join in the programme being shown. I chose this film in order to record the children's response to the mixture of cartoon and actors shown on screen together, and to investigate whether the children could sort out in their minds key differences between the cartoon character and the actors. When talking with the children about this film I was careful not to use the term 'actor', to see whether any of the children themselves would introduce this label.

The third video was an animated film of a favourite nursery story book, *Where's Spot?*[2] This was chosen firstly to see whether the children recognised that Spot was a cartoon, secondly to stimulate talk about other cartoons the children regularly watch. I also wanted to observe the children's attention to this film while viewing and to see whether they could name differences between the film and the book, such as that the film has music, the animals move and talk, Sally goes upstairs in the film, but does not do so in the book. I intended to ask which they preferred: watching the video or being told the story by the teacher.

Trigger questions used when discussing television in general with the children
1. What do you like to do if you are bored? Which of these:
   – Play outside?
   – Play with a friend?
   – Play with toys?
   – Watch TV?
   – Look at a book?
2. Do you watch TV at home?
3. What do you like to watch?
4. Who do you watch TV with?
5. Do you ever watch TV by yourself?
6. What room is your TV in? Is it in the kitchen, the sitting room, or somewhere else?
7. Do you have a video [i.e., a video recorder]?
8. Do you go to the video library/shop?
9. Who chooses the video [i.e., video tape]?
10. Have you got a favourite video?
11. Have you seen a video you didn't like – what didn't you like about it?

12. Can you draw your television for me?
13. What is your favourite programme?
14. What do you like about it?
15. Do you watch the news?
16. Do you like to watch television at school?
17. What do you like to watch at school? Why?

Trigger questions used with the dressing-up tape 17
I introduced the term 'close-up' and explained what it means. I then asked the children to look for, and then shout out, when they saw close-ups during the dressing-up tape. They also had to identify what it was a close-up of.
1. How does the boy talk when he doesn't open his mouth?
2. How does he change his clothes?
3. How does he make the dinner?
4. How does he change toys?
5. Is he a real boy?
6. Is he really doing this? Could you do this?
7. Is it magic? Is he pretending? Or is it something else?
   [I did not introduce the term 'special effects' at this stage.]
8. What is magic?
9. Is magic real?
10. What does it mean when you say something is real?
11. Is it a trick?
12. What is a trick?

Trigger questions used with the kangaroo tape 18
1. what is henry?
2. Is Henry a real kangaroo?
3. Is he a cartoon?
4. Are they real children or cartoon children?
5. What does Henry do next? Why?
6. How does he jump into the television?
7. How does he get in?
8. Could you do that? Could Ellie and her friend do that?
9. When Henry sits on the settee is he big or little?
10. When does he change size and how does he?
11. Is it real or is it pretend?

Trigger questions used with the Spot tape 19
1. Have we got a book in the nursery that tells the same story as this video?
2. The video and the book are slightly different; what is the difference?
3. When we are reading the book, who opens the door, the clock, the cupboard, and so on? Who opens them on the video?
4. Is Spot a real dog?
5. Is Spot a cartoon dog? [Introduce the idea here that a cartoon is a drawing.]

277

6. If a cartoon dog is a drawing, how does it move?
7. How can drawings move?
8. What cartoons do you watch at home?
9. Which is your favourite?
10. Do you like cartoons? Do they make you laugh, frighten you, or upset you?
11. What do you do if a cartoon frightens you?
12. Does anybody else in your family like cartoons?
13. Is anybody else in your family frightened or upset by cartoons? Why? What happens then?
14. Do you like the music that accompanies cartoons?
15. Which do you like best, watching Spot on the video or reading about him in the book? Why?

Doing the Research: Stage One

Talking in depth with the children about their everyday television and video experience was much easier to achieve with the children from nursery A than from nursery B. This was simply because I already knew the children well and our relationship was not complicated by the issue of making friends. As the nursery teacher at nursery A I had had close relationships with the children in the target group for nearly two years. In nursery B, I was a new face, a new adult. The children were very friendly and communication was very clear (English being their first language), but they wanted to talk about themselves and to make friends, not to talk about television. They wanted to tell me about their families, their pets, their nursery. This was why I decided to reduce the number of children that I concentrated on in nursery B from the original thirteen to the four who had been first to establish contact with me and tell me all about themselves and who now appeared to feel they 'knew' me.

I also took in books and magazines to read to the children that would focus their conversation around the issues I wanted to explore: a *Postman Pat* annual, a *Spot* book, a *He-Man* book, a copy of the comic/magazine *Fast Forward*, and the BBC publication *Henry and the Birthday Surprise*, featuring the cartoon Henry from the *You and Me* programme. I decided not to use the audio-tape recorder at nursery B as it was another distraction; the children were unused to being taped, and were not casual about it.

The trigger questions about general television viewing produced a wealth of information. Watching television, videos, or playing outside were the most popular activities to combat boredom; all the children said they watched television at home. Asked what they liked to watch, the only pre-school programmes specifically mentioned were *Rainbow* and *Spot* (mentioned by a child at nursery B). Most popular at both schools were *Neighbours* and *Home and Away*. Other programmes frequently mentioned were *Teenage Mutant Hero Turtles*, *Ghostbusters*, *He-Man*, and *Popeye*. Several children mentioned Freddy (three from nursery A, one from nursery B), and on further questioning, I concluded this to be Freddy from *Nightmare on Elm Street*. The children at nursery B listed more soap operas than those at nursery A, including *A Country Practice* and *Take the High Road* (both broadcast in the afternoons). The target children in nursery A attend

278

nursery morning and afternoon, and the target children in nursery B in the mornings only, suggesting that children not attending nursery in the afternoons watch daytime soaps with their carers.

Asked who they watched television with, the children in nursery A did not report watching alone. Cartoons were watched with brothers and sisters; soaps with the whole family. Two children reported watching horror videos just with their fathers, and this experience was also reported by a child at nursery B. Children in nursery B reported watching television alone, and one child watched with his grandmother. This probably reflects the fact that children from nursery A live as part of very large extended families, whereas the children in nursery B live in smaller family units. Children watching alone have more choice over which programme they view than those watching with older siblings or relations who may control programme choice. Lone viewing children, however, do not have anybody with whom to discuss programme content while viewing. 23

Asked about the location of their television, the most common response was 'in t'room', meaning the family sitting room. One child in nursery B reported watching television in her bedroom, but her minder said this was untrue. (It is possible that the family had a portable set they moved around.) No child reported watching television regularly in their bedroom. 24

Nearly all the children had a video recorder in their homes, and those who did not expressed a desire for one. All the children understood the function of a video and seemed familiar with the idea of video libraries, calling them the 'video shop'. 25

It seemed to be adults who chose the videos. The children made requests but the adults made the actual selections. For example, a child at nursery B reported that his favourite television programme, *Ghostbusters*, was not being shown any more and so his father had gone to the video shop and got the video out for him. He could recognise that the video was different from the cartoon series on television: when asked if they were the same he said no. When asked what was different he described the slime. 26

Asked about a favourite video, the children at nursery A listed videos they watch in the nursery: *You and Me*, the nursery rhyme video, *Fireman Sam*, and the like. The children in nursery B also listed children's videos such as *Postman Pat*, *Dogtanian*. 27

Asked about videos they did not like, most children had a story to tell. A child at nursery A reported a video he had watched with his father: 28

Teacher What about at home, do you ever watch anything at home that frightens you?

Child Yeah – you know that film I watched with me dad, we stayed up right late while half past two, right, well you know that man, right, that was in bed wi' that lady and he were trying to kiss her, right, and he were trying to shoot her head off.

T Oh, and did that frighten you?

C It frightened me dad.

T Did it frighten you?

C Yeah, it did.

T Did the man shoot the lady's head off?

C	Yeah.
T	What did it look like?
C	All blood everywhere.
T	How horrible! Was it real? Did it really happen?
C	Yeah.
T	Or was it pretend?
C	No, it really happened.

A group of children discussed what seemed to be the *Nightmare on Elm Street* films:

Teacher	Do you watch anything that frightens you?
K	Freddy.
T	Who's Freddy? I've heard about Freddy.
K	Pretending.
T	What does Freddy do?
K	Um –, er –, 'e kills everybody with his gun.
T	What does he look like – Freddy?
K	He scrapes all his skin off.
T	Oh, is he frightening?
K	And he eats it.
T	What?
K	And then he eats it for his dinner.
F	And it's all blood.
T	Have you seen Freddy?
C & F *together*	I have – I have.
T	You have, you've seen Freddy.
F	I have, and it's right horrible and my mum and dad doesn't watch it now.
T	You mum and dad don't watch it?
K	Yeah.
T	And what else does Freddy do, because I didn't see Freddy.
K	He shoots everybody's head off [laughter].
T	Does he – weren't you frightened watching that?
K	No, I turned round and [tape is unclear here].
F	And he broke the doll house and [unclear].
T	And was he really doing it or just pretending to do it?
F	Really.
K	[after quite a pause] Pretending.
T	Well, F thought he was really doing it.
F	Really.
T	Why did you watch it if it was so horrible? [tape is unclear] Did it frighten you?
F	Yeah, and I scared of it and I went to bed.
T	Did you? Why didn't you say – Oh, turn it off, its frightening me?
F	And I turned it off and go to bed.
T	Did you?

F	And I watch it at night time.
T	Did it frighten you, K?
K	No.
T	No?
K	No – 'cos I turned around.
T	You turned around – what, so you couldn't see it?
K	[child nodded at this point]

Interestingly, although K had said Freddy was pretending and not real and that she had not been frightened by him, she still looked frightened. She and J, her neighbour and close friend in the nursery (a child not in the target group, as she is younger), often discussed Freddy together; both girls seemed very familiar with the *Nightmare on Elm Street* series of films.

A child at nursery B reported viewing horror films with his father whenever his father was looking after him. 'He's got a right lot of 'em, a right lot of monster films, my dad.' When asked if watching these films frightened him he said no, and he did not seem frightened. Asked if his mum ever watched these films, he was most definite: 'No, me mum don't watch them.' 29

A child at nursery B reported that his small sister was frightened of the Mutant Turtle cartoon and habitually hid under the kitchen table when he watched them. 30

Asked to draw their television, responses ranged from refusals with the child saying 'I can't,' to simple box-shaped drawings, to quite elaborate televisions with lots of buttons, according to the drawing skills of the child. 31

In both nurseries the same four programmes were consistently named as favourites: *Neighbours*, *Home and Away*, *Teenage Mutant Hero Turtles*, and *Ghostbusters*. When shown photographs of the various actors from the *Neighbours* soap in the *Fast Forward* comic/magazine, the children easily named them. At nursery B all the children that looked through *Fast Forward* with me, including several not in the target group, recognised and named the characters and went on to volunteer information about the characters' lives, who they lived with, and where they worked. 32

The children in nursery A also knew a lot about the characters and storylines of *Neighbours*. This is an extract from a tape that began recording a conversation concerned with the short video featuring Henry the Kangaroo. 33

F	His name is Henry.
S	Henry in *Neighbours*?
T	No, Henry in *Neighbours* is a different Henry, isn't he? Do you watch *Neighbours*?
S	I like Henry in *Neighbours*. I kiss him.
T	You kiss him?
C	She goes out with him.
S	Yeah.
	[later in the tape]
T	Has Henry in *Neighbours* got a girlfriend already?

Chorus of	
children	Yeah.
T	Who is this girlfriend? [This conversation took place before the character was involved with the character of Bronwyn.]
Children	What – Don't know – Not sure – I think – Lucy.
T	You think its Lucy?
F	I don't know. Do you watch *Neighbours*?
T	Yes, I do.
S	Do you know Lucy?
T	I do.
F	I watch *Home and Away*.
S	She says 'I don't want to go to school.'
T	She did say that. [The child was correctly reporting a current storyline.]
S	Yeah, she said 'I don't want to go to school' and dad said – her dad – she run away – and she then said it again and run away again and then her dad come with her – he – with her.
T	Lucy in *Neighbours*, is she a real girl?
S	Yeah, I think so.
T	And is that really her dad?
K	No – yeah.
S	No – he bought her.
T	Or do you think it's two people making pretend play for the television.
S	No, I think he bought her.
T	Did he?
S	He make her – she didn't say rude things – she shouted 'I don't want to go to school'.

The most common response to the question, What do you like best about your favourite programme? was a blank look, and if pressed further the response 'Cos its good.' The children could not really tell me what exactly they liked except in terms of naming characters they liked: 'I like the turtles,' 'I like Henry.' The response was not as clear as when they talked about programmes they did not like.

Most children knew the term 'the News'. They didn't like it, though many reported their parents as watching it. In nursery A, F said 'the News is lovely', but K and C said the News was 'not lovely, its right crap' (meaning, I think, that they did not enjoy watching it, rather than commenting on its content).

S complained that after *Neighbours* she liked to watch a film but that if she left the room her dad would put the News on: 'If I'll go, he puts the News on.' I asked if the News showed real events. If she saw a man on the News hurt, maybe shot, would it be a real man or someone pretending? She became very serious, considering this, and answered me slowly:

S	That's a real man, I think – like you. You are a real, aren't you?
T	Yeah – I'm real. Does your dad watch the News every day?
S	I think he does.

I deduced that although S believed both *Neighbours* and the News to be real people she considered the News to be more serious and worth more consideration. Her tone when talking about *Neighbours* was relaxed and happy; when talking about the News slower and more pensive. Only her father really watched the News in her house but she reported 'everybody' – that is, two parents and five children – as watching *Neighbours*.

The children universally, in both nurseries, answered that they liked to watch television at school. In nursery B the children answered *Playbus*, which is what they regularly watch. In nursery A the children listed their favourites from the videos we regularly watch in the nursery, *Humpty Dumpty* coming out top. 37

The response to the dressing-up tape and its trigger questions
In both nurseries this tape was well received. The children like the song, joining in singing the chorus, and they liked the dressing-up clothes, discussing and commenting on them, especially a mask which was featured. They seemed to accept the special effects as quite a normal result of the boy being dressed as a magician, and if I had not pushed the children to question what they had seen, I do not think any of them would have done so. The response at the end of the tape, in both nurseries, was not *how* or *why* but 'Can we see it again?' 38

In nursery B the children usually watch live television only, but I had brought a video recorder and portable television with me. The children demonstrated the knowledge they had brought from home in this area by asking me to 'rewind' the tape using the 'remote control' (using these correct terms). The children also commented on the size of my remote control which was unusually large, again demonstrating their knowledge in this area. They asked me what other tapes I had brought and what other tapes I had, and they offered to bring nursery tapes of their own from home. Discussing video tapes was an area they felt confident to talk about. Had I been reading a story I wonder if they would have engaged me in a similar conversation and made similar offers concerning books! 39

In nursery A I had the opportunity to watch the tape in a separate room, away from the main nursery, with a small group of the target children and a small group from the reception class. (The combined group of children were from the same year, those in the reception class being the September 1989 intake, those in the target group the Easter 1990 intake.) With this group I explained the term 'close-up' in this way: 'a close-up is when the person operating the video camera moves up really close to something or someone so that only that is filmed, only that is framed in the viewfinder, it could be a ladybird or it could be someone's hand or just someone's thumb. When something is in close-up it can look bigger than it is really, a bit like looking at something in a magnifying glass.' 40

The children seemed to understand this, but I was building on knowledge they already had. Video cameras are very popular within the Asian community, a must at weddings, and the children had seen them used. We had talked about viewfinders in the nursery and made them out of Sticklebricks and Lego when making cameras with the construction toys, and we use magnifying glasses in the nursery for looking closely at objects. 41

Asked to identify objects they saw in close-up on this tape the children could do it: shoes, hat, dinner, and so on.

When I asked the children in this group how the little boy talked without opening his mouth, they had no idea. A separate sound track recorded and then added to the visual track was outside their experience and imagination. N went for the most logical explanation – it was someone else talking.

When questioned as to how the little boy did the things the video showed him doing, the children sought what seemed to them to be logical explanations, the key one being 'It was magic.' (The child himself uses the term 'magic' on the video.) N's explanation was that of course he, the boy, could not do it by himself, but he could when he had the wand (calling it 'that thing in his 'and'). When questioned further as to how he made the dinner as he had not held the wand, she patiently explained to me that 'He did it with his fingers, he's got magic in his fingers, he's not like me because I can't do that.' N's explanation was that the boy was not doing any of these things really but that he was dreaming. (I was impressed with the language she was using as a very young ESL child.) I asked her how the video could show the boy's dream and she changed her explanation, abandoning the dream theory, to 'His mum did it,' and considered the matter settled then.

Watching the video again with another mixed group of target and reception children, the comments made during my questioning struck me as a good illustration of the difference in thinking between nursery children and slightly older reception class children. By and large, the nursery target children said 'He did it with his fingers,' the slightly older children said 'He *pretended* to do it with his fingers,' an exact parallel to the difference I often get when asking crying children in the same two age groups where they have hurt themselves. Children from the nursery will often reply 'Over there,' and point to the place in the school yard where they fell. The reception child is more likely to respond 'On the knee', or 'On my arm' and point to the afflicted part of the body, showing a greater depth of thought about how to reply to the question.

All the children were sure the child was real: a real boy. I realised the difficulty of discussing reality with this age group. We got into terrible knots: one child told me that *Popeye* is a real cartoon – I suppose he is. We established that the boy was not a puppet, not a cartoon, not a model, but no child suggested that he was an actor. As actors *are* real people I began to be unsure exactly how to phrase the questions to make the answer 'actor' possible.

The children were very clear that they personally could not do the things the boy in the video was doing, though several children said they would like to. N, always a patient and kindly child, explained to me that if she had magic in her fingers like him then she could have, showing that she thought it was the child himself who was special and that the video was just showing this.

When I asked the children if it was magic, pretending, or something else, they chose magic or pretending. No child chose to explore the idea of something else, or what this something else could be. I did not introduce the term 'special effects' or try to attempt any explanation. The children could not explain the terms 'magic' or 'tricks' to me, except to say 'You

284

know – you know – magic.' When I asked this same question to nursery B, a child said 'Like Paul Daniels,' and another child explained to me a complicated illusion trick he had seen on television the previous night, illustrating magic but not explaining what it is.

Clearly the children took pleasure in watching this video, but they readily accepted what they had seen at its face value. They brought no knowledge of special effects or camera tricks to what they were watching, neither did they seem to have a concept of acting or actors. Although children in nursery A understood filming as using a video camera, their understanding was limited to their own experience that what was filmed was exactly what was really happening, as happens, for example, when filming a wedding as a home video.

Responses to the kangaroo tape and its trigger questions
In neither nursery did the children watch this tape as calmly and accept- ingly as they had watched the previous tape. They were puzzled by Henry jumping into the television set; it was an act unlike anything they had seen on television before.

In answer to the question, 'What is Henry?' all the children could answer: a kangaroo. (In nursery A we had seen Henry many times before on *You and Me* programmes and labelled him thus.) In nursery B the children were quick to label Henry as a cartoon. In nursery A the children were not sure what he was, or even whether he was real or not. S thought he was a puppet made of wood. N, the little girl who had talked of the boy in the previous video as dreaming, decided that Henry was a cartoon. When asked what a cartoon was, she was the only child from either nursery to volunteer, with no prompting or clues from me, that a cartoon was a drawing. This child has an elder brother of twelve who had two years of media education at primary school. He, or other members of her family, may have influenced her thinking; she may have gleaned this information from watching *Hartbeat* or a similar programme; she may have thought it out for herself. The children were all sure that Ellie and her friend were real children, not cartoons, but no child could offer an explanation of how a cartoon kangaroo could sit down on a sofa next to real children.

Recall of Henry jumping into the television was total; it had made a big impression, though no child offered an explanation as to *why* he had done it. There were many explanations as to *how* he had done it, all logical according to the children's way of thinking. The most popular was that he had jumped through a hole, having made himself smaller first. Even when we rewound the tape and watched again and saw *no hole*, many children were still convinced of this explanation. A child at nursery B insisted Henry had smashed the TV screen to get through, although we had seen no evidence of this. The same child later told one of the nursery nurses that she (i.e., the nurse) could not get through ('pass through') the television because she was a girl. I am unclear what he meant by this comment; it may have been purely sexist or it may have been a recognition that normal real people cannot do as cartoons do, a recognition of the world of fantasy. Several answered the question by demonstrating a jump forward, showing 'how' at a very basic level!

285

K (nursery B) thought Henry had been pushed through the television and had gone 'splat'. She did not say who had done the pushing, but she was very clear that somebody had done it and it was not a magical occurrence. R (nursery B) insisted that Henry had jumped into the television by means of magic and was still there. Then he said that he was also inside the television and pointed to his own reflection in the switched-off set.

In nursery A there were two main explanations offered, magic and jump- ing through a hole. One child, showing a touching faith in her teacher, said I had done it, I made it happen, which I quickly denied. S thought it was because his tail was magic.

T	You remember when Henry jumped into the television? How did he do it?
S	He might press the button and that video may and then he might want to jump and then his tail – [tape then becomes unclear].
T	You think his tail is magic, it might be?
F	I don't know how he jumped in that telly.
T	Do you think there is any way at all that Ellie could have jumped into the television?
S	No – she hasn't got a tail!
T	She hasn't got a tail?
S	If you had got a tail, Mrs Van, you could jump in it, but you haven't got a tail.
T	So you think it was the magic tail, and that was how Henry did it?
S	Yeah.

[S then went on to discuss Henry from *Neighbours*, on whom she was obviously smitten, later returning to the theme of the magic tail.]

S	I like Henry in *Neighbours* – I kiss him.
T	You kiss him.
C	She goes out with him.
S	Yeah [agreeing, pleased with this idea].
T	She goes out with him – but could she go out with him? Henry, in *Neighbours*?
S	Yeah – [changing to 'No' as the other children are chorusing 'No'].
T	Why not?
S	Because I haven't got a tail.
T	What, do you mean because you couldn't get into the television?
S	No, I haven't got a tail – if I did I would be magic.
T	I see, and then you could jump into the television and go out with Henry?
S	And then do you know what I'd do?
T	What, what would you do?
S	I'd run away from him.
T	Would you?
S	Yeah – to – ooh – then I'll knock him on the head [laughter from the other children].

The other children continued to give thought to this tape long after we had watched it, and in both nurseries initiated conversations with me concerned with it, mostly pursuing the idea of the hole in the television screen. There was confusion over whether what they had seen was real or pretend. One child told me it was real magic. No child had any idea of this effect being achieved through using electronic special effects: how could they?

Responses to the Spot tape and its trigger questions
This tape was very popular in both nurseries, and I did not need to ask 55 whether we had a book in the nursery telling the same story. This information was freely volunteered.

In nursery B I observed the children actively settling themselves into 56 comfortable positions with expectation and anticipation of enjoyment – they considered this video in the light of a treat. Nursery A was more blasé, having seen the video many times before.

Asked how the book and the video were different, the children could 57 not give me the answers I was looking for. One bright child at nursery B said the video had music. I listed the differences with the children, including music and voices on the tape, but only the teacher's voice when reading the book, the animals moving in the tape, not in the book, writing in the book, but only two words shown on the tape (the title *Where's Spot?*), and so on. It was obvious that they could not have attempted this task without teacher help. They had never made this kind of comparison before in either nursery.

When asked whether Spot was a real dog, like a dog they might have at 58 home as a pet, only one child answered yes. This was a particularly bright child at nursery B and at first I was surprised by her answer. It led me to consider again the nature of a four-year-old. This child was fond of Spot stories, liked Spot videos, was emotionally involved with Spot, and identified with his adventures. To her he was real, a friend in the same way a teddy can be. I concluded that the fault lay in the question, not the answer.

When I asked if Spot was a cartoon dog I was answered with a chorus 59 of 'Yes' at both nurseries. Having introduced the idea of a cartoon dog being a drawing, no child at either nursery could tell me how cartoons or drawings move. I could see a real opportunity for introducing simple flick books and zoetropes to nursery children to explain this phenomenon in principle.

The children listed lots of cartoons they liked to watch at home. *Turtles* 60 was the current top favourite, but many old favourites like *Popeye* were also mentioned. F at nursery A related an entire *Popeye* cartoon to me from start to finish; I was surprised when she described Popeye as 'opening that tin and eating that mud and then his muscles grow'. On reflection, I realised that it does look like mud rather than spinach and, as a second-language child, she may know the English word 'mud' but not the English word 'spinach'. She did not seem to question why Popeye should consider eating mud or why mud should make his muscles grow. Cartoons are not expected to be logical and very young children have absorbed this, F included.

Several children said some cartoons frightened them or younger members 61 of their families. Hiding seemed to be the solution: behind the settee, under the table, or just behind one's hands – anywhere, in fact. No child suggested switching off if they or a sibling was afraid; this was not an option even considered. Despite these stories of being afraid, the majority of children said they, and their families, liked cartoons and liked the music. They could sing me the significant title music accompanying successful cartoon series: *Spot*, *He-Man*, *Popeye*, *Ghostbusters*, *Turtles*, and so on.

Asked whether they liked the Spot video or the Spot book best, many children found it hard to decide. A few clearly stated the video; none clearly stated the book. The majority could not choose, saying they liked them both.

Context

Clearly the context of these conversations and my observation has a bearing on the conclusions that may be drawn. The children from both nurseries involved in this project are working class, with one exception at nursery B. The children's family life experiences include many negative factors: low pay, unemployment, racism, poor housing, overcrowding, the effects of theft and vandalism. In nursery A in particular, the children's spoken English was neither articulate nor rich. The majority of children in this nursery are learning to speak English as a second language and, due to the poverty of their parents in their country of origin (a poverty from which many emigrated to escape), their parents' lack of education (many never attended school at all), and the rural areas from which they originate, many speak at home in a 'restricted code' or rural dialect, rather than a rich, articulate mother tongue.

Attitude to and use of television in the home will govern whether children are used to discussing a programme's or video's content before, after, or during viewing, or not at all. It will also govern whether children are selective about their viewing and watch whatever is being broadcast live at the time. None of the children participating in this project mentioned any sort of censorship by their parents. They were free to watch whatever they wanted to watch, or whatever anyone else in their home was watching. No child mentioned bedtime as a restriction, either; in this context a 'nine o'clock watershed' is meaningless. The child who mentioned that his mother chose not to watch the horror movies did not say that she ever tried to prevent him from doing so. A child discussing a video that had frightened him said he stayed up 'while half past two' to watch it with his father. Perhaps censorship in the home, by parents, is also a class issue.

The media are a major influence in the lives of the children who participated in this research. The media influenced their clothing. I saw Mutant Turtle T-shirts, sunglasses, and shorts, Ghostbuster sweatshirts, He-Man and Batman T-shirts, My Little Pony bags and hairslides, and so on.

The media clearly influence their imaginative play, and I saw Turtle and Ghostbuster games. In nursery A a three-year-old was playing The A Team long after public broadcasting had stopped showing these programmes – maybe his elder brothers have them on video tapes. I constantly heard theme songs sung. The media influence their drawings and paintings and their choice of storybooks in the book corner (*Postman Pat* being a favourite).

According to the children, watching television or videos is their preferred 67
way of spending their leisure time. Certainly their knowledge of programme
content is wide. Most can skilfully operate a video recorder, operating all
the buttons correctly (i.e., FF, rewind, pause, etc.), though they are less
careful with books. This knowledge is brought from home – I do not allow
children to operate the video recorder at school, and nursery B does not
use one.

Although pre-school children's television influences some of the toys the 68
children buy, such as cuddly Spots, Postman Pat bags, Thomas the Tank
Engine bath toys, their stated favourite programmes are targeted at older
children or adults. The children watch soap operas and believe the characters are real people living in real families in real houses. Some watch the
news, some watch adult videos, and in all cases the children believe they
are watching real life. All watch a range of cartoons. Some cannot tell the
difference between a cartoon and an actor, and consider both to be real.
Only one child was able to say that a cartoon was a drawing, and she was
then floored by the question, 'How do cartoons run about?' Several children
could tell me that a cartoon was different from real people or animals, but
they could not tell me what that difference was. Although one child in the
target group and several from the reception class at nursery A used the
term 'pretending', no child used the term acting or talked about actors.
One child differentiated between the news and soap opera in terms of the
atmosphere in the room when they were watched and who watched them.
Her father always watched the news and considered it important, but in
her mind both the soap and the news were about real peoples' lives. The
soap interested her and the news appealed to her father; a matter of preferences, rather than different genres.

When cartoons and actors were shown together side by side it was easier 69
for the children to correctly pick out 'real' people from cartoons. Every
child knew that Henry was different from Ellie, her friend, and her father,
and they could label them as 'real' and Henry as a cartoon. They could not
explain to me how they knew this. It was harder for the children to assess
the reality factor when watching the clip that was only animated cartoons.
They became emotionally involved in the Spot storyline, and Spot became
real to them. At nursery B we watched this video with the whole nursery
group, and when I questioned all the children after viewing, several said
Spot was a real dog and several children were unsure.

Watching the 'dressing-up' video extract, the pre-school target children 70
thought the little boy was actually performing the magic, just as they
thought Henry jumped into the television. Their explanation of what had
happened had no suggestion that they had even an inkling of television
technology, and was confined to logical explanations they could identify
with: his mum did it; you (the teacher) did it; there was a hole; or they
offered the explanation the little boy himself gave: 'it was magic'.

They recognised, however, that things happen on television that cannot 71
happen in real life. No child expected that he or she could jump into the
television or perform magic tricks by flicking their fingers but, having
acknowledged that things happened on television and video that were out

of the ordinary, the children were inclined to accept this and needed pushing to ask how and why.

Conclusion

If there is an unequal opportunity for children to discuss their experiences
of television in the home, does it then fall to the *social agency* of the nursery
to provide this opportunity, and how can it be tackled?

The quality of and opportunity for talk in nurseries varies as widely as
it does in the children's homes. It is dependent on the quality and attitude
of the nursery staff, and the climate and atmosphere they create in the
nursery environment. As well as the degree and freedom from formality in
talk between nursery staff and children, talk about television is dependent
on the nursery staff's own attitude to television and familiarity with the
wide variety of programmes. The under-fives watch programmes broadcast
by satellite, cable, ITV, BBC, and Channel 4, as well as a range of videos.

Many nursery teachers and nursery nurses may not feel equipped to
tackle in-depth talk in the area of television with young children. The
theories of media education are, even now, rarely included in initial teacher
training or NNEB (National Nursery Examination Board) courses, and
in-service courses concerned with primary media education are equally
rare.

Even young children ask questions concerned with technology which
adults not involved with programme-making may be unable to answer and
so may prefer to avoid. As an example, during this project I was asked how
the Invisible Man takes his head off when he takes his bandages off.
Another child volunteered the information that the head was still there but
that it was invisible, offering the intended storyline. The first child did not
understand the concept 'invisible' and preferred to believe that the head
was ripped off. Where should I have started my explanation: the concept
of invisible, or the technology that makes things seem to be invisible?

Some nurseries refuse to have a television as part of their resources,
refuse to allow play rooted in television experiences (e.g., Ghostbusters
imaginative play), and will not discuss with the children their experiences
of television.

> Watching with an adult is an important factor in understanding, even
> discussing the language used in a programme. Nurseries that ban
> television remove again from children who may already be watching
> television alone at home, the opportunity to watch with an adult and
> the opportunity to discuss with the adult what they are watching.

Clearly, there is a role for media education in the nursery. The media
are very powerful, their influence on the pre-school child enormous.
Knowledge is power, and we should be giving pre-school children some
knowledge and understanding of how the media work and what they are.
Language is the key factor. The children need the opportunity to discuss
what they are viewing, and they need the appropriate vocabulary – new
concepts and new words need to be introduced to the children. For
example, unless the words 'actor' and 'cartoon' are part of their vocabulary

290

and are concepts with which they are familiar, how can such young children understand or compare the differences between, say, Henry Ramsey in *Neighbours*, and Henry the cartoon kangaroo in *You and Me*? How can they begin to understand complexities such as: Henry Ramsey is not a real person, but the actor playing Henry Ramsey is. If the child met the actor shopping in the street, they would not be meeting Henry Ramsey but the actor that plays that part. They need knowledge of the appropriate vocabulary to frame and phrase their questions. How can this be achieved?

The project has shown that pre-school children engage with the storyline   78
of what they are watching and react to it, believing it depicts what is really happening, somewhere.

This is the same whether the programme watched be a pre-school pro-   79
gramme or an adult video that confuses and frightens them. As teachers, we cannot control or censor what the children watch in their own homes, but we can give the children the opportunity and the appropriate language to talk about their experiences of television and video with a non-judgemental but informed adult. This is in itself the beginnings of media education. It may also help children develop an understanding of how real what they are viewing actually is.

Notes

1. A national project set up in 1986 by the BFI Education Department with funding from the Calouste Gulbenkian Foundation.
2. The *Spot* videos are based on the illustrated stories by Eric Hill, produced for publishers worldwide by Ventura Publishing Ltd, 11–73 Young Street, London W8 5EH.

Representation

Dot Froggatt

Several years ago I went on an in-service teacher training course that was 1
to have an enormous impact on the teaching and learning processes in my
classroom. That course was entitled 'Media Education', and I thought it
was going to be about language development and have something to do
with television. Little did I realise that within a few months, my class of
seven-year-old children would be in the middle of a number of battles with
major institutions and would leave them bloodied! Media education quickly
became an integral part of our cross-curricular themes, underpinning all
our work, rather than a new subject that had to be slotted in. My aims
were to help the children to understand that the media are involved in the
actual construction of events, information, knowledge, and attitudes, and
not just in their presentation. I wanted them to be aware of this, then be
critically aware, and then independently critically aware. It seemed a daunting task to take on with such young children, but in view of what developed
subsequently, I realise now how much I had underestimated them.

I began with the concept of representation – how the world around us 2
is described or represented. The media have enormous power and influence
over our knowledge of that world, and I wanted the children to realise this
and to scrutinise portrayals in a variety of texts, including greetings cards,
wallpaper sample books, wrapping papers, and magazine advertisements.
Their responses to these products became the material for further investigation, learning, and action. The children commented readily and became
very articulate in expressing their own opinions, particularly as those views
were given recognition and seen to matter.

Our mixed-ability class was multiracial and included a child with a physi- 3
cal disability, so it was with very real involvement that we looked at birthday cards and party invitations to see if a suitable card could be found to
send to each of the children. I had deliberately chosen a selection of cards
showing children, but had been unable to find any depicting ethnic groups
or disabilities, and the majority reflected gender stereotyping. For over a
term we searched for appropriate greetings cards, but to no avail. Eventually the children designed and made their own, after analysing and commenting on the commercial cards:

> This card has a boy on with a football. I have never seen a birthday
> card with a girl on and playing football. Sarah, who is in my group,
> would love to have a birthday card with a girl playing football on it
> as she loves football. [Kirsty, 7 years]

We then turned our attention to magazine advertisements to see what they were selling, what was being implied by the product in the layout, at whom the products were aimed, and what the children thought about the whole marketing process. Those complex issues were well within the emotional and cognitive capabilities of this class. For example, of an advertisement for a diamond necklace featuring a cat, one wrote:

Cats' eyes glitter like diamonds but the cat is soft and furry as well, so the advert people are hoping people will say, oh, look at that cat. And the advert people are hoping people will then say, oh, look at that necklace, isn't it nice? I want it. Please buy it. The cat is next to the diamond necklace to make it more loving, but I would buy the cat instead. [David, 7 years]

The project continued by looking at photographs; a set of biased, ficti- tious school rules; a picture storybook; and the roles played by the children in Enid Blyton's gangs. Throughout, we were analysing representations and responding to them critically, but not necessarily to find fault or be negative about the media. Much of this work heightened an appreciation of aspects of the media, and it was positive, challenging and fun. For example, 'Toadstools' involved looking at dictionary definitions of the fungi. Initially, the children accepted these completely but after several weeks of observations, investigations, fungal forays, and experiments (during which they had become the world's leading experts), they reread those definitions with some dissatisfaction. They felt that too much essential information had been missed out, and so were challenged to write their own. Their first attempts bore closer resemblance to a botanical dissertation than a concise definition and, after many drafts, the children produced simpler statements with which they were reasonably satisfied. However, as a result of this process, their attitude towards the editors of the dictionaries had changed to one of admiration as they came to appreciate the difficulties involved in this sophisticated language task.

While becoming more critically aware, I avoided tearing things to shreds that were important to the children, such as favourite stories that often served as a way of confronting their fears or problems and provided them with security. However, I need not have worried because, when there was shredding to be done, the children did it themselves and with the ruthlessness and killer instinct of which a shark could be proud!

A national arts products company had produced a pencil called 'Flesh' that arrived in our class. It was shrimp pink, and its label caused much concern and hilarity as the children took off socks, pulled up vests, and rolled back sleeves trying to find any patch of skin that matched the pencil. They decided it could not be used to draw any person in the class, and that to have just one colour labelled 'flesh' was inadequate. I asked what they wanted to do about it, and as a result they wrote short but powerful letters to the company explaining the foolishness of a single pencil called 'flesh'.

Your pencil called flesh won't do a right picture of me, because my colour of skin is brown. There is pink, brown, and pale colours of the skin. You should open your eyes and look at the world's skin. [Zeshan, 8 years]

I think your flesh-coloured pencil is a nice pencil but you should mix in brown and pink designs as well as just the flesh. If you look around our class you would see all sorts of blacks, browns, and pinks. Flesh colours, Zeshan, Rekha, and Keith have all got dark brown skins. Marta has got a brownish yellowish skin. Jo has skin which is turning brown. Why can't you make all those colours? All those pinks and browns? [Teresa, 8 years]

The company replied – but not to the children. Our head teacher showed us the letter he had received, which defended the name of the pencil. The children were angry that the reply had not been written to them and disagreed with the company's attitude, both towards themselves and the product. Undeterred, they took red, blue, yellow, and white paints and mixed up all the shades they needed to paint each other, creating just over sixty. They sent these off as their example of what was required to represent flesh. The children concluded that other companies also 'got it wrong' with 'flesh-coloured' bandages and plasters, but when they grew up and were in charge of the world, they would change things like that. However, they did not have to wait that long. The arts products company wrote to explain that, as a result of being 'stimulated by an external suggestion or comment', they had changed the name of the pencil and widened the range of shades, enclosing samples of the new colours for consideration. The children were satisfied with the outcomes as regards both the new product and the company's responses to their criticisms.

Concepts of representation were further developed in a whole-school project on Winter Festivals that involved a multi-cultural celebration of Diwali, Chanuka, and Christmas. My class designed our own Winter Festival, and one of the activities was to decide what qualities and gender to choose if Winter were a person. The children varied in their representations, and Winter became a powerful, cruel, and terrible ice queen; a battered, weak, grey old man; a glittering, radiant snow princess; a merciless, tyrannical god, and so on.

If Winter were a person she would be a woman – naughty, snowy, icy, kind, nice, beautiful, lovely, wonderful. But changing. Evil, horrible, disgusting, terrible. [Louisa, 8 years]

We examined symbols used in festivals and chose our own, then looked at how Christmas is often portrayed by images of deep snow and frozen ponds. None of the children had ever experienced this and had few memories of snow from any winter. They discussed this with their usual animation and concluded it wasn't a misrepresentation because there must have been times in the Olden Days (pre-1981) when Christmas had been like that and it was good that that's how people wanted it remembered.

294

Unlike the coloured-pencil project, the children wanted to keep and perpetuate the images of Christmas they had analysed, despite their awareness of the stereotyping. Their own reaction made me question my own responses to stereotyping, and I realised that, in my attempts to redress imbalances, I had inadvertently created the 'oh-no-not-another-swashbuckling-independent-black-princess-syndrome'. In effect, I had tipped the scales from one extreme to another but, thanks to an awareness created by the sensitivity of the children, a balance was restored and the swashbuckling princess remained, though alongside her stereotyped sisters. That was the first of many examples of just how media-literate many children are.

The concept of representation can be addressed equally well in less media-specific themes. A technology-based project on Romanies, undertaken by another class, generated a gradual understanding of the alternative life-styles and cultures of Travellers. At the start of the topic, the children had been told of the prejudice often encountered by Travellers, but it only made an impact when they experienced it at first hand while spending the day at what they thought was a Romany camp. Although created just for the project, the camp looked so authentic that a neighbouring farmer who did not know the 'Gypsies' were all teachers, gave vent to a tirade of threats and warnings. The 'Gypsies' maintained their role-play and, having established their right to be on the land, promised the farmer that nothing would be damaged or stolen. The children had witnessed the entire exchange, and their immediate reaction of silent incredulity over such blatant hostility developed during the following weeks into a deep concern for the rights and cultural values of Travellers. Articles about real Gypsies in the district appeared regularly in the local newspapers and, without exception, every one created a negative impression of trouble-makers, yet the most common issue was that of official campsites, over which the Travellers had legal rights.

As their knowledge and understanding of Romanies grew, the children increasingly challenged the poor image and social standing portrayed in the newspapers. A television documentary on a day in the life of a Gypsy family was felt by the children to provide a more realistic reflection, although the family under scrutiny was seen in isolation and not integrated within any community. By the end of the project, the children had developed favourable opinions of their own, based on direct practical experiences with authentic and role-play Gypsies that had informed them enough to analyse and reject many of the images presented by the media.

In another example of a study based on representation, a class of children who had had some experience of media education illustrated how quickly their understanding of the concept could be developed and extended through their own heightened awareness.

It began by looking at a selection of L. S. Lowry's paintings, all similar in style and content and featuring the numerous 'matchstick' figures, as well as features of the artist's technique, such as painting on a white background and omitting shadows. The children then watched a video of the Northern Ballet Company's stunning production of *A Simple Man*, in which the biography of Lowry was told through dance, and the paintings with which the children were now familiar suddenly came to life in the form of ballet. The children were deeply impressed by the costumes, scenery, and choreography of the dancers and, after spending several hours rewatching the ballet and returning to the paintings in the classroom for detailed comparison, they concluded that the Northern Ballet Company had represented successfully Lowry's creations via another medium without losing or changing the essential characteristics. This had required sophisticated observational skills, but throughout the work the children had needed very little teacher intervention, and their conclusions were their own. It had been an exciting privilege to watch children who were only in their third year of primary education tackle presentation and representation with such independent, critical awareness.

The results from these few projects were enough to convince me that media education is too important to be restricted to occasional projects about the media. In the same way that there is more to multicultural education than 'doing the festivals', media education is not just about newspapers or television programmes. It is a complex set of concepts that allow children to take an active critical role in their responses to any form of communication, whether from television, books, or cornflakes boxes. Representation was an exciting, challenging introduction to media education in the primary school.

'Nature Park':
A Project with Media Education Focus

Kate Dewar

I teach in a 5–9 school in inner-city Leeds. The catchment area comprises 1
a substandard pre-war council estate with about 50 per cent unemployment,
one-third one-parent families, and only two families from ethnic minorities.
I have recently finished an evening Certificate course on Media Education.

Our school has two 35 mm cameras, an overhead projector, a slide pro- 2
jector, a VHS video recorder, TV, and several audiocassette recorders, and
my class has access to a computer for two days a week. As yet, the school
has no policy for media education, and I am the only member of staff with
an interest, though the other teachers do see a value in the approach and
have been supportive to me in my efforts.

My class had a student for four weeks but the practice was continually 3
being interrupted by illness, leaving me to fill in the gaps. As my class of
twenty-two seven- to eight-year-olds had been enjoying a computer program 'The Nature Park', an adventure game, for several weeks it provided
a fruitful start to a short media education topic, something these children
had not done before. The paint-box colours and stylised computer graphics
of trees and so on were clearly a long way from a 'true' representation of
a park as experienced by my class. The concept of representation in this
context seemed a good place to begin.

We decided to visit the local city park with a view to the children taking 4
their own photographs – their own representations. First, however, we
looked at a variety of pictures. We sorted them and tried decoding some
of them, the intention being that this would help us to talk about, and then
decide, how best to take the photographs. This activity was done in groups
of about six. In threes the children sorted pictures any way they liked,
having been asked to explain their decisions to the other three. This provoked a certain amount of discussion, but the decisions to group the pictures were made on very cursory observations: colour and pastimes were
the main criteria chosen, although comic pictures were grouped together
without hesitation. (One group was unable to come up with the word
'comic', but used the term 'cartoon'.)

The children were then asked to select their favourite picture. They were 5
asked:

> Where do you think I found this picture?
> Who do you think would look at it?

297

How do you think it was made – was it drawn, painted?
What can you say about . . . ?

The children were able to give some response to all these questions. The 6
main problem was their lack of concentration while others were talking.
With hindsight it might have been better to pick on just one of these aspects
at a time, repeating the exercise in slightly different contexts choosing a
different focus each time.

One discussion, featuring Lisa, Nicola, Peter, and me, the teacher, went 7
as follows:

T	What can you see?
L	A lady.
N	She is going to work.
T	How can you tell?
L	She's got a bag.
N	She's got posh clothes on.
T	Where is she when this was taken?
L	At home [related to another picture from the pile].
N	They're probably sisters and she's just come into work [other picture has a lady sitting in a house and looking towards a door].
T	Yes, I see what you mean – the ladies do look as if they are sisters. But supposing we forget this picture for a minute [puts it away] and just look at this lady – where is she?
L	At the office.
T	But where are the office desks?
N	Oh, there aren't any.
L	She must be at home then.
T	But where is the furniture and windows and things?
N	I don't know [gets fidgety and looks away].
L	Hmm. There's nothing there. [Also seems bored with the activity now and looks away.]
T	Think hard. Where was this lady when the photograph was taken? Why is it all white behind her?
L	[flippant] It's snow.
T	Come on – we know it's not snow.
P	[frustrated at listening to the conversation and butts in] She's in a place where they take your photos.
T	Yes – anyone know what it is called? [Silence]
T	It's called a studio. What is this white thing, then?
N	A big sheet.
T	So, do you think this is a lady going to the office?
L	No, it's just a model wearing a posh dress.

Here, the children, with no experience of decoding texts, perceive the text
to be reality – that is, they had no concept of mediation. The confident
identification of 'posh clothes' and the connection with 'the office' provided
a true enough representation of reality to the children without requiring

them to look further for reassurances. Practice at this type of exercise would hopefully start to develop decoding skills. Clearly, a basic vocabulary also needs to be developed to make the discussion of images richer. It is easy to assume that children know simple terms such as angle, studio, photographer, magazine, catalogue, comic, brochure, film, and programme when in fact many children in my class have no such words in their vocabulary.

Before visiting the city park we split into two groups and discussed ways   8
in which one group might make the park seem an unpleasant place to visit, while the other group should try to make it seem the opposite. The children liked this challenge and, as they were familiar with the park, nearly all were able to make valuable contributions in the discussions and when taking the photographs.

The trip was lots of fun, and every child took two photographs each.   9
Back in class they were asked to draw what they expected the outcome of one of their photographs would be. The drawings were on the whole surprisingly accurate and showed far more perspective, detail, and variety than the children's normal pictures. Once developed, the children compared the photographs with their drawings, and enjoyed discussing the differences. A small group then sorted the photographs into two and then mounted them to portray the park as either 'good' or 'bad'. Children were able to express their preferences when making the choices. Another small group was asked to provide single-word labels for each photograph to complete the display. Success was experienced by all, and the children were quick to drag a parent to the display and say, 'I took that photo.'

A spin-off from this was to consider what was 'included' by the camera   10
and what was 'excluded'. Some children used cardboard cut-out frames to choose how they might do observational drawings of a preserved bird or squirrel. Other children were given a photograph they had taken at the park and asked to extend the picture on a larger piece of paper.

A visit to a nature reserve, out of the city, then gave us another opportu-   11
nity to use the cameras, but this time we decided to make a photomap (trail) for a parallel class due to visit the same place the following week. I drew a map and marked the points where the photographs would need to be taken, recording the initials of the child who was to take the photograph. The children passed the map round during the trip. The decision of what they would need to include in their photograph was left up to them. (Unfortunately, this activity did not progress due to incorrect insertion of the film by someone else, and half our photographs were lost!) Nevertheless, the extra attention paid to the characteristics of the nature reserve by looking through the camera made the subsequent class discussion much richer. We were able to compare the park and the reserve, listing their attributes. The computer game was also referred to, and one or two children were able to say that the program was more like the nature reserve than the local city park. This comparison was, however, beyond the majority.

The children were asked to design their ideal park, bearing in mind all   12
they had seen. This was a successful activity, and seasonal differences became a relevant area of discussion: for example, 'Does it make sense to draw someone sun-bathing in the park while someone else is sledging?'

The more able children in the class were asked to make a list of questions 13
to ask the parallel class about their visit. From these individual lists we
discussed which questions were open and which were closed. As a group
we compiled a list of open questions, then each child chose someone from
the other class to interview on audiotape. Ideally, these reports would have
been compiled into a newspaper article, but suddenly Christmas loomed
large and all we managed to do was to look at the 'Front Page' computer
software and for children to write their own experiences in a newspaper
report. This was not a complete success, and it became clear that we needed
to look at newspapers more carefully before trying to produce our own.

Our local Primary Centre lent me a camcorder for a fortnight. I intro- 14
duced it to the whole class, using a monitor, letting each child take it in
turn to be behind the camera and in front of it. Making the most of some
release time (the student was back for a spell) I took a small group of five
children and we embarked on animating the narrative of the computer
'Nature Park' adventure game. The children drew and cut out the main
characters of the story and buildings and furniture and so on that would
be needed, and these cut-outs were then Blu-Tacked to a large board and
moved about to depict the story. Having tried this for a while the children
then made a storyboard on which to base the filming. A final storyboard
was made by me, using their ideas but trying to ensure that we had some
success by not being too ambitious. Next we defined the roles of each child
for the filming process and agreed a system of signals for stopping and
starting filming. One child did the filming, one moved the cut-outs, two
others did the voices, and one directed, with me helping out when necessary. Without editing facilities the final version was full of small mistakes,
but the children were able to experience the complexity of the process and
gained much from working co-operatively.

Designing board games based on the 'Nature Park' narrative required 15
the children to think about a different type of representation. Looking at
commercially produced games would have been another fruitful area to
explore, although we did not have time on this occasion. Making 'twizzlers'
with a net on one side and a butterfly on the other provided a simple
example of the persistence of vision. (When twizzled the butterfly is
'caught' in the net, as in the computer game narrative – a chance also to
discuss nature conservation.)

The topic lasted for about four weeks and although not all the children 16
did all the activities, all were nevertheless able to achieve success in activities pitched at their own levels. The topic gave much scope for discussion
and other language work. It was possible to address different areas of the
National Curriculum (see Topic Web) although English clearly made up a
large part. It provided plenty of first-hand experiences and many situations
where the children could have their own decisions valued. This topic arose
out of unexpected circumstances and to some extent generated its own
progression. The activities could have resulted just as easily from maths
work on maps, a class storybook, or science work on, say, food chains. A
media text-based topic (newspapers, for example) would possibly have been
an alternative way of organising media education, but with this particular

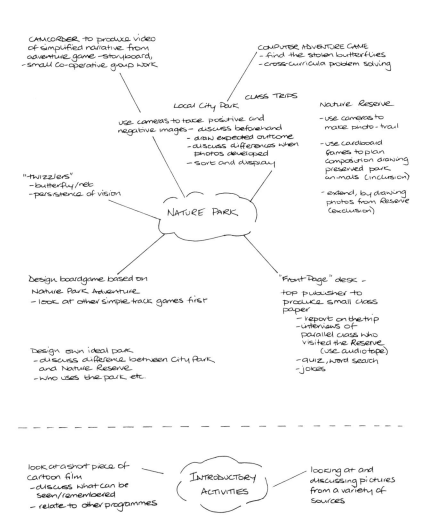

CAMCORDER to produce video of simplified narrative from adventure game -storyboard, - small co-operative group work

COMPUTER ADVENTURE GAME - find the stolen butterflies - cross-curricula problem solving

CLASS TRIPS

Local City Park

use cameras to take positive and negative images - discuss beforehand
- draw expected outcome
- discuss differences when photos developed
- sort and display

Nature Reserve
- use cameras to make photo-trail
- use cardboard frames to plan composition drawing preserved park animals (inclusion)
- extend, by drawing photos from Reserve (exclusion)

"twizzlers"
- butterfly/net
- persistence of vision

NATURE PARK

Design boardgame based on Nature Park Adventure
- look at other simple track games first

Design own ideal park
- discuss difference between City Park and Nature Reserve
- who uses the park etc.

"Front Page" desk - top publisher to produce small class paper
- report on the trip
- interviews of parallel class who visited the Reserve (use audiotape)
- quiz, word search
- jokes

look at a short piece of cartoon film
- discuss what can be seen/remembered
- relate to other programmes

INTRODUCTORY ACTIVITIES

looking at and discussing pictures from a variety of sources class I decided against it due to the large number of children with learning difficulties.

The children have now made a beginning in media education. They have been reading a variety of texts, talking about media agencies, audience, and representation. They have started to become familiar with the technologies, and they have worked with narrative. Building on what they have started will be important. Continuity within school and a steady progression into their secondary education would be ideal. I hope to continue this year, looking at symbols of Christmas, and talking about Christmas cards – their design, the reasons for the images, and the intended recipients. 17

None of what we have done in this topic is particularly new in terms of primary practice. What has been different is the way in which I have started to direct discussions: the questions I have asked, and the vocabulary and concepts I have tried to introduce. I would have found this very difficult to begin without having attended the media education course, and I still have much to learn about approaches with the children. Small group discussions in a lively classroom, where the children are extremely demanding of attention, are very difficult. I hope to include work through drama and movement next term in a topic on animals in literature, television, and film – hopefully starting, at a simple level, to look at stereotyping. I think the children will be more responsive and expressive in a situation where there is more room to move and more opportunity to become individually involved. 18

'He Quickly Changes into his Bikini':
Models for Teacher–Pupil Collaboration
Cathy Pompe

Here are selected moments from two very different projects in which I [1] played a part as a media support teacher, and the parallels between them have helped me to identify dilemmas and critical ingredients for media education work. They focus on the inevitable teacher–pupil divide, which bears upon all classroom dynamics but becomes a central issue in media education. They also raise issues about the nature of the help teachers might offer children. The anecdotes related here suggest that, as a matter of course, children are actively riding the media codes and conventions they know so much about. This forces us to shift our input as teachers away from the instructional mode, and towards attending more closely to the kinds of critical awareness which children already have and which might be built on. Finally, these accounts touch on the question of what we can actually do to empower children in their unequal encounters with the mass media Goliaths that surround them.

Two Media Projects
One class of 11-year-old juniors was working on a project combining science [2] and media work. Their school is set in a large council estate to the north of Cambridge and deals with a complex range of children. The classroom atmosphere was volatile: the teacher knew that important developments were taking place, but the fragmented nature of daily life offered little scope to dwell on the results. Her personal commitment as a teacher was to open out the curriculum so that in any classroom venture all children were moved on creatively, rather than to nurture crack groups and polished end products.

The idea of combining science with media work arose from the conviction [3] that children's interest in science is kindled by the attractive ways science is packaged and presented in the media. As science is itself a constructed discourse with its own set of communications and persuasive devices, a programme in media awareness might help children become more skilled at assessing and communicating scientific information. More importantly still, scientific thinking exists within social and cultural contexts, and scientific discoveries are framed by the narrative structures and imagination of scientists. By making room for the powerful narratives and other media texts in which science and technology play star parts, children might be given the imaginative space within which scientific ideas could be explored.

The second group of children were thoughtful nine- and ten-year-olds in a village school. Some stages in their learning progression are better documented because of the enormous amount of work the project generated. Because they were so co-operative and hard-working, it also took these children longer to dare to take liberties with media conventions, and risk a playful outlook which eventually brought the project alive and put power into their own hands. The class had been 'commissioned' to make a video documentary about the local community by the school governors, who hoped it might lure more parents to the next statutory AGM. The class were baffled by the responsibility of creating a text that would be of interest to an audience that knew everything about the subject already.

For both teachers it was a first attempt at tackling media education, and the first encounter with a media technology like video.

I start with two stories, taken from these two very different classrooms. Between them they go to the heart of the contradictions I have experienced in drawing children's media experiences into the curriculum. Media education sets out to put at the centre of the curriculum the cultures that children know. We want to tap into areas of experience about which children are fluent and confident, yet we are not trying to ingratiate ourselves with them like adults trying to join in on a children's party. We only intrude because we claim to have something to offer. As a result we easily get caught between the recognition we owe to children's opinions and expertise in these matters, and our role as catalysts who want to intervene to challenge their thinking and help release their voices.

The first scene is set in a darkened room in the city school. We are doing 'image analysis' using slides, a stage on the way to children making choices in constructing images of their own. I have somewhat patronisingly chosen stills that will make a succession of careful points, but my articulate questions hover uncomfortably over the uneasy group. In the dark, cosy underworld on the carpet, however, life goes on. Cryptic utterances fly discreetly between friends, furtive and casual asides that reverberate with interest and relevance, giggles and speculative exchanges and authoritative wise-guy pronouncements. The teacher sitting among the children can hear that the children are making statements that are exactly relevant to the discussion I have been trying to draw from them, two disconnected discourses running parallel to each other, above and below.

I show a slide of the Superkings cigarette advert, where an aerial shot of a train on a railway siding makes a pun on the shape of a cigarette, with the train's red lights mimicking the glowing end of the cigarette. Urged to say the first things it made them think of, children called out 'USA!', and 'John Wayne!' These two utterances go to the heart of the hidden associations in the image: while advertisers may no longer connect cigarette consumption with images of healthy outdoor pleasures, the ochre of the harsh landscape edging the railway line in this image leads straight into those old narratives: the Rockies, untamed horizons, the free life, manliness, the rich natural colours of saddle, suntan, and tobacco. The children need no help: decoding this picture for themselves in this way is a matter of course. These throw-away words are typical of the witty, insightful remarks children make to themselves or to each other; to elaborate destroys the potency of the communication.

A teacher-led discussion could not bring them to this point without   9
killing off their interest. Yet the cluster words 'USA' and 'John Wayne' are so tightly packed, so cryptic, that it is impossible for the children themselves to realise the value of what they are saying: perhaps it is even impossible for them to make explicit use of the understanding it implies.

The other scene shows a group of children earnestly reviewing the   10
material they have shot for their video documentary so far. They do not know what they want, but they are nevertheless not happy with what they have. They show me umpteen retakes of interviews and presentations which become more stilted the harder the children try to get the conventions of the genre seamlessly right. The children are puzzled, exhausted, and highly critical. 'We want to make it good, not boring: interesting!' They think it would become more interesting if they could 'make it slick', 'use more TV tricks', 'more magical effects'. At the same time, they are clear they want 'something different from television programmes'. They agree that the main thing that will save the day is humour. 'We try as hard as we can and there is nothing we can do to make it better,' they gloomily conclude. The touching element in this scene is that during gaps in the discussion these children, earnestly seeking for the key to comic entertainment, are in fact falling about with laughter watching the bits of their video that went wrong, or that capture spontaneous moments with messy edges: here indeed is something funny and different, but the children are discounting it.

What these two scenes have in common is that they present an edu-   11
cational stalemate. On the one hand, here are children full of energy and healthy independence, implicitly aware of the codes and conventions of media languages. On the other, we see all the pitfalls and difficulties which lie in the way of trying to access and develop that expertise and put it to creative use.

Getting over the Teacher–Pupil Divide
There is much to drive teachers and pupils apart who tackle this kind of   12
work. On the one side is the teacher, probably fearful that she knows nothing about the media herself, wondering what she can offer children. Her tastes diverge widely from theirs: how can she share her own interests and values without passing judgement on some of the 'rubbish' children watch? Their greater knowledge and exposure to television easily feels threatening. When, after the image analysis session, children in the science project were working on an advertising exercise constructing a collaged still image (trying to lay a trail from their chosen product to 'people's secret wishes', as the teacher put it to them), I made a half-hearted child tell me what his plans were. Listening much later to the recording of his speculations, I realised he had in fact been giving me a detailed rendering of the plot of *Robocop* (Certificate 18), which I had not seen at the time. His clear grasp that I had no idea about where his ideas were coming from, and his choice not to tell me about this, my standing useless and uninvolved at the side of this tangle of poorly expressed ideas, yet having the power to impose

305

on this child the use of his time: it added up to a lifeless and alienating exchange. How much more potent if I had been able to share the conversation as an insider, and we had carried on in that half-stated, comfortable, 'I-know-what-you-mean' talk.

On the other side of the divide stand the children. The private subculture where media pleasures and tough talking are currency is one area of intimate experience which they do not really want teachers to get hold of and trample on. Four children and I were discussing the science project and making further plans, and we had set up the video to record ourselves. A child arrived late and was greeted with the excited tongue-in-cheek warning: 'Don't say anything interesting, you're being filmed!' The message was that children's real opinions are powerful, and potentially risky. The children in the science project did not want to share with us their views on the television they watched, or discuss science in the media, from dental adverts to *Tomorrow's World*. We had to find fresh common ground, a place where children and adults could meet on an equal footing and contribute their respective knowledge and expertise.

With the science project we solved the problem by introducing a class theme. 'Science Fiction' provided a forum and allowed us as teachers to introduce media texts that would call up our varied cultural backgrounds and set up a dialogue. We may not know about *Robocop*, but we might be wheeling in *Frankenstein*, and other real or fictional tales about coping-with-the-monsters-we-have-created, and which would find echoes in the contemporary stories that engage children so powerfully.

The village school tackled the issue in a different way. They found common ground in the actual task they had been set, and which every member of the class was coming to as a beginner. The teacher later identified the most powerful dynamic of the project as having been the experience of 'being in it together', of learning, and been seen to be learning, alongside the children. By taking on a set of real problems that she herself had no idea about how to solve, she instinctively created an atmosphere which was clear of hostility.

This collaborative approach to learning, good practice in general, is indispensable with media work. In my experience, a key to children extending their critical understanding of the media lies in finding contexts which legitimise their own private and subversive voices, for they are the shoots from which their critical faculties will grow. Where children are too busy trying to guess what the teacher wants to hear and what rules will help them survive in the classroom, media work will not reach those areas of experience and opinion which children defend from meddling adults. For the purposes of classroom work they will surrender critical judgement when what they need is to develop a committed two-way engagement with media texts.

I want to turn now to evidence that children do spontaneously engage with media texts in active and critical ways. They tend to dismiss this capacity in curriculum terms, and the contribution teachers can make here is to value, and help children value, this subversive, playful capacity.

Valuing Media Knowledge

Noticing what Children Know
The science class worked on collage posters of sci-fi movies of their inven- 18
tion, like *The Trip to Kalip* and *The Last Galaxy*. The children who chose
Killers of Kane as the title of their movie might not have even known the
story of Cain and Abel, but they did know that Kane was a good name for
a killer. Informal, open-ended work of this kind offered listening ground
that helped locate children's interest and energy, and identify a role for the
teacher.

Taking the New Literacy Seriously
In the first moments of the media and science project the teacher was 19
distressed about the noisy, messy atmosphere that the media work was
generating. At the end of the whole project some classroom assistants
confessed to being relieved the media lark was all over and the class could
settle down to regular work again. What happened here was firstly that the
children needed to learn to take this kind of work seriously. Some quickly
hailed and embraced the 'new literacy'. Other children, however, who
thought they had finally mastered the classroom literacy routines, felt the
tables had turned on them and they were being cheated. On top of that,
by steering close to the children's own culture, we were setting tasks which
gave free rein to energetic and irreverent reactions.

The media programme had started with superheroes. Having watched 20
the opening of *Superman II*, retracing the origins of Superman, the children
were asked to work in small groups on the origins of a superhero of their
own, endowed with exceptional (scientifically interesting?) powers. The
storyboards the children used were later refined to prepare a polished
six-shot video sequence which was recorded as a series of stills, and audio-
dubbed, to give all children a grounding in video skills. As they started
work, however, the teacher was upset at the subversive attitude the children
were taking. Superman had been greeted with enthusiasm, but most of the
stories were send-ups of the genre: *Superduck, Baby Critter*, and the like:

> Super coppe hears her screams with his supper hearing powers. He
> quickly changes into his bikini puts on his headphones and gets onto
> his super scooter. Then he scootes away into the distance.

> It was the 25th centuary when church goers have peirced noses and
> sing acid House. It was an ordinary Sunday when a capsule lands on
> the head of the bishop of cantabury. The capsule opens and out come's
> an odinary Bishop that looks just like the Bishop of Cantabury. Little
> did the pierced nose church goers know BUT the new bishop of
> cantabury [had] extraordinary powers. He originated from heaven on
> cloud 9 with its pearly Gate's and it's welcome matt.

Back in the village, the video documentary children were labouring 21
intensively, believing success was a matter of cleverness and technical skill.
At this point the children had to be helped to see that any text needs to

307

take its viewers 'for a ride', to carry them along a roller-coaster of anticipation and surprise. From that moment onwards the class started to consider wider issues of narrative structure and genre. Suddenly, the abundance of what they themselves enjoyed and knew about television, but had never thought of seriously, came into play. Media conventions came to be seen as a range of open choices and effective persuasive devices, rather than immutable and deadening rules.

Actively Reading the Media Forms

Purposeful contexts for media work – serious without being didactic – provide children with the opportunities to enter into a committed dialogue with media texts. The space for this is probably to be found in the intimate play between children's concern to crack the media codes, to 'get it exactly right', and their desire to resist and distance themselves from dominant media cultures.

Trying to Get it Right

Five children from the science project who were unable to accompany the class on the educational holiday week were entrusted with a video camera and the use of the school library for two weeks. They created the desktop sci-fi horror video *When the Aliens Wanted Water*. What was striking about the way they developed their ideas, whether this offered the best strategy for collaborative work, or revealed the rules that governed their thinking in general, was that *it was abstract considerations of plot, character, and genre which generated the specific incidents and details of the story.* The children started with the genre they wanted, then worked out the need for a goody hero, then planned the number of 'heroes' (six, not four, 'because that's the same as *Turtles* and *Ghostbusters*, so we'll have to have something different'), then decided the heroes would be picked off one by one leaving only one to save the day. ('That's what they always have in horror films: they all die in the end, don't they, so it ends up with one.')

Sitting in and joining in on these discussions during my occasional visits provided many other instances of the children's earnest concern to go by the rules, and align themselves with the respectable coterie of film-makers:

> The video was planned to show still pictures with a soundtrack: I am asking the children how they plan to introduce to the viewers what they have been telling me about the various characters.

> Teacher: How do you show that her parents have died?
> Imran: Show her in the graveyard.
> Liam: That's not very nice – not in a *cartoon*!

> Here the children are wondering about using a coloured figure of an alien against a black-and-white library book picture of the Tower of London:

| Imran: | Colour – with black and white? |
| Johnny: | They do that in *Pink Panther* . . . |

Johnny is saying that if they do it in *Pink Panther*, doing it here will not detract from the credibility and professionalism they are seeking to achieve.

Resisting the Codes
The *Robocop* anecdote raised the spectre of children's 'derivative' ideas. 25
Yet many imitations they produce, from casual, everyday remarks ('Liam, you win our fantastic prize for the most swear-words in this recording') to the stories about Supercopper and Superduck, are barbed with irony: the children are declaring their understanding and their distance, at once irritated and fascinated.

The Enabling Role of the Teacher
Aspirations towards professionalism and sophistication lead to frustration: 26
like the village children, the science class were disappointed with the modest outcomes of their mighty efforts on the six-shot video sequences. They had dreamt of instant Spielberg, but their work was beneath contempt as measured up against television output. And while Imran and his friends were proud of *When the Aliens Wanted Water*, it did not begin to do justice to their ideas and visions. This is where teachers can help children as they measure themselves up against the giants of the mass media.

Tolerating Teacher Interference
Unlike the instructional mode, which achieved little during the dis- 27
embodied image analysis session, my meddling in *When the Aliens Wanted Water* was tacitly welcomed, because it offered the children some of the conceptual levers they needed.

All along I had shown an interest in the categorising and speculative 28
asides that came up during planning discussions. While my interest gave them a sense of the value of what they were doing, I also felt the children humoured my particular line of inquiries with a 'well-that's-teachers-for-you' shrug. Nevertheless, here is perhaps an instance of a specific interest of mine quietly being taken on board:

When the Aliens stars Jack Gadget, a 'mad scientist', who works in a secret laboratory under the Statue of Liberty. I have been trying to trace the sources of influence of the story, and engage the children in a discussion of the films they enjoy:

Me:	Do you reckon this story is a bit like— what's underground? Tunnels . . . in New York: *Beauty and the Beast*?
Johnny:	Yes, when it was on, it's not on now.
Me:	What else, does it remind you of any other ideas? The underground tunnels, it's a bit *Turtles* in sewers. . . . Who else lives underground?

Child:	Wombles [general disowning laughter].
Child:	Batman, lives in a cave.
Me:	The *Superman* baddies live underground.

Not much response here.

The same day, at the beginning of the afternoon: two children who have been subdued when the whole group was together have worked over lunch, and have made up for lost time. Imran walks in, and they announce triumphantly to him:

| Paul: | Guess who we are going to have as the narrator? The Statue of Liberty! It walks and talks. |
| Imran: | I know where you got that idea from – *Ghostbusters*! |

Here, information about sources is coming out because of rivalry: Imran is slightly putting down the others for challenging his dominating influence over the shape of the story. A few moments later, however, this type of information is actually being volunteered by him, free of derogatory implications. It is at least possible he is pursuing the line of analysis which I had initiated, and established as a valid form of discourse. However, shrugged off at the time, he was using it for his own purposes now.

Child:	We could start with that beginning.
Me:	It sounds a bit like *Star Wars*.
Imran:	That's how I thought of it from.
[Other children comment appreciatively]
Imran:	Thank you, thank you. [Raising his voice:] Thank you fans out there!
	[reading:] 'Centuries ago there was a battle between good and bad and now the baddies have invaded earth . . .'

In a later session, while we viewed the video, Johnny explained to me how he had filmed the title-page in a 'jiggly' way to evoke further *Star Wars* connotation, the disappearing-into-the-distance 3-D effect; not so much trying to imitate as simply making an intertextual reference.

While teachers and children can collaborate to widen their choices in creating media texts, resources can never measure up to the multi-million productions children see on the screen. Teachers and children must therefore focus on the most important aspects of the process, which do lie within their reach. Creating their own media texts has first to be celebrated as the opportunity to represent and honour children's own unique voices and points of view. This can be achieved through work which has spontaneity and energy; when it is achieved, glossy production values recede as the overriding concern.

This is the path the village children were able to take. As an antidote to their early and earnest efforts over the video documentary I showed the class some clips from a 'video-letter' made by older children, where the messy edges of the production process had deliberately been included in the editing. The children now needed adults to legitimise and value the quirky events that surrounded the making of their documentary, and to help them believe that the 'mistakes' they were making were precisely the points at which their unique character and energy was coming through. Freed from the tyranny of seamless production standards, the children began to relax and incorporate into their video the humorous asides and private commentaries which they usually kept to themselves. They created a narrative link, wove in counterpoint commentary voice-overs, and interrupted the video with animations and other inserts. The head teacher was interviewed about his favourite books, which were spy novels and thrillers, so the children added their own playful comments: 'We know Mr Jones is a busy man. But could the reality be this?' The next shot showed the head teacher locked away in his office with a pile of detective stories, living in a Sherlock Holmes fantasy, with the *Pink Panther* tune playing in the background. By the end of the project the children had acquired a voice. The governors who had benignly commissioned the documentary for the parents' AGM sat up astonished; they had not been expecting anything like the video the children had prepared.

That term, staff in the school noted that the children from this class 31 were walking tall. They had acquired a new humility and awareness of the complexity of media languages, but they also glowed with a sense of professionalism. Most importantly, they had become confident because their own worth was being made visible to them. Something from the subculture, the underground reservoirs where children are witty, sophisticated, and energetic creatures, had broken through into the official world for others to see and celebrate. This is what teachers have some power both to facilitate and to suppress.

Media Education as an Essential Ingredient in Issue-based Environmental Education

Robin Bower

The School

Peak Forest Church of England School is a small and somewhat isolated village school situated in the heart of the limestone uplands of the Peak National Park. There are, at present, nineteen pupils aged from 4½ years to 11 years, of mixed ability. The school comprises two classrooms which make up the total working, office, dining, and storage space. Staff consists of the head teacher (myself) teaching full time, and an assistant teacher working at present for four days a week.

Through an intensive policy of opportunism, the school is better equipped than might be expected, and has two computers, most audiovisual aids, and a basic kit of equipment to promote video work including a shared VHS camcorder, mains VHS deck, simple edit controller, microphones, tape recorders, and so on. The pupils have extensive access to this equipment and show the confidence of those who have the opportunity for real 'hands on' experience.

The Curriculum

Given the wide age and ability range within the school, it has always been school policy to provide a flexible approach to the curriculum based on individual needs, and providing as rich a range of experiences as possible. The small number of pupils on roll makes it possible to involve all the children in activities which might only be available to small groups in a larger school, just as, conversely, it may be difficult to provide some of the opportunities available in larger schools. All schools must by necessity develop their own strengths.

The introduction of the National Curriculum certainly appeared to threaten the more stimulating approaches used in school and lead to a rigid system geared to an attainment target orientated and segregated subject regime. This presaged a direction which could leave little room for media education, information technology, and the like to fill the cross-curricular role they should.

The approach adopted by many schools has been to work to a more effective whole-school, cross-curricular approach which can genuinely respond to individual needs. The approach makes it possible to exploit the full potential of modern technology as a binding agent, where appropriate, to the whole process. It is encouraging that this way of tackling the National Curriculum is fully supported in the NCC (National Curriculum Council) Curriculum Guidance Series Number 7, which specifically looks at environmental education as an area that is of great importance and which demands a cross-curricular approach.

Media Education

In the primary classroom media education is not so likely to be approached   6
as a separate curriculum area, but rather be an influence that affects the whole learning environment in terms of both the hidden and the stated curriculum. It may be evident in a wide variety of ways:

- The regular presence of photographs and media images in displays, on the notice-boards, news-boards, etc.
- The encouragement of pupils to take photographs and video footage as a record of school trips, projects, etc., and to use them as a resource to allow individual viewpoints to be expressed.
- The effective use of educational broadcasts as a general resource, coupled with the encouragement of a critical response to these and other broadcasts.
- The use of tape-slide presentations and photo stories to present information or creative impressions.
- The use of desktop publishing techniques and the production of a class newspaper or newspaper-type items.

This list could be much more extensive but does, I hope, serve to make the point that aspects of media education can be integral to the ethos of the primary classroom.

I have always felt it important that pupils are helped to understand the   7
nature of media messages, the techniques that can be used to influence them, and the strengths and dangers of such influence. It is also fundamental to me that learning through activity and experience is vital at the primary stage, and it is therefore important to provide involvement in the planning and creation of such messages for a real audience on the subject of a real issue. Such issues are revealed all the time in environmental education.

Many of these issues are the subject of extensive media coverage, which   8
enables children to experience a range of television styles. These issues can also easily offend a child's sense of 'fairness' and arouse genuine concern and worry.

I feel it is irresponsible to generate this sort of concern without offering   9
some way forward, whether this be in terms of a local project at a personal or school level (such as recycling waste materials, planting trees, and so on), or by coming to terms with the structures of influence in our society, communication and the media, and then using them in an appropriate and sensitive manner.

'Trefax': A Case Study

The making of a video was one of the ways of presenting the work done   10

313

in a whole-school project on trees. It was filmed over the last two days of the spring term, drawing together materials created over that term.

The project covered a wide range of English and maths attainment targets, and the video covered those areas that were chosen by the pupils for inclusion. The programme was made by a group of children aged between 5 and 11 with a wide range and depth of experience in making programmes of this type. These areas included:
- The parts of a tree;
- The tree as a habitat;
- Statistics concerning trees;
- Photosynthesis and the significance of green plants in the food chain.

Given that extensive use of a wide variety of IT applications was used to create databases, produce computer graphics, word process documents, and develop video use, most of the Science Attainment Target concerned with Information Technology was covered in depth.

The Stages of Development

It was clear from the project that the children were interested in and concerned about trees. There was the opportunity to care for trees in a practical sense through management of our own school conservation area, but the *issue* seemed worthy of wider expression.

It was decided in discussion that this was a good subject for a video to present before the wider audience of parents and friends, and as an appropriate entry to the Co-operative Retail Society's sponsored 'Young People's Film and Video Festival'.

A format for the programme was discussed, and we looked in detail at a programme in which some of the pupils had been involved. This was from a series called *Animal Album* which was produced by the BBC, and a session had been recorded at school the previous summer. As well as looking at a programme from the series that was actually broadcast and recorded off air, we were also able to look at a video record I had made and edited of the experience which gave a flavour of the process of recording. It also offered an opportunity to identify the various tasks of the camera and sound operators, and so on. The programme was of the magazine type, and used a variety of approaches to look at a different animal each week. The style of programme was snappy and contained factual information with jokes, stories and a cartoon character.

At this stage the audience was targeted (we were making a children's TV-type programme), the general 'ingredients' were identified, and the overall message was understood (trees are important to all of us). The process of choosing material was under way. We had observed that one aspect of the magazine programme which was helpful was that separate items could be linked by a simple image with a 'jingle', thus enabling the items to be prepared independently.

The titles were tackled by one group who naturally wanted to emulate the cartoon character they had seen on *Animal Album*. This was somewhat beyond our budget, so we had to settle for a glove puppet to introduce the video. This puppet doubled as an MGM Lion substitute, and there was a sad story behind this. The original contender for this part in a previous production was to have been the school guinea pig, but clearly the stress of impending stardom was too great and he passed away before filming could commence! Maybe that at least saved us from upsetting the animal rights movement.

The creation of the title apparatus represented a design project for which ideas were first sketched out and then put into practice: the final design needed testing and, with minor modifications, proved satisfactory. The actual titles and a test card were produced using a computer design package (AMX Superart), and the titles were made to scroll sideways by a sliding arrangement. The result was more representative of early cinema than of modern technology; it demanded greater involvement than using a character generator or other gadget, however, and Simon, who was largely responsible for this section, clearly gained a great deal of satisfaction.

The story element used in the programme was one of a set of stories produced in class and word processed on the computer. The class's experiences in the past had shown them the importance of reading to camera and maintaining eye contact. Therefore the jumbo-print text was mounted around the camera lens and referred to as necessary while reading to camera. The desired result took several attempts to achieve, but I was pleased by the patience and determination they all showed to get things right. The way in which Louise imitated the Queen's voice in the story made her performance particularly memorable.

Planning of the programme was done on a committee basis, with meetings being held and ideas recorded. On previous occasions we had invited guest 'consultants' to these meetings to offer their experience, and these had varied from TV education officers to community arts workers. Ideas for the programme were 'brainstormed' on to large planning sheets, and these emerged steadily as an overall production plan for the elements of the video.

The actual production of the programme was very straightforward. Sections were filmed separately and only put together at the editing stage. A fresh tape was used for each section, though it may have ended up with two or three consecutive takes on each one. The use of separate tapes is very valuable as it reduces the risk of recording over valuable material. It does, however, necessitate careful labelling and tape management. It is worth camera blacking (recording a section of tape with the lens cap on the camera) the first minute or two or each tape and commencing recording proper towards the end of this section.

Scripting was not a problem, as the programme was made by selecting material that had, for the most part, already been produced, and this was selected through editorial discussions. The material was displayed, examined, and selected, and then fitted into the overall planning sheets mentioned earlier. Some of the scripting was prepared in detail and rehearsed, whereas some was made up after discussing the scene. Sequences were often shot and then critically examined and modified in a subsequent take.

Editing was carried out with two mains machines and a sound mixer – no electronic 'trickery' was used and, to adapt a phrase, 'what they saw was what they got'. The children did not see an unrecognisably modified

315

version of what they had done, and so felt real ownership of the finished product. This part of the process might be the most daunting to a newcomer to video work, but help is often at hand through staff development centres or colleges. With a little guidance and a lot of patience, however, it is perfectly possible to tackle this yourself, though only very keen primary children are likely, in my experience, to maintain interest.

Developing skills in editing and practice in this area may, however, be approached in a number of less demanding ways over a period of time, and could include:

- working with individual photographs, cropping them to change their impact, selecting photos to suit your message, etc.;
- working with sequences of photos or slides to make tape-slide sequences or photo-stories; this involves making choices and offers opportunities to create an almost infinite number of sequences of (say) five slides from a set of twenty, a truly flexible resource;
- working on editing from short sequences of video; for example, a short piece of footage in the playground could result in a number of edited sequences showing how 'boring', 'frightening', or 'exciting' playtime is to different individuals. The same sequences could have over-dubbed commentaries or music to enhance the desired effect.

These are a few of the ways in which the editing process can be examined by the whole class, whereas only the most serious 'enthusiasts' may have the patience to be truly involved in editing a major production. You will undoubtedly learn as much as the pupils from these experiences.

Sound is obviously very important, and part of the review of each section of tape needs to consider this before you dismantle the 'set' or move elsewhere. You can, of course, add sound later, but it is worth getting spoken passages right the first time. I have found that using an inexpensive tie-clip mike is invaluable in noisy outdoor (or indoor) settings.

Lighting has always been approached in the simplest way possible, using desk lights or whatever comes to hand. The children learnt from observation of a BBC film crew the importance they attach to lighting, and they quickly saw how to use a reflective surface to direct light so as to fill in shadows, a technique of special value outdoors.

Most of the techniques and approaches we have used at school have been developed steadily over a period, guided by experience and experiment rather than any training in the field. I have been interested in still and cine photography for many years, and no doubt this was of value. The real motivation, however, was the capacity to carry immediate results from video, results that allow instant feedback and development. Many complete programmes have been made entirely within an afternoon and, while the results may have been basic, they have given satisfaction and stimulated development. These short programmes have varied from creating a news studio in the classroom, to recording a news programme, to recording impressions of the 'nature area' in spring.

Tree Trivia was a section on 'amazing facts' about trees, and the presentation was supported by suitable props such as a mortar board and gown, as well as graphs produced as visual aids. The whole process of seeing themselves on screen does an enormous amount for the children's self-awareness and, ultimately, self-confidence.

Tree Ticklers was a section where the infants were seated around a desk 29 telling jokes to each other about trees while doing their project work. Good jokes about trees proved rather elusive, but the children enjoyed this part very much.

All in all, the last two days of term, when school became a 'television 30 studio', created an enjoyable atmosphere which affected everyone with a sense of purpose at a time when it is often difficult to achieve anything worthwhile! The stories, graphs, art work, and other achievements were brought together for a real purpose in a presentation capable of being shown to a wider audience, an audience that subsequently included viewers at the National Film Theatre when it was chosen for screening at the Festival.

The video also received an award from the Biochemical Society of Great 31 Britain for the scientific content of the project. The financial awards received have been invested in further materials and equipment, while local sponsorship enabled a group of pupils to travel to London to attend the Festival.

Conclusion
I feel that the programme that was produced was an important and worth- 32 while element of the whole project for the following reasons:

- The children's work in this or any other project is presented in a way that gives it value and boosts their self-esteem and self-confidence. It is just another approach to exhibiting their work.
- Any production of this type requires and develops co-operative work, patience, and constructive criticism to achieve a worthwhile result.
- Over a period of time the children's perception of the way TV broadcasts are produced and what they represent has developed steadily to the point where they are much more critical of the schools broadcasts that we use and discuss. I also hope that if the opportunity arises for them to visit a TV studio, they would soon be able to relate the processes they see to the experiences they have had in school.
- Editorial decisions demand attaching importance to different aspects of an issue, and in this context the production of a programme of this type is a useful means of *evaluating* what attitudes the pupils have developed.
- Asking pupils to articulate their views is a vital step to their own understanding of issues and of their position, and giving them the means to communicate those views is a liberating process which will hopefully empower them to influence others.

Clash of the Titans:
Myth and Legend in Year Seven

Jude Brigley

Context

St Ilan is a mixed-sex comprehensive school of five-form entry, and is predominantly a working-class school. The first three years are housed in a pleasant but overcrowded building overlooking Caerphilly Castle, but the upper school site was recently burnt down and the pupils are now housed in an older building and terrapins. There is only one television and videocassette recorder in the lower school; these have to be booked in advance, and you can make yourself quite unpopular if you consistently book them on the same day. English classes are taught in mixed-ability groups, but as there is only one designated English room travelling between classrooms can bring its pressures.

In planning courses for the new intake to secondary school (year 7, 11 and 12-year-olds), my department chose to take the theme of myths and legends. Meetings with our primary schools had shown us how often the typical texts we had taught in the past, especially those by Roald Dahl, had already been covered. 'Myths and legends' offered us the opportunity to deal with imaginative literature and work which could open up opportunities for 'knowledge and language' – an area of the National Curriculum which many teachers were worried about. From the beginning we were eager to incorporate media approaches to literature as outlined in the appendix to the Cox Report, such as front-page stories, interviews, radio phone-ins, and the like, but although we believe that to do such exercises properly students must understand the media products as well as the work of fiction, we were not happy about media content in the unit. Another local concern for us is the Welsh element, and one of the reasons for taking up the theme was to include Welsh myths and legends and to follow up this work with the study of either the book or screen version of *The Snow Spider*.

Unfortunately, through an administrative error, I was not timetabled to teach the new intake, and it had been intended that I would team-teach with another teacher a unit of work based on *Clash of the Titans* in order to put a film at the centre of a unit of learning. This meant that classes all started off on a book-based approach to the course when ideally there should have been a choice of book or film. Eventually, through tortuous rearranging, I was able to work with a class but they had already started working on Greek mythology. This meant that they had a good knowledge not only of Greek gods and stories but also some approaches I might have taken to studying the film – constructing a board-game, for example, had been done and would have been repetitive in a new context.

Teaching Schedule

A few of the pupils had seen *Clash of the Titans* before but I do not think   4
this spoilt the unit of work at all; later storyboards proved how dimly they remembered it, and the class was enthusiastic at the prospect of studying a film. There are problems, of course, in that, although watching films at school is not a new experience for these children, they carry with them the expectation of past viewing: films were shown at the end of term at primary school as a special treat. The stop/start nature of the viewing did not seem to irritate them unduly, not any more than stopping for questions while reading a book, anyway.

I started with showing the class the titles, because they provide an easy   5
way of getting children to think about audience expectation: how we are lulled into expecting certain events and moods through the use of music and title images. Later in their school career, previews of film can be used for the same purpose, but here, the children take their first steps towards understanding genre construction and simple film language. As the class becomes more adept at reading these signposts, later films could have the soundtrack turned down so the class could guess the sort of music that would fit the images.

I showed the class the opening of the film up to Perseus' arrival at the   6
amphitheatre. Then I held a class discussion in which I questioned them to test their understanding of the film and to see how much they could connect with the stories, as well as encouraging them to examine film language. It was interesting to notice how intently the children watched the first part of the film, and questioning proved how much of it they had understood at a narrative level. Some teachers feel inhibited about the types of questions they ask children about film, and my solution is to try to divide my questions into the following four categories.

What is this I see before me?
Observation-type questions about what they can see and why. These help   7
to develop a sense of film language and montage, and assist the development of skills for reading film in semiological terms.

Anticipation and backtracking
What will happen next? Why? How will it end? Such questions help to   8
develop a sense of a film's structure and shape, and help to involve the audience in what is happening. A sense of narrative and what might follow logically in terms of cause and effect can be explored in this way.

Empathy and other imaginative links
By asking how pupils feel about characters and asking them to compare   9
their own responses to events on screen, we are helping pupils to develop imaginative sympathy. We can move from this to helping pupils explore that involvement and how it is built up by camera angles, music, and so on.

What is it worth?

How is it told? Does it work this way? Are there ways in which it could be improved? Is the story being told well? Eventually pupils can explore their own preferences and give reasons for their opinions.

The initial class discussion on the gods, their clothing, and setting involved all of these types of questions, and the class were eager to point out the details of observation ('white clothes and pillars', 'Zeus looks old and wise') and to anticipate ('Thetis wants revenge, she's angry about her son'). The poems, from the point of view of Thetis, concentrated on either her thoughts or the quality of her anger. This exploration through poetry helped the children empathise with the character and explore the feeling:

> My only son was changed into a monster.
> I hate Perseus so much I will put him
> In a sandwich and crush him.

The discussions on how Zeus could help his son were lively and sometimes argumentative. When it came to the drawing of the storyboard only a few children tried to rely on memory, and that did not always serve them well. One boy who drew the owl found in a tree remembered an object which Perseus was, in fact, given later in the film. Emma's storyboard was typical of the ideas the children came up with. She gave Perseus a sword and a shield which she shaped as a heart to suggest it was a gift of love. The cordial of death was an imaginative stroke, as was the horn of honesty with which Perseus could summon help from the animals. She had also given some thought to the names, which suggested that she had taken on the idioms of mythology, and to her settings – by depicting a tree-stump, for example, she showed an understanding of the genre and of the fact that events often take place out of doors.

Some children found it hard to apply their ideas to the world of the film and had difficulty in thinking themselves into the character, suggesting such things as 'flying trainers' found in a bedroom or 'flying wellies' found in a cupboard. Some children had a colourful sense of setting, as a sketch for a building demonstrated.

There were different responses when the children saw the film's version of the gifts from Zeus. There was an argument between those who were delighted by the sword, shield, and helmet which made Perseus invisible, and those who were disappointed that their own ideas were not included. These activities encouraged anticipation of the story and encouraged thoughts about how events could be appropriately related in a film. Eventually, in watching the film version the class were able to compare results and think about whether the film satisfied their imagination.

Clash of the Titans has been criticised for being episodic in structure, but that is what makes it ideal for this teaching purpose. It can be broken up into its main stories, and its structure can soon be assessed by pupils as being 'And then . . .' The first episode covers the early life of Perseus, which was dealt with in the first series of lessons. The next section of the story revolves around the curse on the princess and the solving of the riddle. This was the next section which the class were asked to look at, and the viewing was only interrupted for a brief time for them to write or draw their views of Calibos' changed appearance. This could be done by introducing the idea of comparison, such as, 'He walks like . . .' or 'His eyes are . . .' Such structures enable children to collect their thoughts. After each section viewed, the children were asked about narrative film language and were quite able to describe what was frightening about the cave: 'wild looking men', 'mist and dark', 'Calibos' voice', and so on.

They really enjoyed the riddle which Perseus answered, and were asked   16
to try some on each other. This would have worked much better if I had asked them to choose an object from the film or if I had chosen objects and written them on pieces of paper. They took a long time to choose and then often chose modern objects, whereas more careful thought could have kept us in the world of film. Thus, near 5 November (Guy Fawkes night) we got:

Pretty in the dark,
They only come out once a year
In different colours and shapes.

Or ingeniously this description of a fork:

It has got one leg,
But it has many arms.
Each arm has a point.
Sometimes found in the garden.
Sometimes found near food.

The children had fun guessing these, and it made them more aware of using language without this being obvious. Although I emphasised the media education content and outcomes of this module, it is important to stress that from the basis of the film many English attainment targets could be covered. There were many opportunities for speaking and listening, for writing and, of course, in the reading of film.

The discussion of special effects was introduced by the children. They   17
were horrified (but interested) when the head of Thetis spoke, and I asked them to discuss how they thought the figures in the film moved and operated. Some children thought they were animated electronically from within, and were rather surprised to hear of the small size of many of the figures. I introduced them to some facts about Ray Harryhausen (the world-famous designer of movie monsters), and after my explanation I asked them to draw a rough outline of how some effects were achieved. This offered an opportunity to encourage children to think about how films are made and to explore the role of a key film worker.

The Medusa sequence is one of the most exciting in the film, and the   18
class were able to put together a good list of things which made it frightening: 'the noise of the Medusa's movements', 'the lighting', 'the dead bodies'. The pupils became more aware of camera operations through

321

describing the approach of Medusa while Perseus had his back against the wall. The end of this sequence, where Perseus holds up the head of the Medusa, seemed an appropriate place to break off, although at the next session it would be a pity to lose the dissolve into the bagged head. I felt satisfied that the class had really understood the film language and how it worked in this instance.

Dividing the class into their groups, I gave them scissors, photograph, glue, and paper, and asked them to make their own picture, an activity which was taken up enthusiastically. This was purely process work designed to make children aware of the way photographs can be manipulated. I introduced it here because of our many discussions about special effects and the illusions created by manipulation. The oral work which came out of this was of a high standard, and the class were deeply involved in the task. Some pupils spontaneously added drawing, and there were different approaches as some thought of the picture as a map and others as a montage. The groups were asked to title their pictures and they chose titles like 'The famous statue by the castle', 'The Village', and 'Over the dark tunnel'. I have in the past used such pictures for writing, but that was not my purpose here.

At this stage I would have liked to have taken Polaroid pictures to create illusions with models, but it was near the end of term and the model had to be finished. Another time, this would be a logical extension of the work undertaken so as to give the class a chance to make their own special effects and see how the camera can provide illusions.

The last section of the film was enjoyed by the class without interruption. By now they understood, to a certain extent, how the illusions were created, but it did not spoil their enjoyment – as John Fowles said:

> I have disgracefully broken the illusion? No. My characters still exist, and in a reality no less, or no more, real than the one I have just broken. [John Fowles, writing about his novel *The French Lieutenant's Woman*]

Hopefully, by the end, the pupils were used to the questions and proved themselves to be close observers of film. Because of the interruptions of Christmas festivities, the class did not get the opportunity to write their responses, which would have helped them to draw their opinions together. Orally most of them named the key scenes of the riddle, and the Medusa and the other Gorgons, as their favourites, so I do not think the detailed treatment spoilt the film for them. The end of the film, with its eponymous legend-like conclusion of pointing to the stars, is typical of many myths and brought the 'And then . . .' structure to a conclusion. Children could be asked to write their own stories or poems accounting for buildings, stones, and the like.

We have long worked with literature-based teaching in the lower school, basing our language work on the text being studied. In the upper school we have often used a film text, such as *Mam* (Red Flannel), *Rebecca* (Hitchcock), or *The Emerald Forest* (Boorman), as the basis for language work as well as a text in its own right. This was the first time we had used a film text in the lower school as the basis of work, and we are encouraged enough to work to develop this approach even further.

Many English attainment targets were either covered or contributed to through this work but many strands from media education are also here. Thus, media categories were touched on through work on genre, media technology through special effects, media language through *mise-en-scène* and music, and media audiences through examining the titles. We feel the work on film was successful and we look forward to developing it further.

23

Comics and Magazines

Julian Sefton-Green

Northumberland Park Community School is an inner-city comprehensive situated in Tottenham, north-east London. It draws from almost exclusively working-class communities, some of which are the most socially and economically deprived in the country. The school's population comes from a range of ethnic minorities, and over twenty-five home languages are spoken. Many classes have pupils who are recent arrivals in the UK and have little English. The school is committed to mixed-ability teaching, and the class who followed this particular course of study in fact had two children who have statements of special need. The range and scope of need in the school is very large indeed, and while it may be typical of any large inner-city comprehensive, it poses considerable challenges to the classroom teacher.

This unit of work took place in year 8 (13-year-olds) English lessons; in fact, I used it to begin the year's work. This is relevant as the class's first year at Northumberland Park was fraught with difficulties and the class had very low expectations of English as a subject. In that sense the group work aspect of the project and its cultural frame of reference were deliberate attempts on my part to enthuse the class and demonstrate both the pleasures and purposes of English, and the pedagogic advantages that media work can often provide. Despite the class's large ability range the diverse nature of this kind of work stretched most children, and the inclusion of oral work, design, and art skills had the effect of bonding the various experiences and enthusiasms the children brought to the class. Because of the collaborative ethos this kind of work establishes, it also enhances the students' mutual respect for the different tasks and skills brought to the class. I would not wish to over-romanticise the situation, but media work can often have a positive and empowering effect where traditional subject-based work devalues the individual student at this level.

National Curriculum

The unit itself was a draft version of the second part of the BFI's *Media in English* publication. The teaching pack aims to meet the full range of National Curriculum requirements through media units of work at Key Stage 3. This particular unit aims to explore both the formal aspects of comics and magazines (layout conventions, styles, front covers, etc.) and the social uses of these media products. There is a special inflection for this topic of study within English. The students at Northumberland Park come to school with traditional utilitarian expectations about English; reading books is not a common pastime (even less so, as one might expect, among boys), and broadening the scope of critical and cultural inquiry was definitely one of my long-term aims. This remained a mixture of silent and spoken values. By including student pleasures as topics of study, or seriously discussing the iconography of wrestlers on the front cover of *WWF* (journal of the World Wrestling Federation) or the sexual explicitness in agony column correspondence, an implicit valuing of student culture takes place. This became explicit when analysing the school's readership habits through consideration of the combined purchasing power of over a thousand students, discussion about appropriate reading material for different age groups, or comparison of the cost of stocking the school library (or even, particularly significant at the moment, the comparative cost of class readers).

In terms of the reading profile components, this project requires students 4 to reflect upon the kinds of skills that are involved in any type of reading. Reading itself involves decoding in the larger sense of the word rather than just speaking and repeating words out loud to a teacher. In the work my class covered, therefore, they were 'reading' all the sorts of visual and graphic codes and conventions that you find in magazines. Within the writing profile component the activity involves a variety of writing for different audiences using different repertoires. This can range from something not particularly demanding, such as creating puzzles appropriate for particular audiences, to parodying the problem page style of the gossip or fashion kinds of writing (or, indeed, all the different kinds of styles that you find in a magazine), as well as typical English assignment-style stories. Within the speaking and listening component there are an enormous number of oral activities. There are whole-group class discussions, as well as individual situations were students have to negotiate, for example, and editorial decisions about what choices to make. There are also a variety of problem-solving tasks, such as setting out a survey or doing a photo-story where the students have to work by themselves or with small groups and come up with products.

Within the terms of the knowledge about language section of the National 5 Curriculum I think the activity encourages students to reflect upon their reading experiences of studying comics and magazines, and this relates to a sociology of reading. By looking at who reads what magazines, when, where and how they borrow magazines, what they and their friends read, they ask broader sets of questions than the interpretive. This type of approach gets the students to think about reading in a larger sense, and therefore perhaps gives them access to reading and notions of literacy in general rather than a specific kind of reading where students only learn about words on the page.

The activity also draws on the multicultural and multilingual strengths 6 that you will find in a school like Northumberland Park, and that you will find in many communities. When students are asked to consider themselves as an audience, and to consider producing media artefacts for their particular kind of audience, it is very likely that their awareness of the kinds of strengths that are often devalued by the wider culture will be raised, thereby foregrounding their strengths.

Media Education

Because comics and magazines are self-evidently composed of many different elements it made the task of formal analysis that much easier. We ended up with a sizeable collection of comics and magazines to use, and again the evident similarities and differences, use of colour, advertisements, layout, lettering, and so on made the process of textual analysis that much easier. Comparison and contrast are obviously the conceptual building blocks in any analytical activity, and having such contrasts to hand made any textual study very approachable. This was a marked difference to their work in English and, although I am not making any great claims here, doing this work when we did, and in the way we did, helped with other close textual study throughout the rest of the year.

Using the class as a sample group and getting them to reflect upon themselves as serious actors in the chain of production, distribution, and circulation is also an important way of enabling students to conceptualise the idea of audience, and because we are dealing with products that were meaningful to the class it gave them a sense of proportion regarding their power. As we developed our own magazine they began to place their own taste within larger patterns of consumption. The work also raised the issue of gender in a useful and explicit fashion. Because tastes and patterns of consumption are so gendered the differences (and similarities, such as agony uncles) are going to be factors in any discussion of the issues. After going through the stage of finding boys terribly immature, gender became more a matter of disinterested concern, and this was one of the rare occasions where gender could appear as an issue of socialisation rather than one of competition. It also turns sexual difference into gender difference, as girls who like football are equally as valid as boys who are interested in hair products.

Discussing audiences is particularly useful for focusing group work and negotiation skills, normally activities which teachers find difficult to manage, and students quite clearly enjoyed working on their cultural experiences and having their values and their pleasures taken seriously. Those were some of the aims that I hoped to achieve with that class, so I felt quite satisfied. I think the students felt ambiguous about the quality of the final product, as I did, but that was also good because you get to the stage where you and they realise through experience and experimentation what they want to do next time. If they get to the stage where they can see what is good and what is bad, what went wrong, and how to improve it, then that is the best outcome of all because that is exactly what much practical and experimental work is centrally about.

I should want to take the process further as they go up the school, by beginning to systematise the kinds of knowledge that I have talked about, the forms of conventions, the representation, the audience and institution, and to compare it more with an actual media product. The obvious natural development is to examine areas of publishing, and the whole relationship between students' reading and book production (agencies).

Managing Practical Work

To sum up managing practical work, you have a whole-class brief to begin   11
with, and you have individual briefs; students will be attempting different
roles and will get a variety of jobs. There will be tight constraints, but
there will be room for negotiation within that, a sense of constraint that I
obviously want to be able to negotiate. Tension between negotiation and
constraint is where the success of practical work lies. One of the problems
of practical work is that students have had little consistent experience of
it, and we are therefore somewhat in the dark about what we should expect
7-year-olds, 14-year-olds, and 16-year-olds to do. It is often the luck of the
draw whether or not a teacher is prepared to venture out and undertake
some practical work.

I have some sense of what I want students to work towards because of   12
teaching GCSE Media Studies. It is always important that the quality of
what the students do is clearly at the top of their skill range and, although
it is difficult to generalise about success, every teacher knows what their
class is capable of and whether they achieve it. I felt happy that this group
were pushing themselves and working together to do this kind of work and
that what emerged was a fair representation of the groups' skills.

'What Does it Mean?'

Deconstructing a Continuity Sequence with 9G

David Sudbery

It is 5.59 p.m. any weekday. Good neighbours have once again become [1] good friends, and the 'Grundy Television' logo is superimposed for a second over Ramsay Street. Almost before it has faded a new piece of music has started, pulsing, twisting, slightly mesmeric, and a series of exotic images appears. A window opens and some yellow and blue balls appear. Are those land masses painted on them, like miniature globes, or are they boules, you wonder, as they land now on rippling sand? The images are intercut almost too rapidly to answer these or other questions; now there is a sun-bather with a map of Africa cut away in her swimsuit revealing a bronze torso, before that image is in turn obscured by swirling blue and yellow sunshades; the suggestion is all of sun and sea, the faraway and exotic.

A voice-over, meanwhile, announcing 'Programmes tonight on One', has [2] made clear the purpose of this piece. For a second the bright, swirling images continue: an exotically sculpted punk coiffure, a bicycle sweeping around an abundant display of fruit on a Mediterranean piazza. The voice-over is plugging the guests on *Wogan*, but it is unclear whether the Robinson Crusoe figure walking on the beach with the frayed sunshade was one of the sequence of images or part of the trailer for 'British Film Classics'. Warren Mitchell makes it easy to identify *In Sickness and In Health*, and the remaining clips are clearly captioned, but the music pulsing gently underneath has kept in our minds the waltzing images of elegant paradises in the sun right up until the final programme summary, behind which all the images are brought together in a dancer's flaring blue skirt printed with the map of the world in yellow.

We have been guided smoothly into the solemn harbinger of the News: [3] the turning world of the BBC logo, where we may or may not connect the continuing rotation, the continental land masses, and the colours with what we have just seen. The sequence has unjarringly achieved the transition from ephemeral soap to the dignity of a world broadcasting institution. It has also, incidentally, set up the new audience, back from work or the kitchen, for an evening's viewing. It is an impressive piece of packaging, doing its job elegantly, hauntingly. A whole family of these continuity sequences appeared in 1990 using a related series of images, movement, and colours, changing according to the season, and they were, according to an artist friend, the most exciting thing on television. They cannot have been cheap to make and, judging by the amount that they were used, the

328

BBC certainly wanted to get its money's-worth. *The Observer* reported that a replacement logo (which it thought at the time might, because of its 'radical format', never be used) cost some £500,000.[1]

Teenagers are impressed by those kinds of production details and like,   4 I think, to be awed by the mention of the big money that is lavished on media productions. There are plenty of programmes of the 'The Making of –' variety, which have a valuable place in educating students in the media processes involved in the products they consume. But apart from those fascinating technical details, I wonder how many students have ever thought about what I suspect to be the real purpose of these spin-offs: the promotion of the product involved?

Similarly with the continuity sequence. How aware are we generally of   5 the way in which media products are promoted? Are teenage consumers of television aware of the ways in which television is packaged to encourage them and others to keep watching? Probably not. Television takes up quite a lot of time in most thirteen-year-olds' lives, but it is there much as water is there in the tap. (Flowing water was, in fact, the dominant image in one of the later examples of this series. Once having thought about the function of these pieces, the yellow and blue shimmering images unmistakably suggested to me the sense of effortless and seamless flow that I imagine programme planners seek to achieve. Why turn off or turn over when there is such an endless stream of goodies on offer?)

This was my starting point for doing some work on television with a   6 group of thirteen-year-olds, trying to get these students to look at why television needs to advertise its products and how it does this. The outcome I was looking for was an awareness of television as an institution, or rather as a series of institutions, all competing to gain a share of a limited market; to show that these institutions are not God-given but are the result of human decisions, and to show the ultimate possibility of the students themselves making these decisions. I wondered if it would be possible to set up a project to give a ninth-year (14-year-olds) mixed-ability class an awareness of some of the institutional practices on which television, probably the dominant cultural form in their lives, depends – and at the same time get them to look very closely at what actually appears on the screen.

This is the kind of work which comes under the heading of 'Institution'   7 in Media Studies GCSE courses and often seems to be the area of the course that provides the most problems in teaching. For the English teachers who set up media studies courses, creating and analysing media products develops comfortably from their own discipline, whereas understanding media institutions involves the disciplines of economics, sociology, even politics. Another problem arises from the difficulty of gaining up-to-date information on such matters as the costs of advertising campaigns, ownership of companies, and the latest viewing figures which this kind of work requires.

I was working with a mixed-ability English group in a large, well-   8 established 11–18 comprehensive. Years 7–9 are fully mixed ability and in January to March of year 9 option choices are made for years 10 and 11. Media studies is included in the technology column, from which the students are required to choose an option, but it is taught by English teachers and the students' main contact with the subject before year 9 will have been in English (and could, depending on the interests and enthusiasm of their teacher, have included keeping a television diary, using video to record a class drama production or news programme, or making newspapers using simple desktop publishing programmes such as Typesetter or Front Page Extra).

Ninth-year English seemed the right place to attempt some serious study of television, quite apart from its use as a taster for the media studies course. The English National Curriculum includes in the programmes of study for reading at this stage the requirement that 'Pupils should be introduced to a range of media texts and should be encouraged to consider their purpose, effect, and intended audience.'[2] With a mixed-ability group of this age it would not be possible, I thought, to get involved in abstruse theoretical issues: a creative approach which offered the opportunity for some detailed observation of what is actually seen and heard on television programmes seemed preferable. It would also have to avoid being judgemental: as soon as I mentioned 'television' to the class I could sense a feeling that their own lifestyles were about to be attacked.

The simplest way to achieve these aims seemed to be to transform the students from consumers into producers. They would set themselves up as new television companies, each seeking a particular, defined audience. They would need to think about what kinds of programmes to show and how they would encourage this target audience to watch. To do this, devices such as the continuity sequence, currently used in television, would need to be observed. This basic framework would give a simple introduction to three of the main concepts used in the media studies course – Genre, Institution, and Audience.

We started with a brief discussion of the present four land-based TV channels: whether there was a difference in what they offered; which channel students preferred (strong loyalties were in evidence here, though fairly equally divided between ITV and BBC 1 – BBC 2 was 'posh', Channel 4 'weird'); how programmes are financed (not much awareness here); and likely future developments. I was quite surprised at the lack of much interest in satellite TV.

Next, some basic work on genre. The word had already come up at the beginning of the year when we were discussing what books the class enjoyed reading. Now, as an exercise in showing what they knew about this concept already, I gave some brief descriptions of the beginnings of imaginary new programmes and asked them to predict what was going to follow ('a brightly lit set with platforms on various levels and flashing lights announcing the name of the programme; a well-known celebrity with a wildly exaggerated smile breezes down the set waving at the cheering and clapping audience'). We soon discovered that we could fit the programmes I had imagined, and most others, into recognisable categories: game shows (in the example given), soaps, news, police series, and so on. We confirmed this by looking at a series of extracts from real programmes, conveniently collected in just the sort of continuity sequence we would be looking at in more detail. These can easily be recorded off-air just before the early evening news on

330

any weekday, or are available on video as part of teaching packs such as *Talking Television*.[3]

We quickly brainstormed on to the blackboard a list of identifiable genres, then the class divided into groups to try to work out what were the characteristics that enabled us to recognise the genres. The way in which most groups coped with this showed that they had already internalised this concept as far as it related to television. The 'News' group, for instance, came up with:

Music: Loud and dramatic, punctual.
Graphics: Neat, simple, eye-catching.
Colour: Not too bright, very formal.
Presenters: Formal dress, speak clearly and accurately.
Studio layout: Simple, up to date, good layout, matching colours.

That was the first part of the project. In the next part I was going to attempt to tackle the issue of Institution. By taking part in a simulation the students could play an active role in promoting their channel, rather than a passive role as viewer, and would have a new perspective for looking at promotional ploys such as the continuity sequence. I hoped that I would be able to introduce concepts such as corporate identity, a controller of programmes, and the linked notions of a target audience and the need for revenue without having to be explicit about them – the students would find out the need for such things as they went along. So, based on their earlier discussions, I now asked the class, again working in friendship groups:

– To create their own television channels, thinking in particular about the kinds of programmes they would transmit, the particular audience they were aiming at, and the logo they would adopt (this gave a concrete focus to the more vague and probably less comprehensible request that I made for them to think about the 'identity' of their channel).
– To think of an idea for one new television programme. The groups were asked to focus on genre, the target audience, some ideas for a title sequence, and a brief synopsis. The aim of this was to link the work we had done on genre with the work on promotion and audience.

Most of the ideas for TV channels were well targeted. 'Teenager TV' was a natural choice; 'Today's National Television' was aimed at an older audience that needed waking up and so became 'TNT – the most explosive channel around'. A lot of discussion about stereotyping and the way in which old people perceived themselves was needed to relaunch 'Granny TV' as 'Sunshine Live', although the logo for this station has remained a humanoid television with a walking stick!

The programme ideas that emerged could be taken either to show how thoroughly the class had studied and learned the conventions of television shows or as a comment upon the sameness of most mainstream British television! Game shows predominated; shows like 'Scrabble' or 'Roulette Winner' were versions of board games while 'Comedy Catchphrase' updated a current hit. Attempts at originality came in the search for a glitzy visual presentation, such as TVE Roulette Winner's 'very own quiz show host Guy Smiley' jumping through the show's logo at the beginning of the show.

There was a likely looking soap called 'Friends' – 'about a group of teenagers living in Colorado in the USA. They have fun, tears and, most of all, trouble'. The synopsis was illustrated with photographs cut from teenage magazines to accompany thumbnail sketches of the all-white, clean-cut, and good-looking cast. All very convincing, and worth a lot more classroom time to examine the representations which are offered in the series which it seems so accurately to reflect. How 'real' is the real world of a soap like *Neighbours*? What 'rules' does it suggest about how to get on? Where are the people who follow, or find themselves judged by different rules – the unemployed, the homeless, the trade unionist? Does it suggest a link between happiness on the one hand, good looks, white skin, and an entrepreneurial outlook on the other? The way to explore this creatively might have been to get the group to dream up an 'anti-*Neighbours*', but time was short (because of timetabling difficulties I was already teaching the class for only two of their three weekly English periods) and I had begun to sense that I might be trying to pack too much into the project! At least I knew that the class would have done some work on stereotyping in their previous year's humanities course. **17**

The idea for this project had grown out of the BBC 1 continuity sequence, and watching it closely at this point gave a focus to the whole project by drawing the various strands together and giving a model to the students for their own work. This was most relevant, because the next task that I was going to give the class was: **18**

– To plan an evening's viewing on their channel, using the programme they devised themselves as a centrepiece.

As the BBC 1 schedule they had studied had been a summer evening's they were to plan theirs for an autumn or Christmas evening. Again, this was aimed to get the class to think about the relationship between individual programmes, the very heavy publicity which some received, and the need to attract an audience. The seasonal element would ask them to concentrate on the visual imagery of the trailer. In the one we were studying I was hoping that they would pick up the yellow and blue and the associations made with sun, sand, and the exotic possibilities of travel – the evening's television viewing, perhaps, was being offered as the equivalent of everyone's dream holiday – and all linked to the BBC's chosen identity through the map/globe motif. What would they see as the equivalent perfect autumn or Christmas series of images? And how could this tie in with the identifying logo of their channel? As a final activity, therefore, students were asked:

– To plan and storyboard their own continuity sequence for this evening's viewing. This would be their chance to demonstrate in a practical way some of the ideas that I had intended to introduce, and in a medium more appropriate than a test, which presupposes a right answer, or an analytical essay, which is a difficult enough genre in its own right!

Watching the continuity sequence was an enormously useful exercise in itself. Textual response and analysis is at the heart of literary and media studies, and it seemed important in a project on television just to observe closely what was there on the screen. Thus, a concentrated series of images in a one-minute discrete sequence was ideal. Because it was short we were able to look at it several times, and in several different ways. The 'Pause' and 'Rewind' buttons were well used and we were glad that we had a video with a good freeze-frame.

At first we just observed. It was important before we tackled the question 19 of connotation – the meanings and associations that the sequence had for each individual – that we established the denotation, exactly what images and sounds were there. This was not as straightforward as it might seem. When I asked the question, 'Can you tell me something that you saw or heard on the programme?' the first answer that I received was 'Comedy'. When I pressed the girl who had answered to tell me exactly what she had seen she replied with something that did not actually appear, 'People laughing.' The second answer, from a boy, was no more accurate: 'On *Panorama* you can tell that it's all political because it's — serious music.' These exchanges make clear how denotation and connotation can become confused and how useful it can be just to sharpen the process of observation. As the same question was repeated the process of description became more accurate. With further discussion and another look at the video a girl called Hannah was able to answer: 'Well, you saw these shutters suddenly open up and then you could see the wall. There was . . . a map on the wall and the balls shot out the window and hit the sand.'

Using the pause button we found ourselves looking at those images in 20 closer and closer detail. Where previously they thought there was nothing, literally a space between programmes, students were now seeing more and more. Now we saw shutters opening in a sunbaked 'crumbling plaster' wall, a 'flask like one used for carrying water in the desert', a curtain billowing out, a lizard (a chameleon, one student claimed knowledgeably) scuttling across; and on looking still closer, a map (of Europe, we decided) discernibly shaped in the roughest wall. All this in the first second of the film. The more we looked at the sequence the more we discovered these maps: Australia sculpted in the punk's scalp, Africa in human flesh through the swimming costume, and again writ large in the fruit on the stall. Yes, the boules *were* painted like miniature globes of the world, and there was the whole world outspread on the skirt. The impetus was simply the process of discovery, of looking at the unexpected.

After a little while, concentrating on just the soundtrack, by getting the 21 class to close their eyes, I was able to elicit a detailed account of the various strands of music, actors' voices, audience laughter, and the varying amount and tone of voice in the voice-over accompanying different programmes;[4] one boy, Sean, was able to give an impressively accurate account of how the quite complicated music script interacted with the programme excerpts.

I asked questions just to help them make clear to themselves what they 22 had observed. As we continued, however, more and more questions arose and these involved making connections in the patterns of imagery and the associations made: 'What colours were used most? Did you see any other maps, or other things turning around? Where else on BBC can you see maps going around?' This close observation followed by questioning was the beginning of a process of critical analysis.

The questions that had finally been prompted were questions about the institution that produced the sequence and how that institution promoted itself. Behind it all was the turning blue and yellow globe of the BBC logo (now finally replaced). I had intended just to establish what was in the film, the denotation, in this lesson. But we did make the connection, and next time I do something like this I would follow it up more explicitly. There are quite complex connections to be made and it might be best to do it while all the images are fresh in the students' minds.

As it was, I did not pursue the whole-class discussion in the next session, but let the students work out in their smaller groups what 'meanings' they saw in the sequence and then feed these ideas into their work on their own sequences. I did not push the analytical work too hard, for the reasons I have already mentioned: I had told them that watching the sequence was just to give them ideas for their own pieces. But again, I think in retrospect that I might have been underestimating them, and next time I would help them to formulate their ideas more clearly. What they should have been doing, I thought later, was keeping a record of all their ideas as they went along so that when they had finished their storyboards they could write a log explaining what decisions they had made and why. These production logs are standard practice in media classes and we are finding them increasingly valuable in English. Time is particularly short in the ninth year and I suppose I was worried about spending too much time on one project, particularly if, without this log, it did not involve much written work.

Nevertheless, there was sufficient evidence of students' involvement in the project, and when they came to write their self-assessments for their English reports several months later many of them singled out their work on 'making our own TV channel' as the part of the course from which they had gained most. For my part I had come to think that, given the limitations of time, perhaps the most important part of the process was the watching and analysing of television material that students might not normally notice. I think that next time I would devote more time to that and have confidence that they would develop the ability to discuss its 'meaning'.

The very process of watching, rewatching, and pausing had necessarily made the class aware of the process of construction. Using a camcorder at home or school can make it seem simple to produce results which seem like the real thing. Students' comments afterwards made it very clear that looking at this piece had made them much more aware of the craft involved in making it.

But what they were really involved in was a process of deconstruction. They were being asked to examine exactly what was in this quite complex piece of film, how it had been put together and for what reasons. In doing this they were starting to deal with such matters as use of imagery, colour, and mood; observing, interpreting, and giving themselves a framework to think about what they saw; and finally to be able to ask 'What does it mean?' Form 9G would probably have been as surprised to know that they were 'deconstructing a continuity sequence' as they would have been to know that they spent forty-five minutes very attentively examining one minute of film.

Notes

1. *The Observer*, 28 October 1990.
2. *English in the National Curriculum*, London, HMSO, March 1990. Programmes of Study for Key Stage 3 and 4, p. 32.
3. *Talking Television*, Southampton, TVS Education and West Sussex County Council, 1989.
4. Ideas on how to make students aware of their expectations of announcers' and newsreaders' tone of voice, and how important these are in establishing meaning, can be found in Julian Bowker's teaching pack *What's News?*, Southampton, TVS Education and West Sussex County Council, 1989.

Newspapers in Education:
Three Case Studies

Ben Moore

The Newspapers in Education Scheme is financed by the industry and organised through the Newspaper Society, a national organisation which represents local and regional newspapers in the UK. There is a widespread recognition on behalf of the regional press that with increasing competition from other media they can no longer assume that young people represent a readership in waiting. There is a trend even among the national dailies to address a younger readership (e.g., *The Young Telegraph, The Funday Times*). Local papers attempt in a variety of ways to form closer relationships with schools and colleges: in Newcastle, *The Evening Chronicle and Journal*, part of the Thomson Group, pay part of my salary as an advisory teacher to organise their programme. Central to this work is the belief that to develop a critical understanding of the regional press, schools should be encouraged to produce their own newspapers, and wherever possible I like to encourage schools to circulate these newspapers to the wider community, generally their own catchment areas.

There is some financial support for this as well as resources, in terms of both personnel (myself and/or newspaper staff) and computer hardware for word processing, layout, and design. The project described operated in both primary and secondary schools and, because of its cross-curricular nature, was often undertaken by teachers with little or no experience of media education. Often, in the frenzy of publication deadlines, the opportunity to reflect upon the experience of production seems distant, and there are so many opportunities for learning in such a project that it is difficult to focus on the specifics of media education.

What follows is an account of the project in three schools. These accounts were first written up by the teachers and supplemented by comments made during an interview I conducted with them, in which they were asked a number of questions which specifically focused on what the children learned about newspapers as a mass medium.

Cowgate Primary School – Denise Wann

Cowgate Primary is a small inner-city school of 175 pupils. The community is well established with its own library, shops, and swimming baths. Housing is a mix of council and privately owned, and the area is largely made up of white working-class families. There were 26 children in my own class, and the project lasted a term, occupying about 80 per cent of the whole week. Although it did not start as such, it evolved into a whole-school project.

Origins of the Project

My interest in newspapers as a topic was stimulated by a course at the local teachers' centre where Ben Moore, the co-ordinator of the Newspapers in Education Project, explained the scope and purpose of the scheme. The aims of the project for media education were: to help children develop a critical point of view; to distinguish between fact and opinion; to detect bias; to understand that there are many different types of newspapers which embody a range of choices made for particular reasons; and that writing for a wider readership imposes certain constraints on what can be said and the way it is reported.

One of the strengths of a small primary school is its flexibility. Thus a beneficial interaction between age ranges, especially during whole-school projects, can be more easily achieved. Building on early interviewing experiences within the school, for example, a group of 6- and 7-year-olds extended their range of interviewees from teaching and non-teaching staff to the wider world of local business, with the help of 10- and 11-year-olds.

Within our whole-school project on newspapers the emphasis was on learning, not only *about* newspapers but very much *through* them. With this in mind, early activities with all the children included familiarisation tasks. These ranged from simulating the setting-up of a newsagent's to monitoring a specific feature in a variety of publications (e.g., weather forecasts) to compare style and symbols. This particular activity was developed into the design of more child-friendly symbols by 5- and 6-year-old pupils. Statistics were explored by dissecting a paper and analysing the proportions of text to graphics, and of news to advertisements. An in-depth investigation in the use of time in print was another valuable learning experience. This involved time in its widest, 'seasonal single', dimension, as well as demonstrating the pluralistic use of analogue and digital notation within a single publication. International time differences were also an aspect of this study.

The project involved visits to both local businesses and international companies for news items. This resulted in a group of children forming an enterprising advertising design team, offering a service to help offset our production costs. Other visits included the local newspaper publisher, enabling a group of representatives to report back their findings, both verbally to their peers and as a special feature in their newspaper. The opportunities for learning in all curriculum areas were understandably diverse – even the science of creating inks and paper was not overlooked. For the purposes of this piece I shall focus on one activity in more detail. This activity was initiated early in the project which, although in this case was used with years 5 and 6 pupils (9- to 11-year-olds) is equally valid with most age ranges approaching media education with little prior experience. It started as a whole-class session, and was then developed into group activities which continued over the space of a week or more for some groups. The class was mixed ability, mixed gender, and mixed age range.

337

The Activity

Sufficient copies of one edition of the local daily paper were available. A single headline caption was distributed to groups of 3–4 pupils who were asked to identify between: (*a*) which page it might be from, and (*b*) which news item was depicted: 'Sudden Halt to City Centre Traffic'. After reporting their own ideas to the rest of the class, the children listened to the actual item, read by the teacher. Their interpretations demonstrated well the sensationalism of the caption, and included a meteorite landing and a volcano suddenly erupting. These were far more imaginative than the actual report, which concerned a court case after a city-centre incident involving a man on a roof dropping debris on to the pavement endangering the public. The recognition that this type of sensationalism is designed to sell newspapers, to excite readers into buying the product, was a useful experience.

Development

With their own copy of the news item to refer to (although not all the children were able to tackle this text, so varying degrees of teacher involvement were indicated), the groups then set about transforming their news items into an alternative way of broadcasting the event. Three activities were undertaken which involved transforming the item into:
- (*a*) comic-strip form, complete with speech bubbles;
- (*b*) a continuous roll of pictures round a 'barrel';
- (*c*) dramatic re-enactment involving what happened next and how the event might have affected the family.

Implications for Assessment

Through this particular activity, pupils were collaborating in their interpretations and displaying a range of skills including the following Attainment Targets (ATs):

English: AT1 Level 2: Statement (1) participating as speakers and listeners in a group engaged in a given task. Plus statements 1–5.
AT1 Level 3: Statements 1–4.
AT3 Level 2: Structure sequences of events, real or imagined, coherently in a chronological account.

Maths: Within this activity the children used Shape and Space awareness.
AT8: Measures.
AT9: Application of Shape and Space to practical situations.

The proposed ATs for Media Education were also covered for Media Categories as outlined in *Primary Media Education: A Curriculum Statement*:[1]

> Level 3. Effect a transfer from one medium to another.
> Level 5. Be able to differentiate most forms of media text: e.g., news, news and comment, documentary, dramatic reconstruction. Effect a transfer from one category to another.

Children learned the differences between local and national newspapers and 12
examined the designs of title-pages. They were able to categorise newspaper
content into features, news, and advertisements, and to identify advertising
features. Newspapers past and present were compared. The children
looked at the way stories were reported in newspapers, with all the important points in the first paragraph and each paragraph being just one sentence
long, and compared it with more familiar methods.

The children had to assess the newsworthiness of stories and choose the 13
way in which each story was to be presented. This led to some discussion
of issues of representation and news values, and if there had been more
time and opportunity to share these and make them more explicit, this
would have been valuable. In terms of language work there was opportunity
for summary and redrafting, and a great deal of work was done on
headline-writing.

Unfortunately, there was less time for reflection on the product than we 14
would have liked, as the newspaper was printed and distributed on the
very last day of term. One point that strikes me from this distance (half a
term away) is that advertisements were placed in the paper without much
consultation with the children, and that in some cases they were accorded
greater prominence than perhaps they should have had. This could also
have been discussed with the children. It might have led to some understanding of the importance of advertising in the newspaper industry and led
to some interesting questioning about the nature of newspapers themselves.

Cragside Primary School – Caroline Gray and Kath Milligan

The piece of work described took place with a class of 35 children aged 15
10–11 years. The children, in National Curriculum year 6, are in their final
year of primary education. The school they attend is in a predominately
middle-class, white area of Newcastle-upon-Tyne. The children involved
are generally very able pupils, self-disciplined and very well motivated.

The interest in producing a school newspaper was initiated by a 'News- 16
paper Day' in school supported by the Information Technology (IT)
teacher adviser. We began our project with a brainstorming session to
discover what the children already knew about newspapers. Who produces
them? What do they contain? What production processes are involved?
How is the news gathered? Why do we need newspapers? Next came a
visit from Ben Moore, the Teacher Adviser for Media Education and the
Co-ordinator of the Newspapers in Education Project, sponsored by our
local newspaper. He gave a presentation explaining in more detail the kinds
of choices and decisions which were made in producing a newspaper. The
children visited the Science and Engineering Museum for hands-on experience with early printing presses to see how laborious and slow the process
was when each sheet was printed individually. We then visited our local
newspaper, *The Newcastle Evening Chronicle and Journal*, where we saw
how quickly and efficiently news can be processed using the latest computer
technology.

This in turn resulted in a general study of newspapers with a view to 17
producing a small school newspaper to be distributed to other children in

the school, as well as members of the public in the immediate locality of the school. In tackling the project our aims were:

- to help pupils distinguish between fact, opinion, and interpretation;
- to provide opportunities for speaking and listening and working in groups;
- to encourage collaborative writing, especially redrafting and editing;
- to develop a sense of audience and purpose for writing;
- to understand the difference between the 'popular' and 'quality' press;
- to discover how to make paper.

The children looked at news stories in pairs. How did the reporters write up their stories, and what questions did they need to ask? Children in pairs acted in role-play as reporters and eyewitnesses. They had to ask relevant questions, take notes, and write a report for the newspaper on the computer using Folio, a simple word processing package. The children also designed fonts for our newspaper. The visit to the newspaper left a number of questions unanswered, so we asked if a reporter might come to visit the school. We were lucky enough to receive a visit from the deputy editor, who found himself closely questioned on such matters as why there was no children's page in the local paper.

It was felt that it would be necessary to have a working knowledge, and a greater understanding, of a range of newspapers before embarking on our own newspaper. The following information was then entered on the computer about these papers: cost; page size; whether the newspaper used colour; number of photographs per page; number of columns per page (text); print size; popularity; number of advertisements per page; number of pages; and whether the newspaper was issued daily, in the morning, or in the evening.

Once the data was entered on disc and stored, the children could request the newspaper to be sorted according to a selected category. Alternatively, it enabled the children to ask the computer to sort newspapers according to two or more categories, such as those tabloid newspapers which contained more than 30 pages and cost less than 30p. This information could be printed and circulated to other class members. A further alternative was for the children to request sight of the information as a Venn diagram, displayed on the VDU or printed as a block graph or pie chart. It is clear from a brief glimpse of the investigation described that a data-base program, such as Our Facts, provides future opportunities for the collaboration and categorisation of a wide variety of data.

In pairs again, the children set about producing a children's page for our own paper *The Cragside Chronicle*. This included jokes, a wordsearch, cartoons, and book reviews.

The project's aim was to produce a newspaper to sell locally, with the children acting as reporters, feature writers, an advertising department, and photographers. When working on their own newspaper, pupils also made jingles (raps) to advertise the newspaper which were subsequently broadcast on Radio Newcastle. On reflection, I think pupils were given too much scope, and more teacher intervention, particularly in relation to design and group organisation and possible relations with outside agencies (e.g., local businesses), would have been helpful. Pupils divided themselves into groups based on both their analysis of the newspaper and their visit to the newspaper offices (sports, features, editorial, layout, advertising, photography). The visit emphasised the need and purpose of collaborative work. We found that the children knew a great deal about newspapers from home, and we were helping them to make this knowledge more explicit (e.g., the difference between daily and weekly, local and national, and quality and tabloid). They had no idea that advertising paid for the paper, though this realisation prompted them to form a strong advertising team rather than ask questions about editorial independence.

Issues of representation emerged when one pupil submitted a letter 23 bemoaning the fact that girls were to be allowed into the scouting movement. The editorial team did not want to publish it on the grounds of sexism but decided in the end to reply to the letter. There was some difficulty in relating tabloid journalism to the production of a school newspaper, and one teacher felt uncomfortable discussing some of the issues raised by these newspapers. The school raised over £200 in advertising revenue. The paper was an eight-page tabloid, and 2400 copies were distributed at a cost of £480. New technology was a motivating factor and gave us easier access to a wider public. Writing for the community meant that pupils had to consider the amount of background information necessary to make the article both comprehensible and interesting to a wider readership ('Think about the grannies'). Design decisions demonstrated a knowledge of the conventions of newspaper layout (where to put the photographs and advertising, how to group articles together, and how to write interesting headlines – trampolining, for example, became 'Hopping Mad').

The children were interested most of all in environmental stories, stories 24 about children, and scandal and violent crime. The editorial team had to ask themselves what makes a good story. Is it news to other people? Is it well written? Is it properly explained? Is it accurate? Is it too long? Is it about the school or the wider community? The front-page lead, for example, was about the closure of the local swimming baths, and they saw this very much as a campaigning piece, although an opportunity to speak to a representative from the council was missed.

The children were aware that because of the time it takes to produce a 25 school newspaper most of the articles did not need to be time-critical. Some children practised writing articles by taking historic events and reporting them for a contemporary newspaper, others designed their own advertisements and needed to make sure that they were both attractive and fair. As a class, they demonstrated their own editorial independence by including an article on the poor provision for disabled pupils at the school (a disabled pupil fell while visiting the school).

These are but a few of the learning outcomes of the study of 'Newspapers' 26 in my class, and I have indicated how useful a resource information technology was in this particular activity. However, most important, I felt, was the sense of control and achievement experienced by the children involved in using the data-base computer program. Since the children wrote their own data, determined the categories to be explored, and asked their own questions, a definite sense of belonging was created. The children felt the file was exclusive to them since they themselves requested the information they required. This in turn gave the whole exercise a sense of ownership. I feel it is a bonus when young children experience such a level of control over information technology. Perhaps then they can begin to dispel some of the apprehensions many of us, as adults, continue to experience with it.

Kenton School Community Newspaper – Gill Hosie and Lynne Clark

Kenton School is an 11–18 city school in Newcastle (mixed catchment area) with 1600 pupils. The group in question were 40 pupils from year 11 (pupils aged 15–16), with two teachers team teaching, and were mixed ability, mixed gender, and mixed race (a small proportion of Asian, Chinese, and black children). Media studies is taught within the 'foundation programme' and is assessed as part of the BTEC qualification. The pupils have a double lesson (2 hours with a 15-minute break) for a 6-week period, then the group changes.

The 14–19 Curriculum Initiative (TVEI Extension) aims to equip the pupils with knowledge, competencies, and skills required for the world of work. It also aims to promote teaching and learning styles that encourage pupils to be enterprising and creative, solve problems, and work in teams. The pre-vocational modules of the foundation programme are an attempt to deliver an entitlement curriculum for all pupils in years 10 and 11 as a means of fulfilling the aims of the 14–19 Curriculum Initiative. We aim:

- to allow pupils to gain experiences in areas which are not on offer within the core or options;
- to relate these experiences as closely as possible to the world of work, and to establish links with industry and commerce;
- to ensure that pupils who opt for subjects to study up to GCSE can retain a balanced curriculum by giving them continued experiences in, for example, languages or aesthetic and creative work beyond year 9;
- to give pupils the opportunity to develop a range of transferable skills;
- to enable all their knowledge, competencies, and skills to be accredited through a nationally recognised BTEC/CGLI certification.

Most work is done in the library, where pupils have access to reference books, an extremely knowledgeable librarian, and four computers. The computer suite is also available through a booking system. Demand for this facility is high, so the library computers are used in the main, and we hope an Apple Macintosh will also shortly be available for use.

One of the major aims was for the children to become more media aware and media literate through the analysis of existing newspapers and through the creation of their own. Another aim was to allow children of all abilities to become more knowledgeable about the use of word processing in newspapers, and the importance of layout. The learning outcome will be the creation of a twice-yearly newspaper (A2 folded to A3). The pupils will create the newspaper themselves by deciding upon articles and where they will go in the newspaper. Through individual and group work they will make their own decisions and work to a deadline.

The main motivation for this piece of work was a similar piece of work 31 conducted with a mixed-ability first year. They wrote their own environmental pieces and, with the aid of Newspapers in Education (NIE) and the *Evening Chronicle*, this was produced free of charge. It was an extremely professional news-sheet, and the children's delight in seeing their work presented in this way was motivation enough to go on to produce further newspapers. The newspaper which is being produced by Year 11 pupils (15- to 16-year-olds) has met with the same enthusiasm. From the outset the pupils are informed that the newspaper will be professionally produced and that it will be distributed among the community. When researching other newspapers for content, layout, and style they are also asked to consider the use of advertisements.

The problems we faced became evident from the beginning. We did not 32 possess the expertise to produce a really professional newspaper. We wanted the children to create the layout but found it would be too difficult, so we enlisted the help of the adviser who put us in contact with the *Evening Chronicle* again. It is hoped that the *Chronicle* will produce the final layout typesetting according to our design.

Prior to beginning the course we wrote the aims for assessment closely 33 linked to the attainment targets for English and Technology. One area which was to be assessed was that of layout, which we solved through using a newspaper software package which allowed us to cut and paste stories. The children were required to think about choice of stories, bias, front page layout, and so on.

Although the pupils wrote to many companies for advertising revenue, 34 very few replied. We had enough money for one edition, but no more. The adviser, however, offered financial assistance and also advice on how to gain further revenue: (*a*) charge money for its sale; (*b*) include a classified section; and (*c*) advertise feature articles. We decided to opt for the first and the third options, as the newspaper would take too long to produce to make a classified section viable. We have not discarded this idea, however, and will take this up in our second edition.

It was initially envisaged that the newspaper would be produced four 35 times a year. However, we decided to produce the newspaper twice a year and choose the articles from two groups, as we found that we did not have enough articles of quality from the first group to produce a newspaper.

The project began with the children looking through newspapers to 36 assess layout, content, and bias, and for this they were given specific questions to work to. Next, they were given the layout sheets and the stories, and they cut and pasted their own front pages from the selection of stories and pictures available. They were then required to make a presentation to the rest of the group to state why they had presented their front page in such a way.

The remainder of the time was taken up with producing articles. Suggestions were made concerning the events in school which could be covered, and local events too. If the children had special interests they could work on them, sending off for further information and using the resources in the library. Feature writers could also decide upon the area in which they wished to work. Everything was then word processed from notes or from taped interviews.

Finally, an editorial team was set up to decide upon the name of the newspaper (they chose *The Kenton Times*); what typefaces would be used; the headlines for the articles; the photographs to be used; and the position of each article in the newspaper. The following equipment was used: a camera, word processors (BBC), newspapers, the layout kit, and tape recorders. The material outcome of the project was, of course, the newspaper itself, particularly the front page layout.

Learning outcomes were identified throughout the course by discussing the children's knowledge about newspapers and discussing their articles and advertisements. The editorial team made decisions on their own without any guidance from teachers as to content and layout, which was based on their own knowledge and what they had learned during the course. A final discussion and writing of their assessment sheet revealed how they felt about the course and what they had gained.

As teachers, we learned that initially we had been over-ambitious and streamlined the course as a result. Our teaching styles had to adapt to the different stages of the course – initially leading and instructing; facilitating during the final stages; giving guidance where necessary.

Three of the children made presentations of their work to a variety of educationalists, which I feel made them value the course and the work they produced. People they interviewed considered them to be serious in their intentions and as such answered the questions with thought and careful consideration, which also made the whole exercise more credible.

I feel that the course has achieved what we intended and has given the pupils more balance and breadth to their curriculum choices. When the first newspaper was produced it was clear that subsequent groups realised that it was a professional production; hopefully they were inspired to work as hard to produce a similar, if not better, newspaper.

We intend to maintain the course as part of the foundation programme, with the hope that in subsequent years we will be able to produce the four newspapers we wanted to. It is obvious that we cannot continue to rely on the local newspaper, so we need to look towards gaining specific knowledge on layout techniques in order that the newspaper can be produced in school using existing technology: Apple Macintoshes and PageMaker.

Note
1. Cary Bazalgette (ed.), *Primary Media Education: A Curriculum Statement*, London, BFI, 1989.

344

Teaching TV Cartoons

Peter Frazer

Using TV cartoons in the classroom may seem to be an activity more
appropriate to the age groups assumed to be watching them, at primary
level rather than secondary students. My experience using *The Flintstones*
and *The Simpsons* at a range of different levels in secondary teaching would
appear to contradict such an assumption, both on the grounds that older
children watch cartoons (and in significantly different ways from those
much younger) and that they provide a fruitful focus for the study of media
studies concepts. I have used both programmes with year 10 and 11 pupils
(15- and 16-year-olds) taking a joint course in English Language and Media
Studies, during a unit on the representation of the family. Slotted in among
The Cosby Show, *Telly Addicts*, *EastEnders*, and extracts from Victorian
novels, they form part of an apparently bizarre concoction, but in practice
seem to engage students in some of their most animated discussion and
raise many questions about the representation of the family more generally.
I have also used the programmes with first years to teach about the conventions of narrative, where again the sophistication of the work produced
illustrated their usefulness.

I initially chose the representation of the family as a unit of work because
I felt that it would afford us the opportunity to look at the notion of
representation without the limitation which either a particular representation (e.g., women or black people) or a particular genre might impose.
Thus similarity and difference, perhaps the two most useful concepts in
media studies, could be raised in this unit across a range of genres and
forms and across a range of representations of social groups.

Each text used was chosen because it raised particular questions in
relation to representation of different social groups and issues. Since the
unit only lasted a few weeks we were limited in our scope, but students
were given the opportunity of one piece of coursework to write about any
programme of their own choice based around the family. Though many
chose programmes we had looked at in class, others chosen included *Bread*,
Neighbours, and *The Gummi Bears*.

Work around *The Flintstones* consisted of screening a single episode
(which turned out to be particularly apposite in terms of its explicit questioning of gender roles), followed by group and whole-class discussion of
particular questions. Among these were the following:

(1) Name the characters. Who is related to whom? What other characters, if any, are usually included?

345

(2) What expectations does the title sequence raise about what is to follow?

(3) Are the settings strange or familiar?

(4) Is it a 'realistic' cartoon? How is it similar/different to other programmes based around the family?

(5) *The Flintstones* are described as 'a modern stone-age family'. What kind of family do you think the cartoon represents? (You may include the Rubble family too).

Questions 1 and 2 were standard for all the programmes we looked at, while Question 4 was included following some discussion of the problematic notion of the term 'realistic', perhaps best approached through Bob Hodge and David Tripp's concept of modality.[1]

In the episode we looked at, Wilma and Betty learn from a TV programme of a method of brainwashing people by telling them what to do when they are asleep. They try the technique out on their husbands, resulting in Fred standing up to his boss and both he and Barney doing jobs around the house. The wives, however, tire of their 'new men' and decide to stop the trick after one last effort, in which they ask for new mink coats. The husbands overhear this plan and 'act up' to their brainwashed roles, pretending they are going to rob the fur warehouse. Just as everything is about to be resolved, daughter Pebbles lobs a brick through the warehouse window and they all get arrested. At their trial, the judge punishes the women with twenty days of being made to take the husbands breakfast in bed.

This raised interesting points in discussion of whether gender roles had changed since the 1960s, as well as what males and females should be expected to do around the home; perhaps this took us away from the analysis of the programme itself rather too quickly, but it did none the less engage students with ideological questions based upon what seemed an unlikely text to raise such questions. The advantage of *The Flintstones* lies in its accessibility while raising many of the questions which more 'complex' texts, media or literary, might do. It fitted well with the other programmes examined, both because it was based totally around the construction of the family and because its narrative structure was very similar to that employed in the sitcom genre. If we take what students wrote about it as a guideline, we can see a number of media studies concepts raised.

> The two wives sometimes plot against their husbands when they've had too much of their male chauvinism and create even more havoc than the men do . . . a situation is set up so that Fred's attitudes can be shown and the faults in them pointed out, either by an outcome in the story or by the other characters . . . the disruptions are almost always started by Fred and are usually resolved by Wilma and Betty.

These narrative and gender roles are intertwined as far as the student's understanding of the ideology of the programme is concerned. He sees the programme in negative terms: 'The Flintstone family is a very American 1960s narrow view of the way certain places should be taken up by members of the family,' and furthermore sees this as having a particular purpose for an audience: 'I feel that this programme is intended for children to be educated about the real world in a comic way . . . the cartoon is an ideal medium for giving the child an idea of what the real world is actually like.' The format of the show is likened to the sitcom:

> As the jokes are not exactly top class, a fake audience is used to create the illusion of the cartoon being a live show . . . the cartoon equivalent of a live comedy like *The Cosby Show*, set largely in one place, unlike cartoons such as *The Smurfs*, who go out on adventures.

The Simpsons proved even more provocative as a text to use. Unlike *The Flintstones*, which I remember from my own childhood, *The Simpsons* is very much part of some of the students' own popular culture. Until one member of the class who had satellite TV taped an episode for me, I had never seen the programme, as indeed neither had most of the class, though all were particularly keen to do so. The 'cultish' nature of the experience, and the 'one-upmanship' from several of the (often less academic) students who had seen *The Simpsons* previously, made an interesting contrast with viewing *The Flintstones*. Students who in previous lessons had not joined in very much became most vociferous in their detailed background knowledge of both characters and narratives.[2]

Again the episode chosen (randomly) was particularly apposite for the unit. In it, what the merchandising label describes as 'the first TV family you can relate to, man' goes on a picnic at Homer's boss's mansion. They try to put on a show of family unity, which does not convince the boss. Both at the picnic and later, peeking through neighbours' curtains, they see other families' apparently idyllic relationships and are shamed into doing something about their own. After seeing an advert on TV (which they watch constantly) for a psychotherapist specialising in family therapy, offering double your money back if he fails, they pawn the TV set to pay for treatment. Inevitably, all his methods fail, including the electric shock treatment which they dish out to one another in such large doses that the city's power supplies fail. They solve the problem, however, as they get double their money back and are able to buy a bigger portable TV which they can wheel into the dining-room at mealtimes to prevent arguments.

What we make of students' writing about the programme is hard to decide when they describe the representation of family life thus: 'Even though it is a cartoon, I feel that it is more realistic than *The Cosby Show* as there problems are resolved too easily. In *The Simpsons*, they go to extremes to get what they want.'

In using the programmes with first years, we concentrated more on narrative patterns, with the students producing diagrams to illustrate how far the narrative of each programme conformed to structural models. *The Simpsons* appeared to be broken into two narratives (the picnic and the psychotherapist) separated by the commercial break, linked only by the theme of familial disunity. The agent of disruption in both *The Simpsons* and *The Flintstones* was seen as the TV, though more refined arguments decided that this was merely the catalyst for pre-existing tensions in both

7

8

9

10

families.[3] The endings were seen in different terms, with *The Flintstones* having a conventional happy resolution, in which the couple laugh at their own silliness, whereas that of *The Simpsons* was viewed more as a truce rather than a resolution, with the pleasure of the programme apparently being in direct proportion to the disunity of its family.

On this question of pleasure, the students were divided about equally regarding which they enjoyed the most, with there being an apparent correlation between finding the programme enjoyable and its family the more 'realistic' of the two. This would, however, need more research on my part as, in discussion, being realistic as a prerequisite of being pleasurable became so entangled for the 11-year-olds that it was difficult to follow the logic of some of their points. Certainly, though, the disunity of the Simpson family, often sparked by the most popular character, Bart, is a principal source of pleasure (for adults too!), while the safe familiarity of Fred and Wilma's light-hearted tussles seemed a cosier world that other children preferred, disliking the stridency of the Simpson family.

Thus I would suggest that students could gain a good deal from the study of TV cartoons. Representation can be approached in a way in which the students own identity is not under threat; after all, these are cartoon characters. Genre, narrative and ideology are all raised, and the programme offers a way into teaching about all these areas and an easy relationship to a range of other texts.

Doubtless, *The Flintstones* and *The Simpsons* seem odd choices to many English teachers – they do not seem 'worthwhile' at first glance – and certainly my own anxiety about using them still lingered as, at one point towards the end of a double period on a Thursday afternoon, it suddenly struck me that elsewhere in the school, parallel fifth-year groups were probably agonising over a scene from *Macbeth*, and doubtless discovering some 'universal truth'. I made this point to the students, asking them, in a moment of angst, whether they felt that what we were doing was justifiable. They could not see my problem at all – 'Well, it's all part of the media, isn't it?' said one.

With thanks to Lorraine Gould and Katherin Sheikh, who also taught this unit.

Notes

1. Modality is a term derived from linguistics to describe the ways we judge the reality of things. Bob Hodge and David Tripp, *Children and Television: a semiotic approach*, Cambridge, Polity, 1986, chapter 4, gives the best account of this.
2. I have no research information other than very loose observation on which to base this footnote, but it has struck me at my school that the students who have been first to acquire satellite TV at home have tended to be Afro-Caribbean and Greek Cypriot. It seems for them to act as a symbol of social status; in giving them access to films and programmes which other students do not have, they seem to act as both providers of copies of these and as receptacles of knowledge about them. I would also argue that some element of the construction of cultural identity takes place via its possession.
3. In debates around popular culture, TV is itself often seen as an anxiety object,

triggering moral panics regarding its supposed effects. Cartoons, as a form popular among children, have often been the focus of such attacks. Interestingly, both these cartoons make use of such a discourse in terms of the narrative, disruption being set off by something the characters see on TV. In *The Simpsons*, however, the resolution comes with the acquisition of a bigger TV but, as the children recognise, this is merely a short-term 'sop' from Homer to keep the family intact; disruption will recur next time. The programme often makes use of TV in this way, and acknowledges the discourse of TV as 'dangerous' while simultaneously mocking such a discourse – after all, its audience in the UK is made up of those who have Sky-TV, the source of much recent furore over 'quality' and children's programmes in particular. Thus a complex set of ideas, of which the children seemed to have a degree of knowledge, circulate in the programme.

Sniffing Out Stereotypes:
Using Fragrances to Explore Gender Images in Advertising

David Brockie

I have been working as part of a tutor team responsible for teaching year 8 pupils (13-year-olds) for half of their week's lessons. This 'mini-school' structure called 'Home Base' brings together subject staff from English, science and humanities areas. The Home Base is timetabled as a block with consistent staffing to enable considerable autonomy and flexibility in terms of the way learning is organised. This team-oriented approach is part of the wider structure and ethos of a community school which is keen to resist the drawing of tight boundaries around learning experiences, in spite of the way that the National Curriculum in its subject-based structure has encouraged the growth of a more narrow 'subject patriotism'.

Although personal and social education (PSE) is a natural part of the cross-curricular projects initiated by the team, it has sometimes felt appropriate to give this area focus in its own right. It was with this in mind that the team decided to use the facility of the whole day timetabled for Home Base each week to launch a unit exploring a variety of health issues. The idea of a Health Day was thus floated, kicking off with a 7 a.m. swim (for staff, too!); a healthy breakfast supplied by the school cafeteria; and then a morning filled with a circus of activities staffed by the Home Base team. These ranged from the making of a one-minute video, with a brief of encouraging junior-age children to take responsibility for personal hygiene, to the use of the Harvard Step Test (in this case stepping on and off a chair via a low bench) in order to introduce the notion of assessing fitness and the reading of pulse rates. More sedentary activities included the focal point of this account, the use of fragrances to unpack sex-role imagery and stereotypes found in advertisements. All of this was to be accomplished before consuming the healthy snack students were to create in the home economics area and, after a suitable pause, taking to the park for the inevitable 'fun run'.

It might be thought strange to site an activity examining gender stereotypes within a health education context. However, this stems from the broader conceptions of health education which emphasise definitions of 'health' beyond narrow 'medical' notions to give due consideration to wider influences on 'feelings of well-being' (for a full discussion see Burrage, 1990[1]). These might include aspects of community health, and certainly a focus on psychological health. The contention here would be that the latter is threatened quite markedly by the clamps that are put around what is defined as gender-appropriate behaviour, particularly in the case of those students who will not, or cannot, meet these expectations and suffer at the hands of peers and possibly teachers too.

Media representations of gender certainly play a significant part in this coercion, one with which the school environment often seems to do much to collude when issues of gender have effectively been confined to lip service, while issues of sexuality have been largely scared off the agenda. In spite of the subtle shifts in masculinity presented by the images of the present (Gazza may be prepared to shed a tear but he is still firmly 'one of the lads'), 'Rocky' and 'Rambo' characters are still ten a penny, encouraging boys towards an unquestioning emphasis and celebration of certain attributes, while girls are still constantly encouraged to align themselves with a pastel and submissive frilliness. As failure to comply in school with the codes supported by this sort of imagery can result in ruthless attack (I would assert that terms of derision which comment on some presumed expression of sexuality, such as 'lessie', 'poof' and 'dog' are among the most common currency of classroom abuse), it seems highly appropriate to give space within a Health Day to an activity which might encourage a climate in which a wider range of behaviour is tolerated and thus greater psychological health is possible.

Fragrance advertising seems to be a rich area for uncovering gender stereotypes as it deals directly with images of what it means to be the socially successful man or woman. However, so common are these soft-focus representations in magazines, on TV, and at the cinema, I felt that an exercise in 'content analysis' would produce a sterile and detached response from students who are often experts in giving teachers the answers they want. In my experience, many of the cues to gender representations are quite apparent to students when they are prompted to examine them. The white lace, the swirling lettering, the soft music, can be quickly identified and yet, although there is a readiness to intellectualise about such stereotyping, there is often a failure to make a connection with the way it relates to their own behaviour and expectations. It is interesting to consider myself in this respect: I feel I switch to analytical mode when watching advertisements, and yet they are still extremely powerful influences on my behaviour. After every Christmas my father is pleased to receive the 'passed-on' bottle of Old Spice aftershave I give to him, which originates as Auntie Maud's present to me. I have to admit that the way the product smells does not actually come into this decision, but the imagery I associate with this brand (older, traditional, 'the mark of a man'), is not something I want to identify with. In short, I have a strong personal response to this product that has nothing to do with its essential fragrant property!

It was partly this recognition which helped me in my search for a more powerful entry point to the session, which would bring the critical experiential element to the activity I was planning. Thus, I considered the potential of engaging students more personally in the process of analysing images through harnessing their own sense of smell. I wanted them to grow in their awareness of the 'hidden power' of advertisements as well as that which they would readily recognise.

351

The essence of the activity lay in separating fragrances from their identity as presented by their 'name', packaging, and advertising contexts. Students would then be set the task of trying to identify which fragrances were aimed at men and which were aimed at women. Having discussed the activity with the rest of the team, their support was supplied in the form of the 'smellies' they had themselves received last Christmas. It was clear from the outset, when our next meeting transformed the Home Base office into a downmarket perfumery, that once separated from their source it was just not very easy to relate fragrance to gender.

Preparation involved the selection of eight fragrances, four aimed at men and four at women. I tried to avoid the most common ones. Meanwhile, I embarked on a magazine-flicking, TV-taping project in order to compile a wide range of advertisements, hoping particularly to find examples for my chosen fragrances. This proved quite difficult, and I had to settle for less than a 50 per cent match given the timescale to which I was working. However, I felt that there was enough of a connection with the fragrances in use for the activity, and most of the points could be generalised to the other examples I had found.

On the morning of Health Day itself, I dripped samples of each of the fragrances on to the cotton wool balls that were nestling inside three sets of eight numbered bottles. As each group of students arrived for their 45-minute session they were asked to sit in a mixed group of four. I wanted the activity itself to form the stimulus for the session and so opted to minimise any preamble, except for asking the students to consider whether they might wear a fragrance they liked even if they knew it was designed for the opposite sex. Unsurprisingly, the stronger reaction to this came from the boys: 'No fear!', 'Only if you were a poof,' or 'People would take the mickey out of you.' The girls seemed to be less convinced of the need to apply the brakes quite so forcibly here: 'My sister wears men's stuff – she says she likes it better,' 'Women's perfumes smell better – they wouldn't want aftershave, it smells boring,' or 'I would wear it if I liked it, but I shouldn't think I'd like it.' Rather than attempt to discuss or challenge any of these comments at this stage I let them ride, feeling the activity itself would do this most effectively.

Each group was asked to assess the four numbered fragrances on their table to enable them to complete the table (Figure 1). As well as recording whether they thought the fragrance was designed for men or for women, I also asked the students to give each a score to show how much they liked it (1 = low, 10 = high).

After the comments made in response to the initial question it now became apparent that the exercise was not the 'piece of cake' some had assumed. There was intense interest in how each other had defined each fragrance. The boys certainly did not want to be seen to be giving high scores to those fragrances they were identifying as female, although clearly many of them were not convinced as to which gender each should be assigned. Asides from one boy to another such as, 'Well, you would think that's a woman's one – you are a woman!' I felt important to leave unchallenged at this point, so as not to stifle the creation of learning points which could form the basis of the later discussion. I was also conscious of not

352

BOTTLE no.	FOR HER ?	FOR HIM ?	SCORE (1-10)	ACTUAL FRAGRANCE	✓ or ✗
1					
2					
3					
4					

Figure 1

wanting to foster a climate of 'teacher-pleasing' behaviour, in which the students would readily identify my aims and agenda – jump through the appropriate hoops to keep me happy, but avoid engaging personally in the sessions.

There was certainly a lot of excitement in the room – it seemed that the sense of smell was a rich vein of learning worth exploiting! Moves to complete the chart were tentative and there was a sense, particularly among the boys, that it was important to be seen to be going with the flow of opinion and so avoid the perceived ridicule which would result from being isolated when the bottles were unveiled. After about ten minutes the 'sniffing' session was over. I asked the students within each group to compare their results to see where there was consensus and where there was disagreement. Again the atmosphere was tentative as it became clear that the results were diverse; there was little overt marketing of presumed 'right answers' even among the most reliably effervescent contributors. As the bottles were revealed the activity had achieved an almost 'game-show' quality. Students completed their chart, registering a number of surprises. Although some of the brands may have been unfamiliar, it was interesting that nobody, having seen the bottles, needed to ask for clarification as to the gender for which the product design was intended, except the occasional statement of surprise disguised as a question: 'Is number three really a men's one?'

In one of the groups I heard a boy comment to another, on discovering that he had made errors in four out of eight cases: 'But then, you're a poof, aren't you?' I found it impossible to let this go completely unchallenged, in spite of my earlier resolution to allow such comments 'air time' so that they could be tools for debriefing the activity. In the event I asked the accuser to look at his own list, drawing his attention to the fact that by his own reckoning he had identified two of the 'female' fragrances as being for men and registered them with scores of 7 and 8.

Only two members of the whole group had managed to make correct judgements about the entire set of eight fragrances. The majority had made errors in two, three, or four cases. The sober bottle of Grey Flannel aftershave had caused most universal upset, in that this had been considered by many as a 'safe bet' in the women's category. Again the comments were largely from the boys: 'I'm not going to wear that one then, that's for sure!' Again I had to resist the temptation to challenge, and proceeded to distribute the magazine advertisements.

My original intention was that each group would use a chart like the one shown in Figure 2 to collect data. However, my mismatch of advertisements collected with fragrances used, and in this case my time constraints, led me to ask groups to divide their sheet in half to record 'messages received about women's products' and 'messages received about men's products'. In terms of the examples I collected, the more 'popular' fragrance ranges seemed to spawn the imagery in a form that I felt would be most accessible for this age group. These included the following:

Impulse Body Spray	(TV/magazine) The women is portrayed as the passive recipient of a stranger's flowers.
Sixth Sense Body Spray	(TV) A similar but more explicit message of the 'wear this and get your man' variety, has our dynamic 'Sixth Sense' wearer as a magnet to the attentions of the good-looking focus of an eighteenth birthday party.
Le Jardin	(TV/magazine) Soft-focus gone mad – a garden in full bloom is visited by a sophisticated 'lady in white'.
Lynx	(TV) Valiant hero saves 'dusky damsel' from bandits who storm their isolated shack situated somewhere in the 'macho' West.
Denim	(magazine) The product range sits proudly above the caption, 'Just add the girl', seeming to suggest that a woman is a willing ingredient of this particular recipe for male completeness.
Insignia	(TV) Bob takes a shower with the assistance of the eight-armed female robot. He is pampered with each variation of the product and spoken to in 'luscious tones' from the robot's control panel which depicts pouting red lips.

MESSAGES Sent by			
FRAGRANCE	PACKAGING	MAGAZINE ADVERT	TV ADVERT

Figure 2

The bottles and advertisements generated a hubbub of discussion and a   16
large number of responses:

– 'The delicate bottles and the frilly writing makes you think it's supposed to be for someone elegant.'
– 'A lot of them have got a man in the picture, as if to say, "If you wear this perfume you'll get a boyfriend." '
– 'Some are linked with fast cars, like Hero and Turbo, they seem to be trying to make out that you can show off to women, like men who drive sports cars often do.'

Screening the TV advertisements then spawned a further flurry of com-   17
ment. My key observation was that the activity of 'content analysis', which I have used previously on a number of occasions, seemed to have bite and relevance here, in that the fragrance activity had made the students sharply aware of how their senses could be manipulated. This came out particularly strongly in the criticisms levelled at the advertisements in our concluding discussion:

– 'They're just trying to make you a certain kind of man or a certain kind of woman.' [girl]
– 'You might end up feeling you're no good if you don't end up like the people in the adverts.' [girl]
– 'I bet they could sell exactly the same smell to women and blokes as long as they called it by different names and advertised it to fit in with what we've seen – just shows how stupid the whole thing is.' [boy]

Asked once more if they would consider wearing a fragrance not designed for their gender, many of the boys remained resolute: 'People will think you're gay.' Interestingly, it was some of the girls who challenged this statement, the essence of which had been present as an undercurrent throughout the session: 'Don't be pathetic, what we just did showed that there's hardly any difference in the smell of women's and men's anyway!'

I asked the group to think about the images they had identified and   18
criticised and then consider their everyday lives at school. I referred to

355

some of the comments I had heard during the session, noting that while they were critical of advertiser's attempts to control the way in which it is acceptable to behave as a man or as a woman, there seemed to be a lot of restrictions placed around what behaviour was judged as acceptable for girls and boys within the group. Asked for their views on this I was pleasantly surprised to see one of the boys willing to speak up. He said he thought it was stupid that there had been two fights the previous lunchtime because some of the boys in his tutor group were trying to 'look tough in front of their girlfriends by getting the people who had been calling them names'. One of the girls agreed with this comment, noting that it often annoyed her how some of the boys 'try to act all hard in front of each other'.

Time had run out – my group was due in the home economics area to make their 'healthy snack'. The next group was already queueing at the door. I felt pleased at the way the activity had seemed to make concrete connections with the students' own experience, but a little concerned that there had been insufficient time to debrief the exercise thoroughly. I had expected the fragile nature of 'masculinity' to be somewhat exposed during the session, and this was borne out by the much more troubled responses of the boys. Perhaps I should have been more keenly aware of the potential the exercise had for exposing those in the group who did not conform very neatly with their peer's expectations in terms of appropriate gender behaviour. I was a little worried that the jibes made by some people as issues of sexuality came to the surface were not adequately countered by the concluding discussion.

With a later group our discussion made the interesting conclusion that it would generally be easier for girls to wear aftershave than for boys to wear 'perfume': 'Boys have to prove they're men all the time, don't they? That seems stupid to me.' Somebody asked me if I had ever worn a 'female' fragrance. I felt a bit of a 'let-down', having never done so, although I did admit that I am very partial to Lux soap, and that I have no qualms about putting that in my shopping trolley even though it is clearly marketed as a 'beauty soap' for women!

In reflecting on the activity, I have been sharply aware of the danger of raising issues in an effective way but then not dealing with them adequately, whether because of a lack of time or, more probably, because of personal discomfort at some level. I regard it as vital that issues of gender and sexuality should be given greater prominence in the classroom, not least because of the pain of my own experience growing up as a teenager at school who offended the norms of 'appropriate' masculine behaviour and suffered as a result. Now, having fought the odds to embrace a positive gay identity, I am confident enough to 'own' my sexuality with most colleagues (if not with students), and wish to play a part in challenging a curriculum, both formal and informal, which has for so long supported society's heterosexual assumption. However, in practice I have to own up to a residue of fear when dealing with this issue in the classroom, sometimes treading that bit too carefully for fear of being seen by my colleagues negatively as proffering my own cause. I do not feel good about this admission, but acknowledge the process in the expectation that in doing so I can work towards a better mode of operation in the future.

However, this is not to knock the validity of the exercise, just to stress the need for a thorough debriefing. The use of smell had certainly been effective in challenging and exposing the process we go through when we respond uncritically to 'representation', even if we tell ourselves that we know how the advertiser is attempting to work on us. Using smell makes clear the extent of the manipulation by mounting a personal challenge to the cosy assumptions in operation in a way that is not possible by viewing or listening to the advertisements in isolation. The activity allowed the students to look at media images from a fresh and involved perspective, and thus enabled them to look at familiar products with new eyes.

Another positive factor contributing to the success of the activity was the context of the Home Base curriculum framework in which it took place. As I was part of the small team of staff in frequent contact with each group of students in the year group, the relationships which existed were an important foundation on which to build a consideration of quite sensitive issues to the developing adolescent. Although I felt the activity had a lot to offer the year 8 students I felt it might be more appropriate still with an older group. In fact, the idea was later taken up by the humanities team for their year 11 unit on aspects of gender. I have since considered the possibilities provided by shifting the emphasis of the activity a little: it might be more powerful to initially choose one of the anonymous fragrances which they would wear, before even introducing the gender question. Then there is the option of beginning the activity with the images and asking the students to try to identify the fragrance that matches.

In conclusion, it is interesting to note the very profitable coalition I have begun to identify between media education and approaches to personal and social education. Looking at media issues through a personal framework, as was exemplified here, seems to harness the power of experiential learning and so enables students to really gain a personal understanding of the way in which the media can affect their own attitudes and behaviours. This contrasts sharply with the personal detachment which can accompany a standard exercise in 'content analysis', (e.g., the exercise as described minus the use of the fragrances themselves). Similarly, I would argue that the use of the media images was pivotal in encouraging the students to question their own gender stereotypes, giving them a tool to aid their personal reflection. A similar complementary relationship could be seen elsewhere on the Health Day, where students constructed their video images aimed at encouraging junior-age students to take greater responsibility for their own personal hygiene. As they considered their 'audience' and appropriate 'media language' they were also dealing with a topic which remained highly relevant in their own lives. They were thus encouraged to consider both strategies for communication about a potentially sensitive area as well as their own approach to their every little nook and cranny!

The effect of working in the sort of environment I have described, with the sort of activities I have outlined, is to make me value such cross-curricular approaches very highly, and trust that National Curriculum 'tunnel vision' will not succeed in drawing tight boundaries around subjects and 'subject teachers' to the detriment of potent learning opportunities, for both students and staff.

Note

1. H. Burrage, 'Health Education: Education for Health?' in B. Dufour (ed.), *The New Social Curriculum: A Guide to Cross-Curricular Issues*, Cambridge, Cambridge University Press, 1990.

Photomontage:
Image and Meaning

Tony Carroll

This project at Ifield Community College, Crawley, involved investigations 1
by year 10 (15-year-olds) GCSE art and design students, entitled 'Photomontage: image and meaning'. It took place between autumn 1989 and
spring 1990, in response to a wider county initiative in 1988 called the
West Sussex Photography Project, funded by the Arts Council and Southern Arts. The schools involved aimed to develop visual literacy and oracy
through photography, linking art and media education.

Montage can be described as the combination of both visual and written 2
texts, usually with other textural surfaces, which are pasted together. One
intention is to transform the meaning(s) of the original texts by deliberate or
accidental juxtapositions with others, in order to communicate associative
meanings to the viewer. The meanings of montage are therefore partly
governed by the intention of the producer of the work itself, while others
are constructed by the viewer. The latter may depend on the viewer's
disposition, or the context in which the work is seen. Montage, then, can
operate on complex or contradictory levels as well as very simplistic ones.

Montage itself has a short but complex twentieth-century history. It has 3
served as a propaganda tool (art in the service of politics), and it has been
developed by Surrealists as a means to create chance combinations which
may lead us to explore our subconscious selves. Pop artists celebrated
popular culture icons such as those seen in billboard posters, transposed
to large canvases, or posters, screen prints, photographs, and even soft
sculptures, where odd juxtapositions were fun. More recently in the 1980s
David Hockney produced photo-montage work, not necessarily for political
or propagandist reasons but to re-evaluate photography's problematic link
with art. Hockney cleverly and decoratively explores cubist motifs. He does
this through informal portraiture and still life to continue the exploration of
fragmented space, often quoting directly from Picasso and Braque, as many
have done before. But this time Hockney makes use of the easy availability
of Polaroids and 35 mm 'snaps' and the 'good fun' element of sticking
images together, to construct a sense of 'realism'. It sounds contradictory,
realism through fragmentation, but my students found Hockney's work
exciting and accessible.

My initial aim was to develop the students' knowledge of drawing con- 4
ventions, using photography. Montage is an effective way of combining art

359

and design processes with key media concepts such as forms and conventions, representation, audience, and, to a lesser extent, institutions. I also wanted to encourage active, critical, and reflective teaching and learning methods with my students, who demonstrated their learning in a variety of ways.

Learning by Doing
They researched visual and written information, both historical and contemporary, and relied heavily on notebooks and sketchbooks for keeping records. They used their books to plan negotiations with me and their groups regarding the how, what, why, and wherefore of project interpretations. Sketchbooks also provided a means of experiment, scribble and stick, and, of course, somewhere to make mistakes.

Oracy
Oracy was a condition of learning. Students talked informally about their ideas, which became more conceptual as the project developed. They discussed choices of subject matter, of design solutions, of materials, of meaning, and asked questions about when a work was finished, or whether or not it was successful. Throughout the process students moved between reading or deconstructing texts to constructing meanings. Then, back again to deciphering the work and meanings they themselves had produced and those intended by their fellow students. Talk was a way in which we could communicate effectively. Interpreting the work of their fellow students, however, created other readings.

Critically Reading Texts
Class discussions, with slides of work by John Heartfield, Hannah Hoih, James Rosenquist, and David Hockney, among others. We looked at and talked about an episode of *The Media Show* which included new video work commissioned by Friends of the Earth relating to the fashion industry and the environment. We also learned from an ex-student, when he came to talk to us, how he uses montage techniques to allow multi-narratives to flow through his comics. The images he constructs set off all sorts of possible readings.
In small groups, informal talk and note-making. Students analysed the formal elements of images and their codes and conventions as part of the overall processes involved in making connections with art and media texts. They also worked out, for example, possible intentions of the artists and how audiences might have reacted at the time and how the work might be read today.

At this time, although the teaching and learning were taking place within 'traditional' art and design education (i.e., formalist elements of line, tone, colour, and texture were the key issues), we were already asking questions about a fresh range of issues, such as: What is a work of art? For whom is the work produced (where the historical and social context takes on significance)? Who funded the work? Is the person who produced the work gifted, therefore suggesting that no one else except other gifted people are capable of producing 'Art'? Practical work and talk had begun, questions were being asked, experiments in image-making were undertaken. As in previous GCSE work, students interpreted the project by negotiating with each other and myself about how their ideas and concepts could be realised in visual form.

In the early phase of this project, Clare Wilson produced a classroom scene, *The Art Room*, which derived initially from her drawing observation exercises. In her record of oral work she reflects: 9

> I wanted to give a sense of time to the picture. I have tried to show this in the composition of the photographs. For example, there are the same figures with different facial expressions. They had moved every time I pressed the button on the camera. With several photographs put together this way I have been able to extend beyond the frame. This gives me a more realistic view of the classroom.

By making a drawing, or taking a conventional photograph, one might say 'a window on the world view of reality' has been created. This phrase has been used to describe 'realism' from the Renaissance to the present day. In photography and film this notion of realism is also taken as unproblematic, ranging from social documentary styles of photography, such as the Magnum Group, Cartier-Bresson, and Capa, to the reportage convention in news presentation today.

Montage, however, shows us many windows on the world and challenges 10 classic realism. Initial ideas were similar to Clare's piece. They ranged from the experience of self in relation to home, family, or friends, to school, work experience, or the environment. With Cherie's *Grand Hotel* montage, the personal and the social combined in an exploration of how one's ideals can be crushed:

> As I got further up the picture I started to break the picture away from the grids making arches. This is for the wedding as people break up from marriages. In the Grand Hotel the walls crumbled and fell. . . . I put flowers in some places, they represent peace.

Cherie's friend Martine, who worked in my other fourth-year group, was invited to unravel the work and decipher its associative meanings:

> This montage has a few different meanings. The image in the middle is the Grand Hotel. I think what Cherie is trying to put across is that the hotel is the kind of place where you would go for a honeymoon. I get this impression because she has showed a wedding. It also looks like the kind of hotel that businessman or couples (rich ones) would go for a 'weekend away'. I think that the small pictures or scenes of flowers etc. could be linked with the honeymoon, but also, if you look closer you can see that the hotel is badly damaged, so she could be trying to show the good and bad sides of life. There are many possibilities.

When talking about the 'language' of images in this way, the question of meaning arises. In progressive and critical education distinctions between 'high' and 'popular' culture are effectively blurred. So in art we can ask, what does this painting, sculpture, or building represent and how does it communicate these messages? Equal weight is ascribed here as to the same questions in popular projects on decoding advertisements in media studies.

The ability to actually produce an artefact, however, is of prime importance in art and design. My students took their own photographs and often used 'found' images, thus critically selecting from newspapers, magazines, and old photographs or postcards. They cut or tore images and words, then reconstructed them or freely combined them with drawn, pointed, or collaged material, as deemed necessary, to alter original meanings and communicate associative ones. This was in part controlled by the maker but, because these images were often 'public', it soon became clear that the audience or viewer would actually play an important role in constructing meaning(s). 'Critical' montage was again the vehicle for a diverse range of second-phase project work, negotiated within this more 'public' self and society theme. Kirsten Fitzhenry was soon able to recognise that she could juxtapose known signs. In other words, her personal statement (an anti-war statement) is communicated using well-known 'public' images. In her book she recorded:

> In the middle went the Remembrance Day poppy. This suggests sadness that war brings. It stands out against the other images which show violence. At the bottom I thought Rowan Atkinson as the Black Adder. His character shows little seriousness as he tried his best in the last series to get away from the enemy. In the very last frame you see him running into enemy lines, losing his life for a cause. I thought, it adds to the effect of the stupidity and horror of war overall.

In Alia's montage, *Rushdie*, a strong feeling emerged for her religion. She makes a claim for Muslim children taking an interest in the debate surrounding this issue. The enigmatic question 'The Beginning' engages our attention but is not resolved. Alia disturbs the viewer. Alia enjoyed the space this project allowed to resolve some of her personal feelings and thoughts as she describes, again to Martine:

> *Alia:* I wanted to portray the view of how Muslim people felt about Salman Rushdie and his book *Satanic Verses*.
> *Martine:* It's so strong . . . it gets the meaning across . . . did you agree with those who did call for his death?
> *Alia:* No, I thought that decision was a bit hasty, you know, the fact that they wanted to kill him.
> *Martine:* But you wanted to punish him?
> *Alia:* Yes, but not kill him.
> *Martine:* This picture is more controversial than others?
> *Alia:* It is more eye-catching.
> *Martine:* You know the word RELIGION you put in, did you mean anything by that?

Alia: I cut the word religion up into pieces, to show how it is breaking up.

Pieces like these bear out the importance of critical work in the active and reflective learning model. This involves developing the ability of students to read, decipher, or decode visual and written texts. I am not sure about the many 'ideas' available on picture criticism. It is often suggested that you must describe, analyse, and then evaluate visual or written texts in order to unravel their possible meanings. I think it is reasonable to suggest that on first contact with visual and written material we are immediately engaged in questions of meaning. In work like this, our critical reading skills can be heightened and developed. At one stage of the project we spent some time looking specifically at the ways in which third meanings or concepts can be produced from the combination of two or more given factors. This idea was derived and simplified from Vertov's and Eisenstein's investigations into film form in the early twentieth century. Some of my students picked up on the possibilities of this work and could see John Heartfield's work in a new light. This was a way of understanding the power of film and photography when it creates a sense of 'realism'. Many could understand the subtleties of montage propaganda, and tried to make contemporary parallels in TV and magazine advertisements.

We thus came to understand that the role of the camera was, like the pencil and the paintbrush, more than just a mechanical reproducer of reality. Images carry the potential for communicating personal and associative meanings and feelings to an audience, which can set up an interrogative interplay with socially grounded meanings. This was highlighted effectively by Simon Pattenden in his mixed-media collages called *One of the Dangers is the Money*. In a taped discussion with his friend Stuart he related his experiences which prompted the work: 'I thought of the places where the homeless have to sleep. The most down-to-earth thing I could say was "cardboard boxes are what they are sleeping in, and they could die over winter".' Many of Crawley's students have lived in London, so this would not be an unusual observation. What I found interesting was the exploration by Simon of his reactions to what he had seen and thought about while he realised them in visual form. He continued: 'There's a place called the bull ring, cardboard boxes everywhere, you know, cardboard city. Drug addicts are so common . . . it's unbelievable.' Simon then explained some of his design choices in the process:

> First of all I put a picture of a syringe down but it didn't look right, then I went on to think about where they might get the money for drugs, and whether or not they might be killed. So I put the phrase 'One of the Dangers is the Money'.

He uses a picture of money instead of the word. There are many stories which seem to be at work in Simon's montage, and the oral communication which followed helped to anchor Simon's intentions more clearly.

In these ways students engaged in a dialogue with media texts. Some examined, for example, the problems of how to represent things without resorting to stereotypes. In Clare Wilson's montage called *The Innocent Suffer* she found that this was one of her main difficulties. How do you represent Ireland without resorting to usual stereotypes? As she says:

> It was hard to avoid stereotypes, e.g., the colour green, shamrock, the Blarney Stone and . . . Guinness. I did feature a small amount of green and one image of Guinness, but only because they were part of a connection. . . . The caption *The Innocent Suffer* was my main theme, underneath there is a picture which illustrates the caption – a woman holding the hands of two children. They're screaming at something behind the camera. The thing that upsets the children could be a riot, or a British soldier with a gun, or an IRA patrol – a number of things. The background for the montage is orange, green, and white paper, signifying the IRA tricolour.

Clare tried to represent her own interpretation of the 'Irish issue', which was that the innocent suffer. She had to use public signifiers of meaning to reach the widest possible audience. In conclusion, Clare was sure that this piece had *more* meaning than the classroom scene, mentioned earlier. There are perhaps a number of reasons for this: *The Innocent Suffer* montage is public. The representation and audience concepts are addressed much more systematically. Clare felt much more in touch with her personal politics and had resolved many contradictions within her own mind on the contentious public issue of Britain's role in Northern Ireland. The fact that she came down to a humanist, liberal, and democratic resolution gained for her a sense of personal success, I think, and a feeling of maturity, especially when her father, on seeing the work at the Arundel Gallery, commented on the fact that he had not realised she was dealing with the 'big' issue in such a mature and visually expressive way. This work expanded Clare, and perhaps the value in the work lay in the fact that she was able to realise knowledge through practical work.

In both the work I have introduced, and the teaching and learning strategies I have briefly outlined, students were taking advantage of the opportunity for making their own compositions, exploring a range of media, styles, and conventions. They learned about cultural artefacts, conventions, and histories, and they explored issues of personal and social significance in more than just propositional and discursive forms. Art and media links highlight the importance of showing forms of reproduction which are social. This means that teachers and students can share in the process of producing knowledge, not simply a teacher giving it out and then students on their own reproducing it. These are what I have come to see as some of the most immediate pedagogical issues which need to be addressed in all areas of curriculum development which are negotiated in discussions of National Curriculum work. The plan now is to broaden art and media links at Ifield Community College to see if the photography and media concepts discussed can be drawn on to produce effective cross-curricular work. I am now thinking acutely about how learning through this kind of work can be evaluated more effectively.

16

364

Publishing:
The Book and the Reader
Julian Sefton-Green

I use this unit of work to introduce year 10 (15-year-old) students to their   1
GCSE English/Literature course (NEA Dual) at a mixed comprehensive in
North Tottenham. The school contains a diverse and changing ethnic mix
of students, mainly Afro-Caribbean, white, and Cypriot (Greek and Tur-
kish), with several early-stage ESL learners in each class. It draws from a
homogeneous working-class community. About a quarter of my class also
study GCSE Media Studies, but all should have experienced media units
in years 7–9. The English curriculum is broadly progressive but is strongly
composed of class readers.

Initially the unit set out to examine concepts of literature and popular   2
fiction by examining a selection of books in small groups, simply looking
at the front and back covers. I chose a range of books from Jackie Collins
to Edmund Gosse, Thomas Hardy to Alice Walker. I devised a simple
worksheet to facilitate the process of comparison, examining styles and size
of lettering, the language of the blurb, the status of recommendations, the
use of pictures and photographs, the price, and the targeted reader. I tried
to stimulate a conversation around the way some books were marketed as
'high' literature and some as popular literature, but this was not productive
as my students had no conception of the class values implied in this distinction.

However, the study of books as objects and the introduction of ideas   3
about genre, audience, and market were clearly relevant to both the students' use of books and their conceptualisation of the social value of reading. For example, girls read the Jackie Collins blockbusters but did not
think such books would be appropriate for study in English as they were
too 'sexy and adult'.

We then looked at some of the catalogues sent to the head of English. I   4
chose one mainstream publisher aiming at the teenage market, one small
black and feminist press, and a 'romantic' imprint also aimed at this age
range, but for reading in own leisure time rather than what teachers might
select as a class reader. We divided into these three publishing houses and,
based on the catalogues, each group had to produce a new title for their
allocated publisher. The students had to make explicit the way each publisher hypothesised their potential readership and the way this readership
was addressed through the marketing of a new title. The students wrote a
catalogue entry for their new book, produced a jacket and a plot synopsis.

365

They then presented their title to the class and we chose the most commercially viable. In fact, the titles themselves are so commercial as to verge on the parodic: *French Exchange*, *Summer Love*, or *Two Sweet-Hearts* were the romantic offerings; *The Macdonalds War*, about a mixed-race runaway's role in a catering feud was set locally, and *Can't Resist*, about a Rastafarian's tribulations with the police, were the radical publishing house's contribution; while *Settle The Score*, about a young American's school and basketball career, and *Jake of the Hills*, a historical novel about slavery, were deemed suitable for the class reader.

This piece of work provided two oral assignments (informal group work and presentation to the whole class) for GCSE work. Insisting that the class chose the most viable forced students to justify and compare their ideas, which acted very well as a form of reflection, making their implicit understandings about genre and audience explicit and showing how their reading practice is part of a larger social pattern.

We then examined the opening chapters from several novels. *The Disappearance*, *Animal Farm*, and a Mills and Boon novel called *Moroccan Mystery*, enumerating the conventions common to each. They then wrote the opening chapter for their title, after which they had to write a comparison of any two opening chapters saying which was the most exciting and why.

I was most impressed with the cynical way the students mimicked the 'teenage concern' style of book. They were clear and articulate critics of the kind of book English teachers and examiners had deemed appropriate for them, and made up stories about broken homes and alienation from school at a great rate. The black/feminist publishing house came up with a gritty realist story about a black youth getting into trouble with the law. They were most competent writing in the 'romantic' style and could reproduce the standard tropes with verve and the sort of parody that borders on irony. The following description from *Two Sweet-Hearts* in the new *Hugs and Kisses* imprint is a case in point:

> Toni slipped her feet out from underneath her pink silk covers and into a pair of pink fluffy slippers that were waiting by the bedside. She picked up her dressing gown which lay across her wicker swing . . .'

Lively, colloquial dialogue, aggravating parents and 'americanised' settings were ruthlessly churned out while the only significant generic variation, the fact that the heroine was mixed race and the boys black, was ignored in best commercial fashion, and perfectly integrated in stylistic terms: 'She looked in the mirror to find her own reflection. She saw a smooth, light-brown face with brunette-coloured hair and brown sparkling eyes.' The deliberate use of description would be praised by many an English teacher, but for me the question would be how aware the writer is of her subordination to the codes and conventions of genre and the ways her awareness might influence her manipulation of the material.

When it came to the discursive piece I was surprised that many of the students used their opening chapter to compare with a real one, chiefly showing how their own were superior. There was a real sense of thinking

366

about the ways books attract specific readers and the ways opening chapters were constructed to facilitate narrative viewpoints and communicate details about character and environment. The opening chapters were well done. Everything flowed with a very good rhythm and the right amount of depth – for example, how the attention slipped from one character to another: 'John, where are you going?' screamed Jade rushing through the cafeteria door after him. Amy lay amongst the baked beans . . .' Or: 'In the first sentence a character is mentioned, you quickly come to the conclusion that the book is based on that character.' Again, this kind of writing, besides being early training for GCSE styles, encouraged reflection and comparison of the students' own ideas against real practice. This strikes me as a fruitful application of media learning to English. It also brings the bookish content of English into students' real cultural experiences.

In many ways this could be considered pure English, but there are some interesting applications of media theory. First of all, there is the making explicit of knowledge brought to the classroom from outside, both in the analysis of front covers and opening chapters. Secondly, the use of generic knowledge and conventions, including quite specific textual analysis such as the use of flashback, and so on, was more accessible when approached from the media perspective and was actually more productive than traditional text-based analysis of, for example, poetry. Thirdly, viewing books as cultural commodities and examining their marketing and the way the book market addresses readers is a development from a more conventional 'English' approach. The unit mixed practical and analytical work and started from the assumption that the student was a 'real' reader subject to a play of cultural and economic forces, in particular those constructed by her or his experience of the school subject, English.

What surprised me, on reflection, was the fact that students had not been encouraged to look at books in this way lower down the school. Work on book jackets had tended to be for its own sake, like filling in an empty homework, or generally expressive, 'your impression of the book', not clearly directed at paying attention to a putative market or aimed at explicating the author's intention towards a particular readership. It would be a good idea to be more rigorous when doing work on book jackets lower down the school and build up to full institutional awareness of how books are marketed, paying attention, for example, to different reviews aimed at different readers rather than the ubiquitous English-lesson book review (see the BFI's *Secondary Curriculum Statement* for learning progressions in work on book covers[1]).

Equally, students should have a knowledge about reading built into an English curriculum. Who reads what kinds of books raises questions of gender and class and, reflecting on what schools are trying to achieve with the kinds of books they choose, makes explicit the cultural values of the school subject, English. Units of work lower down the school, such as the BFI/Nuffield comics and magazines work,[2] also raises the question of popular versus 'cultured' reading habits, and would be a good stepping stone towards the idea of book as commodity.

Finally, there is the question of evaluation. Obviously, the oral and written assignments outlined here were designed to meet English and

367

Literature GCSE criteria, but how would we assess the media objectives in such a unit of work? I would suggest we look for generic understanding in the ways students mobilise other texts and references. The reflexive process involved in several parts of the assignment should enable students to come to a clear understanding of the basic principles of the publishing industry. The articulation of cultural values enables students to grasp important issues in contemporary cultural politics. The procedure of analysis followed by practical work, examining opening chapters, writing one's own, then comparing the two, is a more detailed and rigorous one than commonly employed in English and this shows how skills derived from media education can positively be applied to other subject areas.

This unit of work was devised in collaboration with David Buckingham.

Notes
1. Julian Bowker (ed.), *Secondary Media Education: A Curriculum Statement*, London, BFI, 1991.
2. Tana Wollen (ed.), *Media in English*, London, BFI, 1991.

Playtime:
Learning about Media Institutions through Practical Work

Jenny Grahame

From David Buckingham (ed.), *Watching Media Learning*, Brighton, Falmer, 1990.

Introduction

Among the many conventional wisdoms underpinning the practice of media education, the claims which are most fiercely defended are often the hardest to evaluate. For example, the 'best' classroom practice has tended to be based on assumptions about the intrinsic value of active learning and of practical work as a means of understanding the processes and institutional structures of media production. These assumptions mark a transition from a text-based literary criticism approach to media study to the concept-based experiential model which now informs GCSE and TVEI courses, and they have increasingly characterised the changing shape of classroom practice, curriculum planning, and examination syllabuses.

Yet evidence of the value of hands-on experience of media production is notoriously difficult to assess. Having for many years trusted intuitively in (and argued interminably for) the importance of practical work in media education, and the need for a structured curriculum for it, I had begun to feel increasingly uncertain about how to evaluate its many outcomes, and how those outcomes were perceived and evaluated by the students themselves. When I undertook a piece of practical work, I knew what I wanted the students to learn, and had developed a range of strategies to ensure that they took away with them a variety of experiences and questions according to my own predetermined agenda. But I had become increasingly aware that my agenda was not necessarily synonymous with theirs; that my meticulously preplanned learning objectives were often redefined or amended according to the dynamic of the group; and that my observations and assumptions about what students had understood from the process frequently diverged from their own explicit analyses. I wanted to look at this more closely, to examine the factors that seemed to be important in shaping what and how students learned from practical work.

Like many teachers, the area of the media curriculum I had found most difficult to teach was that of media institutions. Teaching young people about the structure, ownership, and economics of media organisations had always proved a less than motivating task, viewed from both sides of the blackboard. The pedagogic problems of transmitting vast quantities of data about broadcasting legislation, patterns of power and influence, or the economic infrastructure of media production have been well documented,[1]

369

as have a range of valid and accessible ways of exploring the area through more specific, localised study.[2] Nevertheless, the complexity of the topic, and my own very limited access to information, had led me to feel more confident about teaching it through practical activities.

In undertaking some classroom research, I was seeking to discover whether students' understanding of otherwise difficult or 'boring' areas of knowledge could realistically be developed through hands-on experience of media production. I wanted to monitor the social interaction of students during the negotiation and planning stage of a practical exercise, and the ways production roles were allocated and handled, in order to identify the factors which determined both technical performance and students' abilities to draw conclusions from it. I also expected to investigate a few half-formed hypotheses based on previous observations, intuition, and gender theory – for example, how far aspects of the technology were annexed by the boys, whether girls really did take responsibility for editorial decisions and for the 'look' of the work, and how far qualities of physical co-ordination, confidence, and assertiveness contributed to effective group learning.

But somewhere along the line, my focus changed – not once, but several times. At various stages, I found myself shifting from an evaluation of simulation as a methodology to an examination of the significance of social interaction, to an analysis of gender differences, and, ultimately, to reflections on the process of students' own self-evaluation. These changes underline the significant problems involved in monitoring, evaluating, and drawing meaningful conclusions from practical work, particularly where technology adds an extra dimension to the complex dynamic of group interaction. In fact, these are precisely the issues faced by any media studies teacher attempting to evaluate students' practical work. They highlight both the contradictions and limitations of assessment practices, and the understandable problems experienced by students in evaluating their own work. In this respect, my account confirms the very real anxieties about evaluation voiced continually at all levels of media education and most frequently at GCSE moderation meetings. Ultimately, it will argue for more flexible and student-centred criteria, and for a broader redefinition of exactly what it is we are trying to assess.

The *Playtime* Simulation

[*Playtime* is a simulation which involves the production of a preschool children's television programme along the traditional lines of *Playschool*, *You and Me*, *Rainbow*, and, latterly, *Playbus*. It was devised by Hugh Morris at the Inner London Education Authority's Television Studio Workshop which, as well as facilitating student-devised productions, offers a number of structured production simulations and activities.

Playtime includes departments for songs, stories, activities, video extracts, the programme's title sequence, and overall presentation (including number and role presenters, the appearance of the set, and any regular or visiting toy characters). The material on offer has been selected to offer a number of possible links and themes (animals, families, transport, noises, and so on) which an astute producer can exploit. In each case, the departments' decisions are affected not only by their own specific costs but also

370

by the requirements of other departments. Debates about appropriateness to the age group, education versus entertainment, and what makes 'good television' are thus located within 'real' industrial constraints of finance, time-scale, and editorial accountability.

As well as being responsible for the financial viability of the programme as a whole, the producer is required to judge this in relation to a projected series of ten programmes. He or she must weigh up the feasibility of over- or under-spending on this particular programme, and the implications for the rest of the series. Is it justifiable to exceed the budget for a first episode in the interest of attracting the audience, even though at the expense of later episodes, or is it wisest to play safe and stay within the budget, no matter how televisually limiting? A fall-back strategy allows the possibility of injecting extra funding for selling the series to other channels, which can be exercised by the producer at the discretion of the class teacher.

Playtime was designed for groups of between ten and eighteen upper secondary students, and takes a day to complete. The only advance preparation required, apart from basic familiarity with the working of the studio, is the screening of examples of preschool childrens' programmes in the classroom prior to the studio visit. The day itself falls into two distinct stages, each taking about two-and-a-half hours. In the morning students are briefed, volunteer for (or are nudged into) production departments, and plan their individual items. By lunchtime, the producer has approved or amended their selections. The rest of the day is spent in production; the original departments are dissolved, a studio crew is formed, and the overall programme is rehearsed and recorded. The crew consists of three camera operators, two sound engineers, a vision mixer, floor manager, and a variable number of floor assistants, caption-changers, and general dogsbodies. Although the brief is open, most groups choose to have two on-camera presenters, who are the only non-crew personnel. Thus every student is involved in both stages of the process, and encouraged to work on a variety of takes in different groupings.]

Learning What's Been Learned

This section focuses on an all-girls group I worked with, in order to investigate the final, and most crucial, stage of a simulation: the evaluation process. My experience of conventional self-assessment strategies – diary-keeping, log-writing, group discussions, and presentation – has been that these frequently reveal more about the limitations of a simulation itself, and the social interaction of the participants, than the media learning that has taken place. Teachers have always assumed the acid test of practical work to be the extent to which it enables students to transfer their conceptual understandings to other media processes and institutions. Yet recent experience of GCSE assessment has revealed only too clearly the difficulties students face in articulating and applying their learning within the limitations of existing forms of evaluation.

In the double lesson immediately following a studio visit, the students reviewed their work far more objectively and analytically than during their initial debriefing. The first part of their discussion focused almost exclusively on the technical weaknesses of their programme, of which they were both proud and critical. Each image, camera angle, and line of dialogue was deconstructed and accounted for, initially anecdotally, but increasingly in relation to the meaning it might hold for its preschool audience.

This close scrutiny revealed two contradictory features. Firstly, it was immediately apparent that their understanding of their audience had in fact informed their programme, however flawed, and that they were very aware of the ideological nature of the material. For example, their story had been selected because it was the only item in the programme to offer multi-cultural images; yet in evaluation, they were critical because there was no girl in the narrative, and the women were represented in conventional domestic roles. Similarly, they had consciously decided against the use of a doll in the programme because they wished to avoid sexism. The songs had been chosen for the physical activity and repetition they entailed, but students were highly critical of their middle-class settings and performance. Discussion of the sequence and variety of items revealed a sophisticated understanding of the concentration span and needs of their audience, and considerable dissatisfaction with both the nature of the material on offer, and their own use of it.

At the same time, only in close analysis did students begin to realise the range of choices that had been open to them, and the opportunities they had missed. For example, their story, which was presented as a series of illustrated captions, was the most difficult of the alternatives to record, and they shot it very badly, misframing particular images, moving others, and so on; it was also far too long to hold its audience. The episodic nature of the story would have enabled them to edit it into a far tighter and more manageable unit, but this possibility did not occur to them until after the event. It was immediately clear to them how much this was a function of the institutional context: the division of labour, time-scale, and financial constraints had militated against clear thinking and forward planning.

Threading through the discussion was a sense of bringing to the surface and making explicit knowledge and understanding about television which students had not previously recognised. Analysis of their botched story led into a discussion of rostrum camera-work; an inspection of the way they had spent their budget raised questions about the economics of series production and scheduling; there were constant references to the *mise en scène* of *Wogan*, the conventions and constraints of the News, and so on. Clearly the simulation had activated a fund of experience and knowledge they already had but had never valued. The most frequent comment was, 'I sort of knew but never really thought about it like that before.'

What also began to emerge was the way in which they perceived their work to be inhibited by their interaction as a group. Although this group was much more conciliatory and co-operative than other groups, it did not always function effectively. Nevertheless, the students' loyalty to each other precluded direct criticism, just as the group's desire to maintain equilibrium in the studio worked against the coherence of their programme. This sense of shared responsibility and unwillingness to apportion blame was unique among the groups, and must in part have derived from their unusually strong sense of group identity. But the priority given to social interaction and collaboration in both oral and written evaluation is typical of many students' responses to practical media work. For many students it may be far more significant than the conceptual learning it is designed to encourage.

Following this discussion, students were asked to produce a written evaluation for the GCSE coursework folders. In comparison with the class discussion, however, these seemed to tell a rather different story. They were invariably descriptive, anecdotal, and bland. Although we had provided a carefully structured help-sheet, the majority tended to be chronological accounts detailing the minutiae of the production process, involving interminable lists of who did what, what the choices were, and what the end result looked like. This was entirely compatible with all my previous experience of log-writing, which I have always found a profoundly disappointing exercise. Several students ignored our guidelines altogether, and all bar the two most able girls omitted the more difficult questions about what they felt they had learnt from the process. None of them reflected the excitement, intensity, and pleasure of the experience; nor, for the purpose of assessment, did they offer much explicit evidence of how their understanding of media institutions had developed during the simulation. In the main they focused squarely on the limitations of their own product, but far less analytically than in discussion.

However, a few students did attempt to identify what they thought the experience had taught them. In the hands of a more academically able student, the account reads like this:

> My experience of producing *Playtime* taught me a lot about the television industry. I never realised how much work went on behind the scenes, how much preparation and time was spent on the programme before the actual filming. I also never realised so many people, departments and money were involved in just one programme. The fact that more time was spent on preparing the programme than the actual filming shocked me, I think now the filming is quite easy and quicker. I think it's a shame that the presenters are so well praised and looked up to for the job they do and that no attention is directed towards the people behind the scenes as they do a very hard and important job. [Sharon]

On one level, these are fairly mundane insights, but they do indicate a genuine sense of demystification directly related to Sharon's personal investment in the experience: she had been responsible for the choice of story, and, as camera operator, for recording it – perhaps the weakest part of the programme. Although throughout her log she attempts to predict how the programme might have looked without constraints of finance and time, her focus is strictly on the parameters of her own experience. When she attempts to make more general points, her writing sounds like common-sense knowledge rather than the analysis she was able to apply to other forms of television in group discussion:

> From my experience any TV programme is affected by having to produce within a very tight budget because their choices are limited

373

in each department, with more money you could improve the set, have better standard videos, more enjoyable songs, cartooned stories etc. On the whole have a much better standard of programme, but the reasons why programmes are strictly organised is so that the series has been fairly put together, it could be stupid to spend a lot of money on one programme leaving only a small amount for the following. So with these strict rules each programme is equally produced.

In fact, this rather laboured and generalised comment implies considerable understanding not only of the constraints imposed on the genre, but also of the economics of series production; what is missing is an ability to reference other examples, to make broader comparisons, and to raise questions about how and why the industry works in this way. But is not that ability an awful lot to expect from a 15-year-old, no matter how able? How many teachers could articulate more clearly their understanding of a complex and inaccessible system of power relationships and industrial practices from the basis of a simulated experience?

The following extract from Ann's log seems to epitomise the difficulties many students experience in trying to meet the agenda we as teachers set for them. Ann was the presenter who carried the show and improvised through the various disasters. A band three student, described as academically weak, she was a lively and committed participant throughout the production process, quick to improvise, and intuitively responsive to the needs of her audience. Her contributions to the group follow-up discussion were bright, funny, and intelligent. But committing her experiences to writing resulted in work like this:

> [The producer] had made decisions that I disagreed with because she said that I should use paint which I would like to use colour pencil. She should had made a decision on useng the toys and showing it to. The Producer role is important to the programme makers because if there was no producer everyone will not know what to do and will be uncontroled and confused. . . . The decision were not made sensibly they just happened. There was a lot of teamwork help in this programme. . . . The professionals only stick to one job because if they swop around something can go wrong so they need to know who made that thing to go wrong to make things right.

Ann's writing suggests a struggle to make sense of her own experience and articulate it in a form with which she is not at ease. She wants to make connections between what actually happened and what she thinks we want her to have learned; but she is doubly handicapped both by her limited writing skills and by the limitations of her own intensely felt experience. We can read her learning from between the lines, but not on the page itself.

In some ways, the evaluative skills we expect in log-writing are not dissimilar from those required in a conventional 'A' level English Literature essay, a form which many teachers have found deeply unsatisfying in itself. The field may be different, but the skills are not: 'objective' deconstruction balanced against personal response; a body of conceptual knowledge about how language works, whether literary or televisual; and the articulation of personal experience, whether of reading or production, into an acceptable framework in appropriate language whose parameters are defined according to criteria far removed from those of the students. Add to this the extra dimensions of writing in literary mode about experiences which are essentially audiovisual, and the influences of the group dynamic on what is learned, together with the informational and technical aspects of knowledge about media institutions and processes, and it is hardly surprising that students' work so rarely meets our expectations. Reading these laboured accounts of *Playtime* has confirmed my view of the inadequacy of written self-evaluation, whether as a means of assessing what students have learned or of helping them to identify and articulate their own learning. There has to be a better way.

An Alternative Production

In addition to the written log, we designed a follow-up task which   20
attempted to gauge how far students were able to apply the institutional understandings they might have gained from *Playtime*. This involved devising a proposal for a Channel Four preschool programme, without financial constraints. The submission was to include a detailed outline, a title sequence, a storyboard for an opening sequence, and rough costings, together with a detailed rationale. By deliberately reducing the importance of the financial element, and by prioritising the question of audience needs, we hoped students would produce very different types of programme, and that they would then be able to reflect on these differences and on the institutional factors which gave rise to them.

Furthermore, we wanted to offer students the opportunity to develop   21
their ideas creatively, to draw on their own cultural experiences and identities, and to set their own agendas for preschool learning. We had been unhappy about the white middle-class bias of *Playtime*: while it was necessary for the purposes of the simulation, we were concerned that it might have reinforced rather than challenged dominant conventions and representations. We were therefore relieved when students actively took up these issues in their discussion and began to articulate critical notions of representation, rather than simply resentment.

The writing which the students delivered was of a very different order   22
from that of their logs. It was unequivocally subjective, full of anecdote and personal reminiscence:

> For starters I remember when I was a child, I enjoyed making things like paper airoplanes, plastersine models, etc. These are fun to do and also teach the child how to use their hands. . . . I enjoyed creativity. I like creating my *own* things. Paper collarges with different substances such as milk bottle tops, feathers, different coloured paper is a creative activity so I'd include that. [Sharon]

This informal, direct mode of address was evident in most of the students' work. It was obviously an assignment perceived on one level to be much closer to autobiographical writing, and therefore less threatening; but it was also clearly much more pleasurable as a task.

In addition, the writing invariably demonstrated a meticulous sensitivity to the concerns and educational needs of their target audience. Among the topics mentioned were items about the arrival of a new baby, a whole range of lively strategies to develop an understanding of road safety, and (surprisingly frequency) activities designed to promote books rather than simply to develop reading skills. Notions of 'everyday life' recurred throughout the work – in pointed opposition to what students perceived to be an unrepresentative view of the world constructed by adults for children in existing programmes. Furthermore, everyday life, for several students, was far from the world of leaping penguins and 'Alex and Roy' games represented in *Playtime*:

> So for my programme I would like a story to do with a child going out to different places. I'd like the story to describe the surroundings of the child, the busy roads, the big buildings, the people they see, etc. And for the video, the dangers of their surroundings. I think the video should show the dangers of children straying from their mothers, the dangers of the roads, the dangers of children going off with strangers . . . a child so young and innocent and I feel that is vital it knows the dangers around it. [Sylvia]

Here Sylvia may be voicing her own adolescent anxieties and privileging her preconceptions about children's vulnerability over her sense of appropriate content. But these sorts of issues emerged throughout the students' work, indicating a very different agenda from the one determined for them in *Playtime*.

Despite a completely free hand in terms of programme content and structure, most students' work remained fairly close to the magazine format of *Playtime*, but significantly made it their own. Most felt that a combination of short, varied items would be most appropriate for preschool children's concentration span, but then constructed elaborate and often innovative variations around it. This was the point at which they began actively to make use of what they had learned from the *Playtime* experience, for students almost invariably emphasised the importance of a theme to each programme – a direct reflection on their own problems in achieving this in the studio:

> For example if one week they were doing something on farms, there will be a story read which would relate to farms, there would be videos shown of children who live on farms talking about what they do and what it's like on the farm. The people reading the stories would dress up in a costume that would go with the theme like dressing as a farmer, a stereotype of a farmer with straw and hay sticking all over them, something that would keep the children watching amused. [Adeswa]

Adeswa's work relates to a further issue raised in their own experience with *Playtime*, that of the identity of the programme's presenter. Her projected programme was a theme in itself: aimed at 4- to 6-year-olds 'who are showing signs of intelligence and like to read. . . . It would educate them and show them how to pronounce words and read sentences also a little about pronunciation so that they would understand a little about why they have to use it.' But her *pièce de résistance* is:

A funny little assistant called Bookworm. The programme will include a book club where the children can write in and obtain books at a reasonable price, and a story session. . . . The story will be short because it will be read again with the words coming up on the screen. Bookworm will go underneath each sentence pronouncing the words for the children and encouraging them to repeat. At the end the Bookworm will ask the presenter questions and the presenter will answer them.

Her work is lavishly illustrated with full-colour pictures of Billy the Bookworm.

While other students were less earnestly educational there was a range of genuinely inventive presentation ideas. Several opted for animated characters or puppets, including Sylvia, one of the *Playtime* presenters, who invented Freda the Space Alien glove puppet, 'who'd look all green and fluffy but very lovable. The person operating this puppet should sound gentle and happy. I'd like my programme to be called *Stop, Look and Listen to Freda*.' This implied connection between the programme's identity and the persona of its presenter relates directly to their experience of *Playtime*, where they had rejected the use of the toys on offer, mainly on grounds of gender and ethnicity. Interestingly, few of the presenters suggested here were human, and most were more or less androgynous, apart from their names.

Two further features reflected students' awareness of TV as an institution. In the rationales submitted with their proposals, many students argued coherently for appropriate budgets for their series, adjusting these according to the technical sophistication of the programmes. This was the section of the assignment which was not always completed; it seemed to indicate how far students felt confident with the concept of institution, and predictably students such as Ann, who had enormous difficulty expressing her ideas coherently, omitted this part of the work.

The second indicator was the detail with which students conceived and visualised their work. Although not all students produced a storyboard, in almost every case the 'look' of the programme, its *mise en scène*, and the sorts of conventions it would observe were recorded lovingly in minute detail. Many students included colour illustrations of presenters, logos, titles, and floor plans. Adeswa's work included a convincing representation of the presenter (a black woman) sitting in the studio surrounded by cameras, monitors, and microphones, to illustrate the effect of Billy the Bookworm's subtitles. This work suggested not only a sophisticated understanding of television conventions and industrial practices, but also a clear development from the random and unvisual way in which they had approached the production of their own programme. To this extent, *Playtime* seemed to have transformed the ways in which they thought about the construction of television.

What might we conclude from these different attempts at evaluation? Of all three approaches, the formal log-writing exercise seemed the most problematic, for reasons outlined above. The *Playtime* simulation, and much other production work, is often most valued by students for its difference from other kinds of learning, its connections with the real world of professional broadcasting, however tenuous, and the opportunities it offers for both individual responsibility and collaborative enterprise. It is also conducted outside the normal context of school, its pips and lesson-changes, and its conventional classroom hierarchy. Yet the form of log-writing which is required for examination purposes cuts across these differences: it brings it all back into school, into a conventionally teacher-directed context, where personal experience is ultimately secondary to a series of predetermined learning objectives. This may devalue what for students was a genuinely radical learning experience and, judging by the evidence of students' logs, it almost certainly defuses the excitement and pleasure of the experience.

This may account for the curiously flat and impersonal tone of many students' logs, which in my previous experience is characteristic of formal self-assessment. It may also account for the enormous differences between the responses made in informal group discussion and those which surfaced in the *Playtime* logs. Perhaps this illustrates a mismatch between what students themselves perceived as appropriate language for examination assessment, and what they saw as classroom 'chat'. Certainly the interpersonal dynamic, which they identified in their discussion as one of the most significant areas of learning, was not adequately reflected in their writing; their perceptions of the nature of exam assessment may have discouraged them from explicit comment which might have reflected unfavourably on other members of the group.

The kinds of learning demonstrated in the more open-ended follow-up task seem to offer a far more positive approach to evaluation. The task enabled students to move outside the economic and ideological constraints of the original simulation. They were able to set their own agenda and to build upon their extensive and active experience as an audience, an aim which is frequently voiced by media teachers, but rarely fully addressed in practice. By offering a range of forms (storyboards, scripts, visual aids, as well as descriptive and transactional writing) it offered a wider range of opportunities for students whose skills are not conventionally literary. It made space for oppositional or innovative practices without actively penalising those who feel safer in replicating conventional modes.

What this sort of task does not entail is an explicit account of the production process or an abstract definition of the concept of institution. Yet, as previously noted, these may be aims which are ultimately unrealistic and even counter-productive. So why do we routinely demand them – and demand them in a written form which experience has proved to be inhibiting, unrewarding, and undermining for many students?

One major function of 'objective' written evaluation is to enable us as

teachers or examiners to identify the contributions of individual participants, and on this level it is a potentially useful recording strategy. Yet
there is also a sense in which we demand it because we need evidence to
justify practical work in traditional academic terms – and perhaps also
because we are insecure about what students might be learning from it.
However open-ended the project, we seem to need strategies which bring
academic knowledge back to us in a safe and acceptable form, but by
insisting that students must locate their individual accounts within a predetermined 'objective' framework, we may be putting several important learning outcomes at risk. It may be that only by allowing students to write
freely and subjectively about their own personal perceptions of the production process can we begin to reconcile *our* notions of appropriate learning with what *they* perceive as important to them. Perhaps it is at this
interface between 'our' theory and 'their' practice that a new agenda for
media education may be constructed.

Conclusion
Despite carefully structured learning objectives, there were tensions
inherent in the *Playtime* simulation which are typical of much practical
work in media education. We were requiring students to work within
tight institutional constraints, in unfamiliar working relationships, with
intimidating technology. At the same time, we sought creative or innovat-
ory responses to the brief which were incompatible with the hierarchical
division of labour we had imposed. In effect, we had three distinct aims:
to develop students' technical and production skills; to offer them the
experience of working within institutional constraints; and to generate creative programme-making which questioned existing practices. While all of
these were touched upon during the simulation, it became clear that these
aims were both too demanding and potentially contradictory.

The evidence of *Playtime* suggests that, however structured a framework,
the physical intensity of production work militates against explicit reference
to 'theory', and that previous analytical work may not simply transfer into
practice. On the other hand, the students' final evaluations and follow-up
work offer clearer evidence of a movement in the opposite direction, from
practice to theory. What *Playtime* and other media simulations tend to lack
are opportunities for reflection during the process itself. This might have
been aided, for example, by introducing interim production meetings at
various points to create space for reflection, for judicious teacher intervention, and for conscious consideration of their working practices, both
in terms of the 'institutional' questions and in terms of the group dynamic.
Relatively small organisational strategies would thus serve to contextualise
the production experience for students and offer them a clearer sense of
the purpose of the exercise, as well as enabling us as teachers to monitor
more effectively what is actually being learned. We cannot assume that this
sort of learning happens by osmosis; we need to actively construct the
conditions and practices which will make it explicit for students.

Clearly, for many students, the most memorable and valuable aspects of
the production process were to do with the experience of collaborative
group work.[3] Yet this aspect of production work has never been fully

acknowledged by media studies theorists, and is explicitly omitted from assessment practices, which are geared towards evaluation of the individual rather than the group. It is as if this crucial aspect of students' learning is considered part of another order of knowledge, subject to other criteria, unrelated to the conceptual framework of the syllabus. Yet the potential learning outcomes of practical work are multiple and diverse: we need to devise strategies which will enable both teachers and students to evaluate these, without reducing them to a set of abstract skills or understandings.

I would like to thank Eddie Lobo for his collaboration on this research.

Notes
1. For example, Len Masterman, *Teaching the Media*, London, Comedia, 1985.
2. For example, Gill Branston, *Teaching Media Institutions*, BFI Advisory Document, London, BFI, 1987; Manuel Alvarado, Robin Gutch and Tana Wollen, *Learning the Media*, London, Macmillan, 1987.
3. Interestingly, advocates of practical work within a broader media education approach have long recognised the importance of collaborative learning in terms not only of language, communication, and social skills, but also of subject-specific skills: see C. Lorac and M. Weiss, *Communications and Social Skills*, London, Wheaton, 1981.

Tackling the Tabloids

Angela Devas

I work in an inner-city college with a large cultural and racial mix, which   1
brings an exciting variety of students into the classroom. I am a white
teacher with many Afro-Caribbean and Asian students, along with others
from very diverse backgrounds. Many of them retake GCSEs, but for most
16-year-olds GCSE Media Studies is a new subject; they come with a very
open-ended set of expectations, without any sense of having 'failed' this
particular subject. This provides a freshness and appeal which I feel it is
important to maintain and build on.

Teaching media studies necessarily entails the teacher in selecting appro-   2
priate areas of study from an extensive field, and though tackling the
press as one of the central media institutions is important, my previous
experience of teaching it as an industry had left me feeling that the students
had remained uninspired, and without any real grasp as to the object of
the exercise. I had also not previously confronted teaching the tabloids,
but some of the students did read them, and for some it was a source of
news, presenting a certain shape and understanding of the world which I
did not feel I could continue to ignore. I was aware that many of the
students thought that the tabloids offered racist and sexist representations,
but did not think it would be useful to launch into an attack on a particular
newspaper, or to denigrate any of the students or their family or friends
who might read the tabloids. Nor did I in any way want to deny those
students the pleasure of reading about something in which they took an
interest.

The teenagers I have taught did not initially display much enthusiasm   3
for any kinds of newspapers, or newspaper reading. From initial surveys
conducted in class it generally emerged that most of them read whatever
newspaper it was that their parents had lying around the house; virtually
none would have bought one of their own accord. When they do read them
it is very much the 'soft' items that gain their attention: the TV listings,
the horoscope, or the more gossip-oriented pages. There were several things
here which I wanted to tackle but I limited my aims (*a*) to encourage some
sense of critical analysis and understanding of what they might see and
read in the tabloids; (*b*) to give them an idea of the content base of certain
popular newspapers, looking at what may or may not constitute news; (*c*)
introducing the idea of newspapers trying to reach a specific audience. The
stumbling block was to find an appropriate way to gain and maintain their
interest in what was for them a rather dry and dull area of the syllabus.

Knowing what I wanted to teach did not solve this problem. Thinking   4 about the GCSE Media Studies syllabus, I was aware that some parts could claim to be more 'fun' orientated than others; pop music is one area which teachers anticipate will interest their pupils, while the structure of the press industry cannot claim the same glamour. I assumed it would be relatively easy for teenagers to build on the knowledge they already had about who controls what in the pop music world, how to make a hit record, how a band puts its image together, and so on. This part of the syllabus is particularly accessible to the students, and I have received a great deal of pleasure myself in learning from them about particular bands, radio stations, DJs, music programmes, and so on. In addition, the students I teach at GCSE, unlike the older ones, are not yet aware that the purpose of a youth subculture is to keep adults in the dark, and are therefore happy to share information and trade pop gossip as part of a classroom exercise. There was clearly a contrast between the excitement and enthusiasm that this part of the syllabus generated, and the rather dry and pedantic way I had been teaching the newspaper industry, and indeed newspapers themselves. I therefore decided to try and link together these two areas: the institutions of the press and the pop music industry, and so make the press seem relevant and challenging.

Previously, I had used different parts of the *Wham! Wrapping*[1] pack for teaching different aspects of the pop music industry, such as image analysis (record sleeves), textual analysis (Wham! videos), and industry (the construction of a particular pop group). For my current purposes, I decided to tackle work on the tabloids using the part of the pack devoted to the newspaper industry, seeing if we could move on from the purely pop specifics to a fourth aim, which was to encourage a more generalised understanding of the workings of the tabloid press in terms of two of my aims listed above – news values and targeted readership.

I decided to concentrate on two tabloids, the *Daily Mirror* and the *Sun*, as these are both specifically aimed at the youth market, and I also felt the comparison of two newspapers would be more straightforward than attempting to include too many. I contemplated having a general discussion at first about which students read the *Sun* and the *Daily Mirror* but felt that this might aggravate the very kinds of problems I wanted to avoid – although stimulating and useful discussions can arise spontaneously in the classroom these should never degenerate into a finger-pointing slanging-match (in one discussion, for example, my own censorship of the tabloids, exhibited by my not giving them the whole newspaper, was thrown back at me by certain students, while others defended the right to have laws that suppressed racist and sexist material). When spontaneous discussions bubbled up during the project, and to avoid a situation where the students just talked at each other, or worse, I appointed a chair whose job it was to sit in front of the class and encourage their fellow students to make points one at a time. At the end of these discussions, I insisted on a written summing up of the different points that were made, even though no particular conclusions may have been reached. Later, this material was usefully incorporated into their written assignments.

I started the project by putting the students into groups and giving each group the front page of the *Sun* or the *Daily Mirror* from the same day. I did not want to give them a copy of the complete newspaper since it would have meant the entire lesson taken up with them going through it all and not necessarily concentrating on the parts that I wanted them to look at in detail. They were asked to study the front page, looking at the major stories covered there which were then continued on the inside pages, and to analyse the front pages in detail, assessing how much space was given over to banner headlines and photographs. Then they compared and contrasted the different stories covered in the two papers.

The exercise was intended to give the students a general overview of how 8 the front page of a tabloid worked to catch attention and demand the reader look at it. This stage also offered an opportunity to broach the subject of news itself: did the students consider that what they were reading was in fact newsworthy? Many of the students had little interaction with 'news' as such – they avoided those parts of the paper which might be considered to have some hard news, and they rarely, if ever, watched it on television. They already realised that the news belonged to a separate category, which for most of them was not the part of the newspaper that interested them; but in the discussions over the two tabloids about what constituted news and what did not, there were considerable areas of disagreement among us all, and in the end we had to settle for a continuum. The purpose of the discussion and the worksheet was not in any case to settle for hard and fast rules, but to illustrate how difficult it was to effectively delineate the different categories of news, gossip, and entertainment.

I felt we needed more specific examples, and it was at this point that it 9 seemed appropriate to introduce students to the interesting relationship between the music industry and the press which is characterised by the blurred boundaries between news and gossip. I decided to use the *Wham! Wrapping* pack as it includes photocopied front-page tabloid coverage for the week which featured Andrew Ridgeley's nose job. Apparently, he had undergone cosmetic surgery on his nose, but a story was invented by Ridgeley's manager and was deliberately leaked to the press that he and a friend had fought in a nightclub, and the friend had broken his nose with an ice bucket. Because of Wham's massive popularity at the time this story was considered newsworthy, and the subsequent revelation of the truth took up an enormous amount of tabloid space between Tuesday 3 July and Saturday 7 July 1984. I used the worksheets in the pack, which revealed the ploy, in conjunction with the career sheet of Wham's ex-manager, Simon Napier-Bell, extracts from which revealed some very useful quotations about the power relations between the music industry and the tabloid press:

> Being notorious is more valuable than being anonymous in the music business. You may cringe at what they write, and the people around you may get hurt, but in the long run any publicity is better than no publicity,

and, 'As a manager, you must be able to manipulate the press and the other media to the benefit of the artiste.'

The students (and myself) were fascinated by the behind-the-scenes 10 shenanigans of the pop and press industries, and there was much animated discussion as to whether this sort of behaviour was morally defensible, with strong positions taken on both sides. Many of the students were immensely taken with this story of outright duplicity and gleefully reproduced it in their written work. However, whether concentrating on this particular example led them to question further the literally constructed nature of certain news items in the more 'hard' news sections of the papers was difficult to assess. They did appear to be able to spot apparently made-up quotes and press releases, but to lead from this into the nature of the news process itself proved to be conceptually quite difficult for them, partly because they could relate to the world of pop stars as being part of a world they owned in a way that did not apply to the news as a whole.

Pursuing further the notion of what does or does not constitute news, I gave the students an exercise in comparison between a story in a tabloid and a broadsheet. It proved more difficult than I expected to find stories that were covered by a broadsheet and a tabloid without having too many or two few details, and it certainly proved impossible to find ones that related to the pop world. In the end I used an article on the State Opening of Parliament. The exercise concentrated on differences in style, photographs, mode of address, and vocabulary. What I had hoped, perhaps over-ambitiously, was that this would lead on to an examination of bias in considerably more detail, but whereas the students certainly showed an awareness of differences in approach, it proved difficult to translate the concept of 'two sides to a story' to an examination of institutional bias.

I used some of the general worksheets on the tabloids in *Wham! Wrapping* to emphasise various points, such as what was omitted from a story being as important as what was included, but the work around pop did not really get them any closer to the idea of newspapers and the news constructing a particular world view for them. There seemed to be a large conceptual gap between the notion of a story having two sides, an idea the students readily assimilated, to the idea of news construction itself. They did appear to understand from these exercises, however, the relative nature of 'facts' and how they can be manipulated.

I wanted the students to explore more about agenda setting, how news was constituted and defined as news, how it could be reported, and how it finally ended up packaged in particular ways for particular newspapers. To do this I would need to follow a 'hard' news story over a period of time, using several different papers and different media. This might present difficulties at GCSE level, but I feel the students could well benefit from such an approach if it could be related to their own interests in the way that the pop music industry is; I shall certainly consider it next time.

From work on news values we moved to the notion of audience; initially, we undertook work on content analysis of the different types of stories that featured in the two major tabloids we were studying. News about pop stars spilled over from the two main pop pages into every other aspect of the newspapers, including part of the news pages themselves. We concluded that while personality stories featured very strongly in all parts of the papers, there was a special emphasis on stars who would be popular with young people, and we briefly compared this coverage in the newspapers with some selected items from *Smash Hits*, including the use of colour, headlines, coverage, and gossip. The students had already done some work on image analysis at the beginning of the course, using the BFI *Reading Pictures*[1] pack, so were able to return to this area. I also reproduced for them the table in *Wham! Wrapping* which shows the age range of the readership of the *Sun* and the *Daily Mirror*.

Finally, we moved from notions of audience to the industry itself. We examined why it should be important for the two major tabloids to woo a youth audience. We looked at the pop pages from the *Sun* and the *Daily Mirror* – 'Bizarre' and 'Sky's the Limit' – to see how they specifically set out to attract a youth audience. Students conducted surveys among themselves and their friends to ascertain whether they turned to the pop pages first when they opened a tabloid. We then compared advertisements from the two tabloids with advertisements from *Smash Hits*. The majority of the advertisements in the former, unlike *Smash Hits*, are not aimed particularly at young people; they are for goods and services, such as cars, supermarkets, home loans, holidays, and sexlines, which relatively easily break down into gender divisions and are obviously geared towards adults. We also touched on different social categories as evinced by marketing strategies, but shortage of time led to a very sketchy outline of what was a very hazy area to the students. 15

My students concluded that the advertisements were probably not the main reason why the two tabloids were keen to attract a young readership. I informed the class of the demise of the *Daily Herald* in 1964 which had a flourishing circulation but failed because it had an ageing, working-class readership with very little spending power,[3] and they appreciated the importance of establishing a young readership that would stay loyal to the paper. 16

I then gave them a simplified handout based on an article in the *Guardian*[4] about ownership and control of the press, in so far as it related to the activities of Rupert Murdoch and Robert Maxwell, and especially looking at the cross-media ownership of Murdoch's satellite and press empire. The introduction of such formal, institutional information at this stage placed it within a context that made it more comprehensible and relevant. Even so, it was still rather a jump for the students, who do not necessarily have the economic and political background knowledge that would help them process this. However, they did gain some understanding of the institutional powers and restrictions that govern the press in Britain. Some of the students from other countries, in particular one from Pakistan and another from Iran, were very quick to pick up on the idea of press censorship and were disappointed at its existence in the supposedly free press of Britain. Other students emerged with a much more questioning attitude about what they thought the press should be like. 17

Unfortunately, I did not allow enough time to let the students devise their own ideas of how to build and maintain a free press, but later on, in a debate about the broadcasting system, they came up with some very compelling arguments for and against having ethnic minority channels on British TV (some arguing that it would ghettoise certain groups, others saying that it would give a voice to those who were not normally seen or 18 heard on television). Many argued from a personal point of view that, while everyone had to pay the licence fee, there were no programmes in their own languages for those who had family members who could not speak English. Others argued that this would mean too many programmes in too many languages. In future I would allow time for a similar sort of debate about the press at the end of a project.

Various assignments emerged from this whole exercise on the press: comparisons between the front pages of two tabloids and between two articles dealing with the same subject in a tabloid and broadsheet. The students also wrote a press release about a band of their own choosing, and then turned this into an article suitable for publication in the pop pages of the tabloids. (This latter exercise proved much more difficult than any of us had anticipated, and gave me a new respect for tabloid journalists!)

They also had to write up a staged classroom incident (two students fighting) in a limited number of words and from various points of view: that of the students concerned, the teacher's, and a 'neutral' observer's. They also had to suggest reasons as to who or what would have to be involved in order to make the incident newsworthy enough to merit coverage in tabloid or broadsheet or both. The students wrote essays on the role of the tabloids in the newspaper industry, and there were some generally clear and competent overviews of the press, drawing on material they had covered in class as well as coming up with their own examples.

An enormous amount of work was crammed into this six-week period, but I felt satisfied that I had at least managed to approach the subject of the news and the newspaper industry in a way that would not intimidate the students, and had also demonstrated the symbiotic relationship between the press and the music industry as powerful media industries. The project also threw up questions for me that remain unanswered, particularly around the role of the tabloids and newspaper-reading in general among young people. Both the *Independent* and the *Guardian* have reported a drop in tabloid sales,[5] and suggest a plethora of reasons why this might have happened. My own small amount of work with the students showed that they were not particularly concerned with reading newspapers, and certainly did not interact with them in the way they did with television. There were areas I felt I had not covered in this particular project – there had been little room to cover representation, for example, but then again I taught this as a separate area, looking at different representations of Australia in *Neighbours* and *Crocodile Dundee*.

Making links across the syllabus, as well as including a variety of media texts in the limited time available, is one of the challenges of GCSE Media Studies. Time will inevitably continue to act as a restraint on how much can be covered, but I did feel that the students ended up with a greater awareness than they had at the beginning of the course of how the tabloids construct news for a particular readership, and, because of the approach through pop music in particular, that the whole area of the syllabus was rendered more appealing and enjoyable for them.

Notes

1. Lilie Ferrari and Christine James, *Wham! Wrapping: Teaching the Music Industry*, London, BFI, 1989.
2. *Reading Pictures*, London, BFI, 1981.
3. See James Curran and Jean Seaton, *Power Without Responsibility: The Press and Broadcasting in Britain* (3rd edn), London, Routledge, 1988.
4. *Guardian*, 12 June 1989.
5. *Independent*, 17 April 1991; *Guardian*, 1 July 1991.

PART IVB
In-service Training

In-service Training
Introduction

It is interesting to note that this second section exists because advisory teachers and initial training providers have responded to individual subject specialists who want to incorporate media education in their classroom practice. The INSET context provides a valuable site for exploration of thematic issues which weave, as in the case of geography, across areas of a subject often unconnected and separately taught. Exploring the symbolic referential aspects of subject specialisms through media education approaches clearly catalysed curriculum developments in these three accounts.

In 'Mapping the Media', Gill Branston identifies a wide range of media artefacts and materials which can be related to the particular concerns of geographical enquiry. Through collaboration, teachers developed ideas around the notion of 'mapping' personal and cultural identity. Other subject specialists could also deal with representations of people, places, and events through a media education approach.

Jan Mulreany, in 'A Positive Sense of Self', relates the experience of working with teachers to produce units of work for personal and social education. In the training sessions teachers used official health education media materials to explore the values and attitudes contained within them. Media education approaches were employed alongside group evaluation techniques (personal and social education) to investigate individual and group attitudes brought out during the exercise.

Steve Brennan describes in 'Signs and Symbols' the links made with media education by a group of specialists convened to explore common areas of understanding under a performing arts umbrella. He identifies what media education might contribute to drama and music, but at the same time argues that differences in the forms and conventions between the media have to be recognised. The account offers an important starting-point for exploring the relationship of theatrical melodrama to film and television genres and vice versa.

Mapping the Media

Gill Branston

In November 1989 part of a conference of teachers involved in media   1
education in Wales was devoted to discussing 'Images of Wales'. Emerging
from this session was a sense that it might be possible to organise work
around the concept of 'mapping' for both geography and media studies in
schools and colleges.

In their sections on geography, the BFI Primary and Secondary docu-   2
ments[1] summarise much current work that can be applied well above primary
and even secondary level. Materials which can be drawn on include stamps,
weather forecasts, food packaging, charity images of the Third World,
tourist advertisements, holiday programmes, and soaps, which often construct a very particular sense of places which also exist in the real world,
whether Dallas, Australia, or the East End. *Neighbours*, for instance, represents Australia in a particular way (suburban and nearly all white, for
starters) with some very striking exclusions (class conflict, Aborigines, bad
weather, cane toads). It is interesting to begin to make sense of these as partly
determined by the needs and constraints of soaps, even as we try to hold on
to a sense of how inadequately they map important realities of Australia.

Turning to news forms, it can be fascinating to watch them for a week   3
with an eye to where foreign correspondents are located[2] and to observe
how this determines the duration and prominence of stories – and our sense
of where the world's hot spots, or 'important' places are. A big royal visit,
for instance, will have reporters and satellite link-ups in place for days
beforehand, producing 'stories' about their own presence there as build-up
to the tour. Because the Queen's visit to the USA a few years ago coincided
with exceptional weather, we had expensive satellite stories giving us drop-
by-drop accounts of the gales, even though bigger stories were thereby
squeezed out of the bulletins. How are these links decided on? Why are
some spots deemed 'newsworthy' and therefore have expensive teams sent
out to them? How do news agencies trade news around the world? How
does that trade[3] tend to produce its own key 'trade routes' across the world's
million-fold happenings in a 12- or 24-hour span? Can students map the
coverage provided by satellite news, for example, and see which parts of
the globe are thereby rendered familiar (sometimes more familiar than
nearby parts of it) and which are made strange or exotic?

At the Welsh conference we became interested in one of the key concepts   4
of geography mapping. One way of opening up an often enclosed and defensive sense of Welshness in some students is to get them to draw maps of

where they have come from. Such mapped journeys, whether they involve other parts of the world or the next village, could then include images, of how the places along the way have been imaged by the media, whether these be Birmingham or Bangladesh. Or (and this idea works interestingly for a region or nation, like Wales, which is strongly represented by tourist image) students might be given a blank outline map of the area and five minutes in which to draw appropriate images of its various areas.

For Wales, such a quick exercise often produces male industrial workers in the south, sheep in the middle, and assorted daffs, leeks, and mountains elsewhere. The group can then discuss where these images come from, and how they become routinely used and emphasised. Students in rural areas, for instance, often have internalised imaginative maps which suggest that rural equals innocent, natural. This may be even though they have relatives who know quite well that tractor deaths are one of the commonest kinds of industrial accident; that Welsh farming should be understood as an outpost of the multinational chemical industries, as 'agribusiness'; or that 'batteries' (rather than 'flocks') might be a more adequate term for sheep and cows as well as hens. Here media studies (in its full sense, claiming language as a king of mediation of the world) can really open up discussion within geography. Students may go on to investigate, for Wales and many other regions, the ways that tourist or historical-heritage images are often in a kind of tension or even struggle with 'enterprise zone' imagery offered elsewhere in the media.

In relation to Wales there has been a determined effort by the Welsh Tourist Board in the last few years to swing around the image of the principality from one associated predominantly with greyness or blackness to one embodying a greener Wales. We discussed how that 'black' image, while corresponding to the historical reality of parts of the coal and heavy industries of South Wales, might also persist because of the numbers of black-and-white 30s and 40s documentary films and photographs of the region which, recirculating in the present, certainly seem to be part of an overall imaginative sense of Wales held especially strongly by those living outside it. It was, incidentally, very easy to obtain Welsh Tourist Board and Welsh Development Agency materials with which to study these shifts and attempted shifts in image. Often, too, it can be an eye-opener to overlay transparency maps of different realities, such as the preponderance of women part-time workers in areas which are often imagined as being full of male hard-hat industrial workers.

Such work might enable the concept of 'mapping' to be developed in relation to broader meanings. Having seen how maps work in geography, some classes might explore how we routinely 'grid for meaning' in books, films, TV, and advertisements. Just as the grid reference which combines 'G' with '6' will enable you to find the road you want on a map, we bring familiar 'grid references' to cultural products, otherwise we could make no sense of them. We 'grid for meaning' along the intersecting lines of our knowledge of speaker, context, genre, and so on. A film like *Witness* produces certain surprises if read as a detective thriller (the switch to a rural setting; the romantic rather than street-sexy love element; the resolution to conflict by community rather than lone, armed action) and quite other surprises, and familiarities, if read according to the reminders of a Western it holds out to experienced viewers (the echoes of *Shane*; the 'schoolmarm/saloon girl elements in the representations of the two women; the use of an agricultural rather than heroic rural landscape, and so on).

Both maps and media products can be explored as representations, as accounts of the world. Maps do not just miniaturise space in their representations, they also employ elaborate codes *of* representation.[4] We learn to read maps just as we learn to read media products, and often the codes with which we have grown so familiar bear very little relation to the local experiences and needs of those being 'mapped' by both. Different maps of an area will embody very different purposes and histories, just like media products. The familiar Ordnance Survey maps actually originated in the Napoleonic Wars and at first covered only the South Coast of England, for military ('ordnance') purposes. The medieval Mappa Mundi put Jerusalem at the centre of the world, and Britain at the edge, for religious purposes. When Ireland was mapped by British troops in 1824 'ancient boundaries were not always left undisturbed and place names were Anglicised, either directly or more subtly in an attempt to arrive at spellings that looked acceptable to an English eye',[5] as had already happened with seventeenth-century maps of North America in relation to American Indian names. (A parallel study of the Western would be tempting here.) The very familiar Mercator projection maps were made in 1569 for trading purposes, to enable all compass points to be drawn straight, and thereby excluded the sense of scale with which the Peters projection shifts our sense of a world centring on Europe.[6]

Of course, such maps are not only *like* the ones produced by the media (organising, miniaturising experience to us), they also often *make up* media products, such as TV news. What kinds of maps get used in TV news programmes? (And in weather forecasts, for that matter, where the cheery national identity confirmed by a map that never gets localised is perhaps an important part of the news.)

How do the very names used for certain places produce a sense of our place in the world? Much has been said of recent years about 'the Middle East' but the name rarely receives critical examination. Why is it used? What are Iraq and Saudi Arabia in the middle of? Where are they east of? Like other concepts – 'Down Under' or 'the West Indies' or even 'the Home Counties' (whose Home?) – these are usually accepted as given. (Even stranger new maps are produced when a newsreader describes Japanese people fleeing over the Kuwait border as the first *Westerners* to escape.)

Carol Mathews[7] suggests that these taken-for-granted centres can be shifted by, for instance, getting students to produce their own Pacific-centred maps by cutting and pasting, tracing, or free-hand drawing. Suddenly North America appears in the same global space as the 'Far East', and Russia suddenly *looks* as close to the USA as parts of it really are. Similarly, students can consider the way the term 'problems' is one that implies that the 'First World' has no such dilemmas, or is not causally linked to Third World problems.[8] Does the very word 'famine' used of food crises similarly reproduce a sense, a map of such events as Biblical, as

Hollywood epic, existing outside modern history and means of regulation?[9]

Clearly, though these re-orderings can give a much fuller, more adequate understanding of the exclusions and personalities of both news and cartography, such work does not make one kind of map a 'lie' and another 'true' but should help students understand the representational nature of both maps and media products, each of which can be more or less adequate for particular purposes. 12

TV, like cartography, can never produce one complete and objective image of any subject because it, too, produces different representations, with different exclusions, emphases, codes, depending on which specific purposes are being pursued. While horror films will often map fears about the body and its limits, science fiction will take the whole universe as its terrain. Detective thrillers often work to suggest one map of meaning (the maid was guilty) and then remaps the contours of events at the end of the story (so we feel 'Why didn't I spot it was the butler all along?'). 13

One of the media equivalents of re-ordering the centrings of geographical maps would be work rearranging the shapes and emphases which different narratives impose on their material. What kind of film would *Psycho* be, for example, if it were re-ordered so as to be told chronologically, beginning with young Norman Bates's childhood, and giving access to the mother's character and story? What other kinds of questions would such a 'psychological case study' (rather than horror film) involve? How would they organise our pleasures as audiences? What kinds of pleasures would they be if we knew 'who did it'? Would that process be anything like the remapping of the globe to put Africa or Antarctica at the centre? 14

Just as some maps work best when *least* realistic or 'lifelike' (think of how the London Underground map distorts the relationship of the places it names compared with an 'overground' map of London), so some media representations of certain realities will work best as fantasy or deliberate exaggeration. We inhabit a world where millions of pounds can be transferred millions of miles from one Stock Exchange or bank account to another, all in a matter of seconds. It is also a world where countries with nuclear weapons are no longer only connected at their borders with their neighbours. As Bunge wrote a few years ago: 15

> The Russians are not 'ninety miles off our shores', they are literally 'up there', and we from them, since we occupy each other's heavens and can mutually destroy to the depth of 500 feet anything on each other's surface. Political maps have not even attempted to show this fact.[10]

Maybe living on such a globe we need new imaginative as well as geographical maps to situate ourselves in that world, perhaps the kinds of 'maps' provided in science-fiction, or fantasy, or photomontage?[11]

The term 'mapping' while referring to a geographical image might help us hold on to the feeling that there is, figured in most representations, a knowable reality getting mapped in different ways, for different purposes, and that the uses of these maps depends partly on where the user is, and where he or she want to go. Some areas, of course, have remained for a long time 'off the map'. 16

Of course, some maps or TV programmes are more fun than others, and we may prefer them for certain purposes, like cheering ourselves up, or relaxing. But though, for instance, fun tourist maps look as though they just record a place neutrally, if jokily, they actually help to produce a new reality in that place, traffic flow, attitude to work, to the past and present. Maybe the term 'mapping' could help students to connect emphases, exclusions, 'griddings' in the media which help or prevent us from situating ourselves in relation to the world so as to be able to change it. If both areas of work converged, they might develop our sense that what gets represented is a place where we all have to live.

Notes

1. Available from BFI Publications.
2. See *Watching the World*, teaching packs from Manchester Development Education Project, Manchester Polytechnic, 801 Wilmslow Road, Manchester M20 8RG.
3. *Watching the World* is also a good source of material on the activities of news agencies.
4. See Merryn Hutchings, 'Maps', in *Primary Teaching Studies*, January 1989, for an interesting account of primary school children's difficulties in grasping the codes of overhead perspective mapping.
5. From Mary Hamer, 'Putting Ireland on the Map', in *Textual Practice*, vol. 3, no. 2, Summer 1989.
6. The *Peters Atlas of the World* is the first atlas to show each country in its true size in relation to the rest of the world. It is thus based on the principle of the equality of scale and area. It was published by Longman in 1989.
7. See Caroline Mathews (Brentside Middle School, Ealing), 'When East is West', *Guardian Education Supplement*, 1990.
8. See Peter Mason in *Teaching Geography*, January 1989, and the Oxfam Education Department, Oxfam House, 274 Banbury Road, Oxford OX2 7DZ, for further teaching suggestions around this key term.
9. See the excellent video *Consuming Hunger*, available for hire through Metro Pictures, 79 Wardour Street, London W1V 3TH, for an illuminating account of how Western media constructed or mapped the Ethiopian food crisis of 1984. Michael Buerk's comment on his famous footage is especially striking: 'The curious thing – it came out in the first film we did – is the Biblical business. People looked like those depicted in the colour illustrations in my old school Bible. Sort of sackcloth and a certain nobility of features.' The video implies that it was this already familiar 'grid' of reference which helped ensure the impact of Buerk footage over other, earlier reports.
10. Quoted in Dawn Gill and Ian Cook, 'Power: The Fourth Dimension', in *Contemporary Issues in Geography and Education*, vol. 1, no. 3, 1984.
11. For a more elaborate argument around this issue, see Fredric Jameson, 'Cognitive Mapping' in Nelson and Grossberg (eds), *Marxism and the Interpretation of Culture*, Champaign, Ill., University of Illinois Press, 1988. Interestingly, on the subject of montage, the film-maker Alexander Kluge, writing in *New German Critique*, nos. 24–5, has compared it to the calculations of navigators measuring the distance between stars and horizon to find out where they are. 'Montage involves nothing more than such measurements; it is the art of creating proportions . . . it does not measure the location itself but the relationship – it is this relationship that is contained at the cut, at exactly the point where the film doesn't show anything.'

A Positive Sense of Self:
Media Education and Personal and Social Education

Jan Mulreany

The context of this description of media education used within personal and social education (PSE) is the in-service training of teachers of personal, social, and health education (PSHE). The specific occasion is a four-hour session on a Teachers' Certificate in Health Education course, which offers teachers and lecturers the opportunity to look at their work in greater depth. Course participants come from a range of schools and colleges within the London area, and from a variety of subject areas and specialisms. Although they will use media education concepts and conventions in their own work, often without realising it, none has had any formal training in media studies or teaches it as a main subject.

This practice has been reinforced with the recent publication of *National Curriculum Guidance 5: Health Education as a Cross-curricular Theme*,[1] in which several general and specific references to the influence and use of the media are set down in recommended statements of intent. Recent public health crises have led to government and voluntary agency-produced packages for classroom teaching which incorporate examples of the exploration of print and broadcast media for use in PSE lessons,[2] and textbooks to support the theory and practice have advocated the study of newspaper and magazine references to, and portrayals of, health.[3] Teachers' notes often include exercises which use media education pedagogy, though without the references which might help teachers identify them as such, and without suggestions for their most effective use by teachers unskilled in media studies.

Teachers of PSE need the skills to 'analyse image/screen' in order to help their students do the same. The in-service training session described here attempts to address the teachers' personal development as well as offering strategies for working with students in this area.

References made in the National Curriculum Guidance to studying 'the influence of the media' fall into two categories: those which help develop content for lessons, and those which, especially given the mutually-supporting pedagogies of PSE and media education, fulfil aims regarding process, personal confidence-building, an ability to co-operate, and working individually and in groups, which are also referenced in the English Statutory Orders.[4] Examples of the former are: at Key Stage 3, in the study of the environmental aspects of health education, understanding the impact

397

of the media and advertising on attitudes towards health; at Key Stage 4, the ability to discuss the role of the media in influencing attitudes towards drugs, especially smoking and alcohol, and to be aware of the influences of the media on self-image.

It is in the context of this latter statement of intent that we can develop work which uses the process of deconstruction of media conventions as its basis. A major aim of personal and social education is the development of a positive self-image, raising students' self-esteem and reinforcing their own identity. Key Stage 1 in the health education guidance also stresses the 'importance of valuing oneself and others' as 'essential to mental health'.[5] Links between a high level of self-esteem and educational achievement, as well as the acquisition of positive health habits, have been long established.[6] The pedagogy of PSE assumes that, ideally, teachers should experience the methods they are to use with their students, and the session entitled 'A Positive Sense of Myself' draws upon the use of media studies to create positive images. At the same time it is 'direct' media education, addressing the use of technology to create the images, studying the process of construction of meanings by understanding the means of, and motivation for, production.

Initially, the session links the personally-familiar world of being a media consumer with the professionally-familiar aims of PSE, and, in this case, the use of health education as an example. In an experiential style, the group members are invited to introduce themselves in a 'round', adding an alliterative adjective to their name which offers a positive reflection of their present feeling or state (e.g., eager Eileen, confident Calum, etc.), and to tell the rest of the group about one media artefact or text they saw the previous day which reminded them of 'health'. A brainstorm to gather a 'map' of which media gives images and messages relevant to health education, with as wide a range as possible being encouraged, is next, with the questions, 'What is our aim in analysing them? How can we analyse them?', to generally focus in on the theme.

A brief 'foundation course' in media studies is introduced with still-image analysis, to explain denotation and connotation, using a choice of materials – black-and-white photographs of everyday objects is one example,[7] as described in the BFI Secondary Statement,[8] or the 'Teddy Bear' activity from *Reading Pictures*.[9] Next, we deploy the concept of 'anchorage' by using alternative captions created by members of the group for a range of images taken from teaching materials such as *Reading Pictures, Eyeopeners*,[10] or from easily available sources such as magazines. When all captions have been considered, the teachers, working in pairs, will choose an image and work to place it within a health education context, manipulating the image (after some instruction) using technology such as the photocopier, cropping, editing, and adding further appropriate captions such as 'inequality in health care', and so on. By the midpoint of the session an understanding of how meanings are created is reached, by presentation and discussion of the newly created artefacts or texts.

Obviously, this could be an end in itself, but in this example the objective for personal and professional development is the use of such understanding and technical skills to create a sense of 'myself', a positive self-portrait/

self-image which reinforces one's own identity. One well-developed activity in PSE is the creation of a 'personal shield', a badge or a larger piece of art work which identifies the creator to others; it can then be used as an agenda for personal discussion with others in tutorial time, for example, though its use is found in other areas of the curriculum where the sharing of 'self' is traditional, such as drama and religious education. This exercise takes it at least one step further.

The development of technological skills and the resulting self-confidence can stand apart from the furthering of self-esteem, but with the goal of this INSET as it is, the two go hand in hand. Placing parts of the body on to photocopiers for this self-portrait, manipulating technology, can be an enjoyable experience for teachers used to its more mundane operation! The realisation that, by making multiple copies of photographs, enlarging and reducing, using coloured paper or OHP foils for emphasis, moving when taking a photograph and manipulating the chemicals during its developing, offered ways of depicting oneself literally as having more than one role, some of which are larger/more important or smaller/less important than others. Showing mood or stereotype by use of colour, emphasising one's personality, is an interesting exercise for teachers, for their own personal reflection as well as for transferring to the classroom context. The activity is personally-directed, though with the knowledge that they will share what they wish from the experience afterwards, when debriefing.

The size is generally A3 maximum, mainly because of the limitations of the photocopier and time available. People take about thirty minutes to create their portrait, their representation of what it is like to be 'Me'; some are able to produce two or more images, based on different aspects of their lives or feelings about themselves. They can experiment with how meanings change with the different positionings of images, and their motivations for the changes.

After the images have been developed, each person will then write something positive about themselves that has come out of the activity, completing the sentence 'I am . . .' five (or more) times. This is an exercise familiar to person-centred psychology, which forms a framework for the PSE curriculum such as 'Active Tutorial Work',[11] and which, here, helps to summarise the identity by concentrating on feelings generated by the immediate task. Statements could include 'I am good at the technical bits of this,' 'I am a person of many facets, some more important than others,' 'I am able to see now how all the parts of me fit together'. The debriefing of the activity is as important as the image-construction exercise – the reflection, and the voicing, the expressing of that reflection reinforces the positivity of the identity. In my experience teachers, for example, often play down their creative skills, unless their work is in the creative and expressive area, and saying something positive about oneself is not an easy adult activity. Having 'a positive self-image' by Key Stage 3 might be a requirement for teachers, too!

The debrief instruction is to share two things. One is the image, displayed in the room, perhaps, so that everyone can walk around, look at them, and see what their responses are, what they read of others' self-portraits, as well as how the artefacts were constructed. The other is to share how they arrived at this positive sense of self: how easy was it, what were the difficulties? Again, this can be separated into considering the content and the process; depending on the climate of trust and acceptance within the group, a decision about sharing what is there as the image, and why, will be a personal choice.

In the particular context described, the group climate was already established, group-building had been a specific part of the instruction to the course, and group maintenance was ongoing. The feedback from the process, however, is important in that everyone will be able to discuss the facility of their use of the technology, and how that contributes to (a) their own feelings of competence and (b) how the activity might be developed for classroom use in their own location. Identification of the skills needed, and how teachers will acquire and develop these, is the next step in the enhancement of their professional expertise. In the development of curriculum planning it is necessary for them to consider what might be available in their institution in terms of other colleagues' knowledge and skills and what materials are available which support classroom work for the study of the media in PSE, and to look to the co-ordination of the cross-curricular themes.

Feedback from the session at the time, and since, has proved positive in terms of knowledge and skills acquisition, from both personal and professional points of view. This INSET, which was developed from several activities which concentrated on specific health issues such as drugs education and advertising, was seen as a valuable tool in the teachers' understanding of the media, previously typically described as an unknown quantity, as 'them', to be blamed for society's ills.

Subsequent advisory work with individuals from this group has been easier to develop, in that levels of interpersonal understanding, as well as the professional relationship, have been enhanced; one could say that the identification of a positive sense of self has helped to procure 'health' (in its widest sense) benefits for the course participants and facilitator!

Notes

1. *Curriculum Guidance 5: Health Education*, York, National Curriculum Council, 1990.
2. *DoubleTake* drugs education pack, *Minder* episode, London, Department of Health, 1986; *Chasing The Bandwagon* teaching pack with Lenny Henry, London, National Council of Young Men's Christian Association, 1985.
3. Judith Ryder and Lesley Campbell, *Balancing Acts in PSHE*, London, Routledge, 1989.
4. *National Curriculum – English*, York, National Curriculum Council, 1989.
5. Key Stage 1 statements, Curriculum Guidance 5, op. cit.
6. Introductory Booklet to Schools Council Health Education Project (SCHEP) 13–18, London, Forbes Publications, 1980.
7. *Everyday Photographs*, London, ILEA Learning Resources Centre, 1986.
8. Julian Bowker (ed.), *Secondary Media Education: A Curriculum Statement*, London, BFI, 1991.
9. *Reading Pictures*, London, BFI, 1981.
10. Andrew Bethell, *Eyeopeners* 1 & 2, Cambridge, Cambridge University Press, 1981.
11. J. Baldwin, *Active Tutorial Work*, Oxford, Blackwell, 1982.

Signs and Symbols

Steve Brennan

From *Secondary Media Education: A Curriculum Statement*, London, BFI, 1991, pp. 56–8.

Certain sections of the advisory support service within the authority – namely, drama, dance, music, and media education – have been constituted as a performing arts team to provide formal in-service courses for teachers of the arts. These courses have been intended to act as 'springboards' for arts projects within schools and to provide a forum for project dissemination and evaluation. Much of the recent work of the performing arts advisory team has been looking at the ways in which the arts can function symbiotically. A weekend course for teachers within the authority was organised with the express purpose of exploring ways in which the various arts subjects can function together on mutually enriching projects, and to try to define some of the fundamental commonalities which bind them together.

We started the process of searching for a shared language in the arts by looking at the media notion of codes and conventions. A group of fifteen teachers from a variety of arts subjects was asked to consider some quotations about codes and conventions, but to replace the word 'media' with the words 'arts':

> The first principle of media education from which all else flows, and to which teachers and students will continually return, is that the media are symbols (or sign systems) which need to be actively read, and not unproblematic, self-explanatory reflections of external reality.[1]

All media use a sign system, but do they use the same system? Clearly, some signs may be 'media specific'. It is difficult to think of an equivalent to the sound of guitar feedback on a rock record or an image produced in a video game. However, the study of sign systems (semiology or semiotics) can be applied universally.

The codes will be used in what have come to be seen as conventional ways – what do we expect from a news programme, how long is a pop single, where do we expect to find the problem page in a magazine? These formal conventions have developed through history, often deriving from earlier forms and being modified by the constraints outlined above. All media production is in this sense 'conventional' – it must be, or most of us would not make any sense of it. The extent of its conventionality is exposed by the independent or avant-garde practitioners who attempt to break the conventions of mainstream media codes.[2]

In the discussion which followed, the notion of a shared language for the arts was developed further, with a consideration of a whole range of key terms which appeared to have a 'generic relatedness' as words originating in one art form and becoming used by others, creating a body of shared vocabulary across the arts. Words such as harmony, discord, form, structure, symbol, metaphor, sign, image, style, mood, and, crucially for this particular course, genre.

A group task was then devised which attempted to point out, primarily in filmic terms, that we all actually do understand exactly what the codes and conventions of various genres are.

Codes and Conventions: The Task
You have three imaginary props: a hat, a gun, and a cigarette. Devise a short scenario, no longer than two minutes, using those props. You must work within the film genre of:
1. The Western. 2. The Musical. 3. The Gangster Movie.

The groups were also asked to consider the following questions:

- What sort of hat is it? Who is wearing it? How is it being worn?
- What sort of gun is it? Where is it?
- What sort of cigarette is it? (not the brand!) How is it being held?
- Describe the characters – what are they doing, what are they wearing?
- Describe, briefly, the setting.
- Any music or sound effects being used?
- What is the role/function of the objects within the scene?
- Briefly plot the narrative just before and just after the scene.

They then looked in depth at the codes and conventions of the various traditional art forms, and how they might go about constructing these, by asking some of the traditional questions of media education, centring on the relationship of producer, text, and audience, and its ideological frame.

In the light of these discussions, the group were then asked to try to 'read' some of the codes and conventions of the various art forms. They brainstormed the implication of certain terms within their art form, asking 'What is your "reading" of each? What "meaning" does each convey?' The terms were: proscenium arch, perspective, black-and-white photograph, oil paint, steel drums, a tutu, a chorus line, agit prop, a black dicky bow, the madrigal.

After operating on a 'carousel' system and undergoing an introduction to the basic codes and conventions of each art form, the course culminated in group presentations. These were multimedia, and were devised through looking at the codes and conventions of one genre and using these as a vehicle to communicate the traditional 'content' of another, keeping in mind all the sensory modes of engagement and their relevant sign/

meaning-producing systems. In short, it became an exercise in identifying codes and conventions of contrasting genres and combining them in performance. These included: the disaster movie and pantomime; film noir and Punch and Judy; 'rap' and Greek tragedy; soap opera and the blues.

While most people had an instinctive familiarity with most of the conventions of each genre (film noir needed some explanation and illustration) the difficulty arose in maintaining a close observation of the perceived codes and conventions of each genre while avoiding slipping into superficial pastiche as the dynamics of the performance began to shape the work. The teachers, on the whole, found these concepts stimulating, and they encouraged the development of a common strategy and approach which can be shared with other arts teachers. 6

The work in this project was media education-led, with the analytical framework and vocabulary of media education providing the 'way in' to a cross-arts project. Each new project would draw more heavily on some of the art forms rather than others, depending on the nature of the work – it was not felt necessary to strain for absolute equality between the arts subjects in every project undertaken. One other point which it was felt needed stressing was that all the arts need not work together all the time. This could easily lead to unnatural liaisons and superficial links which pupils would soon perceive. 7

Notes

1. Len Masterman, *Teaching the Media*, London, Comedia, 1985.
2. Roy Stafford, 'Construction', paper for BFI Easter School, 1988.

PART IVc
Strategies

Strategies
Introduction

Scotland has a longer and more coherent curriculum development in media education than England, Wales, and Northern Ireland, and the two examples here have been selected to highlight broad issues of curriculum development and organisation of advisory support.

One piece focuses on the national and the other on regional perspectives. Eddie Dick, in 'Developing Broad Strategies and Interventions', evaluates the effects of a concerted attempt to develop media education within the Scottish educational context. Eddie Dick is Education Officer for the Scottish Film Council, which has lobbied successfully for media education within the formal education sector. An independently produced set of curriculum guidelines for media education exists in Scotland, from which schools might derive frameworks for development. As there is evidently a fair degree of good practice in schools, Eddie Dick asks why there is variation in its effectiveness in Scottish secondary schools and suggests criteria for securing long-term development and effective integration of media education.

Angela McEwan's 'Renfrew Raises the Media Standard' is a description of a TVEI development in one authority in Scotland. From her perspective as an advisory teacher she outlines the structures, strategies, and training she believes are required to establish a long-term programme of development.

Developing Broad Strategies and Interventions

Eddie Dick

In 1988 the Scottish Film Council, in association with AMES (Association for Media Education in Scotland) and the education department's curriculum service, published the *Media Education Curriculum Guidelines*. These guidelines served a number of purposes, the first of which was to support media education teachers, for the Guidelines legitimised media education in a way that had never been done before. Teachers used this document in many different ways: it became a defence of existing courses and an argument of expansion; it became a key to unlock training; it was quoted in budget claims for materials and equipment. The second purpose was to argue for the importance of media education. This was done within the document itself and by the free distribution of the Guidelines to every school and college in the country.

We were also able to outline the curriculum: with confidence and accuracy in the secondary sector, a good bit more speculatively in the primary sector, where our experiences were weaker and more limited. Nevertheless, the outline was there and it aided the final purpose, which was a mapping exercise of expectations and needs from primary to tertiary, within the formal education sector and in the community at large. We began to look at the implications of our suggestions and demands.

One of the principal implications flowed from the consensus that media education is not a subject. Not only did we believe this, it would have been politically inept of us to try to develop a new subject in the subject-crowded secondary curriculum. A second-level choice would have been to try to locate media in English. But what would we have been giving away in trying to locate media in that diffuse and troubled subject? What would have happened to the balance of the media curriculum? What about all the art and sociology teachers who have invaluable insights and experiences to offer?

The curriculum model in the Guidelines is based on permeation, which is the coherent, organised development of those aspects of media education which relate directly to the interests of established subjects. It is a kind of planned suffusion of relevant aspects of the curriculum. This will involve teachers in almost all subjects, at all levels, drawing attention from time to time, in ways appropriate to the individual subject, to issues such as the constructed nature of media products, the influence of media institutions on those products' formation, distribution and consumption, the contribution of the mass media to specific areas of culture, and the kinds of pleasures that the mass media afford.

In the primary sector in Scotland, this would result in media education appearing with language, environmental studies and expressive arts. In the secondary sector, in English, for example, media-related work will continue to contribute to writing, to the study of narratives, to listening and talking, to the promotion of reading. In the art department, work will concern visual message systems in comics, fashion, television, advertising, and photography; work in music will enhance the understanding of a major media industry; work in modern studies might deal with the evolution and structures of media institutions, such as newspapers and television.

Permeation should progress in relevant areas in ways which result in media education being the focus of attention. In other words, permeation represents a sort of sliding scale of opportunity which will gradually and appropriately build towards the emergence of discrete courses.

Aside from the value of this in its recognition of administrative and pedagogic realities, this scheme welcomes the existing experiences of teachers from a wide range of disciplines. Teachers in primary, of English, art, music, modern studies, and so on, can see what it is that they are bringing to this seemingly new and occasionally intimidating discipline. Media education can then be seen as an extension to their skills and experiences rather than a rejection of them.

In addition to permeation, discrete cross-curricular courses have been developed in which media studies provides the organising ideas that were the leading edge of development. However, cross-curricular media education in Scotland is still not uniformly developed, and in certain areas of the curriculum it is in better shape than others. Where media education exists in primaries (and it is not yet as widespread as it could be), it tends to be provided on a cross-curricular basis. The *Media Education Curriculum Guidelines* suggestion of locating media education in projects, practical work, and permeation of other subjects has tended to be interpreted in a thematic or medium-specific way. Both approaches result in the inclusion of linguistic, aesthetic, technological, and social aspects drawn from a broad range of the curriculum.

Sometimes the 'big bang' approach is used. One school gave over its whole curriculum to media education for a week. The themes used were mainly children's media, news, and advertising. The whole school worked on a wide range of topics within these themes, including old and new media, interviews, animation, desktop publishing, still photography, newspapers, comics, soundtracks, radio drama, and TV news. A taste of Media Week can be seen on the Scottish Film Council's video *Primetime*, in which some of the classwork is depicted and the teachers interviewed on how the experiences benefited them and the children.

Media Week was exceptional. Most schools take a class-based approach. In any case, the principal long-term objective is to provide experiences which can be integrated into the normal curriculum.

In the secondaries, some interdepartmental work is organised on a cross-curricular basis but the main achievements have been as a result of working with the catalogue of Scotvec modules. There are now seventeen forty-hour modules from which to choose, and all of them call for learning and teaching which transcend the traditional curricular boundaries. As well as a complete range of medium-specific modules, the catalogue includes Representations, Advertising Analysis and Production, Fashion, Broadcast Narratives, Graphic Design, and Photography. These modules are taught in just over half of the secondaries and all the further education colleges.

The development was beginning to look something like this: 12

Primary and Lower Secondary (5–14)

Permeation		Environmental studies
Practical units	*via*	Expressive arts
Discrete topics		Language

Middle and Upper Secondary (15–18)

Permeation meant a general commitment to an engagement with media education in 'all modes and courses', but it was emphasised in language and communication, creative and aesthetic subjects, social and environmental studies. Inserts in standard grade English, modern studies, art; higher grade English, modern studies, art, Scotvec modules (currently fourteen short courses).

Further Education

Scotvec modules (pre-vocational)
Higher National Certificates (vocational)
Higher National Diplomas (vocational)

Higher Education

Communications degrees
Film and Media Studies degrees
Vocational training (e.g., Film and TV Production)

As can be seen, we are attempting three different ways of including 13 media education in the primary curriculum, in three different broad areas. This breadth continues in the early years of secondary (and this is as yet an underdeveloped area) and moves into specialisation via short courses and modules. We also have an important insert in English provision. The modules bridge across into post-school experience which is mainly vocationally oriented. The higher education sector has a range of academic and vocational provision. The main point to stress is that we were beginning to get a sense of flow, of movement in the media provision from the early years through to adults.

Thus, in the Guidelines we had a document which talked of the curricu- 14 lum, on the one hand in clear and descriptive ways and on the other in ways which were highly political and rhetorical. These latter parts of the document were speculative and generally abstract, which was both a strength and a weakness. It was a strength in that it meant the Guidelines were not tied too closely into the moment of their writing – they had a shelf life which is useful in a time of rapid curriculum change. They could also be applied to different schools in different places. Their weakness was that they did not always provide direct evidence of the implications of developing media education in the Scottish curriculum. We had, of course, been aware of this from the outset and even before the Guidelines were published had begun to plan to provide this missing evidence.

We established a development and research project which was designed 15 to address two issues: (a) What counts as media education? and (b) What counts as policy for media education?

Clearly, what we wanted to count as media education was the model 16 which we had been developing for the previous five years. The Guidelines were the common starting-point for a small number of pilot project schools. These schools were not chosen as media education 'centres of excellence' but as being interested and willing. What we did was to tell them about our ideas on media education, have them find out what was happening in their own schools, and try to establish what their teachers' training needs were. The Scottish Film Council provided them with ideas and in-service training but, while we were important to the development, we tried hard to avoid being essential.

We needed evidence from these schools which we could extrapolate 17 across the country. The application of that evidence would have been badly damaged if we had placed the Scottish Film Council at the centre of things. We are a small cultural agency which could not possibly hope to provide intimate support for all Scottish schools. We do not aspire to that role, which is the responsibility of the education authorities. Our role was to make them realise it was their job.

What we wanted from the schools were general policy scenarios. We 18 were interested in the curriculum developments, but the focus of our attention were those arrangements which facilitate development. Policy in these cases did not merely mean pieces of paper with a few high-sounding phrases and never-to-be-achieved aspirations. What we wanted was the application of media education in the daily activities of each school. A common starting-point in the Guidelines was sensible and flexible development which fitted into real schools, with real teachers who taught real kids.

In the meantime I approached the Scottish Council for Research in 19 Education (SCRE), convinced them that media education was a priority, and together we applied to the Economic and Social Research Council for funding for research into the development. The successfully secured money was used to employ a researcher based at SCRE. This again deliberately reduced the importance of the Film Council, and it means that when the research results are published they will be seen to be independent.

What did the researcher find? Firstly, and not surprisingly, that there 20 was a very high degree of consensus as to the nature of media education. In the secondary schools she found that, to begin with, there was more activity in the upper school. As time went on and confidence grew, more teaching took place in the earlier years. The initial emphasis on older students was probably influenced by certificates being available. All the schools either started off with an approach which balanced analysis and practice or, in one instance, began with a heavy practical emphasis and gradually realised the benefits of blending practice with analysis.

Much of this confirmed things which we thought we knew already. To have it independently confirmed was important but not exciting. The excitement was in the primary schools. Before the project, media education was not taught in an organised way in any of the pilot primaries. Each school began with a particular project – video, tape-slide, newspapers, representations of gender, and so on – and then developed permeative strategies. The integrated day of the primary school with one teacher responsible for almost all of the teaching of each class was, of course, more conducive to permeation than was the subject-based curriculum of the secondary, where teachers' contacts with students were more fragmentary and decisions about courses are the province of subject departments or national policy-makers. Furthermore, the primary teachers brought an openness, an expectation of flexibility and integration, which proved ideal for media education development.

All the staff in the primaries were involved in the pilot scheme; in the secondaries, small teams undertook the work. Certification led the secondaries' interest and development; the primaries were not bedevilled with certification and showed more creativity and diversity. This may partly have been of necessity. The primary teachers were much less experienced than their secondary colleagues at the beginning, and it was the perceived importance of establishing a common base of experience which led the primary schools to start with projects. Whole-school projects provided experiences upon which teachers could build together, and this in turn encouraged attention to progression of analysis, skills acquisition, and practical competence from Primary 1 (five-year-olds) to Primary 7 (twelve-year-olds). For instance, advertising and representations provided the structure for media work, where five-year-olds asked 'Is this me?' and worked with media representations of themselves and their families. Eight-year-olds studied shopping and the manufacture of shoppers. Eleven-year-olds looked at foreign places and their media construction as holiday locations.

In the secondary schools, the general policy scenarios were characterised by the development of interdepartmental teams which brought together senior management and unpromoted teachers who had a high profile new to them. All aspired to permeation and, though none fully achieved it by the end of the pilot scheme, at least all the teams had taken the first steps to integrate media into the broad provision of the schools' curricula.

The most important resource which was made available to the teachers was time. Staffing cover allowed planning and in-service training to develop quickly. Per capita funding under the team's control brought in resources such as teaching materials. Equipment, viewed as a whole-school resource, was sought and argued for, often successfully.

Co-ordination was a team responsibility which benefited teaching and curriculum development. The team knew what its members were doing and what was expected of them. They also kept colleagues informed and, as interest grew, this enabled them to broaden the teaching group.

Decision-making and accountability were the areas which differed most greatly from school to school. In one, both areas were devolved to the team within the general pattern of the school's policies; in another, the head teacher chaired a formal team meeting and was effectively its manager. In all cases, however, decision-making was open and argued through, and accountability was clear and flowed up as well as down through the management structures.

In the primary schools, the head teachers were uniformly closely involved. The teams were small, and consistently worked to involve all staff. Like the secondary schools, organised support was crucial and also took the form of resources, co-ordination, and decision-making and accountability.

In implementing their policies for media education, schools were conscious of constraints. These could be referred to as hurdles, because many were overcome as the teachers gained experience. Anyone contemplating media education on a wide scale would have to take account of such hurdles which would include:

(1)   The need for at least minimum allocations of staff, time, in-service training, funding, and equipment;
(2)   The limited initial conceptual understanding about the nature of media education;
(3)   The lack of relevant skills among teachers;
(4)   The problems of creating flexible staffing and timetabling structures;
(5)   The scarcity of existing models of good practice (particularly in primary schools);
(6)   The difficulties of persuading teachers to consider media education as an integral part of all aspects of the curriculum.

As well as these hurdles, there were rewards and incentives to encourage teachers to build for the future:
(1)   The students were very enthusiastic and motivated to learn;
(2)   Teachers enjoyed working in the field of media education;
(3)   Teachers were motivated by their sense of ownership of media education – they knew they had developed it themselves, and their achievements were quite clearly their own work;
(4)   The professional development of special expertise gave teachers a great deal of satisfaction;
(5)   The new experience gained was valuable for promotion;
(6)   Some unpromoted teachers experienced decision-making normally restricted to senior staff.
(7)   School managements could use media education to fulfil national requirements for curriculum balance, whole-school policies, and enrichment.

One interesting recurrence was how teachers' anxiety about equipment diminished. As they gained more experience their demands for equipment did not lessen but they felt they understood better.

Renfrew Raises the Media Standard

Angela McEwan

Introduction

Renfrew Division's TVEI Extension is a unique implementation of the government's Technical and Vocational Education Initiative. In general, the scheme aims to enhance the curriculum for 14- to 18-year-olds by relating it to the society of which they are a part. I joined Renfrew's team of staff development officers at the beginning of the TVEI Extension in August 1988 (the start of the academic session in Scotland). One unique feature of the Renfrew model was the creation of a central team seconded on fixed contracts for the project's seven-year duration.

The staff development officers (SDOs) are all subject based and represent academic areas in which there have been significant curriculum developments. The subjects were often organised on a cross-curricular basis rather than in traditional terms. My own remit as Staff Development Officer in Media Education involves work with English departments but also with art, social studies, religious education, music, and modern languages (particularly French), and, of course, with individual media enthusiasts who can come from any subject background. Links between media education and Enterprise Activity are also strong in a number of schools. Other SDO remits include expressive arts, design, and educational computing.

Renfrew Division is one of six which make up the Education Department of Strathclyde Regional Council, the largest education authority in Western Europe, and each division has its own proposal for TVEI Extension. With its permanent central team, the Renfrew Extension specialises in in-service training and material provision for special curriculum initiatives. The development of media education since 1988 has been built on the foundations of one such initiative, a mandatory curriculum TVEI insert.

The provision of a cross-curricular insert for 15-year-old students (year 10; secondary education in Scotland begins a year later than in England and Wales) was a major priority for the newly established Renfrew TVEI Extension. The Scottish Consultative Council on Curriculum had recommended that educational provision for 14- to 16-year-olds should include 5 per cent technological study. Some students, depending on their choice of standard grade subjects, failed to meet this figure and a method of enhancing their programmes of study was therefore required. (Standard grade is the Scottish National Certificate administered by the Scottish Exam Board for 14- to 16-year-olds and is equivalent to GCSE standard in England and Wales.)

Faced with the possibility of an additional subject column in a crowded curriculum, or the difficult curriculum audit of a wide variety of subjects in an *ad hoc* fashion, the proposal to enhance the core subjects of English, mathematics, science and social subjects emerged. A forty-hour course, with time divided equally between the four elements, ensured the minimum requirement of technological provision for *all*, with some students going well beyond the 5 per cent target. As all students are involved in the selected core subjects, the audit could also be made with ease.

Discussions between the advisers for the core subjects and the SDOs 6
who were to write the course (e.g., media/English; educational computing/ maths) led to the decision that a common theme would not be the best way forward. Instead, all of the components were designed to encourage problem-solving skills and enhance these with the use of technology. The portion of the course to be taught within the English curriculum was to comprise the study of the mass media and culminate in a media production.

Early problems which this presented included (*a*) the problem of having 7
all students taking part while grouped in classes of up to thirty-three, and (*b*) teachers who were, in many cases, unfamiliar with the concepts involved and who, by their own admission, lacked the necessary production skills. Nor did the schools have the hardware required since there was not yet a course for them to teach. If those issues seemed to represent a challenge, the fact that we were talking to about 180 English teachers, across 29 schools, with a client group of 4500 14-year-olds, completed the development scenario.

The diagram shows how the cross-curricular nature of the course was 8
planned:

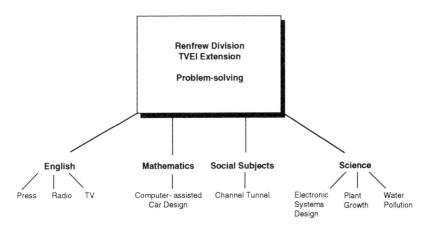

The Course

The choice of case study for the media course was finalised as 'public 9
relations'. I selected this subject because it lent itself to short productions of a promotional nature, rather than epic dramas. There was also the hidden agenda of encouraging pupils to look positively on their own environment. My own teaching experience had been in the East End of London, where I constantly used the study of images to promote the creation of positive images of the pupils themselves. I found that enhanced self-esteem could

415

be built in as a side-effect or perhaps a self-fulfilling prophesy. The final production was, therefore, to be a newspaper page, a radio magazine, or the 'and finally' item for television news, which featured their own school and showed it in a positive light.

As part of the TVEI agreement all English departments offer at least one class in press, one in radio, and one in television. Beyond that, departments offer additional classes in a pattern of their own choice. For example, at Gourock High School two classes study each medium, while at Castlehead High School the emphasis is on the press and television, with five and four classes respectively, and only one class studying radio. Port Glasgow High School, on the other hand, offered three classes on television, two on radio, and only one on the press. Departments created quite distinct patterns. Given the limited time available (twelve hours of classroom time for each course), focusing on one medium rather than a variety seemed more appropriate. Specialising allows students to develop a deeper understanding of the concepts involved.

The learning outcomes of the course are that the student should:

(1) Plan a problem-solving specification;
(2) Carry out a problem-solving specification;
(3) Evaluate solutions to a problem.

Each of the components emphasises the part of this model most appropriate to the core subject involved – for example, mathematics stresses the planning, while social subjects highlight the evaluation. Science and English assess the student's ability to carry out a plan. All the courses include an early period of investigating the problem. In the media courses this takes up a significant amount of time, about eight of the available twelve hours. It is at this point that analytical and production skills are also developed.

I was concerned that pupils should *not* be asked to produce a media artefact before they had experienced the various jobs involved and reached an understanding of the contributions being made. It was also clear that the students, like the teachers, would have to be trained in the use of the computer, the sound mixer, or the camcorder, depending on which medium they were studying. Investigation of the principal media roles is undertaken by examining media products and establishing the contributions made, as well as the connotations intended. This inductive methodology has been at the centre of media education since its formal introduction to Scottish schools in 1984 when Scotvec (the Scottish Vocational Education Council) created National Certificates in Media Studies.

During this period of investigation, students are given the opportunity to try out each of the roles under investigation. Such opportunities include simulating the key roles of editor, producer, or director, and the development of principal technology and non-technological skills. Another of the hidden agendas of the course was the requirement that pupils should work in groups. The courses are essentially student centred, with the teacher acting as both tutor and facilitator. It is intended that the classes should be mixed-ability groupings and the later production period, in particular, simulates the real world of media production by offering jobs which

416

demand different levels of contribution to the final product. Essentially, there is differentiation in the work demanded during the final production when students perform only one role.

Interesting examples of creative implementation can be seen in two 14 schools which offer the choice of press, radio, or television to the pupils, and reorganise classes according to that choice. The pupils are not told which teachers are responsible for the particular media, and are usually allocated at least their second choice. One principal teacher of English commented that regrouping classes encouraged student motivation, particularly since students felt that they could plan their own curriculum.

The radio course was welcomed by teachers because of its coherent 15 approach to 'talk' which also, in fact, represents a third of the assessment of standard grade English. The possibility of using the 'investigation' unit of the radio course, which involves pupils writing for radio, presenting, and interviewing, as well as sound-mixing, was raised very early by several schools. All pupils must reach the level of writing a short script and recording it, mixing from a jingle and to a cartridge. Teachers felt that the course provided an invaluable link between the earlier work within the 5–14 syllabus and that demanded at standard grade.

The television course, with its emphasis on reading television, was also 16 recognised as extremely valuable as preparation for another aspect of standard grade assessment – extended response to reading a media artefact. One assistant principal teacher of English commented that the analytical skills required in media transferred well to the study of other texts, particularly literature.

In-service Training

It would be misleading to suggest that every one of the 180 English teachers 17 approached the requirement to teach one of these courses quite so positively. However, efforts were taken to accommodate staff worries. All English teachers with S3 (secondary year 3, 14- to 15-year-olds) classes were assigned to either press, radio, or television, and attended centrally based courses with similarly assigned staff from other schools. Their absence from school was covered by supply teachers. The response to these courses was overwhelmingly positive, as can be seen by the evaluation sheets:

Expectations of the course realised

A great deal	53.26% ⎱	92.72%
Quite a lot	39.46% ⎰	
Partly	6.9% ⎱	7.28%
Not very much	0.38% ⎰	
Hardly at all	0.00%	

Technology In-service Training

In order to allow teachers to be involved in a production and to develop 18 their skills *before* discussing how such skills would be used in the classroom, training in the use of the hardware was undertaken first. This training lasted one day for the press, one day for radio, and two days for television. Teachers were grouped in classes of no more than twenty. Involvement in a group production led to realistic expectations of students, and a great deal of enthusiasm as budding directors, producers, and editors emerged from the ranks of the sometimes less than confident participants.

An important factor in the planning of these technology courses was that I assumed no prior knowledge on the part of the teachers and began with the basic steps of setting up the computer, sound mixer, or camcorder. It was clearly important to encourage teachers to believe in themselves as, for many, this was their first attempt to use a computer or a camcorder, let alone an eight-track sound mixer. Principal teachers were very accommodating, and the majority of teachers were allowed to opt for the medium which interested them most. It was also important to ask each teacher to become proficient in only one medium, though in subsequent years they have opted to retrain in a second and even a third medium. However, retraining remains optional: 23 per cent of teachers identified retraining as their future need, while 46 per cent saw practice as the immediate need. A significant amount of time was spent in hands-on access to the hardware, and the second half of each course simulated the student courses by assigning teachers to a group of four and giving them a deadline for the production of a newspaper page, a radio feature, or a television news item. As a division taking this enormous step forward together we had to establish team spirit very quickly, and the emphasis on fun during these technology courses was very important.

Methodology In-service Training

Once we had established with teachers that they *could* cope with the hardware, I felt we were ready to move on to an examination of the course content. I wrote all three courses by basing them on my own classroom experience and developed the theory section (the investigation period) in as practical a way as possible. Basically, pupils worked through a detailed and demanding simulation of the principal production personnel after studying their contribution. Each stage saw them changing role to that of yet another principal contributor. All of the examples used were local, allowing us to build up a course which is culturally relevant to the west of Scotland, and this was particularly important as materials are frequently based on an English model.

Classes viewed programmes which are part of Scottish Television's *Time to Think* series on production in the chosen medium: press (featuring the *Glasgow Herald*), radio (*Radio Clyde*), and television (*Take the High Road*). Each class had its own videotape which had one of these programmes along with another programme, which was a study examining the Bank of Scotland's 'Friend for Life' campaign, used during the final production stage. The in-service methodology included a lecture on the aims of the courses, making specific reference to their articulation with standard grade and the 5–14 Language Report (the Scottish National Report which sets attainment targets for years S1 and S2), and their place within the provision of media education for secondary schools. During the day the teachers actually undertook most of the investigation exercises which their students were given. Again, the discovery that the work can be fun was a significant factor in motivating the group.

The specific problem-solving objectives and an overview of the course 22
were given as follows:

Investigation assignments:	– non-technological;
	– technological;
plan, carry out, evaluate	– production.

The in-service courses also included details and advice on assessment procedures. The problem-solving process, and not the product, was assessed.
This is very important in terms of how students and teachers view the
experience. These mandatory courses for fourteen-year-olds are but one
stage in the development of media awareness and skills, a fact further
emphasised by our allocating only a third of the available time to production, even though it incorporates the assessable problem-solving
elements of plan, carry out, evaluate. Students often want to repeat the
exercise, but this may be tackled later for standard grade or for 16+
National Certificates.

The final product was a whole-class production of one artefact. Students 23
also considered the example of a school which had been featured in the
media, before moving into production. Classroom management is obviously
of crucial importance in such a course, and the staff guide which each
teacher received included advice on this, as well as very detailed lesson
plans for the whole course. If anything, this is the area which teachers found
more challenging than the media concepts or the technological hardware.

The jobs demanded different levels of contribution which teachers were 24
advised about at the in-service course. During the production, pupils
worked in groups of between two and four, depending on their role, and
contributed to the final page or programme by taking on one role, which
may be, for example, that of sub-editor or sound effects technician or
set-designer. The class worked as a 'crew' to produce a positive representation of their own school and, by so doing, the nature of media representations itself is raised.

Technological Provision
For each TVEI insert, students are provided with specially printed instruc- 25
tion booklets which can be used with both younger and older classes.

Press Studies
Each Press Studies class is provided with a BBC Master system including 26
printer. The software used during the course is Newham's Front Page
Special Edition. This simple program allows students to print preselected
column widths with justified text; offers a second size of type for lesser
headlines or subheadings; a third size for major headlines, and also six
fonts. Each student learns to use the program by saving and printing the
headline for his or her story.

Radio Studies
Each Radio Studies class is provided with an eight-track sound mixer with sources allocated as follows:

Channels 1–4   Microphones: cardoid and directional (2 × tie-clips);
Channels 5–6   Cassette (stereo);
Channels 7–8   Record deck (stereo).

The cassette source is used to provide both sound effects and 'live' broadcasts from pre-recorded cassettes. Each student learns how to operate the mixer by recording the introduction to a specified interview. This scripted piece has to be mixed from record, recorded, and mixed to cassette.

Television Studies
Each Television Studies class is provided with a camcorder. This allows recording of visuals and the later audio-dubbing of sound. The facility for insert editing of both sound and vision is also available. Each student learns how to operate the camcorder by recording a sequence of stills from an investigation exercise on montage. This provides experience in the use of the zoom and focus pulling, and avoids the initial student embarrassment of appearing in front of a camera. Students are, once again, provided with specially printed instruction booklets and, as in the other courses, these hardware manuals are used by teachers with pupils from secondary years 1–6.

I feel that the positive response to the inclusion of media studies within English has been a result of the security which such support has provided. It encourages teachers to 'go the extra mile' and that is what many have done. In the second part of this case study I have illustrated the developments which have occurred in response to the 5–14 Language Report at secondary years 1 and 2, and which have taken place in the senior school curriculum. As a local authority, we have very clearly established patterns of progression along which students travel as they move through the secondary school. It is significant that these developments have followed quickly from the implementation of the third-year courses.

Changes Made to the Courses
Taking on board teacher comments, students' reactions, and the evidence of my own observations (I visit every school during the teaching of the insert and see, at least, one class in each medium) there have been a number of changes to the material over the past two years. The amount of material has been reduced to allow more discussion. We moved from sheets of paper, to booklets, and ultimately to text and printed notebook format. The notebook has all the necessary pictures, grids, and information for the student activities, while the text has all the exemplars. This has significantly eased the classroom management of the course. Time to redraft copy or scripts has also been added, this time having been gained from the removal of the initial lesson which is now covered in the 5–14 TVEI media materials. Materials are printed centrally in class sets, and a substantial

amount of graphics have also been added to make it easier to read information, especially important in a course designed for *all* students. The press, radio, and TV courses also relate very closely to the three standard grade English components: writing, talking, and reading.

PART IVd
Media Education Across the Curriculum

Media Education Across the Curriculum
Introduction

The National Curriculum Statutory Orders for English and Welsh, and the Common Core for Northern Ireland, includes reference to media and non-literary texts in other subjects. The requirement to teach media education in other subjects is entirely voluntary, but many teachers carry out some form of media education.

Several media education journals have appeared in recent years in which writers have described scenarios for cross-curricular linkage between overlapping themes or through common projects. With the advent of the National Curriculum in England, Wales, and Northern Ireland the possibilities for actual intervention and lobbying of curriculum content became a real possibility. Certainly, the debate within media education circles was not without contention, with one school of thought concerned that the radicalism of media studies would be watered down if sprinkled throughout other subject specialisms. Another view, which became predominant, was to argue for an entitlement for all children to have access to media education and not limit it to media studies and English specialists.

These two pieces have been chosen because they demonstrate what many educators sensed in the period of consultation, 1988–92, between legislators, the Department of Education, and the teaching profession about constructing a new English and Welsh National Curriculum. The feeling was that there were opportunities for reciprocation between media education and other subject areas in terms of both pedagogy and content. For example, art and technology are eminent contenders for media education work, and the two pieces included here explore how both contribute to the development of media education as well as being enhanced by it. Writing about other areas such as humanities or science exists, but more actual examples of co-ordinated and structured whole-school work would help identify the best approaches and possibilities.

A further review of media education nationally and globally would attempt to draw together examples of institutional planning and evaluation of co-ordinated programmes which involved a cross-curricular approach. David Allen, a lecturer in education, writes about the links between media education and the arts in 'Media, Arts, and the Curriculum'.

In 'Media Education, Technology, and the National Curriculum' Norrie Porter, an advisory teacher for technology, and Judy Bennett, an advisory teacher for media education, collaborated to write about the opportunities for media education within the National Curriculum guidelines. The emphasis on process work and on the investigation of primary sources in the statutory orders suggests that there is plenty of scope for media education production which is not really emphasised in the English statutory orders.

Media, Arts, and the Curriculum

Dave Allen

From *Independent Media*, no. 88, April 1989

Since the earliest years of film studies in schools and colleges, debates have centred around the most appropriate place for film and media teaching in the curriculum and the relationship of that work with other subject areas. Even the increasingly popular implementation of cross-curricular work in media *education* often depends upon a member of staff establishing media *studies* on the timetable and using that position to create links with other teachers and subjects.

It has never been easy for media teachers to seek space in a crowded timetable, and the situation is complicated by the current implementation of the National Curriculum. This has re-established the image of the curriculum hierarchically divided into discrete subjects and, despite official assurances that space and time exist for other subjects and that the core and foundation subjects may be delivered through interdisciplinary work as long as they meet the requirements of the subject working parties, doubts must exist about the security of unnamed subjects like media studies.

One possible strategy for media teachers is to pursue links with other subjects which have a stronger hold on the curriculum, and there is already some encouragement for media teachers in the working party report on English 5–11. In recent years the growth of media education supported by a range of institutions and publications has made it easier for teachers to find a place for the key ideas of media teaching across the curriculum, although it does not follow that the majority of teachers have accepted the educational importance of a media dimension to their subjects. Neither does it follow that all the work involving, for example, television, video, or photography actually corresponds with what media teachers understand as media education, despite some of the claims made for such work.

Traditionally, many media teachers have been drawn from the areas of English, the arts, and the humanities. This article is concerned with the links between media education and the arts, not in order to appropriate media education for one curriculum area at the expense of others, but to consider the possibilities of developing existing links for the mutual benefit of both.

To talk of 'the arts' as a single curriculum area is, however, not without difficulties. Most publications on the arts in education tend to define them as art and design, dance, drama, aspects of English (poetry, literature, creative writing, or perhaps, generically, the verbal arts), and music. In

426

some cases film (or photography or both) are included – less often media studies. Even when described generically, these discrete subjects enjoy dramatically different histories and status.[1] For example, art and music have been named as national curriculum foundation subjects while English, with its place as one of the three core subjects, includes work in drama, poetry and literature, and media education. Drama and dance (omitted from the list of named subjects) may be increasingly identified respectively with English and physical education. This uneven picture makes it some-what difficult to speak of 'the arts' as a coherent curriculum area, and there are also powerful groups representing specific arts subjects that view attempts to describe the arts as a single curriculum area with suspicion, if not hostility.

Given these differences, how useful is it to speak of 'the arts' as a generic curriculum area? It is partly possible because of our shared idea of the arts as related through cultural institutions, not least of which are representations of 'the arts' in the media. In the schools context, the past twenty years have seen increasing attempts to develop a common conception of the arts in education. These include the Schools Council's 'Arts and Adolescent' project; the Assessment and Performance Unit's 'Aesthetic Development' document; publications by Ross,[2] Abbs, and most recently SCDC/NCC's 'Arts in Schools Project'. Significantly, there has also been increasing willingness among many arts teachers and advisers to seek links with each other and to draw upon each other's experiences to improve the delivery of the curriculum, although it is important to stress that none of these developments necessarily implies the development of 'integrated' or combined arts courses. The broad concern is to develop a common conceptual base for the teaching of the arts.

The functions of particular arts disciplines in schools are often described in limited ways, but in fact the histories of the various subjects reveal a range of contributions which the arts make to children's education. For the purposes of clarity, I would wish to suggest that the arts can and should offer three specific yet related experiences for all pupils:

(1)   The opportunity for making their own work, exploring a range of media styles and conventions;
(2)   The opportunity to learn about cultural artefacts, conventions, and histories;
(3)   The opportunity to explore issues of personal and social significance in more than merely propositional and discursive forms.

With an apology for the inadequacies of generalisation, I should like to extend these ideas by suggesting that, to an extent, it is possible to identify each of these with traditional arts teaching in a specific discipline. For example, art and design has provided regular contexts for the first area through its emphasis on studio work, a great deal of music teaching of the past century has been 'about' rather than 'in' music, while drama is often acknowledged to be a particularly powerful medium for enabling children to address and examine issues of personal and social significance. *Some* examples of English teaching offer perhaps the clearest example of a balance between the three experiences, but I would suggest that all arts subjects should seek a pedagogy which integrates all three.

To an extent, this has been happening recently although the process is somewhat slow. Art and design, having focused on studio practice, has been emphasising the need to develop what are usually called critical studies;[3] music teachers in secondary schools have responded to the recommendations of John Paynter's Schools Council project to develop practical music-making[4] (not least by using new technologies and popular music forms), while drama teachers, who have often promoted drama as a learning medium over theatre as an area of study, are increasingly recognising the importance of working with drama as an art form. The value of teachers of the various arts developing a common strategy and approach is that they can then share with other arts teachers their particular experiences of working in any of the three ways without necessarily having to make old mistakes or 'reinvent wheels'. Rather, they may be able to share a common pedagogical approach to work in the arts – again, without *necessarily* moving towards integrated or combined arts teaching.

Mention of pedagogy enables me to claim that one of the most significant contributions of the arts to the development of English education has been in terms of pedagogical methods, not least through recognising the importance that pupils attach to the experience of making their own work. By this, I do not simply mean the importance of self-expression (a central but somewhat clichéd concept within arts education) but more broadly the value of 'learning through doing' and the sense of ownership and personal value which is so important to most children.

So let us assume that, however the arts are organised within the primary and secondary school curriculum, each arts subject continues to develop the three ways of working outlined above, seeking, wherever possible, to relate the three, and that schools increasingly work towards a common policy for the arts – where does this leave media education in relation to the arts?

The first point is that media education has not historically functioned in the way that I have described for the arts. Despite a range of practices and objects of study, all of which might be described as media education, the emphasis has been on encouraging pupils to understand the ways in which television, cinema, newspapers, advertising, and so on construct and present particular views of the world and how they (the pupils) create meanings from those presentations. Because of the central concern with analysis and understanding (increasingly through key concepts such as institution, audience, and representation), media educators have been less concerned with 'practical' work. Indeed, in some cases, media educators have been opposed to the apparently unproblematic way in which other teachers believe that attempting to reproduce the forms of classical Hollywood or broadcast television on a single camera portapak leads to an understanding of what Manuel Alvarado, Robin Gutch, and Tana Wollen describe as 'the essence of a media artefact . . . its dual form as commodity and text'.[5]

The move in media education away from film studies and towards popular TV and advertising has enabled media teachers to address important social institutional issues through artefacts with which children readily

428

identify. However, in an article on media education which I believe to be of central importance to arts teachers, Cary Bazalgette described how there is currently a common-sense idea of 'an established canon of media theory' but one which, in the past, rejected as 'atheoretical' certain ideas of importance to arts education. She concluded her article with a sentence which seems to me to invite arts and media educators to work more closely:

> But just because we may have been right then, does not mean that aesthetics, production, and pedagogy will never be needed, cannot be theorised. If we really want to make sense of the media, we need these theories too.[6]

Clearly the arts have something to offer in the areas of aesthetics, production, and pedagogy (although there is no room for complacency), and this is one important reason for seeking to establish links between the two areas. However, this relationship must be reciprocal. In the area of critical studies, the arts lag a long way behind the practice of media education principally because they still view artefacts predominantly in terms of (*a*) formal properties, (*b*) context, and (*c*) the maker (notions of genius). Issues of the institutional, economic, or industrial bases for the promotion of certain artefacts over others, the role of the media in establishing a hierarchy of arts form and styles, representation (race, gender, etc.), are dealt with less frequently, often because arts teachers have comparatively little experience in 'reading' artefacts in this way.

Neither have the new technologies or popular forms established a broad   13
base in the arts curriculum. While media educators explore advertising, popular music, family photography, television drama, and so forth, the arts in school still draw strongly on the 'high' arts of Western culture or are influenced by the need to prepare pupils for vocational opportunities (particularly in the area of design). An increasing number of schools are beginning to develop work in video, computer graphics, sound recording, synthesisers, and the like, but the number is still small and they are often introduced as an alternative to traditional media within a familiar skills/ expression paradigm. Too often, video production in schools attempts to replicate the models of popular television and cinema without addressing the key theoretical issues which should underpin such work. Even in the few schools with access to mixing desks or edit suites, it is almost impossible to approach the appearance of broadcast television and many attempts to reproduce *That's Life* or *Wogan* are recognised by pupils as inadequate. With a genuine media education dimension to such projects, the differences can become a fruitful area of discussion and the task can be less ambitious technically, in order to give pupils a sense of the difficulties of producing work of a high technical quality while addressing issues of construction and institution, but that alone will not satisfy pupils who wish to produce work of which they can be proud.

So where does this leave production? One solution can be to find and   14
utilise models of practice better suited to the relatively modest facilities in schools. In the area of 'moving images' this might be primitive cinema, avant garde or independent work, or contemporary video. This work can

still address issues of construction, narration, audience, and representation, and places questions of aesthetics and production within the field of media education. In addition, it will extend pupils' experiences of what is possible within the field of cultural production. The development of work on popular TV, newspapers, and advertising has been very important in media education in recent years, and I would not wish to argue against it since one can see this as an attempt to make media education more accessible to younger pupils and also as a reaction against a certain kind of film studies rooted in an élitism typical of the benevolent liberalism of state education. However, it is still important that all pupils should be enabled to see (and hear) cultural artefacts which, for reasons of access and circulation, might otherwise remain outside their experience.

By drawing upon these other artefacts in a range of projects which integrate production and theory, the old separation between the two can be challenged in the classroom and pupils can simultaneously experience the creative processes and the value of working with, understanding, and eventually questioning, established forms and conventions.

Moreover, pupils today are not entirely unfamiliar with the conventions of these less 'popular' forms because of their appropriation and use in advertising, pop videos, and television trailers and credit sequences. Through these, the forms and conventions of computer graphics, opera, abstract cinema, surrealism, expressionism, be-bop, and so on are part of an increasingly common cultural language. By bringing together the most powerful contributions of arts and media education, it is possible to enable pupils to be aware of the context in which such work is produced and understood, through analysis *and* through their own creative work.

If we can manage to bring together the best practices of media and arts education I am sure it can only be to the benefit of our children. In order to do this we need a flexible approach to our own theory and practice as teachers. To conclude, I find it helpful to paraphrase Walter Benjamin: asking whether media teaching should be a part of the arts curriculum is the wrong question – we should, rather, ask how the presence of media teaching develops and extends our conception of arts education.

Notes

1. Peter Abbs, *Living Powers*, Brighton, Falmer, 1987.
2. M. Ross, *The Creative Arts*, London, Heinemann, 1978; M. Ross, *The Aesthetic Impulse*, Oxford, Pergamon, 1984.
3. R. Taylor, *Education for Art*, Harlow, Longman/SCDC, 1986.
4. J. Paynter, *Music in the Secondary School Curriculum*, Cambridge, Cambridge University Press/Schools Council, 1982.
5. Manuel Alvarado, Robin Gutch, and Tana Wollen, *Learning the Media*, London, Macmillan, 1987.
6. Cary Bazalgette, 'Making Sense for Whom?' in *Screen*, vol. 27, no. 5, September–October 1986.

Media Education, Technology, and the National Curriculum

Norrie Porter and Judy Bennett

From *Initiatives*, no. 12, Spring 1990

Technology might not appear at first glance to be a likely home for the aims and practices of media education. However, there are a number of pressing reasons why we should examine it with this possibility in mind:

1

- A degree of technical education has always been necessary for media production;
- The technological 'design and make' process is very similar to the planning and production of a media artefact;
- Information technology has a great and increasing influence on the form and content of the media;
- Teachers of subjects designated as technology in the National Curriculum are already teaching media-linked topics (e.g., advertising, theatre design);
- Timetable pressure in both primary and secondary schools means that a secure home has to be found for media education; this is best accomplished through the National Curriculum core and foundation subjects.

Progress Towards a National Curriculum in Technology

Where are we? Publication of the draft order, which took place in December 1989, is the penultimate stage in the process of producing the National Curriculum in Technology. Change is less likely now than at any earlier stage, as it would require full debate by Parliament. The statutory order was approved in 1991.

2

The Nature of Technology in the National Curriculum

What does the National Curriculum mean by 'technology'? Most media education practitioners, and indeed technologists, have a rather foggy notion of what technology actually is. Some confuse the output of design and technological activity, that is the artefacts, systems, or environments themselves, with the process as whole. Others think it is a mechanistic and deterministic application of science.

3

However, technology is a creative process, which should be sensitive and responsive to aesthetic, environmental, and cultural factors. The NCC technology working party is to be applauded for the recognition and promotion of such a definition. One definition of technology, although rather

4

dry, encompasses this, and is acceptable to almost every technologist. It comes from a 1986 HMI report:

> Technology is concerned with the identification of some of the material needs of man (*sic*) and the endeavour to satisfy those needs by the application of science and the use of materials, resources, and energy. The guidance to the technology working group directed the group to view design and technology as 'that area of the curriculum in which pupils design and make useful objects or systems, thus developing their ability to solve practical problems.

In the final report, we are directed to see this as happening in the contexts of home, school, recreation, community, business, and industry. We are also told that the attainment targets 'encourage the co-ordination of the knowledge, skills, and values necessary for design and technological activities . . . to be found at present in art and design, business studies, CDT, home economics, and information technology'. All the reports also make it plain that technology is a cross-curricular activity, and that teachers from a number of areas will have to collaborate to cover the programmes of study.

Curriculum Aims for Technology
If technology is a creative and integrative curriculum area, what ought its curriculum aims to be? We would suggest technology education should enable students to:

- Be aware of and make full use of available technology;
- Develop a critical understanding of technology;
- Make decisions of a personal, community, or national character based on this understanding;
- Appreciate the process by which technology artefacts and systems are made, including the improvement and extension of existing artefacts and systems;
- Use imagination and creativity to design and make technological artefacts and systems.

Together these form a statement of design and technological capability, and help individuals to operate successfully in an increasingly technological world and to take part in the decision-making processes which shape that world. In delivering this experience, the process which includes designing and making is clearly very important. It is, in fact, central to design and technological activity, and is so characteristic that it is referred to as the technological process.

The process starts with an identified human purpose and has as its outcome human achievement, whether this is an artefact, system, or environment. We believe that this process closely parallels the production process in media education, and the two processes should inform and develop alongside each other. This is particularly true when the technological process produces a media artefact, such as an advertisement or packaging. Some current media studies coursework could be suitable for assessment as part of National Curriculum Technology. With careful design of assignments, these links could be extended.

This process is the basis for the attainment targets in the first profile component, design and technology. Each circle has been translated into an attainment target. However, it is important to remember that these attainment targets are linked circles – one cannot be assessed in isolation from others.

Attainment in Technology
The four design and technology attainments targets (ATs) are:

AT1   Identifying Needs and Opportunities
Pupils should be able to identify and state clearly needs and opportunities for design and technological activities through investigation of the contexts of home, school, recreation, community, business, and industry.

AT2   Generating a Design Proposal
Pupils should be able to generate a performance specification and explore ideas to produce a design proposal and develop it into a realistic, appropriate, and achievable design.

AT3   Planning and Making
Pupils should be able to plan to achieve their design, and to identify, manage, and use appropriate resources, including knowledge and processes in order to make artefacts (objects made by people); systems (sets of objects or activities which perform a task); and environments (surroundings made by people).

AT4   Evaluating
Pupils should be able to develop, communicate, and act upon an evaluation of the processes, products, and effects of their design and technological activities and those of others, including those from other times and cultures.

The fifth attainment target relates to information technology and is the only attainment target in the second profile component, Information Technology Capability.

AT5   Information Technology Capability
Pupils should be able to use information technology to communicate and handle information; design, develop, explore, and evaluate models of real and imaginary situations; measure physical quantities and control movement. They should be able to make informed judgements about the application and importance of information technology, and its effect on the quality of life.

All these ATs have some obvious links with the processes of media

433

education. For example, a typical activity in media education might be the design and promotion of a media artefact. For the purposes of illustration, consider the writing and recording of an extract from a radio drama. It is important to differentiate between the media artefact that is the outcome of a process of media production, and any technological artefacts which the pupils design and make to facilitate the media production.

On the media education side, pupils will study the possible forms of the production, the way meaning is constructed within that form, and the techniques of presentation required. Integrated with this, pupils will consider the impact of the media on society: namely, make critical appraisals of the personal, social, and economic implications of the artefacts and systems as well as the impact of the message itself. In their study of the radio industry they will consider the economic factors linked to the introduction of past, present, and future technologies.

They will also learn to set up and use technological systems linked with the recording and editing of sound (microphones, mixers, recorders, amplifiers, etc.). Pupils could also be required to improve and extend the use of these systems (novel ways of interconnecting equipment to produce certain effects, construction of microphone windshields/vibration dampers, making new cabling, etc.). In addition, pupils will also have to design, make, and appraise new artefacts. The type of artefact produced will depend on the knowledge and skills the pupils already possess. In radio production this could range from the design and construction of a soundproof studio, through the construction of electronic effects generators, to the design and construction of sound effect props such as slapsticks, shakers, and so on. Pupils might also produce packaging and advertising materials. These will use technological skills in graphics and design, and will contribute knowledge of audiences and meaning construction to the common resource base.

Many examples of this kind can easily be found in all media. Indeed, there are many examples given in the non-statutory examples section of the programmes of study in the National Curriculum – for instance, planning a stage set for a school play, developing proposals for a company logo, producing slide, animation, or video sequences for promoting a product, producing scripts, and designing the school magazine are all examples from the design and technology profile component. The information technology profile contains a wealth of desktop publishing and multimedia examples, such as producing a class newsletter or a set of information screens to give information about the school.

How can these opportunities be exploited in the classroom? There are two ways. The first is to move some media education into the technology classroom. The second, not surprisingly, is to move some technology into a media education setting. Both methods are possible because technology is not defined as a subject in the National Curriculum, but as an umbrella covering aspects of a number of subjects. As a result, technology courses are likely to be designed, if not taught, by teams of teachers from a number of disciplines. We have seen that they are likely to include an element of content which we would normally identify as media education.

Designing Courses

The first method, then, is to ensure that media teachers are involved in the design of these courses. Their job will be to put topics like advertising and animation into a media education context. They will also be able to make sure that where some of the opportunities offered to students for technological activity are linked to the media, such as in the examples given in the NCC document, the activity takes place in a proper media context and is supported by the study of the relevant media education concepts. Media production systems are also a suitable topic for study, and their design and use can be a valuable activity in both media and technology education. Finally, the production of media artefacts themselves can be a technological activity (such as the production of a tape-slide sequence). [19]

We might also eliminate the worst excesses of desktop publishing, where ill-conceived, ill-assorted jumbles of badly written articles are squashed together without reference to audience, style, or taste. The input which media education practitioners can make to the design of courses will, we believe, be welcomed by technology departments, who are generally aware of their needs in this area. There are, however, two disadvantages to this approach. Firstly, it has considerable INSET implications for the technology teachers who are expected to teach media education. Secondly, this is very time-consuming and needs some resourcing in terms of additional time and support if it is to be successful. Nevertheless, the possibility of preparing materials in this way is being explored in a BFI Education project assisted by funding from the Nuffield Foundation, and is certainly a fruitful first point of contact between media and technology education. [20]

Incorporating Attainment Targets

The second method is to take on board the attainment targets of technology as part of media production exercises in the media classroom. It is not possible to deliver all the technology programmes of study through media education, so these options would have to be part of a wider study of technology. In this case, extended media production projects would be designed to include substantial elements of technology, such as the designing and making of sets, props, and costumes. This method is ideal in the primary school, and in the secondary school ensures a timetabled place for media production. However, it involves study of the methods and content of technology education by the media teacher, and will require co-ordination and moderation of assessment by teachers in different disciplines. [21]

Perhaps the most effective way forward for linking media and technology education is a combination of the above methods. It should be possible to become involved in the design of technology courses in such a way that technological activities linked to the media can be co-ordinated with activity in the media classroom, adding an extra dimension to both. [22]

There are a great number of opportunities opening up for collaboration between media education and technology departments. However, given the pressures on technology teachers in the run-up to implementation of the National Curriculum, the impetus for this collaboration will need to come from media teachers. We hope this article will help build effective and fruitful links between media and technology education. [23]

Index

Numerals marked in **bold face** indicate a chapter/section devoted to the subject entry.

436

438

441

442

447

448